HONOURING CHILDREN

PUBLIC CONCERNS

Honouring Children is the second volume in a new series on Public Concerns being published jointly by the University of Edinburgh's Centre for Theology and Public Issues, and Saint Andrew Press. The aim of the Centre and of this series is to offer informed studies of contemporary issues where a theological perspective can make a constructive contribution to matters of public concern. Books in the series are written for church members and concerned citizens, practitioners and policy-makers, and students and teachers in secondary and higher education, as well as academic researchers.

WILLIAM STORRAR and ALISON ELLIOT, *Series Editors*

God in Society: doing social theology in Scotland today
edited by William Storrar and Peter Donald (2003)

Honouring Children: the human rights of the child in Christian perspective
Kathleen Marshall and Paul Parvis (2004)

Forthcoming:
Netting Citizens: exploring citizenship in the internet age
edited by Johnston McKay

Public Practices: essays in Practical Theology and Christian Ethics
edited by William Storrar and Heather Walton

HONOURING CHILDREN

The Human Rights of the Child
in Christian Perspective

KATHLEEN MARSHALL
PAUL PARVIS

CENTRE FOR THEOLOGY AND PUBLIC ISSUES
NEW COLLEGE
THE UNIVERSITY OF EDINBURGH

SAINT ANDREW PRESS

First published in 2004 by
SAINT ANDREW PRESS
121 George Street, Edinburgh EH2 4YN

Copyright © Kathleen Marshall and Paul Parvis, 2004

ISBN 0 7152 0810 1

British Library Cataloguing in Publication Date
A catalogue record for this book
is available from the British Library

Typeset by Waverley Typesetters, Galashiels
Printed in Great Britain by Creative Print & Design, Wales

Contents

Preface

This book aims to inform policy development and enrich human relationships by helping people look critically at how Christian theology, and Christians, view the rights of children.

Christianity has always had a concern for the welfare of children, and there has been a great deal of Christian support for the rights of children as set out in the United Nations Convention on the Rights of the Child. Nevertheless, there is some discernible hesitation, in some quarters at least, about locating these concerns within a 'rights' framework, where this is vulnerable to accusations that it is egoistic, confrontational, and has a tendency to 'fragment' social and family life.

The book explores the concept of rights in general, and human rights in particular, before proceeding to an analysis of the rights of the child. Information and exploration are accompanied by theological reflection. While this is basically Christian, reference is also made to some insights from other belief systems.

The book is the product of collaboration between a lawyer who specialises in the rights of children, and a Christian theologian. An accompanying Study Guide for use by church groups is also available.

ABOUT THE AUTHORS

Kathleen Marshall is a lawyer with fifteen years' experience of child law and children's rights issues. She was formerly Director of the Scottish Child Law Centre and is currently a child law consultant, undertaking work for a wide range of academic, statutory and voluntary agencies.

Paul Parvis began his study of theology at Emory University, Atlanta, and received his doctorate from the University of Oxford in 1975. After teaching history and doctrine of the early Church for many years at Blackfriars, Oxford, as a member of the Faculty of Theology, he and his wife moved to Edinburgh in 1998, where he is currently an Honorary Fellow of New College.

ACKNOWLEDGEMENTS

This book would not have been possible without the financial support of:

- ✤ The Joseph Rowntree Charitable Trust;
- ✤ Lloyds TSB Foundation for Scotland;
- ✤ The Church of Scotland Board of Parish Education;
- ✤ The Russell Trust;
- ✤ Action of Churches Together in Scotland; and
- ✤ The Scottish Episcopal Church.

The authors would like to thank the funders for their support, and also all who have helped guide this project, including members of the Project Reference Group, and friends and colleagues at Edinburgh University's Centre for Theology and Public Issues. In particular, thanks are due to Elizabeth Templeton for her stimulating contributions during the early stages of the production of this book.

I

Introduction

1.1 What is the Issue?

Attitudes and practices towards children have changed dramatically over the past one hundred years. This development has been made more explicit and more focused by the debates surrounding implementation of the United Nations (UN) Convention on the Rights of the Child, which was passed by the UN General Assembly in 1989. Since that date, it has been ratified by all but two of the world's nation states.[1] However, this high degree of endorsement masks some lingering concerns which manifest in the reservations which states are permitted to make to their approval of the Convention, and in their dialogue with the UN Committee charged with monitoring implementation.

There appear to be two strands to this concern:

1. A concern about the concept of 'rights' generally, and its contribution towards the shaping of an increasingly individualistic society; and

2. A concern about 'children's rights' in particular, and the respect in which this might work to undermine the stability of the family and the authority of parents.

In the USA, which has still to ratify the Convention, some of the above concerns surface as questions raised by Christian politicians about the potential impact of the Convention on the stability of family life and the authority of parents.

Most believers would consider Christian theology and practice as benevolent towards children. They would point to the New Testament portraits of Jesus as welcoming little children, and to charitable practices of Christians throughout the centuries in opposing infanticide, promoting education and providing care for orphaned or homeless children. On this view, Christian belief is not only consistent with the rights of the child but also sets the standard for them. Others would argue that Christian theology devalues children as the initial inheritors of original sin and as perverted wills that need to be tamed. They would point to Christian reliance on Old Testament proverbs that justify and even command the physical punishment of children,[2] and argue that many of the 'charitable' practices of Christian institutions for children were oppressive and cruel.[3] This view tends to consider Christian theology as antithetical to the rights of the child, thus raising a question about what Christian theology actually says about children and their place in the family and in society.

This book is produced under the auspices of Edinburgh University's Centre for Theology and Public Issues (CTPI). 'Public issues' about children and young people tend to surface in media portrayals of children as either the powerless victims of abuse or the irresponsible perpetrators of crime or simple nuisance. Children and young people are either those who have to be protected or those from whom the adult world needs to be protected. In the realm of child abuse, these portrayals become confused: there is concern and anger about the sufferings of children and young people where abusive behaviour towards them has been 'proved' and outrage and anxiety about children's perceived power of accusation, manifesting in the paralysing fear many adults have of being the object of 'false accusations.'

In the legal author's experience, adults often reply to promotion of children's rights with the question, 'What about adults' rights?' Suggestions about the need to educate children about their rights are met with the response, 'They know too much about their rights already.' In fact, children tend not to know about their rights when it really matters. They have vague ideas about them, culled from the same ill-informed sources that feed the views of many adults. At one level, therefore, the issue is lack of information about the justification for, and content of, children's rights.

Even where adults are well disposed to children and young people and wish actively to pursue what is best for them, they can experience concerns about the impact on both general and family life of a 'rights-based' framework. This may be particularly the case where such people have a commitment to a Christian belief that promotes a more 'loving' construct of the world and human relations. A second issue is therefore the extent to which 'children's rights' cohere with the beliefs and values of Christians.

1.2 The Aim of this Book

This book aims to show that promotion of the rights of vulnerable people, especially children, is an effective way of promoting the Christian agenda. We hope to address the first issue referred to above by providing information about children's rights and their relevance to the lives of children. We address the second issue by exploring some of the philosophical and theological issues related to human rights in general and children's rights in particular, and by showing how some of the reservations about children's rights have been discussed by states in dialogue with the UN Committee on the Rights of the Child.

Vigorous academic debate continues about the legitimacy and usefulness of the concept of human rights, including children's rights,[4] and we hope that the 'information' content of this book will provide a useful resource for anyone interested in human rights, particularly when applied to children. The authors are, however, particularly concerned with the attitudes and assumptions of reflective Christians, who are neither philosophers nor moral theologians, and who have questions about the meaning and implications of adopting a rights-based approach to human relationships, particularly within the family and other arenas of the lives of children. Our target audience also includes activists, policy-makers and academics who have questions about the place of children's rights in human relations in general and within families and local communities, and also those who have questions about the attitude of Christianity towards the rights of the child. This means we hope to attract both general readers and those with backgrounds in different disciplines, primarily law, social policy, philosophy and theology. And this in turn has implications for the degree of prior knowledge assumed of our readers, and actually existent within ourselves as authors. Some of what we say, for example, about the philosophy of rights, may be both too simple for experts in that field and too complex for readers from other disciplines. We can only hope that we have managed to negotiate an appropriate 'middle way' that, if it is not perfect in every respect, promotes our agenda of building bridges between these disciplines and facilitating a synthesis of law, philosophy and theology about children.

One of us is a lawyer, specialising in children's law and children's rights, the other a theologian. We have found that our dialogue on the question of children's rights has challenged each of us to reassess our semi-instinctive perceptions about what it is to be a human person, especially a young one, and what must be done to ensure that such young ones have the best possible and most fulfilling lives.

Much of the discussion that follows is about concepts of rights, responsibilities, virtues, etc., but we hope to show also how these are relevant to the lives of real children.[5] At various points, scenarios such as the following will be discussed:

Robin and Maria are drug addicts whose three children, damaged by several unsuccessful attempts at keeping the family together, have been made available for adoption. Maria is pregnant again and consideration is being given to removing the child at birth.[6]

Margaret, a single mother, has been reported to the authorities for leaving her children (aged 7 and 9) alone for half an hour in the morning after she leaves for work. She says she has no family or other support, nor money for childcare.[7]

Thirteen-year-old Jennifer was removed from home because her parents cannot control her. She is placed in a children's home where she becomes the focus of attention of three sexually active teenage male residents.[8]

Mary is 11 years old and afraid to tell anyone her grandfather is abusing her because she fears she will not be believed.[9]

Kevin is 14 and is resisting all attempts to make him comply with a court order to spend time with his mother at weekends.[10]

The project involving production of this book also commits us to publication of a short discussion leaflet for groups wishing to address the subject.

It is our belief that true dialogue can only be maintained when the position of each side to an argument is represented fairly, rather than in caricature. We have tried to access, understand and reflect upon the perspective of those whose views differ from our own in a way that is honest and non-polemical.

1.3 The Authors' Perspectives

We feel we owe it to our readers to be open about our own beliefs and starting points, which we present here as personal statements. At the end of the book we will return to these and assess what we have learned in the process of this dialogue and whether our perspectives have changed.

1.3.1 The Legal Author

I have been working on the rights of children for fifteen years and am an ardent supporter of the Convention on the Rights of the Child.

A legal perspective tends to be practical, with the emphasis on what one can do with concepts and commitments. Much of my work has involved campaigning for changes in law, policy and practice to incorporate the principles of the Convention and thus make it easier for children and young people to pursue their rights and for others to pursue them on their behalf.

I embarked upon this project with a concern about the practical implications of any subversion of the concept of rights. It seemed to me that there was a growing aversion to 'rights' in general, and a related resistance to the concept of 'children's rights'. My concern was that moral discourse aiming to reclaim the idea of a society based upon community, virtue and duty might transfer into the world of politics and law in a way that undermined rights as concepts that can 'do things'. The protection for vulnerable individuals and classes of people, so carefully built up in modern times, might be eroded or destroyed by an unthinking translation into the 'real world' of constructs developed on an idealistic, moral 'high ground'. That is not to say that law should not be informed by philosophy or theology, but that philosophers and theologians should be aware that their pure ideas, if accepted without proper concern for the realities of human life – you might say for our 'brokenness' or 'original sin' – can work to the detriment of vulnerable people.

My work on this book has been paralleled by study for a degree in theology, compelling me to look at my presuppositions through another lens than that to which I am accustomed.

1.3.2 The Theological Author

I approach the problem of children's rights from the perspective of a historian. My main interest is in the thought and literature of the early Church and in the development of doctrine. But it is essential to try to see the history of the Church and the history of Christian thought as a coherent whole and to try to see the way in which different branches of the tradition are related to one another and to the problems we face today.

My own theological training, apart from historical studies, has been in the disciplines of New Testament criticism and Thomist scholasticism, and the latter is where I feel at home. But I believe that in the Church of the early centuries it is often possible to find a freshness and vitality of thought that has much to contribute to our understanding of the demands of the world we live in today.

In any event, my interests are more theological than philosophical, though I hope that I have not proved totally immune to the rigour of argumentation which Aquinas deploys. What I have tried to do in my contribution to this book is above all to make connections – to suggest how what is being said in the public arena about children's rights fits in with and indeed illumines other deep concerns of the Christian tradition. Moral theology, like any academic discipline, can at times become inward looking. I hope that in this book we have managed to open discussion up, rather than close it down. If we have succeeded in that – just a little – I shall be satisfied.

Another perspective has coloured the closing stages of this work. As it was being completed, war broke out in Iraq. Whatever else the war may bring, we now face the prospect of more children dying in a country in which something like one-seventh of all children already die of disease and malnutrition, and over half the population are under 18. The outbreak of war was marked in this country (Scotland) and in England by large-scale demonstrations of schoolchildren protesting against the war – children demonstrating for children. So the tragic vulnerability of children and evidence of their moral autonomy here go hand in hand.

1.4 The Structure of this Book

As this book focuses on the rights of the child, it seems appropriate to start with a brief description of the UN Convention on the Rights of the Child, its history, content and progress in implementation, especially by states with a religious commitment. That is the focus of Chapter 2. Chapter 3 explores the concept of 'rights'. Chapter 4 moves on to historical and philosophical perspectives on 'human rights', with the religious dimension being addressed in Chapter 5. This process is designed to take account of the point made above about resistance to the concept of rights in general, and to human rights in particular. If rights are dismissed as an appropriate framework for human community, then children's rights will have little chance of any sympathetic consideration.

Chapter 6 moves the focus back to children with a more detailed discussion of the 'human rights of the child'. This description is used to emphasise both that children are entitled to (virtually) the whole range of human rights ascribed to adults, and that 'children's rights' are not a class apart but a further specification of human rights in their application to the young of the species. Chapter 7 takes a more in-depth look at the theology of children's rights. Chapter 8 then explores children's rights within the context of visions of human destiny. It looks at the Christian concept of what it is to be a human person, and what it is to be a child. Chapter 9 takes the form of a concluding reflection by the authors on what they have learned from the research and dialogue involved in writing this book.

This book focuses largely on Christian theology, merely because casting the net more widely would have made this a very complex task, which would have had to involve many people from different religious backgrounds. We have never-theless included a case study on an Islamic country (Saudi Arabia) because it is a good example of explicit religious-secular dialogue between a State and the UN Committee on the Rights of the Child, and seems to us to raise some general issues about the characteristics of such dialogue. There are also sporadic references to the perspectives of other cultures, particularly within Chapter 4. Our aims in that regard are, however, modest, and we hope that this contribution might stimulate similar reflections from other faiths, which can be brought together at some point.

Notes

1. At the time of writing, it remains to be ratified by Somalia and by the USA.
2. P. Greven, *Spare the Child: The Religious Roots of Physical Punishment and the Psychological Impact of Physical Abuse*, New York: Alfred A. Knopf, 1991.
3. See, for example, C. W. Atkinson, '"Wonderful Affection": Seventeenth-Century Missionaries to New France on Children and Childhood', in M. J. Bunge (ed.), *The Child in Christian Thought*, Grand Rapids, MI: Wm. B. Eerdmans Publishing Co., 2001, pp. 227–46, which discusses the catalogue of well-meaning cruelty perpetrated upon the Huron Indians by Catholic missionaries adhering to a particularly strict and pessimistic version of Augustinian theology (p. 241).
4. The legitimacy is challenged, for example, by Alasdair MacIntyre in *After Virtue: A Study in Moral Theory* (2nd edn), London: Duckworth, 1985, particularly p. 69; and the usefulness of a rights-based approach is challenged in T. Campbell, K. D. Ewing and A. Tomkins (eds), *Sceptical Essays on Human Rights*, Oxford: Oxford University Press, 2001.
5. Further detailed information about the impact, or potential impact of the Convention on the lives of children can be found

in the documentation of the UN Committee on the Rights of the Child, some of which will be discussed below, and which can be accessed via the UN website. Also valuable are the alternative reports submitted to the Committee by non-governmental organisations, for example, C. Morrison and C. McCulloch, *All Children All Ages: The NGO Alternative Report (Scotland) to the UN Committee on the Rights of the Child*, Edinburgh: Scottish Alliance for Children's Rights, 2000 (Based at Save the Children, Scotland Office, in Edinburgh).

6. More fully discussed at 6.2.3 below.
7. Discussed at 6.5.1 below.
8. Discussed at 6.5.1 below.
9. Discussed at 6.5.3 below.
10. Discussed at 6.5.3 below.

2

The UN Convention on the Rights of the Child

2.1 History

On 20 November 1989, the General Assembly of the United Nations unanimously passed the Convention on the Rights of the Child.[1]

The twentieth century had shown an increasing interest in and commitment to the rights of children. The first international statement was the Declaration on the Rights of the Child, passed in 1924 by the League of Nations. A simple, five-point document, this focused on the rights of children to be protected, cared for and educated towards a means of earning a living.[2]

The Declaration was expanded to seven points by the United Nations in 1948, and more extensively expanded in 1959. It retained its largely protective character, although more 'developmental' rights were included, as well as the 'civil' right to a name and nationality.

In 1979, the International Year of the Child, the Polish Government suggested that the occasion be marked by the drafting of a Convention on the Rights of the Child. A convention is a stronger statement than a declaration. It is a part of international law, rather than a mere exhortation, and it is backed up by a monitoring or enforcement mechanism. Poland submitted a draft convention, which was referred to a Working Group set up by the UN Human Rights Commission. It was ten years before the Working

Group had a draft that could receive the approval of the General Assembly of the United Nations. The main points of debate and/or difference were:

1. The beginning of childhood. Opposing views regarding whether it began at conception or birth led to an ambiguous formulation in the Preamble that could be interpreted as parties saw fit.
2. Freedom of religion. While already existing international instruments (which also applied to children) proclaimed the right to 'adopt' a religion, Islamic opposition led to a change in the initial formulation involving omission of the specific right of the child to 'choose' a religion. The amendment was made 'in the spirit of compromise'.
3. Adoption. As adoption is not possible under Islam, the text was amended to avoid any expectation that an adoption system had to be introduced.
4. The lowest age for enlistment in the armed forces. The most controversial provision of the Convention was its setting of this limit at 15, as a response to strong opposition from the United States, supported by other countries, to a higher age. [3]

While some were unhappy with some of the compromises made to secure general acceptance, it must nevertheless be counted a great achievement that such a degree of consensus as the Convention does represent could be achieved by nations representing such cultural diversity. This approval of the Convention was borne out by the speed with which it was ratified and thus brought into effect. The Convention on the Rights of the Child has been the fastest and most widely ratified document in the history of international law.

2.2 Content

The Convention has fifty-four articles. The first forty-two are substantive, and the remainder procedural. There are a number of possible ways of analysing the rights contained in the Convention; perhaps the most common of these refers to the three 'Ps', that is to say, the Convention proclaims the rights of children to:

- Protection – from abuse, neglect and exploitation;
- Provision – of services to promote survival and development; and
- Participation – in decisions about matters that affect them.

The first two categories of rights represent clarification and expansion of what had been contained in earlier statements. The 'participation' category is new, and it is this that has been the subject of greatest debate.

2.2.1 Application

Article 1 defines a 'child' for the purposes of the Convention as:

> Every human being below the age of 18 years unless, under the law applicable to the child, majority is attained earlier.

It is clear that a child moves out of the definition on attaining the age of 18. It is not so clear when childhood begins. The Preamble to the Convention states:

> *Bearing in mind that*, as indicated in the Declaration of the Rights of the Child, 'the child, by reason of his physical and mental immaturity, needs special safeguards and care, including appropriate legal protection, before as well as after birth'.

While some might see this as a proclamation of the general right to life of the unborn child, others interpret it as recognition only of the retrospective rights of the child who is born alive.[4]

As indicated above, the beginning of childhood was one of the areas of disagreement among the drafters of the

Convention. In the end, they reached a compromise which recognised that agreement would never be forthcoming. A statement was placed in the *Traveaux Preparatoires* indicating that the matter was open to interpretation by States.[5]

2.2.2 Subjects Addressed

The following is a brief summary of the subjects addressed and the content of the rights proclaimed. It should be noted that these provisions represent the *minimum acceptable standards*. Article 41 insists that the Convention should not be used to lower standards in states that already operate at a higher level.

Family Life

The Convention upholds the ideals of family life, while acknowledging the need for support, and even intervention, where the child's rights are not met within the family. It proclaims the family as the fundamental group in society, which should be helped to fulfil its responsibilities in the community. It affirms that children grow up best in a family environment, in an atmosphere of happiness, love and understanding (Preamble). States must therefore respect the responsibilities, rights and duties of parents and other carers to direct or guide children in the exercise of their rights. The degree of direction or guidance that is appropriate will change according to the evolving capacity of the child (Art. 5).

Children have, as far as possible, the right to know and be cared for by their parents (Art. 7). Both parents should be responsible for the upbringing and development of their children. They have the primary responsibility to promote the interests of their children. States should assist them, for example, through the provision of appropriate services. This is particularly important for working parents (Art. 18).

A child must not be separated from his or her parents against their will, unless a lawful authority, subject to judicial review, decides that this is necessary for the best interests of the child. This might happen where a child has been abused or neglected by parents, or where the parents live apart and a decision has to be made about where the child is to live. If a child is separated from a parent, he or she has a right to maintain regular contact, except where this is against the child's best interests (Art. 9).

Moreover, States have a duty to protect children from abuse or neglect by parents or other carers. They must establish services for prevention, identification and investigation of such abuses, and for support for those involved (Art. 19).

Where a child cannot remain with his or her family, the State must provide appropriate alternative care. This should, as far as possible, respect the child's ethnic, religious, cultural and linguistic background (Art. 20). Where national law permits adoption, this must be carefully regulated and must focus on the paramountcy of the child's interest. This is particularly the case with inter-country adoption (Art. 21).

Children should be taught respect for parents (Art. 29).

There are also international dimensions to the rights of children. States should ensure that decisions about who can enter or leave their countries respect the rights of children to maintain contact with their parents, and not to remain separated from them (Art. 10). States should enter agreements to combat international child abduction (Art. 11). Refugee children should be helped to trace their parents or other family members. If they are without family, they should receive the same protection as other children in the country (Art. 22).

Childhood

Children are not miniature adults. The Convention affirms that childhood is entitled to special care and assistance.

Children should be prepared to live an individual life in society, in accordance with the ideals of the Charter of the United Nations and, in particular, in the spirit of peace, dignity, tolerance, freedom, equality and solidarity. It is important also to take account of the traditions and cultural values of the community within which the child is raised (Preamble). Children from minority groups should be able to enjoy their own culture (Art. 30).

Mentally or physically disabled children should be helped to be a part of the community. They should receive appropriate services free of charge whenever possible (Art. 23).

Children have a right to a standard of living adequate for physical, mental, spiritual, moral and social development (Art. 27). They have a right to rest, leisure and play (Art. 31). Their rights to education, leisure and development should not be undermined by economic exploitation. The State must set and implement limits to the employment of children (Art. 32).

Children should be protected from abuse of narcotics (Art. 33), sexual exploitation (Art. 34), abduction or sale (Art. 35), and any other form of exploitation (Art. 36). Children under 15 should not take direct part in armed conflicts. Under 15s should not be recruited into the armed forces. States should try as far as possible to protect children affected by armed conflict (Art. 38).

Where children have been neglected, exploited, abused or tortured, the State must try to promote their reintegration into society (Art. 39).

Identity

Children have a right to a name and a nationality (Art. 7). The Convention affirms that family relations are also an aspect of identity, and should not be subject to unlawful interference (Art. 8). Children have a right to privacy, and to freedom from unlawful attacks on their honour or reputation (Art. 16).

Health

Children have the right to the highest attainable standard of health. States must provide appropriate and accessible services. In particular, they should aim to diminish infant and child mortality, combat disease and malnutrition, ensure appropriate pre- and post-natal care for mothers, and family planning education and services (Art. 24).

Education

Children have a right to education. School discipline should be administered in a manner consistent with the child's human dignity (Art. 28).

Education should be directed towards development of the whole child. The child should be taught toleration and respect for the rights, freedoms and culture of others (Art. 29).

Freedom

While acknowledging that children are not miniature adults (see above), the Convention insists that, as human beings, they have a right to enjoy certain fundamental human rights. Thus, children have rights to freedom:

- of expression, except where this transgresses the rights or reputations of others, breaches national security or public order, or offends against public health or morals (Art. 13);

- of thought, conscience and religion, except where this breaches public order, health or morals, or the fundamental rights or freedoms of others. Parents or carers have a right to provide direction to the child in a manner consistent with the child's evolving capacities (Art. 14).

- of association and peaceful assembly, except where lawfully and necessarily restricted in the interests of national security, public safety, public order, public

health or morals, or the protection of the rights and
freedoms of others (Art. 15).

- of access to appropriate information, to promote
social, spiritual and moral well-being, and physical
and mental health (Art. 17).

Child Offenders

The Convention recognises that some children will offend
and will be subject to a variety of legal processes and
consequences in different countries. It says that children
should not be subject to extreme punishments. If they
are arrested, their deprivation of liberty should be mini-
mised and regulated. They should not generally be placed
with adult offenders or suspects. They should be able to
maintain contact with their families. They should have
prompt access to legal and other appropriate assistance
(Art. 37).

Child offenders or suspects should be treated with dignity
and respect. They should be treated in a way that takes
account of their age and promotes their reintegration into
society. They should be treated fairly. Their privacy should
be fully respected.

The Convention urges States to establish systems specific
to children. These may operate outside the court system so
long as human rights and legal safeguards are respected.
Disposals should include care and supervision orders, and
other alternatives to institutional care (Art. 40).

2.2.3 Basic Principles

In implementation of all of the above substantive rights,
States must observe the four basic principles of the
Convention:

> *Article 2: non-discrimination* – States are to ensure that
> the rights apply to all children and are to protect children
> from discrimination.

Article 3: best interests of the child – Whenever decisions are made about children, the best interests of the child must be a primary consideration.

Article 6: survival and development – Every child has an inherent right to life. States must ensure to the maximum extent possible, the survival and development of the child.

Article 12: the child's views – Any child who is capable of forming a view, has a right to express that view freely on any matter affecting the child. The child's views must be given weight appropriate to the child's age and maturity. In particular, children have a right to be heard (either directly or through a representative) when decisions are being made about them in courts or in administrative proceedings.

It should be noted that the right proclaimed by Article 12 is not so much to *make* decisions as to *contribute appropriately* to the decision-making process. Features of Article 12 are:

- The threshold condition for application of the article is that the child is 'capable of forming a view'. This is a very low threshold. Children can form views at a very young age.
- If the child is capable of forming a view, then the child has the right to express those views freely on any matter affecting the child. This is a basic human right.
- When decisions are being made about the matter in question, the expressed view of the child must be given due weight 'in accordance with the age and maturity of the child'.
- When decisions are being made by formal bodies, the child must be given the opportunity to be heard, either personally or through a representative.

Thus, Article 12 does *not* say that children have a right to *make* decisions. Their right of expression and participation must be seen against the background of Article 3, which says that the best interests of the child must also be 'a primary consideration' when any decision is made. This means that the factors feeding into the decision-making process should include *both* any expression of views by a child *and* an objective assessment of the child's interests. The relative weight to be given to these factors will depend upon the age and maturity of the child and the nature of the decision under consideration. For example, if parents were separating and each sought to have the child live with them, an objective assessment might conclude that, in a particular case, the child's interests might best be served by living with one of the parents; let us say the father. If a 5-year-old child expressed the view that he or she would rather live with the mother, this would certainly be taken into account and given due weight. However, it *might* be considered that the objective assessment of the child's interests outweighed the child's views. If the child were 15 at the time the decision was being taken, it would be much harder to argue that the child's views should be countermanded. Apart from the greater maturity and insight which the young person might have at that age, one would also be faced with the very practical difficulty of trying to implement a decision that went against the young person's views. The extremes to which one would have to go to force the young person to remain with the mother might be more damaging to that young person than any assessed disadvantage of living with the mother as compared with the father.[6]

2.3 Ratification and Reservations

When a convention is passed by the United Nations, it becomes open for 'signature' and 'ratification'. Signing a convention is an indication of an intention to ratify it. Ratification represents a formal commitment to be bound by its provisions. In some countries, ratified international treaties automatically become part of national law (they are 'self-executing') and can be cited in court like any other act of their legislating body. This is the general situation, for example, in the USA.[7] In other countries, such as the UK, incorporation into national law requires an act of parliament.[8]

International law allows states to make 'reservations' or 'declarations' when signing or ratifying conventions. A reservation identifies a provision which the state does not intend to be bound by. A declaration sets out the understanding or interpretation of a provision underpinning its approval by the ratifying state. This mechanism is designed to avoid rejection of a whole document on account of particular 'sticking points'. The United Nations will encourage and support a state towards a position where it feels able to withdraw its reservation and accept the document in its entirety. The reservation mechanism should not be used to undermine the basic purpose of a convention and allow a sham adherence to it. Article 51.2 of the Convention on the Rights of the Child states:

> A reservation incompatible with the object and purpose of the present Convention shall not be permitted.

Reservations and declarations in connection with the Convention on the Rights of the Child covered most of its articles to a greater or lesser extent, but tended to group around a few specific issues. Several states objected to the setting of 15 as the lowest age for involvement in armed combat. This had been a compromise position designed to close the debate and move towards approval of the Convention. In May 2000, an Optional Protocol (which states can choose to subscribe to) was added to the Convention raising the age to 18. Several states were keen to ensure that the provisions of the Convention about refugees and about reunification of families, entering and exiting countries, did not undermine their laws on immigration and nationality. There were also a number of reservations about the mixing of child and adult suspects in the criminal process. The motivations for these reservations might be seen to be largely political and practical.

Another group of provisions subject to reservation or declaration might be considered to be fuelled more by religious or cultural attitudes, which are often difficult to separate. At a very general level, many (but by no means all) Islamic states made sweeping reservations indicating their intention to abide by the Convention insofar as it was consistent with Islamic law. This approach was objected to by a number of European states as inconsistent with the purpose of the Convention in terms of Article 51.2. Many Islamic states also reserved their position on adoption, as not compatible with Islamic culture, adding that they had alternative provisions for relevant circumstances.

The question of the threshold age/stage for application of the Convention attracted nine reservations/declarations,[9] attached either to the Preamble, to Article 1 (definition of child) or to Article 6 (right to survival and development). While some of the reservations are general and do not specify what the issue is (Botswana, Indonesia, Malaysia), others specifically state that they regard childhood as starting at conception (Argentina, The Holy See) or following a live birth (China, UK). Some safeguard their domestic laws on termination of pregnancy (France, Luxembourg, Tunisia).

Article 24.2 (f) of the Convention includes a commitment to the development of family planning education and services. Argentina observed that this was 'the exclusive concern of parents' and that the State's obligation should be focused on 'guidance for parents and education for responsible parenthood'. The Holy See indicated that it understood the provision as meaning only those natural methods of family planning which it considered to be morally acceptable. Poland limited its approval to what was 'in keeping with the principles of morality'. Kiribati made an unspecified reservation to this provision.

As might be expected, Article 14 (freedom of thought, conscience and religion) attracted a large number of specific reservations.[10] Most states making reservations did not specify any particular concern. Belgium and The Netherlands made declarations aimed at expanding the scope of the article by linking it with other international documents which explicitly say that the right to freedom of religion includes the right to change one's religion.[11] On the other hand, Iraq and Oman specifically objected to any right of children to choose (Oman) or change (Iraq) their own religion. Algeria indicated that a child would be educated in accordance with the religion of his or her father. Several other states (Holy See, Kiribati, Poland, Singapore and Syria) made the child's right subject to the general authority of parents in matters of religion.[12]

The concern with parental authority and rights is also reflected in more general statements made in the context of reservations to articles 12 (views of child), 13 (freedom of expression), 15 (freedom of association), 16 (protection of privacy) and 17 (access to appropriate information). Kiribati and Poland made such reservations with respect to articles 12–16; the Holy See with regard to articles 13–16; and Singapore, with regard to articles 12–17. The Holy See linked this with a reservation to Article 28 (the provision of education), but made no reservation to Article 29 (aims of education).

It would seem then, that while the Convention makes strong statements about its commitment to family life and to respect for parents, which have been acceptable to the vast majority of states, there are indications of some religious concern about how this might interface with traditional religious values. This has been most explicit in the attitude of some Islamic states, and in the caution expressed by the Holy See, which is otherwise an explicit supporter of human rights and the rights of children generally. It is also manifest in the approach of some members of the North American religious community, causing them to oppose ratification of the Convention. As one might expect, the more secular states of the Western world generally express no such concerns. Those that do (e.g., Argentina and Poland) would seem to have a sizeable religious community with considerable influence. One might speculate that the concerns made explicit in such countries might also reflect some views of the less vocal and influential religious communities in other secular states.

2.4 Monitoring

Implementation of the Convention is monitored by the UN Committee on the Rights of the Child. States must report to the Committee two years after ratification, and every five years thereafter. Representatives of the state are called to answer questions. The process concludes with the formulation by the Committee of concluding observations and recommendations.

In order to examine how the religious dimension impacts on thought about the rights of children, and the response of the international children rights community to any religious-based concerns, it is proposed:

1. to take one Islamic state as a case study and to examine its dialogue with the UN Committee (on the basis that this was the occasion for an explicit dialogue about the interface of religious and secular thinking);

2. to examine the dialogue between the Holy See and the UN Committee (to allow consideration of the issues raised by both parties where the state has a unique Christian religious character);

3. to take Poland as a further case study (it having initiated the Convention while a communist state, and implemented it as, in practical terms, a Catholic one);

4. to examine some Protestant support for the Convention; and

5. to explore concerns expressed by conservative Protestant Christians, particularly in the USA, in opposition to the Convention.

The influence of the Protestant tradition is more difficult to discern within the UN documentation. The purpose of items 4 and 5 is to allow some exploration of this perspective. While the fundamentalist Protestant voice is vocal in its opposition to the Convention, there is also mainstream support for it.

2.5 Case Studies: Saudi Arabia, the Holy See and Poland

2.5.1 Saudi Arabia

As indicated above, many Islamic states submitted reservations to the Convention. Saudi Arabia was among those entering 'reservations with respect to all such articles as are in conflict with the provisions of Islamic law'. [13] The state's initial report to the UN Committee on the Rights of the Child contains a description of the rights of the child in Islam, and the thinking behind the Kingdom's accession to the Convention. [14] The preface explains that Islam is embraced by the nation 'as a creed, a constitution and an integrated way of life'. The introduction claims that:

> A careful review of Islamic law clearly shows that Islam has guaranteed comprehensive rights for the child before as well as after birth. Islam makes the world of a child a beautiful world, full of love, happiness and joy. It ardently seeks to instil the love of children into adults and urges them to plan and form a family that can ensure harmonious development, respect and equality for all its members, particularly children. It also emphasizes the importance of protecting children, safeguarding their right to life and preserving a healthy environment conducive to their sound development.

It is said that the teachings of Islam 'are in harmony with, and even surpass, the provisions of the Convention'. This perspective is consistently maintained throughout the report.

On receipt of a state report, the UN Committee identifies a 'List of Issues' with regard to which it seeks further information. The list drawn up for Saudi Arabia included a request that the state *identify all the relevant articles of the Convention which are in conflict* with the provisions of Islamic law'.[15]

When the Committee subsequently met with representatives of the Saudi government to discuss their report, the latter observed that the general reservation to the Convention had no real practical effect. It should be understood as a preventative measure designed to avoid possible interpretations of the Convention that might be incompatible with the Shariah.[16]

In terms of particular provisions, committee members questioned whether the *position of females* in Saudi society met the non-discrimination standards of the Convention. The delegation replied that men and women were equal before the law, but that a certain number of customs and traditions tended to limit practical respect for the rights of women:

> Although there was no religious text prohibiting a woman from driving a car, the scholars had established general principles designed to protect the stability of society and to preserve its norms and traditions. It was unwise to discard those norms for purely personal motives. When the majority were in favour of a change in existing traditions, the rules would be amended to reflect that change.

The Committee asked whether the State had considered undertaking an article by article analysis of the Convention in order to ascertain the extent to which there was actual conflict with the Shariah as opposed to conflict with national customs and traditions. Only that kind of analysis, carried out by Islamic experts, with the full confidence of the population, would help a movement towards implementation of the Convention's provisions. The delegation responded that:

> [T]here was an important distinction between Islamic law and traditional customs. While the Government tried to raise public awareness with a view to eliminating harmful practices, the importance of traditions could not be completely ignored.

The Committee asked what importance was given to the *views of children* in matters affecting them. In case of divorce, was it possible, out of respect for the child's view, to breach the rule according to which infants under 7 were given to the care of their mother, and children aged 7 and up to their father? The delegation responded that, once a child reached the age of reason (7), it could choose which parent to live with.

In terms of its *relationship with non-governmental organisations* (NGOs) engaged in promotion of the rights of children, the delegation reported that:

> [T]he government maintained an ongoing dialogue with NGOs engaged in human rights activities. It had, however, encountered some difficulties in dealing with certain organizations which refused to accept the State party invoking Islamic law in discussing human rights.

The concluding observations and recommendations issued by the Committee included the following:

6. Noting the universal values of equality and tolerance inherent in Islam, the Committee observes that narrow interpretations of Islamic texts by State authorities are impeding the enjoyment of many human rights protected under the Convention.

In particular:

7. The Committee is concerned that the broad and imprecise nature of the State party's general reservation potentially negates many of the Convention's provisions and raises concern as to its compatibility with the object and purpose of the Convention, as well as the overall implementation of the Convention.

8. The Committee recommends that the State party withdraw its reservation ...

24. ... [T]he Committee encourages the State party to consider the practice of other States that have been successful in reconciling fundamental rights with Islamic texts. The Committee recommends that the State party take all appropriate measures, such as comprehensive public education campaigns, to prevent and combat negative societal attitudes in this regard, particularly within the family, and train members of the legal profession, especially the judiciary, to be gender-sensitive. Religious leaders should be mobilized to support such efforts.

29. The Committee is concerned that respect for the views of the child remain limited owing to traditional societal attitudes towards children in schools, the courts, and especially within the family.

31. The Committee emphasizes that the human rights of children cannot be realized independently from the human rights of their parents, or in isolation from society at large ...

32. The Committee recommends that the State party take all effective measures ... to prevent and eliminate *discrimination on the grounds of religion or belief* in the recognition, exercise and enjoyment of human rights and fundamental freedoms in all fields of civil, economic, political, social and cultural life ...

33. ... [T]he Committee is seriously concerned that persons under 18 may be subject while in detention to *corporal punishment*, such as flogging ... It is also disturbed that persons who committed crimes when they were under 18 may be sentenced to a variety of methods of cruel, inhuman or degrading treatment or punishment such as flogging, stoning and amputation, which are systematically imposed by judicial authorities ... Moreover the Committee is concerned about reports that members of the Committee for the Propagation of Virtue and the Prevention of Vice routinely harass and assault persons under 18 for, *inter alia*, dress code infractions.

35. ... [T]he Committee is concerned at the incidence of ill-treatment of children in schools and within the family. It is further concerned that *domestic violence* is a problem in Saudi Arabia and that this has harmful consequences on children.

39. ... [T]he Committee ... is seriously concerned that the State party's policy on education for girls ... discriminates against girls ...[17]

The following comments might be made upon this dialogue:

1. As an Islamic state, Saudi Arabia regards the language of the Koran, supplemented by authoritative tradition, as its primary framework. It is willing to take account of the language of the Convention on the Rights of the Child as a secondary framework, judged not incompatible with the Koran.

2. The UN Committee (and the NGOs) adopt the Convention as their primary framework and want States to use it as a yardstick for assessing the acceptability of their laws and practices.

3. It is acknowledged by both parties that traditional customs which breach the Convention often represent interpretations of religious texts which might not be upheld by many religious authorities.

4. The UN Committee wants the State to audit its laws and practices to separate out any breaches arising from custom and any arising from the Koran and authoritative tradition. This would allow the State to take action to combat the former, and to replace its general reservation with any specific ones deemed necessary because of the latter.

5. While the Committee made adverse comments upon the State's respect for the views of the child, the delegation indicated that, as regards which parent the child should live with, there is traditionally more respect for the views of the child in Saudi Arabia than in Western States.

6. The Saudi delegation's claim that the teachings of Islam sometimes 'surpass' the Convention might be seen as an invocation of Article 41 of the Convention which protects any existing higher standards from potential dilution through application of the Convention. This raises a question about the criteria for identification of a higher standard.

7. Because it is framed in religious terms, the Saudi report speaks to the ideal that is encouraged, rather than the reality of human failure towards which law and rights are generally targeted.

2.5.2 The Holy See

The Holy See is a State recognised by international law, with jurisdiction over a small geographical area (The Vatican City State). Citizenship is limited to those who work for the Holy See. There are no children within its territory.[18]

The Holy See is also the 'highest organ of government of the Catholic Church'.[19] It was influential in the drafting of the Convention on the Rights of the Child, and one of the first to ratify it, though with some reservations, discussed below.[20] In its dialogue with the Holy See, the UN Committee recognised that its unique status justified some deviation from the standard form of report and interrogation, while its acknowledged influence over other States justified a close examination of the philosophy underlying its approach to the Convention.[21]

On ratification, the Holy See submitted the following reservations and declarations:

Reservation

a) That it interprets the phrase *'family planning* education and services' in article 24 (2) to mean only those methods of family planning which it considers morally acceptable, that is, the natural methods of family planning;

b) That it interprets the articles of the Convention in a way which safeguards the *primary and inalienable rights of parents*, in particular insofar as these rights concern *education* (arts. 13 and 28), *religion* (art. 14), *association* with others (art. 15) and *privacy* (art. 16);

c) That the application of the Convention be compatible in practice with the particular nature of the Vatican City State and of the sources of its objective law (art. 1, Law of 7 June 1929, n. 11) and, in consideration of its limited extent, with its legislation in the matters of citizenship, access and residence.

Declaration

The Holy See regards the present Convention as a proper and laudable instrument aimed at protecting the rights and interest of children, who are 'that precious treasure given to each generation as a challenge to its wisdom and humanity' (Pope John Paul II, 26 April 1984).

The Holy See recognizes that the Convention represents an enactment of principles previously adopted by the United Nations and, once effective as a ratified instrument, will safeguard the rights of the child *before as well as after birth,* as expressly affirmed in the Declaration of the Rights of the Child (General Assembly resolution 1386 (XIV) of 20 November 1959) and restated in the ninth preambular paragraph of the Convention. The Holy See remains confident that the ninth preambular paragraph will serve as the perspective through which the rest of the Convention will be interpreted, in conformity with article 31 of the Vienna Convention on the Law of Treaties of 23 May 1969.

By acceding to the Convention on the Rights of the Child, the Holy See intends to give renewed expression to its constant concern for the well-being of children and families. In consideration of its singular nature and position, the Holy See, in acceding to this Convention, does not intend to prescind in any way from its specific mission which is of a religious and moral character.[22]

Initial Report

The Holy See's Initial Report starts with an affirmation of the 'inherent dignity of the child, in his or her capacity as a human being, which is the source of children's rights and society's duties towards children'.[23] It describes some of the activities of the Catholic Church throughout the world that promote the welfare of children, including 'mobilizing children themselves to help other children'.[24] It lists statements made by the Pope and Holy See representatives in support of the Convention, commenting that:

These statements indicate the importance the Church attaches to the promotion of the Convention for improving the observance of the rights it proclaims. They emphasize in particular the right to life and the role of the family.[25]

This emphasis is reflected in the concerns expressed in the reservations. The report explains that reservation (a) rests upon the Church's prohibition of artificial contraception, sterilisation and abortion. With regard to reservation (b), the report comments:

It is obvious that children's rights must be protected in cases where it is proved that abuses have been committed within the family. However, under normal circumstances, the civilian authorities must not intervene, because of the 'primary and inalienable rights of parents', in particular in all matters relating to education, religion, association with others and privacy ...[26]

The report explains that parents have expressed concern that their rights to educate their children free from state control are not adequately protected by the terms of the Convention. The rights to freedom of religion, association and privacy:

> might imply, in some cases, that children would have the right to make certain choices that might be against their own interests and the integrity of family life and values. In order for articles 14, 15 and 16 not to be used to enable children to join certain religious sects, to associate with corrupt individuals and to live a life of vice, they must be interpreted in the light of the rights/duties of parents and the family. This interpretation is in conformity with that of the Human Rights Committee in its General Comment No. 22 (48) on article 18 of the International Covenant on Civil and Political Rights (CCPR/C/21/Rev.1/Add.4).[27]

The Holy See's commentary on this reservation concludes that:

> A serious study should be conducted of the problem of implementing specific articles of the Convention in certain social and political situations. It is true that some safeguards of the rights of parents and the family have been included in the Convention, but they need to be explained and clarified, in order to guarantee the rights and well-being of children without undermining the rights of their parents and the well-being of their families.[28]

In general, the Holy See presents an idealised portrait of the family. For example:

No country on earth, no political system can think of its own future otherwise than through the image of these new generations that will receive from their parents the manifold heritage of values, duties and aspirations of the nation to which they belong and of the whole human family.[29]

It does recognise that families sometimes fall short of this ideal:

[I]n order to palliate family shortcomings, the Church has set up a large number of institutions which provide children with the family environment they need for their development.[30]

It is suggested that such shortcomings may require children to be placed outside the family, although the relevant paragraph speaks first of orphaned children and secondly of children who are 'deprived of the assistance of their parents':

Orphans or children who are deprived of the assistance of their parents or guardians must receive particular protection on the part of society. The State, with regard to foster-care or adoption, must provide legislation which assists suitable families to welcome into their home children who are in need of permanent or temporary care. The legislation must, at the same time, respect the natural rights of parents.[31]

The Holy See's 1983 *Charter of the Rights of the Family* is generally referred to as a fuller exposition of its perspective. This declares:

A. The rights of the person, even though they are expressed as rights of the individual, have a fundamental social dimension which finds an innate and vital expression in the family ...

D. the family, a natural society, exists prior to the State or any other community, and possesses inherent rights which are inalienable;

E. the family constitutes, much more than a mere juridical, social and economic unit, a community of love and solidarity ...

F. the family is the place where different generations come together and help one another to grow in human wisdom and to harmonize the rights of individuals with other demands of social life ...

L. the Catholic Church, aware that the good of the person, of society and of the Church herself passes by way of the family, has always held it part of her mission to proclaim to all the plan of God instilled in human nature concerning marriage and the family, to promote these two institutions and to defend them against all who attack them ...[32]

Dialogue

The dialogue between the Holy See and the Committee on the Rights of the Child touched on many issues concerning health and family planning, choice of education and freedom of religion. However, the main point of difference between the parties to the dialogue rested upon the identification by the Holy See of the 'inalienable rights of parents' and the implications for the rights of the child. Members of the Committee asked how the identification of parental rights as 'inalienable,' especially in the context of child abuse, could be reconciled with the fundamental rights of children, both within the family and in the school.[33] The delegation commented:

> The Holy See recognised that violence occurred within the family. In the case of incest – an especially egregious form of violence – the best interests of the child must be foremost and the interests of the family could no longer be seen as taking precedence. Action must be taken to protect the child from psychological and moral trauma and the case be brought before the appropriate authorities.[34]

In response to a question from the Committee about points of conflict between its *Charter of the Rights of the Family* and the Convention, the Holy See reported that, in January 1996, it planned to produce a document on the theme of the child to celebrate World Peace Day. This would make reference to the situation of children who were victims of domestic violence, armed conflicts and various forms of exploitation and was based on the principles of the Convention.[35] This document does indeed refer to these issues. However, it observes that violence towards children is 'infrequent' in wealthy and affluent families. [36]

In relation to the *physical punishment* of children, a delegate commented:

> Corporal punishment ... was a matter of considerable controversy ... [H]is comments did not constitute the set doctrine of the Holy See. In his view, corporal punishment should not be banned until such time as psychoanalysts, sociologists, jurists, doctors and educators agreed.[37]

Regarding the respective rights of *parents*, *children* and *the state*, delegates pointed to Article 5 (parental guidance and the child's evolving capacities) as support for the Holy See's perspective.[38] This was acknowledged by the Committee, which nevertheless pointed out the connection between that article and Article 12 (concerning the child's views).[39] The Holy See said it accepted the right of the child to express an opinion. Respect for opinion was a fundamental principle of the Catholic Church.

The Holy See said that its position as regards *freedom of religion* was clear: a parent could give their religion but did not have the right to impose it.[40] Further, the delegates reported:

> Recently, there had been a certain evolution in the Church's thinking about the right to freedom of religion, especially where the child was concerned.[41]

With regard to *education*:

> The Holy See recognises the rights of children to participate in the running of and life of the school, in a manner corresponding with the child's capacities.[42]

The Committee also made comment upon the Holy See's perspective on *gender* in education. The Initial Report had referred to a 1965 Vatican II *Declaration on Christian Education*, which had stated that:

> [E]ducation should be suitable to the particular destiny of the individuals, adapted to their ability, sex and national cultural traditions.[43]

The Committee said it could not subscribe to the idea that education must conform to national culture and traditions. Sometimes educators had to struggle against established practices prejudicial to children. It was, to say the least, surprising that education was to be designed to take account of differences of gender. Emphasis was also placed by the Holy See upon the role of the family in the education of children, but in many poor countries the parents were often illiterate and ignorant of educational needs. While they ought to be able to have a say, the matter could not be left to their entire discretion.[44]

The Holy See defended its position with respect to the need for respect for people from other cultures. Reconciliation between opposing values could best be achieved through dialogue. A delegate observed:

> A child has a gender. A mother does not speak with her daughter in the same way that she speaks with her son. Nevertheless, in a broad sense, there is not an education directed specifically at boys or at girls. The present situation is the product of a past in which there was a neat division between the sexes. It had to be recognised that the Holy See had demonstrated much understanding and humanity.[45]

Concluding Observations

The Committee's Concluding Observations welcomed the Holy See's general support for the Convention as well as its positive efforts to disseminate and translate it worldwide. The document also sets out the Committee's principal subjects of concern:

The Committee is concerned about reservations entered by the Holy See to the Convention on the Rights of the Child, in particular with respect to the full recognition of the child as a subject of rights.

The Committee is concerned that discrimination between children may arise in Catholic schools and institutions, in particular with regard to gender.

The Committee is concerned at the insufficient attention paid to the promotion of education of children on health matters, the development of preventative health care, guidance for parents and family planning education and services, in the light of the provisions of the Convention.[46]

The Committee also made some recommendations, including the following:

The Committee emphasizes the need for professionals and voluntary workers involved in the education and protection of children to receive adequate training and education, taking into account the principles set forth in the Convention. The Committee also recommends that the Convention be included in the curricula of Catholic schools ...

The Committee recommends that the position of the Holy See with regard to the relationship between articles 5 and 12 of the Convention be clarified. In this respect, it wishes to recall its view that the rights and prerogatives of the parents may not undermine the rights of the child as recognised by the Convention, especially the right of the child to express his or her own views and that his or her views be given due weight.[47]

The following comments might be made upon this dialogue:

1. The Holy See is amenable to the 'rights' language of the Convention, but understands it in the context of 'inherent rights' endowed as part of the 'plan of God'.[48]

2. The Holy See acknowledges the existence of individual rights, but insists that they have a social dimension, particularly with regard to the family.

3. The Holy See's understanding of the significance of gender may also reflect a particular cultural anthropological perspective. [49] As with Islam, it may be useful to attempt to separate out the cultural and specifically religious dimensions of such anthropology.

4. The Holy See tends to speak of the family in idealistic terms, in a similar way to the Islamic delegation from Saudi Arabia, although it also makes reference to family shortcomings and child abuse.

5. The main source of tension between the Holy See and the UN Committee is the concern of each that family rights and children's rights respectively might be undermined by an excessive focus on the other.

6. In most other respects, the Holy See heartily approves of the Convention.

The Holy See's perspective upon the question is illuminated by the Pontifical Council for the Family's 1999 document entitled, *The Family and Human Rights*: a publication designed to celebrate the fiftieth anniversary of the Universal Declaration of Human Rights. While it also expresses a strong endorsement of the UN Convention on the Rights of the Child, this is oddly located entirely within those sections of the document relating to the unborn child, where not only the Convention in general but also specific substantive articles are explored in that connection.

The Family and Human Rights expresses strong support for the family:

> The family is thus a whole which should not be divided up when it is being dealt with by isolating its members ...[50]

The concern about state interference manifests as a fear of abuse of secular power:

> During the last decades, a negative impact has been produced because the family has suffered the same attacks which the State has made on other intermediate bodies by suppressing

them and trying to govern them in its own image. When the State claims the power to regulate family bonds and emits laws that do not respect this natural community, which is prior to the State, it is feared that the State may make use of families in its own interests, and instead of protecting them and defending their rights, it will weaken or destroy them in order to dominate peoples.[51]

[A]s the example of many countries indicates, including countries that are considered 'developed', an effective means of destroying the family consists in depriving it of its educational function under the false pretext of giving all children equal opportunities. In this case, the 'rights of children' are invoked against the rights of the family. The State often invades areas proper to the family in the name of democracy which ought to respect the principle of subsidiarity. We find ourselves before an omnipresent and arbitrary political power. The State or other institutions appropriate the right to speak on behalf of the children and remove them from the context of the family. As so many unfortunate past and present experiences reveal, the ideal for a dictatorship would be to have children without families. All attempts to substitute the family have failed.[52]

This fear of the subversion of families by totalitarian governments for their own ends was indeed one of the factors motivating and shaping the Universal Declaration of Human Rights. It is a danger that cannot and should not be ignored. However, it might be argued that too much emphasis on State tyranny of families might blind commentators to the disastrous effects of family tyranny of individual members. The question is, in this situation, whose job is it to identify the situation and to do something about it? This issue is further discussed at 6.2.4.3 below.

2.5.3 Poland

Poland's embrace of the Convention on the Rights of the Child is of interest for two reasons:

1. As indicated at 2.1 above, the drafting of a Convention on the Rights of the Child was an initiative of the Polish (at that time communist) government.[53]

2. Since the political changes of 1989, the influence of the Catholic Church has been more explicit.

According to a Polish delegate interviewed by the UN Committee, approximately 90 per cent of schoolchildren were Catholic. Seven per cent were associated with other denominations. Only 1 per cent professed no religion.[54] A 'situation analysis of children and families in Poland', published by UN Agencies in 1993, noted the 'growing influence of the Catholic Church' since the political changes of 1989. While that report focused upon the impact in terms of the reduction in the number of divorces,[55] a member of the UN Committee noted (without specific reference to any religious motivation) that, while twenty years previously Swedish women wishing abortions (a subject on which the UN Committee remained neutral) had made their way to Poland, this situation was now reversed.[56]

The draft Convention first proposed by Poland in 1978 was modelled closely on the 1959 Declaration on the Rights of the Child, on the basis that these had already secured the approval of the international community and might therefore be upgraded into a 'convention' quickly enough to be a fruit of the 1979 International Year of the Child. It has also been suggested that the 1959 Declaration's emphasis on economic, social and cultural rights, rather than civil and political rights, was compatible with the Polish political vision at that time. However, other states commented that: the language of the Declaration was not suitable for a legally binding treaty; that a Convention should be backed up by measures of implementation; and that the range of rights needed to be extended.[57]

Poland's specific interests can be identified in its contribution to the Working Group's revision of its first draft:

Poland was responsible, at an early stage in the drafting, for proposing the paragraph in the preamble that expresses support for the family as the fundamental group of society.[58]

Poland's original draft had echoed the 1959 Declaration in proposing protection before as well as after birth. This was later deleted, but restored to the Preamble (but not to the definition in Article 1 of the Convention) through the compromise proposal referred to at 2.2.1 above, involving insertion of an interpretative statement in the *Traveaux Preparatoires*. Poland supported the compromise.[59]

Poland submitted the original text of Article 28.2, concerning the need to ensure that school discipline took account of the child's dignity and rights.[60]

Poland ratified the Convention on 7 June 1991, subject to the following reservations:

(a) With respect to article 7 of the Convention, the Republic of Poland stipulates that the rights of an adopted child to know its natural parents shall be subject to the limitations imposed by binding legal arrangements that enable adoptive parents to maintain the confidentiality of the child's origin;

(b) The law of the Republic of Poland shall determine the age from which call-up to military or similar service and participation in military operations are permissible. That age limit may not be lower than the age limit set out in article 38 of the Convention.[61]

The following declarations were also made:

The Republic of Poland considers that a child's rights as defined in the Convention, in particular the rights defined in articles 12 to 16, shall be exercised with respect for parental authority, in accordance with Polish customs and traditions regarding the place of the child within and outside the family.

> With respect to article 24, paragraph 2 (f), of the Convention, the Republic of Poland considers that family planning and education services for parents should be in keeping with the principles of morality.[62]

Despite the political changes that took place in the intervening period, the Polish approach seems fairly consistent.

Initial Report and Dialogue with the Committee

Poland's Initial Report manifests clear parallels between its concerns and those of the Holy See, although Poland justifies them with reference to traditional values rather than religious considerations. The Polish declarations reflect the Holy See's reservations about *parental authority* and family planning. While Poland makes no declaration about its understanding of the application of the Convention to the unborn child, its Initial Report identifies the extension of legal personality and protection to the unborn child as a measure of compliance with the Convention.[63] In a section of the Report entitled 'Final Remarks', Poland emphasises the correlation of rights and duties:

> The Convention is a document which widely describes the rights of the child but does not point to his/her duties. The Convention states that 'the child, by reason of his physical and mental immaturity, needs special safeguards and care'. For this reason the *separation of a child's rights from his/her duties* may hinder the process of directing his/her proper psycho-social development, thus being to his/her disadvantage.[64]

While the Holy See's report lacks such an explicit reference to duties, this approach is consistent with the communitarian approach of the 1983 Charter of the Rights of the Family, which speaks of the family as the place where members learn 'to harmonize the rights of individuals with other demands of social life'.

Gender is also an issue for Poland. The legal age for marriage, lower for girls than boys,[65] and differing rates of enrolment for girls and boys in non-compulsory secondary education,[66] were the subject of adverse comment by the Committee.

The Committee was particularly concerned at the identification of a 'loss of moral sense' (referred to in the report as 'juvenile demoralization')[67] as a criterion for the detention of a young person in an institution. The Polish delegation explained that this was a flexible criterion to be applied by the judge, but generally related to alcoholism, drug abuse, prostitution or vagrancy.[68] The Committee considered this to be too ill-defined and open to subjective interpretation.[69] In its Concluding Observations, it condemned this provision in very strong language:

> The situation in relation to the administration of juvenile justice … is a matter of concern to the Committee. In that regard, the Committee deplores the provisions relating to 'juvenile demoralization' which do not appear to be compatible with the Convention.[70]

The Polish report acknowledges the existence of child abuse, in all social environments.[71] There are legal criteria for depriving parents of their authority and placing children in substitute care, 'should the parents abuse parental authority or neglect their responsibilities towards the child in a blatant manner'.[72] The Committee was concerned that this *threshold for intervention* might be too high, and that there might be situations in which the social agencies and tribunals needed to act sooner.[73]

Article 95 of Poland's Family and Guardianship Code provides that:

2. The child under parents' power should be obedient to parents.

3. Parental authority should be exercised in accordance with the well-being of the child and with the social interest.[74]

The Committee expressed some concern about what it saw as an over-emphasis on *obedience* at the expense of the child's rights.[75] A committee member expressed concerns at the possible consequences of a dominant ideology of child obedience.[76]

Comment

One might ask about the extent to which the Polish perspective is shaped by religion, tradition or by more recent political experience. The religious perspective is not explicit, but may be latent, shaping the values of the society. It is clear that Poland regards the preservation of certain values as critical to the stability of society and the development of children. Its recourse to 'loss of moral sense' as a criterion for intervention presupposes a shared morality. The Initial Report refers to the importance of values in family life:

> The family is the most important educational environment, where all the major decisions are made concerning the child's development. An increasing number of factors negatively affecting the family's stability, covering the spheres of values, human relations and economic conditions, bring about a growth in the number of children partly or completely bereft of parental care.[77]

Political sensitivities may also be significant. The Polish delegation observed:

> The first step towards changing traditional attitudes and doing away with stereotypes was to promote an awareness that change was indeed necessary. Non-governmental organizations had a very important role to play in that field, for changes in patterns of thinking could not be imposed by governmental edict, particularly as the legacy of the socialist era had left the public somewhat reluctant to accept central government regulation. Non-governmental organizations were thus at an advantage in that regard.[78]

The UN Agencies' situation analysis of children and families in Poland had observed:

> The dismantling of institutions and social norms of the socialist regime has not been accompanied by an equally

rapid and extensive development of adequate substitutes thus causing social costs beyond those due to economic factors ... A considerable institutional vacuum has emerged, with negative consequences for youth socialization and the crime rate. At the same time, the disintegration of the old value system and the absence or slow development of new values has given rise to a new ideological vacuum on which pseudo values and deviant behaviours can take root easily ... faced with declining real incomes, greater economic insecurity, the erosion of customs and values and the need to struggle hard just to ensure basic survival (often entailing long absences from home), many families – already weakened during the socialist period – have seen their supervisory and control role further weakened.[79]

In the light of this history, it may seem unsurprising that there is some resistance to anything presenting as state control of families. The identification of the family as the basic building block of society is a cornerstone of both the Convention on the Rights of the Child and Catholic social teaching. Fear engendered by recent experiences and current vulnerability may well explain Polish suspicion of anything that might present as a threat to parental authority. One might even speculate as to the influence such thinking might exert upon the Polish Pope.

At the close of the final Committee session considering Poland's report, a member observed:

> One has in fact often the impression that Polish society is hesitant about accepting the very notion of the rights of the child.[80]

This may seem a surprising comment to make of the country which initiated the drafting of the Convention. It reflects what has become a significant focus upon participatory rights as central to the Convention. The first draft Convention prepared by Poland had been largely protective in character, and lacked any provision about respect for the child's views. The intrinsic connection between the protection of children and participation by them is explored at 6.5 below.

Second Report and Dialogue with the Committee

Poland's Second Report to the Committee,[81] dated 6 February 2002, was discussed in October of that year. Poland described itself as 'one of Europe's most rapidly developing countries',[82] with a new Constitution, adopted in 1997, that included international agreements such as the Convention on the Rights of the Child in the country's sources of national law. Article 48.1 set out the right of parents to rear their children in accordance with their own convictions, together with their obligation to take into account the *child's degree of maturity* as well as its *freedom of conscience, creed* and *conviction*. Education law had been revised to provide that:

> Acknowledging the right of parents to provide their children with religious training, public primary schools shall organize religious instruction at the request of parents and post-primary schools at the request of parents or pupils; on attaining the age of majority, pupils shall decide the question of instruction themselves.[83]

Among the new state agencies that had emerged since the publication of the Initial Report were a number with specific responsibility for children, including a 'spokesperson for the Rights of Children'.[84] Poland now felt able to move towards withdrawal of the reservations and declarations made on ratification,[85] and it was hoped that this would be achieved in 2003.

While acknowledging these positive developments, the Committee, in dialogue with the Polish delegation, observed that their report focused too heavily on legislation, paying insufficient attention to implementation. Nor was any specific reference made to the follow-up to the Committee's Concluding Observations on the Initial Report.[86]

The Committee's questioning of the delegation about specific issues seemed sometimes designed to probe the impact of the Roman Catholic Church on implementation. For example, a member of the Committee asked about sex education in school. 'How did the Government deal with the question of teenage sexual activities in a society that was so attached to traditional and religious values?'[87] A delegate explained that schools proposed two types of programmes: one oriented towards family values, and the other towards sex education as such. However, a plan was being elaborated which would allow more systematic coverage of the subject.[88]

In its Concluding Observations to the Second Report, the Committee welcomed the commitment to withdraw the reservations and declarations and also the legislative measures designed to implement the rights of the child. However, it recommended that Poland:

> Provide educational information to, among others, parents, teachers, government officials, the judiciary, the Roman Catholic Church and other religious groups, and society at large, on children's right to have their views taken into account and to participate in matters affecting them.[89]

As regards freedom of thought, conscience and religion, the Report notes:

> The Committee is concerned that, despite regulations guaranteeing that parents can choose for their children to attend ethics classes instead of religion classes in public schools, in practice few schools offer ethics courses to allow for such a choice and students require parental consent to attend ethics courses.

> The Committee recommends that the state party ensure that all public schools permit children, in practice, to choose freely whether to attend religion or ethics classes with parental direction provided in a manner consistent with the child's evolving capacities.[90]

The Committee expressed concern about the relatively high rate of teenage pregnancies and recommended the institution of health education and awareness programmes, specifically for adolescents, on sexual reproductive health.[91]

Conclusions

The following comments might be made about the UN Committee's dialogue with Poland:

1. Poland initiated the drafting of the Convention while still a socialist regime (1979). The draft it proposed was protective rather than participative in character.

2. From 1989 (the initiation of political change and the date of the passing of the Convention by the UN General Assembly) to the time of its dialogue with the UN Committee, Poland became increasingly subject to the visible influence of the Roman Catholic Church.

3. In spite of these changes in political structure, there is no obvious discontinuity in Poland's approach to the rights of the child.

4. The Initial Report reflected the fact that the institutional vacuum caused by the dismantling of the socialist regime had given more cause to emphasize the need for family stability and parental authority.

5. Nevertheless, Poland is more aware than the Holy See of the reality of familial child abuse across all social classes and the need to tackle this.

6. By the time the second report was produced, decrease in fear of the state and the increase in institutional supports had lessened the need to rely exclusively on parental authority and allowed a greater focus on the rights of the child.

7. The first step in implementation of the Convention is to embed its principles in domestic law. Poland has

done much towards this. The Committee's lingering concerns are focused on the influence that traditional and religious attitudes might have on the implementation of the rights of the child.

2.6 Protestant Support for the Convention

As indicated at 2.4 above, it is more difficult to identify a Protestant than a Catholic perspective from the documentation of the UN Committee on the Rights of the Child. This section identifies some explicit Protestant support for the Convention, both globally and within the USA. The national support referred to focuses on the USA because this is the locus of the most vocal Protestant opposition to the Convention, the character of which will be explored in the section following.

2.6.1 World Council of Churches

The World Council of Churches (which includes the major Protestant and Orthodox communions) has consistently advocated for effective implementation of the Convention on the Rights of the Child, including recognition of the need to empower children towards active participation in activities affecting their welfare. It has supported the establishment of the Global Network of Religions for Children, an initiative of the Arigatou Foundation, a Buddhist peace organisation based in Japan.[92]

2.6.2 Baptist

In January 2000, the Baptist Peace Fellowship of North America, in an Open Letter to the eighteenth Baptist World Congress, urged all member bodies of the Baptist World Alliance to encourage their governments to give active support to the Convention on the Rights of the Child.[93] The Alliance has published a booklet on *The Rights of the Child*, written by the chair of its Human Rights Commission.[94]

2.6.3 Episcopalian

In September 2002, the Anglican Consultative Council (an international body representing the churches of the Anglican communion) passed a resolution in support of the Global Rights of Children, with a particular focus on support for the UN Convention on the Rights of the Child.

The Episcopal Church in the USA has frequently spoken in support of the Convention and produced *The Children's Charter for the Church*, which speaks of: the *nature* of the child (quoting Psalm 127:4, 'Children are a heritage from the Lord, and the fruit of the womb is a gift'); ministry *to* the child (quoting Mark 10:16, 'Then Jesus took the children in his arms, placed his hands on each of them and blessed them'); and the ministry *of* the child (quoting Isaiah 11:6, 'A child shall lead them').[95]

2.6.4 Lutheran

The Lutheran World Federation officially supports the Convention on the Rights of the Child. In 1990, the Federation's General Secretary described it as 'one of the most important human rights instruments ever approved', and urged universal adoption and compliance. The Federation has worked actively to encourage ratification. Its Council has also adopted a number of resolutions urging action in relation to specific provisions of the Convention and its Optional Protocols.[96]

2.6.5 Methodist

In 1998, the Council of Bishops of the United Methodist Church, meeting in the USA, adopted a resolution urging ratification of the Convention on the Rights of the Child.[97] Members of the United Methodist Board of Church and Society had earlier been asked to write to their US senators to encourage ratification of the Convention.[98]

2.6.6   Reformed

The World Alliance of Reformed Churches (of which the Church of Scotland was a founder member and which includes the main Reformed and Presbyterian churches) does not have an explicit, official position on the Convention. However, its twenty-third General Council, in 1997, adopted recommendations relating to human rights set within a report of its Public Issues Committee, which referred with approval to The Universal Declaration of Human Rights and the UN Convention on the Rights of the Child.[99]

Within the USA, The General Assembly of the Presbyterian Church (USA) has been a long-term supporter of the Convention on the Rights of the Child and other UN initiatives. It has repeatedly urged ratification of the Convention (in 1991, 1995, 1996). In 1997 it approved a Resolution on Children, which again called upon Presbyterians, the church and the United States government to continue work to guarantee the rights of children.[100]

2.7   Protestant Resistance to the Convention

In spite of this mainstream support, there has also been vocal and effective Christian opposition to the Convention. This section discusses some of the resistance particularly, but not exclusively, within the United States of America.

While the religious and cultural concerns of countries that have ratified the Convention manifested in reservations and declarations by the states involved, they have had a more dramatic impact in the USA, which has not yet ratified. A UNICEF document explains this omission as follows:

> By signing the Convention, the United States has signalled its intention to ratify – but has yet to do so.
>
> As in many other nations, the United States undertakes an extensive examination and scrutiny of treaties before proceeding to ratify. This examination, which includes an

evaluation of the degree of compliance with existing law and practice in the country at state and federal levels, can take several years – or even longer if the treaty is portrayed as being controversial or if the process is politicised ... Moreover, the US Government typically will consider only one human rights treaty at a time. Currently, the Convention on the Elimination of All Forms of Discrimination against Women is cited as the nation's top priority among human rights treaties.[101]

The USA was an active participant in the drafting process, shaping many of the articles towards conformity with American law. It was one of the first to sign (and has now ratified) the two optional protocols to the Convention passed by the General Assembly of the United Nations on 25 May 2000, relating to the Involvement of Children in Armed Conflict, and the Sale of Children, Child Prostitution and Child Pornography. Yet, despite much pressure to do so, and the personal support of the former First Lady Hillary Rodham Clinton, the USA remains one of the two states in the world yet to ratify the Convention. Why should this be so?

Within the USA, ratification of the Convention on the Rights of the Child is a controversial question. Amnesty International USA locates the main opposition to ratification within certain Christian organisations that are politically conservative. It identifies the Christian Coalition, Concerned Women for America, Eagle Forum, Family Research Council, Focus on the Family, the John Birch Society, the National Centre for Home Education and the Rutherford Institute as having 'spearheaded opposition to the Convention'.[102] Amnesty comments:

> These organisations have made a significant effort to portray the Convention as a threat. The majority of the opposition's claims stem from unfounded concerns related to national sovereignty, states' rights, and the parent-child relationship. The most common concerns voiced by the opposition include:

The Convention usurps national and state sovereignty.

The Convention undermines parental authority.

The Convention would allow and encourage children to sue parents, join gangs, have abortions.

The United Nations would dictate how we raise and teach our children.

These claims and perceptions are a result of misconceptions, erroneous information, and a lack of understanding about how international human rights treaties are implemented in the United States. Notably, in many cases, the Convention's opponents criticize provisions which were added by the Reagan and Bush Administrations during the drafting process in an effort to reflect the rights American children have under the U.S. Constitution.

These public efforts are reinforced by a number of Senators which oppose ratification of the Convention. Opposition in the Senate is led by Senator Jesse Helms (R-NC). Citing his opinion that 'the United Nations Convention on the Rights of the Child is incompatible with God-given right and responsibilities of parents to raise their children,' and that 'the Convention has the potential to severely restrict States and the Federal Government in their efforts to protect children and to enhance family life,' Senator Helms, along with 26 cosponsors, introduced a Senate resolution in June 1995 which urges the President not to transmit the Convention to the Foreign Relations Committee (which Helms Chairs) for review. It must be noted, however, that, since 1990, five resolutions have also been introduced in Congress which **support** U.S. ratification of the Convention.

The senator's perspective reported here raises two questions relevant to this book:

1. What are the 'God-given right and responsibilities of parents to raise their children'?

2. Are they incompatible with the Convention?

These questions will be addressed in chapters 6 and 7. In the meantime, it may be helpful to explore the thinking, and fears, behind the position of those politically conservative Christian groups.

2.7.1 The Position of Politically Conservative Christian Organisations

Where there is Christian opposition to the Convention, this may be based on religious or political justifications, although the two often come together. The religious basis is put forward by the Center for Reclaiming America:

> Scripture is clear on the rights and responsibilities of parents and children. The Fifth Commandment, 'honour your father and mother,' is God's standard for domestic order. For that reason, those who seek to elevate the rights of children at the expense of parents are at war with God's original design and, therefore, with God himself.[103]

The political resistance manifests in a general suspicion of, and indeed hostility to, the United Nations.[104] It is sometimes portrayed as an explicitly secular or humanist organisation, whose unelected executives are working towards the establishment of a world government based upon secular or pagan values.[105] It is presented as having a particular concern to promote abortion.[106] The Constitution of the United States, whose drafters were reportedly 98 per cent Christian, is perceived as anchoring the country's law and culture in the law of God.[107] Suspicion is further fuelled by the Convention's origin as an initiative of the then communist Polish government.[108]

Against this background, it is perhaps not surprising that the UN's work on children is specifically resisted. As one commentator observed:

> The intention of people who want to change the world is to gain control of other people's children.[109]

Opponents of the Convention on the Rights of the Child interpret UN documents, and statements by the UN or related agencies, against this background. For example, Article 34 of the Convention on the Rights of the Child states:

> States Parties undertake to protect the child from all forms of sexual exploitation and sexual abuse. For these purposes, States Parties shall in particular take all appropriate national, bilateral and multilateral measures to prevent:
>
> (a) The inducement or coercion of a child to engage in any unlawful sexual activity;
>
> (b) The exploitative use of children in prostitution or other unlawful sexual practices;
>
> (c) The exploitative use of children in pornographic performances and materials.

An Australian commentator identified the inclusion of the words 'unlawful' and 'exploitative' as 'the sleight of hand of the conjuror' designed to severely limit the scope of any supposed protection. In his view, the article legitimises the involvement of children in prostitution or pornographic performances, so long as it is legal in terms of their national laws, is undertaken voluntarily by the child, and is subject to appropriate remuneration and working conditions.[110] Is this true?

The *Traveaux Preparatoires* show that there was thoughtful debate about inclusion of these words.[111]

China and the USSR questioned the reference to 'unlawful'. The delegate from the Netherlands explained that it was necessary to include this because it was not the case that all sexual activity by under-18s was unlawful. This was supported by the United Kingdom representative who pointed out that 16 was the age at which sexual activity and marriage were permissible: 'the draft convention could not declare unlawful sexual practices between husband and wife under the age of 18'. The USSR accepted this explanation and withdrew its objection.

Norway and Australia were uncertain about the use of 'exploitative'. Representatives from France and the Netherlands replied that the reference to 'exploitative' was indispensable; the purpose of the provision was not to regulate the sexual life of children but rather to combat the sexual exploitation of children.

China eventually agreed to the retention of 'unlawful' on the understanding that the exploitative use of children in sexual matters could never be lawful, thus linking the two debates.

It clearly made sense to retain 'unlawful', given that the age of consent to sexual activity and the age of marriage (which appear to be related in all states) varies from 12 to 18. This does not mean that the UN approves of early involvement in sexual activity. The UN Committee on the Rights of the Child has consistently expressed concern where it has considered the age of consent to be too low. Further, Hodgkin and Newell note that:

> The definition of sexual abuse of children covers more than non-consensual activities, including sexual activities with children below the age of consent, whether or not they appeared willing and even initiating partners.[112]

Any lingering concerns about the implications of the inclusion of 'exploitative' should be laid to rest by the UN General Assembly's adoption of an Optional Protocol on the Sale of Children, Prostitution and Child Pornography. Passed on 25 May 2001, it entered into force on 18 January 2002, following its ratification by ten states. The first two articles state:

1. States Parties shall prohibit the sale of children, child prostitution and child pornography as provided for by the present Protocol.

2. For the purpose of the present Protocol:
   (a) Sale of children means any act or transaction whereby a child is transferred by any person or group of persons to another for remuneration or any other consideration;
   (b) Child prostitution means the use of a child in sexual activities for remuneration or any other form of consideration;

(c) Child pornography means any representation, by whatever means, of a child engaged in real or simulated explicit sexual activities or any representation of the sexual parts of a child for primarily sexual purposes.

Other provisions of the Convention are also misunderstood by its opponents. Thus, it has been said that it: 'deems children (age 18 and under) as autonomous from their parents'.[113] This is clearly not an accurate interpretation of Article 12 of the Convention (respect for the child's views), especially when interpreted in the light of articles 3 (the best interests of the child)[114] and 5 (parental guidance and the child's evolving capacities).

Opponents give examples of breaches of parental rights, which are presented as legitimised by the Convention. The Center for Reclaiming America cites the following examples:

1. A claim that the American Library Association's policy allows children unrestricted access to any material, including pornographic books, films and internet websites;

2. A reported incident in Pennsylvania in 1996, involving the vaginal examination of fifty-nine sixth-grade girls without the consent of the girls or their parents;

3. A child being forced to attend a 'live seminar' about safe sex, against the child's express wish not to attend.[115]

Far from legitimising or encouraging these occurrences, a true interpretation of the Convention on the Rights of the Child would lead to their condemnation.

As regards example 1, Article 17 of the Convention sets out the child's right of access to *appropriate* information. Paragraph (e) requires States Parties to:

Encourage the development of appropriate guidelines for the protection of the child from information and material injurious to his or her well-being, bearing in mind the provisions of articles 13 [freedom of expression] and 18 [recognition of parental responsibilities for the upbringing and development of the child].

It is difficult to see how total freedom of access could be consistent with the Convention. Indeed, Hodgkin and Newell give examples of the UN Committee's criticisms of States that had failed to provide adequate protection for children. Similarly, the other two reported events would seem on the face of it to breach several provisions of the Convention, including: Article 12 (the child's view to be given due weight in any matter affecting the child); Article 5 (the rights and duties of parents to provide direction and guidance to the child consistent with the child's evolving capacities); and Article 18 (parental responsibilities).

If such things are happening in the United States, one might argue that there is very much a need for a Convention on the Rights of the Child to promote the rights and interests of children, young people and their parents.

One explanation for this concern may be that the concept of 'children's rights' can mean different things to different people. An Australian commentator cited statements by 'child liberationists' who proposed that children:

should be able, at any age, to choose with whom they should live;

need to be liberated from the oppression of childhood, masquerading as protection;

should be free to design their own education;

should be free to conduct their own sexual lives with no more restrictions than adults; and

should have the right to work.[116]

The children's rights movement is not homogenous, but represents shades of opinion. Anyone who wishes to do so will no doubt be able to identify within the children's rights literature liberationist statements with which they disagree. However, this is a characteristic shared by most academic or policy-oriented bodies or movements, including religious organisations. What should be clear from a reading of the Convention, and the content of this chapter, is that extreme liberationist interpretations cannot be founded in the text of Convention. In fact, they are contrary to the Convention's provisions.

To sum up, the following comments might be made upon the position of the politically conservative Christian organisations:

1. Opposition to the Convention in the USA is 'spear-headed' by those organisations, and based upon:
    (a) The perceived threat to the sovereignty of the state; and
    (b) The perceived threat to the authority (sovereignty?) of parents.

    Implicit in these might be a threat to the sovereignty of God. Related arguments are supported with references to Scripture.

2. Despite the suspicion of the communist Polish origins of the Convention, the concerns expressed by politically conservative Christian organisations reflect some of the concerns expressed in the Polish declarations; both states place emphasis on child obedience, and both are resistant to the state control of families.

3. Two particular questions require the more detailed consideration which will be afforded in Chapter 7 below:
    (a) What are the 'God-given right and responsibilities of parents to raise their children'? and
    (b) Are these incompatible with the Convention?

2.7.2 Assessment of the Politically Conservative Christian Position

Is the case made out by opponents of the Convention completely without foundation? It is difficult to argue against the fears about the aims of the United Nations as a whole without descending into assertion and counter-assertion based upon one's own perspective. In the authors' view, the case for a conspiracy aimed at undermining religion and setting up a secular world government is not substantiated; nor are such suspicions evident in the statements and actions of the states and religious bodies that have supported the Convention. In particular, it was concluded at 2.5.3 above, that there is no obvious discontinuity between Poland's approach before and after the demise of communism. Nevertheless, some religious supporters of the Convention agree that there are areas of 'ambiguity' within it, which might cause understandable concern.

Thus, while the Convention itself avoids the issue of *abortion*, this might be a service facilitated for pregnant teenagers by the right to family planning education and services set out in Article 24(2)(f), combined with the right to privacy, proclaimed by Article 16.[117] As indicated above, some states have reserved their position as regards *family planning*, or set out their particular understanding of what it covers, in order to make it clear that their approval of the Convention as a whole must not be understood as approval of abortion. The Convention at least provides a mechanism whereby they can do this, thus allowing them to resolve any ambiguity on their own terms.

Another area of disagreement, about which much has been written, concerns the *physical punishment* of children. Article 19 of the Convention sets out the right of the child to protection from 'all forms of physical or mental violence', while in the care of parents, guardians or other carers. While this does not explicitly mention physical punishment, the UN Committee on the Rights of the Child has nevertheless stated that such punishment is 'incompatible with the Convention' and has urged states to take both legislative and educational measures to change attitudes and practice.[118] This is a matter of particular concern to those Christians who regard physical chastisement of children by their parents as not so much a right but a religious duty. It is further discussed at 6.9 below.

Education is another sensitive issue. Article 29(1)(b) includes among the aims of education:

> The development of respect for human rights and fundamental freedoms, and for the principles enshrined in the Charter of the United Nations.

It has been said that some Christians understand this as a requirement to study secular, humanist materials.[119] This concern appears to be related to their more general suspicion of the aims and character of the United Nations.

There has also been some concern about the possible flexibility of interpretation of the 'child's best interests', the standard set in Article 3 as 'a primary consideration' in any decision affecting a child. This, it is said, might mean different things to traditionalist Christians and secular humanists.[120] This is of course correct. However, the Convention has to be read as a whole. Article 3 is identified as a 'basic principle' which permeates all others. This is a two-way flow. Any assessment of the child's best interests in the context of the Convention would be informed by the other standards set out in the Convention.[121]

The best interests of the child are already generally recognised as the standard to be applied in court systems when decisions are being made about children. The same questions arise in those situations: who decides, and on what criteria? Should parents have an unopposed right to determine where their children's best interests lie? The courts may, for example, override parental rights where the parents' religiously justified refusal to consent to medical treatment for their child would result in that child's avoidable death.[122] Is this an unjustified undermining of the rights of the parents, or a vindication of the rights of the child? Would those who insist on the primacy of parental rights take the same view of the rights of all other parents no matter what they proposed to do? Is it a parent's right to force an abortion on a 14-year-old girl who does not want one? Might a parent insist that their 8-year-old stayed off school and went out to work? Is it all right for a parent to insist that a Christian child convert to a sect that worshipped idols and believed in free and early sex?

These 'parent liberationist' arguments might be derided as 'bizarre', but they could well be legitimised in a system that provided no external checks upon the authority of parents.

The 'best interests of the child' is indeed a subjective concept. Within the international community, it is interpreted against the background of the UN Convention as a whole. Within any particular society, decision-making bodies will interpret it against the background of their own laws, culture and traditions. In ratifying the UN Convention, states agree to accept the Convention as a common standard informing and shaping those laws and evolving traditions. Anyone concerned with the welfare of children should of course be watchful for unhelpful interpretations and should identify and oppose them. That is indeed what many of the Christian opponents of the Convention believe that they are doing. There will always be potential for disagreement in particular matters. The question is whether opponents of the Convention are basing their opposition on an accurate understanding of its content and application and the motives behind its promulgation.

2.8 Conclusion

The UN Convention on the Rights of the Child is a document widely respected by politicians and policy-makers. It is remarkable in its attraction of broad religious support. There remain nevertheless pockets of concern about the potential impact on family life of what might be interpreted as, or evolve into, a child autonomy which undermines both the welfare of children and the authority and stability of family life. These issues will be central concerns of Chapter 6, which explores the human rights of the child and how they impact on the lives of children and families. In particular, this chapter will address:

freedom of thought, conscience and religion, and the implications for education;

freedom of association;

protection of privacy;

physical punishment; and

the child's duty of obedience to parents.

Chapter 7 observes that, throughout the history of Christian reflection on the relations of parents and children, the power of parents over their children has not been left unqualified. Some checks, some controls have been presupposed. Some limit cases have been delineated. But in the past this has been done piecemeal, in fairly random and haphazard fashion. The Convention at least provides a framework within which the complexities of such cases can be teased out.

However, some of the disagreements about the concept, content and implications of human rights, especially when attributed to children, arise from different understandings and usages of the concept of rights itself. The next chapter, therefore, explores these differences.

Notes

1. S. Detrick (ed.), *The United Nations Convention on the Rights of the Child: A Guide to the Traveaux Preparatoires*, Dordrecht: Martinus Nijhoff, 1991, p. 640. The major part of the text of the Convention is reproduced here as Appendix 1.

2. For the text of this document and a short commentary on the development of children's rights in international declarations – see K. Marshall, *Children's Rights in the Balance: The Participation–Protection Debate*, Edinburgh: The Stationery Office, 1997. For more detailed information about the history and drafting of the UN Convention, see Detrick, *Traveaux Preparatoires*.

3. Detrick, *Traveaux Preparatoires*, p. 26.

4. This is consistent, for example, with the Scots law *Nasciturus* principle. See E. E. Sutherland, *Child and Family Law*, Edinburgh: T&T Clark, 1999, 2.05–2.07.

5. In international law, the *Traveaux Preparatoires*, or 'preparatory work' can be consulted to clear up any ambiguities of wording by reference to the intention of the drafters. The actual statement read: 'In adopting this preambular paragraph, the Working Group does not intend to prejudice the interpretation of article 1 or any other provision of the Convention by States Parties' (E/CN.4/1989/48, pp. 8–15, quoted in R. Hodgkin and P. Newell, *Implementation Handbook for the Convention on the Rights of the Child*, (rev. edn), New York/Geneva: UNICEF, 2002, p. 3).

6. For an analysis of the relationship between Articles 3 and 12, see Marshall, *Children's Rights in the Balance*.

7. Although ratifications of human rights treaties by the USA have sometimes been accompanied by statements to the effect that they are not to be regarded as 'self-executing', an act whose legitimacy is questioned by some. See D. Sloss, 'The Domestication of International Human Rights: Non-Self-Executing Declarations and Human Rights Treaties', 24 *Yale Journal of International Law*, 129 (1999); synopsis accessed 10 March 2003 on www.yale.edu/yjil/v24ia3.html.

8. For example, the European Convention on Human Rights only became unequivocally incorporated into national law on the passing of the Human Rights Act 1998. There has been no similar Act of Parliament incorporating the UN Convention on the Rights of the Child, although particular pieces of legislation, such as the Children (Scotland) Act 1995, have been designed to implement some of its provisions.

9. This is an estimate, as reservations and declarations sometimes cover a number of provisions of the Convention and the precise aim is not always clear from the text.

10. The UN document CRC/C/2/Rev.8 of 7 December 1999 lists 16, but one must also take into account the likelihood that

many of the general reservations made by Islamic states might also be addressed to this provision. The states listed as having specific objections are: Algeria, Bangladesh, Brunei Darussalam, Holy See, Kiribati, Malaysia, Maldives, Morocco, Netherlands, Oman, Poland, Singapore, Syrian Arab Republic, United Arab Emirates. There also appear to be reservations to this Article by Indonesia, Iraq and Jordan (see text of the same document).

11. See Article 18 of the International Covenant on Civil and Political Rights of 19 December 1966, and Article 9 of the European Convention for the Protection of Human Rights and Fundamental Freedoms of 4 November 1950.

12. Syria did not refer to this in the text of its reservation, but in a later clarification set out in UN document CRC/C/2/Rev.8.

13. UN Document CRC/C/2/Rev.8, 7 December 1999. It should be noted here that Saudi Arabia is not being presented as *representative* of Islamic states, whose approach is rooted in a variety of traditions. The interest is rather in the explicitly religious focus of the dialogue between this state and the UN Committee.

14. UN Document CRC/C/61/Add.2, 29 March 2000.

15. UN Document CRC/C/61/Add.2, 13 October 2000.

16. The discussions in Committee took place over two meetings. The Summary Records are to be found in UN Document CRC/C/SR.687 (at the time of writing available in French only) and CRC/C/SR.688.

17. Concluding Observations. See UN document CRC/C/15/Add.148 of 26 January 2001. Note: Emphasis added.

18. UN Document CRC/C/SR.255, 24 November 1995, para. 19 (at the time of writing available only in French).

19. The Holy See's self-description in its Initial Report to the UN Committee: CRC/C/3/Add.27.

20. The *Traveaux Preparatoires* disclose the Holy See's particular interest in issues relating to the protection of the unborn child, freedom of religion and the rights of parents to choose their child's education. It was also largely responsible for ensuring that the spiritual dimension was included in references to the child's developmental needs.

21. UN Document CRC/C/SR.255, para. 2 (at the time of writing available in French only).

22. See UN Document CRC/C/2/Rev.8 of 7 December 1999 (emphasis added).

23. Initial Report – UN Document CRC/C/3/Add.27, para. 4.

24. Ibid., para. 20.

25. Ibid., para. 17.
26. UN Document CRC/C/3/Add.27, para. 16.
27. Ibid.
28. Ibid.
29. Ibid., para. 4, quoting Pope John Paul II, address to the General Assembly of the United Nations, 2 October 1979.
30. Ibid., para. 26.
31. Ibid., para. 8, quoting Article 4(f) of the *Charter of the Rights of the Family*.
32. Preamble to the *Charter of the Rights of the Family*, Holy See, 22 October 1983.
33. UN Committee on the Rights of the Child, Summary Record CRC/C/SR.255, paras 11, 12 and 37.
34. UN Committee on the Rights of the Child, Summary Record CRC/C/SR.256, para. 23.
35. Ibid., para. 8.
36. *Let us Give Children a Future of Peace: Message of His Holiness Pope John Paul II for the XXIX World Day of Peace*, 1 January 1996, para. 6: 'Sadly, violence towards children is found even in wealthy and affluent families. Such cases are infrequent, but it is important not to overlook them. Sometimes children are taken advantage of and suffer within the home itself, at the hands of people whom they should be able to trust, to the detriment of their development.'
37. UN Committee on the Rights of the Child, Summary Record CRC/C/SR.256, para. 23.
38. UN Committee on the Rights of the Child, Summary Record CRC/C/SR.255, para. 24.
39. UN Committee on the Rights of the Child, Summary Record CRC/C/SR.255, para. 31.
40. UN Committee on the Rights of the Child, Summary Record CRC/C/SR.255, para. 44.
41. UN Committee on the Rights of the Child, Summary Record CRC/C/SR.256, para. 7.
42. UN Committee on the Rights of the Child, Summary Record CRC/C/SR.255, para. 29.
43. Initial Report, UN Document CRC/C/3/Add.27, para. 9.
44. UN Committee on the Rights of the Child, Summary Record CRC/C/SR.255, para. 40.
45. Summary Record CRC/C/SR.255, para. 51 (author's translation from French original).
46. UN Document CRC/C/15/Add.46, 27 November 1995, paras 7–9.

47. UN Document CRC/C/15/Add.46, 27 November 1995, paras 12 and 13.
48. See the 1983 *Charter of the Rights of the Family*, quoted above.
49. The Pontifical Council on the Family, *The Family and Human Rights*, 9 December 1999, accessed via Vatican website: www.vatican.va/roman_curia/, speaks of the 'reciprocity of the genders' and says of men and women, 'they must unfold their existence according to two complementary modes: the masculine and the feminine' (para. 59). However, Prof. Mary Ann Glendon, presenting the *Holy See's Final Statement at the Women's Conference in Beijing*, 15 September 1995, stated: 'The Holy See ... dissociates itself from the biological determinist notion that all the roles and relations of the two sexes are fixed in a single, static pattern.'
50. Pontifical Council on the Family, *The Family and Human Rights*, para. 9.
51. Ibid., para. 65.
52. Ibid., para. 70.
53. The relevance of this will be identified below in the context of suspicion by the USA.
54. Summary Record CRC/C/SR.192, 23 January 1995, para. 46.
55. Office of the High Commissioner for Human Rights, *The Situation Analysis of Children and Families in Poland: 6 November 1993*, United Nations Human Rights website, Treaty Bodies Database: accessed 12 October 2001.
56. Summary Record CRC/C/SR.194, para. 16.
57. Detrick, *Traveaux Preparatoires*, p. 21.
58. The Polish version had said 'basic' group, but this was amended by agreement. See Detrick, *Traveaux Preparatoires*, pp. 91 and 108.
59. Detrick, *Traveaux Preparatoires*, pp. 109–10.
60. Detrick, *Traveaux Preparatoires*, p. 383.
61. CRC/C/2/Rev.8 of 7 December 1999 refers to part B of the same paper for notification of withdrawal of this reservation. However, part B makes no reference to Poland.
62. It should be noted that the declarations are sometimes referred to also as 'reservations' both within the Initial Report by Poland, and in the dialogue with the UN Committee.
63. Initial Report, CRC/C/8/Add.11, paras 25–8.
64. Ibid., para. 296 (emphasis added).
65. Summary Record CRC/C/SR.193, paras 48 and 52.

66. Ibid., para. 55.
67. The correlative French phrase, used in the Committee Reports for the first and third meetings of the dialogue (CRC/C/SR. 192 and 194), is 'la perte de sens moral'. 'Sens moral' may be interpreted as either moral sense or conscience.
68. Summary Record CRC/C/SR.194, para. 37.
69. Ibid., para. 24.
70. Concluding Observations, CRC/C/15/Add.31, para. 19.
71. Initial Report, CRC/C/8/Add.11, para. 83.
72. Ibid., para. 88.
73. Summary Record CRC/C/SR.194, para. 22.
74. Initial Report, CRC/C/8/Add.11, para. 84.
75. Summary Record CRC/C/SR.192, para. 23.
76. Summary Record CRC/C/SR.194, para. 45.
77. Initial Report, CRC/C/8/Add.11, para. 102.
78. Summary Record CRC/C/SR.193, para. 19.
79. Office of the High Commissioner for Human Rights, *The Situation Analysis of Children and Families in Poland: 6 November 1993*, United Nations Human Rights website, Treaty Bodies Database: accessed 12 October 2001.
80. Summary Record CRC/C/SR.194, para. 43.
81. The Second Report is available as CRC/C/70/Add.12. The discussions with the Committee are to be found in CRC/C/SR.827 and 828, and the Concluding Observations in CRC/C/15/Add.194.
82. Second Report, para. 7.
83. Second Report, para. 123.
84. Second Report, para. 63.
85. Second Report, para. 122.
86. First meeting, para. 7.
87. First meeting, para. 48.
88. Second meeting, para. 27 (French).
89. Concluding Observation 31(b), in CRC/C/15/Add.194.
90. Concluding Observations paras 32 and 33.
91. Concluding Observations, paras 42 and 43.
92. Information from Religions unite for children (excerpt from WCC News) by Sara Speicher (2000), accessed 21 January 2003 via www.wcccoe.org.wcc/what/interreligious/cd35-21.html.
93. www.bpfna.org/openltr01.html, accessed 21 January 2003.
94. T. Lorenzen, *The Rights of the Child*, Baptist World Alliance, Human Rights Booklet No. 2/1998, Virginia: Baptist World Alliance, 1998.
95. Accessed at www.dfms.org/myp/ccres.html 21 January 2003.

96. Information obtained from personal communication with the Lutheran World Federation's Office for Inter-national Affairs and Human Rights, Geneva, 24 January 2003.

97. Resolution adopted by the Council of Bishops of the United Methodist Church, meeting in Lincoln, Nebraska, USA from 27 April to 1 May 1998. Information accessed 28 August 2003, via www.umc-gbcs.org/issues/resolutions.

98. From the *Methodist Daily News*, produced by the United Methodist News Service (official news agency of the United Methodist Church), accessed on 21 January 2003 on http://umns.umc.org/News97/mar/jscience.htm.

99. Proceedings of the Public Issues Committee and the twenty-third General Council accessed from www.warc.ch.23gc/report/pub.html and www.warc.ch.23gc/proced.html on 5 March 2003. Supplementary information obtained through personal communication with the Communications Secretary of the World Alliance of Reformed Churches.

100. Information from The Associate for Child Advocacy, Presbyterian Church (USA) in response to an inquiry by the legal author, 21 January 2003.

101. *Convention on the Rights of the Child: frequently asked questions*, UNICEF, www.unicef.org/crc/faq.htm.

102. Amnesty International USA at www.amnesty-usa.org/children/crn_faq.html.

103. The Center for Reclaiming America www.leaderu.com/issues/fabric/chap16.html.

104. While most of the material on which this section of the book is based emanates from the USA, it also draws upon Canadian and Australian writing.

105. See J. Woodward, 'The UN Quietly Wages War on Religion', *Calgary Herald* (11 August 2001); R. Karolis, *The Convention on the Rights of the Child: The Making of a Deception*, www.biblebelievers.org.au/right1.htm, downloaded 24 October 2001.

106. Woodward, 'UN Quietly Wages War on Religion'.

107. A study of the websites of the opponents of US ratification named above demonstrates the close relationship between national/political and religious concerns.

108. H. Richman, 'UN Child Rights Treaty', reprint of an article published in the Opinion Page of the *Pittsburgh Tribune-Review*, 13 June 1995, obtained from www.pahome schoolers.com/untreaty.html; Karolis, *Convention on the Rights of the Child*, Ch. 2.

109. Dykxhoorn, quoted in Woodward, 'UN Quietly Wages War on Religion'.

110. Karolis, *Convention on the Rights of the Child*, Ch. 3.

111. See Detrick, *Traveaux Preparatoires*, pp. 433–4.

112. Hodgkin and Newell, *Implementation Handbook for the Convention on the Rights of the Child*, p. 513.

113. C. Hurlbert, *UN Convention on the Rights of the Child: A Treaty to Undermine the Family*, on the website of Concerned Women for America, September 2001.

114. Discussed at 2.2.3 above.

115. Accessed at www.leaderu.com/issues/fabric/chap16. html.

116. Points distilled from Karolis, *Convention on the Rights of the Child*, Ch. 2, accessed 22 October 2001. The 'child liberationist' position is considered further at 6.4.1 below.

117. An area of ambiguity identified, for example, by R. Traer, *Fight over the Rights of the Child*, www.geocities.com/Athens/Parthenon/7185/Ratification/ushr.fight.child.htm, accessed 13 July 2001.

118. Hodgkin and Newell, *Implementation Handbook for the Convention on the Rights of the Child*, p. 265.

119. Traer, *Fight over the Rights of the Child*.

120. Karolis, *Convention on the Rights of the Child*.

121. The 'comprehensiveness' of the Convention and interdependence of its provisions is discussed in E. Verhellen, *Convention on the Rights of the Child*, (2nd edn), Leuven-Aledoorn: Garant, 1997, particularly at p. 77.

122. See J. K. Mason and R. A. McCall Smith, *Law and Medical Ethics* (4th edn), Edinburgh: Butterworths, pp. 222–4.

3

Talking About Rights

3.1 'Rights' in Everyday Use

What do we mean when we talk about rights? That is not an easy question to answer, partly because the idea is so familiar to us. Returning a stale packet of crisps to the manufacturer will not affect my statutory *rights*. My neighbour has *right* of access to our garden for purposes of maintenance, while the pub reserves the *right* to refuse me entry. 'You have no *right* to talk to me like that.' The word is used in a variety of ways for a variety of purposes, and those different senses can, if we are not careful, get in the way of each other. Indeed, the word can degenerate into empty bombast or mere rhetoric.

But if the word *is* overused, it is only because it is so useful. In the twenty-first century, the concept of rights is an inescapable part of our moral furniture. We have to try to be clear about what we mean when we use the word. In this chapter we explore some of the ways in which academics have tried to analyse what we mean when we talk about rights. In the abstract, this can appear as a difficult and possibly obscure debate. We have tried to clarify some of the points made by means of case examples.

We explain:

the difference between assertions of legal and moral rights;

the famous distinction made by Hohfeld between rights as: claims, powers, liberties and immunities, each linking into a different correlation with another party;

how these different kinds of 'rights' might be ranked;

the implications of theories of rights based upon the exercise of a choice ('will theory') and the protection of interests ('interest theory');

some objections to rights language;

the relationship between rights and duties; and

questions for Christians.

3.2 Legal and Moral Rights

'Rights' may be:

1. Moral: proclaimed or believed in by some on the basis of religious or moral authority or reasoning, but not universally recognised (such as the 'rights' of the unborn child, or of transsexuals);
2. Mixed: formally endorsed by the international community and set out in a statement or declaration, but not reflected, or fully reflected, in domestic law (which, as explained in 2.3 above, is the status of the UN Convention on the Rights of the Child within the UK); or
3. Legal: recognised and enforced by domestic law (e.g., contractual rights, or those set out in the Human Rights Act 1998 which incorporates into UK law the greater part of the European Convention on Human Rights).

Reflection about the meaning of rights tends to arise in two main contexts. On the one hand there is the need for clarity in the *legal* understanding of an important contractual word. And on the other hand, the notion is used in the discussion of *moral* problems, by both philosophers and theologians, in an attempt to articulate the complex networks of obligations that bind human beings together. Some tension between these two domains is inevitable, and also some confusion, as it is not always clear whether someone is making a legal or a moral claim.

The *tension* can be fruitful. The language of the law is concerned with concepts that can *do* things. The language of rights in a legal context has to be put to work and earn its living. The language of morals – both secular and religious – can, and often has, been prophetic. It can, and often has, given expression to a vision of human dignity and equality which is both proclamation and challenge, a statement of both faith and hope for the whole of humankind. The *confusion*, in contrast, is unhelpful and can nudge a debate towards a sterile process of assertion and counter-assertion where one party is, for example, asserting a moral right which is resisted by the other on the basis that no legal right exists, and the differences of category are not acknowledged.

The two domains of moral and legal meet uniquely in the sphere of human rights.[1] The concern of this book is with the meeting of those two domains in the special sphere of the rights of those human persons who happen to be children.

3.3 A Story Analysed

Let us start by imagining a scenario which is all too plausible. Suppose that three students are sharing a flat. Sandy is revising for finals, Angus relaxes by playing the bagpipes, and Fiona vaguely hopes for a quiet life.

Angus is practising 'Flower of Scotland' at midnight. (1) Fiona asks him to think of the neighbours. (2) Angus does think of the neighbours, but continues playing. (3) Sandy says, 'Surely I have a right to some peace and quiet.' (4) Angus says, 'They're my bagpipes, and I have a right to play them if I want.' (5) 'But,' Fiona says, 'you have no right to mess up Sandy's exams.' (6) Angus thinks about it, decides to practise on the Meadows in the future, and everyone lives happily ever after.

What is going on in this little drama? What do the players mean by what they say? Why do they appeal to the concept of rights? Why does it work, and how does it work?

3.3.1 Legal and Moral Dimensions

In this scenario, it is not always clear whether the actors are appealing to legal or moral rights. On the one hand, there may be legal rights related to the statements at (1) and (3), based upon the general law of nuisance or the provisions of the tenancy agreement, of which, at the time this exchange takes place, the participants may be aware to varying degrees. On the other hand, both of these statements, and the statement at (5), could be assertions of moral rights.

In dealing with legal rights, the answer to the question 'Why appeal to rights?' is, at least on one level, obvious. The rights which I am promised on my packet of crisps flow not from the goodwill of the crisp manufacturer but from statute law. Similarly, some of the rights claims in the scenario may be enforceable because they are founded on general law or the conditions of the lease.

In dealing with moral claims, the matter is less clear cut. We said above that conceptual clarity was needed if the appeal to the language of rights was not to become mere rhetoric. But there is in itself nothing wrong with using the language of rights as rhetoric. For most of us, in the society in which we live, the language of rights provides a powerful and emotive vocabulary. It can, if used responsibly, summon up within us an attitude of seriousness and concern.

But far more important is the basis for the appeal that is being made. Sandy and Fiona both appeal to a common understanding, to a set of shared moral assumptions, that they presume (correctly, as it turns out) they have in common with Angus. In ordinary moral discourse the language of rights can often appeal to these shared assumptions without even spelling them out. Indeed, the deeper they lie and the more they are taken for granted, the more powerful they are.

Here these shared assumptions involve things like: the general need of any human being for some measure of peace and quiet as a necessary condition of human flourishing; or the stronger and more focused need of flatmates to give each other space and be aware of each other's needs; or the still more sharply focused need of someone revising for exams to be able to get on with it.

The language of rights can tap into these shared assumptions and apply them to a particular situation. In effect, Angus is being told in (5), 'You, as a member of the student community, realise how important it is to be able to revise for finals. OK, here's how you can make it work.' Angus recognises the reasonableness of the claim and accepts the fact that that imposes a duty on him. So off he goes to the Meadows with his bagpipes under his arm.

3.3.2 A Hohfeldian Analysis

Rights are appealed to at steps (3), (4) and (5), but not in quite the same way. In (3) Sandy is making a general *claim*; the claim to a reasonable amount of peace and quiet. And it is a claim that points to a duty – a duty of others *not* to encroach on Sandy's peace and quiet. That duty falls, potentially, on anyone who happens to be around, but falls in a particular way on the bagpiper, Angus. Fiona at (5) is implicitly asserting a claim on Sandy's behalf, as she could have done even if he had been out of the room: 'Surely Sandy has a right to some peace and quiet (for the sake of his revision).'

When Angus says at step (4) that he has a *right* to play his bagpipes, he means that he is at *liberty* to do so whenever he wants to and no one else has a right to stop him. But, unlike the rights claimed by Angus and Fiona, there is no correlative duty falling on anyone else. The others have no obligation to further his project. They have no duty to listen. And they would have no duty to turn down the stereo, were it on, so that Angus could concentrate on his own music. The most that Angus can claim is that they have *no right* to stop him.

In ordinary, everyday language this kind of assertion of a freedom to do something is often not distinguished from the kind of right Sandy and Fiona are claiming; it too is often simply called a *right*. We, like Angus, are often tempted to say, particularly in moments of exasperation, 'It's my money, and I have a right to spend it on what I want (and you have no right to constrain me).' But in order to bring out the difference between the right to (do something) being claimed by Sandy and Fiona in (3) and (5) and the freedom to (do something) being asserted by Angus in (4), the latter can be called, not a right, but a liberty.

This is a distinction made by the American jurist Wesley Hohfeld in his enormously influential study of the terminology of rights, published in 1919.[2] Hohfeld was particularly concerned with rights within the legal system. He wanted to help judges make better decisions by providing them with a set of concepts that would assist judicial reasoning. However, his approach has been used as a tool for analysis of moral rights as well.[3] For Hohfeld a *claim-right*, which is a *right* in the strict sense of the word, is something that has attached to it, or correlative with it, a *duty* that falls on others, while a *liberty-right* is an 'it's up to me – I can do it if I want to' sort of freedom.[4] A liberty has correlative with it what Hohfeld calls a *no-right*' – that is, other persons involved have no right to stop me; they have no valid claim to stop me from doing what I want to do. All that can be diagrammed:

Claim-right	Liberty-right
correlative with	correlative with
Duty	**No-right**

3.3.3 Ranking Rights and Liberties

If we apply this classic distinction of Hohfeld's to our story, we can see that in (4) Angus meant to assert that he had a *liberty-right* to play his bagpipes when he wanted to, and from that it would follow that the others had *no-right* to stop him. It might look as if Fiona's reply in (5) undermines that, for she counters the assertion of Angus's liberty by claiming Sandy's right.

What is going on there? Fiona is *not* denying the liberty that Angus is asserting. She is producing another, quite distinct claim; we might say that she is implying that the right based on Sandy's need to revise *trumps* the liberty to which Angus can – validly (in general) – lay claim. That would be to appropriate a metaphor which the Oxford philosopher Ronald Dworkin has developed in a similar context but to different effect.[5] In any event, it will generally be the case that, as here, the appeal to a right in the strict sense – that is, a claim-right – will trump the appeal to a liberty-right. For one thing, the latter is really an assertion that I enjoy the freedom to do something, other things being equal. But other things are often not equal. As an example of the assertion of a liberty-right, we looked earlier at the statement that 'It's my money, and I have a right to spend it on what I want (and you have no right to constrain me).' Most people would agree that the status of that statement is quite different if the 'I' is a teenager talking about the deployment of pocket money from what it would be if the 'I' is an alcoholic father talking to his hungry family. Liberty-rights are so general that they often bump up against countervailing claims occupying part of the same moral space.

But there is a second, and perhaps more important, reason why a claim-right will normally trump a liberty-right. And that has to do with the question of waivability. There are limitations on the extent to which many claim-rights can or should be waived. And that is particularly true of claims made on behalf of somebody else, including claims made on behalf of the most vulnerable, who cannot speak for themselves. But liberty-rights are more flexible. In many cases not much depends on *when* they are exercised.

In our story, the claim Fiona made in (5) on Sandy's behalf, based on his particular need for quiet, trumped Angus's assertion in (4) of a general liberty-right. And in step (6) Angus gave in and abandoned his intention to play his bagpipes in the flat.

3.4 A Child's Story Analysed

Emily, aged 7, is the child of Jane and Henry. Her parents believe that girls should be brought up to be good wives and mothers, and should not be distracted from that aim by an academic education. They decide not to send Emily to school, but to educate her at home on that basis.

If Jane and Henry have, in Hohfeld's terms, a claim-right to direct Emily's education, where does the correlative duty lie? Does Emily have a duty to submit to that education? Do others have a duty to support it? Or is the parents' 'right' more appropriately identified as a *'liberty'*, with a correlative 'no-right' on the part of anyone else to interfere? If it is a liberty then, on the reasoning set out above, it can be 'trumped' by Emily's claim-right, supported by articles 28 and 29 of the Convention on the Rights of the Child, to an education directed to 'the development of the child's personality, talents and mental and physical abilities to their fullest potential'.

Emily becomes ill and agitated. Her parents reject conventional medical or psychological support in favour of a regime of energetic exorcism and ingestion of exotic vegetable substances.

If Jane and Henry have a 'claim'-right in respect of Emily's medical treatment, where does the duty lie? Does Emily have a duty to submit? Does the State have a duty to support the regime? Or is this also the exercise of a liberty-right which must be qualified by respect for: the child's right to survival and development; to responsible parenting that takes account of her best interests; to protection from abuse or neglect at the hands of her carers; and to health services, supported by articles 6, 18, 19 and 24 respectively of the Convention on the Rights of the Child?

This scenario might also be analysed in terms of a third legal relation discussed by Hohfeld. Some so-called 'rights', he said, were better described as 'powers' on the part of one person to change the legal relations of another person – the person subject to a 'liability.' A *power* is the ability to exert control over another. The giving of consent to medical treatment is an exercise of a legal power, in respect that it is a legally effective consent that allows a trespass on the person and protects the practitioner from charges of assault. It is an exercise in control, which is also qualified by the rights of the child.

Jane and Henry believe in physical punishment, and Emily is regularly chastised with a leather belt. This is consistent with their religion, and they advance it as a moral right. It may also be a legal right as the law in their country allows parents to administer 'reasonable chastisement' to their children.

This brings in Hohfeld's fourth set of legal relations, consisting of a class of 'immunities' of which the correlative is a *disability* of the other party to the relationship. In effect it is a freedom from the control of another. If the punishment meted out by Jane and Henry is considered to be 'reasonable', then they are *immune* from the criminal law relating to assault. The state is *disabled* from convicting them; and Emily is *disabled* from suing for compensation for her hurt. Thus, in addition to the categories of claim-right and liberty-right, we can add:

Power	Immunity
correlative	correlative
with	with
Liability	Disability

3.5 Exploring Hohfeld's Analysis

One benefit of Hohfeld's analysis is that it moves the debate on from the usual correlation of 'rights' and 'duties'. There are some things that we call 'rights' that impose no active duty on anyone else, but may, all things being equal, indicate that no-one else has a right to interfere (as with a liberty), or a right to challenge (as with an immunity). When the right asserted is a 'power', we must ask whether it is absolute or qualified with respect to some particular end which it is conferred to serve. These distinctions will become important when we come to discuss the debates about 'inalienable parental rights,' when it will be argued that some parental 'rights' are more accurately classified as liberties, powers or immunities, qualified by the rights of the child.

Hohfeld's system has not been without its critics,[6] and there can be legitimate debate about the category into which any particular 'right' should be included. 'Rights' can also change categories; for example, what might have been a liberty-right as regards the education of a child, can be changed into a claim-right, if the law recognises a legal right to have one's education choices supported by the provision of appropriate services, thus imposing a duty on the state to provide them.

The scenario about Emily and her family focused on the analysis of parental rights, but children's rights might also be analysed in this way. The Convention might be said to include: 'claim-rights' such as the right to a name and nationality, and to an education; 'liberties' in terms of the 'freedoms' of expression, thought, conscience and religion and association; 'powers' to have decisions influenced by one's views and best interests; and 'immunities' from criminal prosecution below a specified age.

However, while the above categories might apply to relations between the child and other individuals or agencies, there is also a sense in which all can be categorised as 'claim-rights' against the ratifying states, given that Article

4 of the Convention imposes a duty on them to 'undertake all appropriate legislative, administrative, and other measures for the implementation of the rights recognised in the present Convention'. Thus, for the purposes of this book, 'claims' when used in relation to children should be understood as embracing all of the rights set out in the Convention.

3.6 'Will' Theory and 'Interest' Theory

The debates around 'will' and 'interest' theory bear upon the question whether children can truly be regarded as the holders of rights. Proponents of the 'will' theory argue that possession of rights is intrinsically related to the ability to choose to exercise or (sometimes) waive them. Proponents of the 'interest' theory hold choice as irrelevant; rights exist to protect a person's interests. This is significant for debates about the rights of the child, because many young children, incapable of making choices, will be excluded from the category of rights-holders by advocates of the 'will theory', but included by advocates of the 'interest theory'.[7] Some believe the will theory can embrace the rights of the child if parents or guardians are identified as the persons entitled to exercise choice on behalf of their children. However, given that some of the child's claim-rights (e.g., to maintenance) relate to the duties of parents or guardians, this would result in the anomaly that the duty-holder would be the one with the ability to choose whether or not the right should be exercised. There are also some kinds of 'rights' (in the broad sense) that cannot logically be exercised by others on someone's behalf, such as the right to freedom of speech, or immunity from prosecution.

For some, the inability of the will theory to accommodate the rights of young children to nurture and care undermines its claim to be the basis of rights. Thus, MacCormick concludes:

Either we abstain from ascribing to children a right to care and nurture, or we abandon the will theory.[8]

Instead he favours a 'variant' of the interests theory which, applied to children, would mean that something was a 'right' if it was a significant 'good' that it would be wrong to deny to any child. Such a 'good' must satisfy, promote or advance some need, interest or desire of each child.[9] 'Choice' comes into it in respect that, in its application to 'normal' cases, there would be an ancillary power to decide whether to waive or insist upon, enforcement of the right. However, such an element of 'choice', which is not constitutive of the right itself, cannot be said to exist in the cases of young children and mentally incapacitated adults.[10] Thus, MacCormick concludes:

> [T]he will theory fails as an explanation of rights because it cannot account for such important rights as the children's rights discussed in this essay. The presumption that people are the best judges of what is good for them and of whether to have it or not is not and should not be extended to children, certainly not to young children. Neither in law nor in what I take to be sound morality can children's rights be regarded as carrying the option of waiver or enforcement by themselves or on their behalf.[11]

The question arises whether such an interests theory of rights, especially when not accompanied by a power or waiver or enforcement, is any different from a theory based upon duties. MacCormick explains the thrust of this objection, which is associated in particular with H. L. A. Hart:

> The principal advocates of benefit or 'interest' theories of rights correlative to obligations have shown themselves sensitive to the criticism that, if to say that an individual has such a right means no more than that he is the intended beneficiary of a duty, then 'a right' in this sense may be an unnecessary, and perhaps confusing, term in the description

of the law; since all that can be said in a terminology of such rights can be and indeed is, best said in the indispensable terminology of duty.[12]

It is possible, however, to distinguish between 'rights as interests' and 'duty-based' theories in the following way:

Under the will theory, the child to whom the duty is owed would be able both to waive implementation and insist upon its enforcement.

Under the interest theory as advanced above, the child would not be able to waive implementation, but would be able to insist upon its enforcement were the duty breached.[13]

If the child were not the subject of rights, but merely the object of duties, he or she would not be able to waive or insist upon enforcement of the duty. If one responds that legal systems do allow for procedures for enforcement of duty, then one might ask whether that did not therefore mean that the person to whom the duty was owed actually had a right in all but name.

It is this right or power to insist upon enforcement (even accepting this is often possible only with the help of adults) that differentiates a rights approach based upon the interests theory and a society based upon the performance of duty.

Within the Convention on the Rights of the Child and within the UK system, the capacity of children increases in line with their maturity and understanding. One might conclude that the interests approach is to the fore for young children. Children and young people gradually step into the will-based approach. Article 3 of the Convention, and associated principles of domestic law, may imply that there is an 'interests' test lurking somewhere in the background, although this is not universal.[14] Indeed, Hodgkin and Newell comment that:

Interpretations of the best interests of children cannot trump or override any of the other rights guaranteed by other articles in the Convention.[15]

3.7 Some Problems with Rights Language

At this point, we would like to note four objections which are often raised to the use of the language of rights in general and which reappear, with a particular spin, as objections to the language of children's rights in particular. They will recur in later discussions. What we want to do here is introduce them and see how they work in the scenarios we have sketched in this chapter. These objections identify rights language as:

redundant;

confrontational;

egoistic; and

individualistic.

3.7.1 Redundant?

The first objection to the language of rights reflects Hart's objection to the interests theory that, if every right has a correlative duty, then rights are redundant. Why not just specify the duties and leave it at that? What, apart from a sort of rhetorical punch, is added by talking about rights?

The deficiencies of an approach based simply upon duty will be further discussed at 4.10 below in relation to the traditional Chinese and Islamic systems. The Chinese supplemented their duty-based system with a right to rebel against an oppressive ruler; thus, it is said, leading to a history characterised by successive rebellions. The Islamic approach left the remedy for breach of duty to the judgement of God in the next world, a prospect that might be the source of some comfort to suffering believers, but would do nothing to alleviate their situation.

Focusing exclusively on duties involves looking at things from the standpoint of the party with the upper hand. Introducing the language of rights shifts the discussion to the perspective of the party in need of protection. So even if there were a logical equivalence between talking about rights and talking about duties, even if the two modes of discourse were perfectly symmetrical so that either language could be translated into the other without loss, there would still be a point in shifting the discourse on to the language of rights, for it brings in an eye-opening shift of perspective. If rights language is logically redundant, the redundancy exists only in the pages of textbooks on ethics, and not in the real world of human need – whether it be the relatively trivial need for an absence of bagpipe playing or the great and terrible needs of the hungry and poor of the world.

But there is a further point to be considered. In the first scenario discussed above, the introduction of the category of rights at stage (3) of our dialogue gave Sandy a *locus standi*. It gave him – precisely – the right to say what he had to say, just as it gave Fiona a right to intervene on his behalf at stage (5). Sandy was not asking Angus for a favour; he was lodging a just and reasonable claim. And in the case of Emily, it was her rights that worked to qualify her parents' liberties, powers and immunities, and that might empower others to intervene on her behalf where those rights are breached. In the real world of significant problems that is important: the language of rights can empower the weak and give a voice to the oppressed.

Thus, approaching a problem from the angle of rights rather than from the angle of duties can help give the claimant a stronger sense of self-respect and self-worth. It can perhaps contribute to a greater sense of human dignity all round. This point has been made forcefully by the philosopher Joel Feinberg. It is part of what he means when he says that rights are 'essentially sturdy objects to 'stand upon', a most useful sort of moral furniture'.[16]

The use that Feinberg makes of the metaphor of 'standing upon' one's rights is clever because, by inviting us to see it in a new way – quasi-literally – he manages to deconstruct a commonplace image which usually calls to mind unpleasant associations. And those unpleasant associations raise two further objections to the use of the language of rights, one based on what it does to community and the other based on what it encourages the individual to become.

3.7.2 Confrontational?

We might think that rights language is by its very nature confrontational and aggressive. Does not appeal to rights tend to polarise society, to encourage conflict between claimants and respondents? Would it not be better if things were sorted out on the basis of mutual goodwill? Would not Angus, Sandy and Fiona have been better off if they had simply talked things out as friends and never brought up the subject of rights at all? Would not Jane, Henry and Emily remain a stronger family unit if the outside world, with its concerns about rights, were kept at bay?

Resolving matters by agreement would clearly be a happier option, if it achieved the desired end. But it is not quite true to say that society would be better off without appeal to rights. Rather, in a better society there would be no need to appeal to rights; perhaps there would be no need to think about them at all. But in the real world, in the fallen and broken world in which we live, problems do occur. Interests clash and conflicts arise, and there has to be some way of dealing with them. Some people will insist on playing the bagpipes at midnight; some parents will persist in exercising their legal and physical power to the detriment of their children; and there has to be some way of talking about things rationally. Rights are, as John Hardwig has said, 'like the net underneath the tightrope act'.[17]

It is important in this connection to remember that rights are not things. They are a way of talking about claims and duties, a way of articulating and formalising relationships, a way that can be useful when matters go awry.

So this objection is in a way like saying games would be better if there were no referees or umpires. Referees are not supposed to occasion conflict (even if they are often accused of doing so!); they are supposed to resolve it.

3.7.3 Egoistic?

An objection, similar in some ways, can be based on the action of the individual right-holder. Does not the concept of rights put the interests of the individual above those of society? Is not the whole idea inherently egoistic and me-centred?

This objection has been put philosophically by thinkers as diverse as Jeremy Bentham[18] and Karl Marx.[19] And it can be put more poignantly still by a Christian ethic which can point to the fact that we are not meant to be aggressive and self-assertive, but are rather meant to turn the other cheek, 'putting up with one another in love with all humility and gentleness'.[20] From this Christian point of view it may be objected that the language of rights is not only egoistic but also egotistical.

One of the things that can be said in answer to the stronger form of the objection is that I, as a Christian, may indeed feel that it is appropriate for me in certain circumstances to waive my rights – to forgo a claim rather than press it. But, as we have seen, the language of rights gives me a basis not only for asserting my rights but also for asserting the rights of someone else, as at stage (5) of our story Fiona spoke up for Sandy's rights. And that at times means looking to the needs of those who are in no position either to assert or to waive their own rights, such as the very young and some of the very old and those of the handicapped, the disabled and the oppressed who have no voice of their own.

3.7.4 Individualistic?

The more general form of the egoistic objection assumes that the assertion of rights is inherently individualistic. But rights are a tool, an instrument, to be used when the network of claims and duties that binds people together gets torn and needs repairing. Any tool can be misused. It is of course possible to appeal to rights in an imprudent or clumsy or self-seeking or frivolous sort of way. But in and of themselves, rights build community rather than destroy it. Or, rather, the network of claims and obligations described by rights language itself constitutes community. At least that is true in the sense in which different but complementary pictures of the surface of our planet can be produced by looking at things through different filters and mapping different features. The network of claims and obligations described by rights language provides one significant mapping of a functioning society.

What constitutes the community comprised of Angus, Sandy and Fiona? The three of them have a number of things in common. They are friends, they are all students, they share the same physical space. But their joint tenancy establishes a further bond. It establishes a little community which is structured by a set of (more or less consciously formulated) expectations and demands. The others, for example, have the expectation that if Angus has bacon and eggs for breakfast he will wash the frying pan. And if he does not, they feel they have the 'right' to yell at him.

An example such as this may appear trivially simple. But even here, things are much more complicated than they seem. Each of the three expects, and is expected by, each of the other two to wash the frying pan after use. So each is twice over a claim-holder and twice over a duty-bearer. Each of these expectations is a one-to-one relationship. But the sum total of all these one-to-one relationships, woven together like wicker work, builds up a solidly structured community.

3.8 Correlation of Rights and Duties

So far in this chapter, in looking at the correlativity of claims and obligations, we have been thinking only of the way in which my right is correlative to your duty (right of A/duty of B). But, as our last example shows, we could also talk about the relationship between my rights and my obligations (rights of A/duties of A).[21]

The reason why hitherto we have stressed the other side of the coin, the my-rights-and-your-duties side, is to avoid any suggestion that those who cannot fulfil obligations are somehow second-class right-holders, not quite full members of the community of rights. If Fiona had been looking after a baby, the infant would have had a right to get some sleep (which someone else would have to claim on his behalf) and a right not to be frightened out of his wits by the bagpipes. But it would make no sense to say that the baby had an obligation not to disturb the others by crying. (Fiona might have a duty to try to quieten the child, both for his sake and for that of the flatmates, but that is another matter.)

And yet sometimes it is useful to put in focus the way in which my rights go hand in hand with claims others have on me. This particular bundling of rights and duties helps define my place in a society of mutual relationships. And it provides an answer to the egoistic objection discussed above in 3.7.3. The debate about a correlation between rights of A/duties of A is further discussed at 4.10 below.

3.9 Conclusion

In this chapter we have tried to understand rights primarily as claims. We have seen that claim-rights are correlative with duties. We have seen how the language of rights operates in everyday usage, embracing concepts of liberty, power and immunity, and we have seen how rights build community. In the next chapter we shall look at what it means to say that there some rights that are held by all human beings.

Notes

1. For an excellent introduction to legal and philosophical discussions of rights and an attempt to relate those discussions to a Christian context, see Kieran Cronin, *Rights and Christian Ethics*, New Studies in Christian Ethics, Cambridge: Cambridge University Press, 1992.
2. Wesley Hohfeld, *Fundamental Legal Conceptions*, ed. W. W. Cook, New Haven: Yale University Press, 1919.
3. See for example, W. E. May, *The Difference between a 'Right' and a 'Liberty' and the Significance of This Difference in Debates over Public Policy on Abortion and Euthanasia*, accessed on 6 March 2003, at www.christendom-awake.org/pages/may/rights.html.
4. Hohfeld actually referred to the 'liberty right' as a 'privilege', but commentators consider 'liberty' to be more appropriate. See J. W. Harris, *Legal Philosophies* (2nd edn), London, Edinburgh, Dublin: Butterworths, 1997, p. 87.
5. Dworkin does not use his metaphor to attempt to rank rights in relation to each other. Rather, he is thinking of a card which the individual can play to protect him from the collective goals of society, a card that will trump the general considerations that would otherwise tilt a decision in the other direction. See Ronald Dworkin, *Taking Rights Seriously*, Cambridge, MA: Harvard University Press, 1977, and 'Rights as Trumps', in Jeremy Waldron (ed.), *Theories of Rights*, Oxford Readings in Philosophy, Oxford: Oxford University Press, 1984, pp. 153–67.
6. See, for example, Harris, *Legal Philosophies*. Ch. 7 explores some criticisms in the context of a generally favourable appraisal.
7. See, for example, D. N. MacCormick, 'Rights in Legislation', in P. M. S. Hacker and J. Raz (eds), *Law, Morality and Society: Essays in Honour of H. L. A. Hart*, Oxford: Clarendon Press, 1977, pp. 189–209 (192).
8. N. MacCormick, *Legal Right and Social Democracy: Essays in Legal and Political Philosophy*, Oxford: Clarendon Press, 1982, p. 158.
9. Ibid., pp. 160 and 163.
10. Ibid., pp. 164–5.
11. Ibid., p. 166.
12. MacCormick, 'Rights in Legislation', p. 199, quoting Hart.
13. Here, the ability to insist upon enforcement is an 'option' only in respect that the child, or some person acting on his or her behalf,

has the ancillary power to call attention to the transgression of the right and to initiate proceedings for enforcement.

14. For example, in Scotland, the law on medical consent relating to children and young people with understanding of the issues was designed specifically to exclude an 'interests' test. See the Age of Legal Capacity (Scotland) Act 1991 and Scottish Law Commission. *Report on the Legal Capacity and Responsibility of Minors and Pupils*, Scot Law Com No 110, Edinburgh: HMSO, 1987, para. 3.77.

15. Hodgkin and Newell, *Implementation Handbook for the Convention on the Rights of the Child*, p. 39.

16. Joel Feinberg, 'The Nature and Value of Rights', *Rights, Justice and the Bounds of Liberty: Essays in Social Philosophy*, Princeton: Princeton University Press, 1980, pp. 143–57, at p. 151.

17. John Hardwig, 'Should Women Think in Terms of Rights?', *Ethics*, 94 (1984), pp. 441–55, at p. 453.

18. Jeremy Bentham, 'Anarchical Fallacies; Being an Examination of the Declaration of Rights Issued during the French Revolution', in Jeremy Waldron (ed.), *'Nonsense upon Stilts': Bentham, Burke and Marx on the Rights of Man*, London: Methuen, 1987, pp. 46–76.

19. Karl Marx, 'On the Jewish Question', in Waldron (ed.), *'Nonsense upon Stilts'*, pp. 137–50.

20. Matthew 5:39 and Luke 6:29; Ephesians 4:2.

21. Some have attempted to distinguish the concepts of 'duty', 'obligation' and 'responsibility'. Etymologically, for example: 'duty' relates to something that is 'due'; 'obligation' to something that binds; and 'responsibility' has connotations of 'response' and accountability. 'Responsibility' and 'obligation' tend to be used in a more general sense than 'duty'. However, these distinctions are by no means applied systematically. In this book we have followed the normal practice of using the words more or less interchangeably.

4

Attitudes to Human Rights

4.1 Introduction

There is a paradox at the heart of our society. At the same
time as 'human rights' are becoming more entrenched in our
legal systems,[1] there appears to be an increasing wariness
about positing rights as the framework for human relationships.[2] Some wish to redraw the boundaries by ensuring
an equal and correlative emphasis on human responsibilities
or duties. Others wish to return to 'virtue' as the standard
of human behaviour. Some doubt whether the concept of
universal human rights makes any sense at all.

It therefore seems appropriate to preface our consideration
of attitudes to the human rights of the child with a discussion
of attitudes to human rights in general, so as to be better
able to identify what concerns or issues relate specifically
to children, and what to the concept of 'human rights'.

This chapter will consider:

what is meant by 'human rights';
the philosophical history of human rights;
resistance to the development of human rights; and
current issues.

4.2 The Meaning and Justification of 'Human Rights'

The term 'human rights' is used to denote conditions for
the realisation of human dignity justified with reference to

moral, religious or legal authority or reasoning.[3] The first two modes of justification depend for their legitimacy upon acceptance of the reality of moral or religious truth. Insofar as religious truth is rooted in revelation, the reality of that revelation can be rejected by non-believers without logical contradiction. Both moral and religious reasoning may seek support from a 'natural law' whose tenets are accessible by reason (discussed further below). Thus, the seventeenth-century philosopher John Locke perceived 'natural law' as the basis of 'natural rights',[4] but this has also been contested, most famously, by the utilitarian philosopher Jeremy Bentham (d. 1832), who insisted:

> Rights is the child of law; from real law come real rights; but from imaginary laws, from 'law of nature', come imaginary rights ... Natural rights is simply nonsense.[5]

More recently, Alan Gewirth asked, 'Are there any moral or human rights?' He concluded that one could found moral rights (including human rights) in reason because: a rational agent needs freedom and well-being to exercise his rationality; therefore these are 'necessary goods'; and therefore that rational agent is logically committed to asserting a 'rights' claim to them. This reasoning was challenged by Alasdair MacIntyre who accused Gewirth of 'illicitly smuggl[ing] into his argument a conception which does not in any way belong';[6] 'the introduction of the concept of a right needs justification'.[7] As, in MacIntyre's view, no good reason has ever been given for belief in human rights, his oft-quoted conclusion is:

> There are no such rights, and belief in them is one with belief in witches and in unicorns.[8]

However, MacIntyre adds – almost as an 'aside':

> By 'rights' I do not mean those rights conferred by positive law or custom on specified classes of person; I mean those rights which are alleged to belong to human beings as such ... the rights which were spoken of in the eighteenth century as natural rights or as the rights of man.[9]

This means that, whatever their ontological provenance, the 'rights' set out in documents of international law are unarguably real 'rights' at least as the subjects of formal agreement. *How* real and substantial such rights are will depend upon the degree of authority with which they are promulgated and accepted. While the 1948 Universal Declaration of Human Rights is declaratory only, with no monitoring or enforcement mechanism, it has been argued that it has attained the status of 'customary law';[10] at the very least, it has provided a vital impetus for the more explicitly binding treaties following from it, including the 1950 European Convention on Human Rights and the 1989 UN Convention on the Rights of the Child. Therefore, as the rights we are addressing in this book *are* set out in positive law as the product of agreement, translated into legal authority, it is proposed to proceed on the basis that they have some kind of reality and substance, irrespective of one's view of their moral or religious basis. The focus of the exploration below will be largely upon their articulation, scope and utility, and the extent to which they *cohere* with religious belief, and in particular with Christian theology. The legitimacy of the vocabulary of 'human rights' within Christian discourse is discussed more fully in Chapter 5 below.

4.3 The Evolution of Ideas of Human Rights

While declarations of human rights are a modern phenomenon, dating back to the late seventeenth century,[11] the idea of human rights has a much longer history, stretching back to ancient ideas of 'natural law'.

'Natural law' (*ius naturale*) is a term used to denote belief in an idea of justice common to all humankind. There are different shades of meaning attached to the concept. Natural law may be understood as the content of a divine 'fiat', or as the rational extrapolation of standards of conduct from the common nature of humanity. In the seventeenth century,

Thomas Hobbes retained the concept of 'natural law' as the only admissible curb on the authority of an essentially absolute ruler, who was responsible only to God.[12] At about the same time, Hugo Grotius, a seventeenth-century Dutch jurist, promoted a more secular idea of natural law, based upon humanity's essential nature. The jurists of ancient Rome also spoke of a law of nations (*ius gentium*), which comprised those precepts perceived to be common to the peoples within their domain.[13]

Natural law is posited both as a source of, and a critical measure of, positive law – the concrete law that actually applies within a state. Some have indeed argued that positive laws which deviate from natural law are not law in the true sense and need not be obeyed.[14] Others consider natural law to be a discredited myth.[15]

Today, natural law theories still hold sway in some religious circles, particularly within the Roman Catholic Church, justified with reference to both Scripture[16] and Church tradition, heavily influenced by St Thomas Aquinas who, in turn, took much from the philosophy of Aristotle.

Whereas Aristotle and other early philosophers tended to restrict the benefits of natural law to persons of a particular standing, the Stoics from the third century BC adopted a more egalitarian attitude. It is this approach which is said to have allowed the development from natural law to 'natural rights,' although such terminology was not adopted until the sixteenth century,[17] and was particularly espoused by John Locke in the seventeenth century.[18] Natural law had initially followed religious practice in focusing upon duties or responsibilities. The move towards the concept of natural rights is said to have followed upon: the rise of the middle classes, with a thirst for freedom;[19] the Reformation movement towards religious individualism;[20] and the writings of the Christian humanists.[21]

The culmination of this progress was the formulation of what are now referred to as the 'classical declarations of human rights' emanating from the eighteenth century.[22] In particular, this refers to the declarations associated with the American and French Revolutions: the 1774 American Bill of Rights; the 1776 American Declaration of Independence; and the 1789 French Declaration of the Rights of Man and Citizen. These started from an understanding of individual rights as absolute and inherent, 'natural and inalienable' to quote the words of the French Declaration.[23]

The eighteenth-century declarations focused upon civil and political rights. The nineteenth-century human misery following on from the industrial revolution led to the acknowledgement of a further class of social and economic rights.[24] This development was given a particular impetus by the Russian revolution and the philosophy of Marxism,[25] and later by the legacy of the depression of the 1930s and the two world wars.

In 1945, the United Nations was established with a founding charter that proclaimed:

WE THE PEOPLES OF THE UNITED NATIONS
DETERMINED

to save succeeding generations from the scourge of war, which twice in our lifetime has brought untold sorrow to mankind, and

to reaffirm faith in fundamental human rights, in the dignity and worth of the human person, in the equal rights of men and women and of nations large and small, and

to establish conditions under which justice and respect for the obligations arising from treaties and other sources of international law can be maintained, and

to promote social progress and better standards of life in larger freedom ...

HAVE RESOLVED TO COMBINE OUR EFFORTS TO ACCOMPLISH THESE AIMS.

It has been observed that the effect of this Charter was to 'transform individuals from mere objects of international compassion into actual subjects of international law'.[26] This perspective is supported by the convictions of war criminals in Nuremberg and Tokyo, establishing the principle that international law applied to individuals as much as to nations.[27] In 1948, the UN passed the Universal Declaration of Human Rights, embracing both civil and political rights (Articles 1–21) and social and economic rights (Articles 22–8).

4.4 The 1948 Universal Declaration of Human Rights

This seminal document for modern life rests upon the basic premise that:

> Recognition of the inherent dignity and of the equal and inalienable rights of all members of the human family is the foundation of freedom, justice and peace in the world.[28]

Recalling the 'barbarous acts' resulting from contempt for human rights, the members of the United Nations pledged to cooperate to promote 'universal respect for and observance of human rights and fundamental freedoms'. A precondition of such cooperation was a common understanding of the content of such rights and freedoms. The Universal Declaration was devised and presented as 'a common standard of achievement for all peoples and all nations' which would promote the establishment of universal freedom, justice and peace.

The Declaration was accepted by the United Nations with forty-eight votes in favour, and none opposed. Eight nations abstained: Byelorussia, Czechoslovakia, Poland, Saudi Arabia, Soviet Union, South Africa, Ukraine and Yugoslavia.[29] Saudi Arabia objected to the right to change one's religion, set out in Article 18 of the Declaration, as not conforming to Muslim belief and practice. The Soviet Union was concerned about national sovereignty, and the breadth of the right to freedom of opinion, which might be construed as permitting the expression of fascist or racist views. South Africa objected to the Declaration's statements about equality.[30]

The characteristics of the human rights proclaimed by the Declaration are that they:

recognise the *inherent* dignity of all members of the human family;

apply *equally* to all; and

are *inalienable*.

In terms of content, the rights proclaimed include:

life

freedom

equality

dignity

justice

property

freedom of thought, conscience and religion

freedom of opinion and expression

freedom of peaceful assembly and association

protection of family

participation in civil society

work

rest and leisure

an adequate standard of living

education

freedom from want.[31]

The rights are qualified only to the extent lawfully determined in any state as necessary to recognise the rights and freedoms of others, or 'meeting the just requirements of morality, public order and general welfare in a democratic society'.[32] They are accompanied by a reminder that, 'Everyone has duties to the community in which alone the free and full development of his personality is possible'.[33]

4.5 Philosophic Themes of the Twentieth-Century Human Rights Documents

Before drafting the Universal Declaration, the United Nations appointed the UNESCO Committee on the Philosophic Principles of the Rights of Man to consult scholars across the world about changes in intellectual and historical circumstances since the eighteenth century that might justify a different approach to the articulation of human rights.[34] A selection of the responses to this 1947 consultation was included in a book published by UNESCO in 1949.[35]

The consultation is of interest, not just because of its historical importance in the evolution of the Universal Declaration, but also because it explores significant concepts, such as the inalienability of rights and the correlation of rights and duties, which still appear in debates about rights in general and about the rights of parents and children in particular.

The period from 1948 to 1986 witnessed a mushrooming of international human rights documents, including the promulgation in 1966 of two International Covenants; one on Civil and Political Rights, and one on Economic, Social and Cultural Rights. At the regional level: 1950 witnessed the passing of the European Convention for the Protection of Human Rights and Fundamental Freedoms; 1969 was marked by the promulgation of the American Convention on Human Rights; and 1981 saw the promulgation of the African Charter on Human and People's Rights. Other international instruments promulgated during this period addressed particular issues such as slavery and sexual exploitation, torture and other maltreatment, and discrimination based upon race, sex or religion.[36]

In 1986, UNESCO commissioned a further philosophical consultation to take a fresh look at the contexts that had shaped the human rights language of the seventeenth century, and re-examine it in the light of perspectives arising from other cultural traditions.[37] The consultation also asked about the implications of developments since 1948, in particular, the increased emphasis on economic and social rights, as compared with civil and political rights.

The fiftieth anniversary of the Universal Declaration in 1998 provided a further opportunity for reflection, focusing in particular on the still lingering concerns about the relative priority to be given to economic and social rights as compared with civil and political rights, especially in the light of the recent demise of European communist regimes.

The following sections identify and explore some of the themes arising out of these consultations and reflections, including:

the possibility of universal human rights transcending different times, cultures and conditions;

the relevance of natural law and implications for belief in 'inherent' rights;

whether rights are based upon needs;

the meaning of 'inalienability';

the relationship between rights and duties or responsibilities;

the relative attractions of approaches based upon rights and virtues;

the relevance of spiritual considerations; and

individualism versus community, including the relative importance to be given to civil/political and social/economic rights.

4.6 The Possibility of Universal Human Rights

4.6.1 The 1947 Consultation

The eighteenth-century declarations of rights had confidently proclaimed human rights to be absolute and inherent, but the passage of time had raised questions about their adequacy in terms of scope, and their capacity to reflect changing human conditions and the emergence of new interests.

The memorandum circulated by UNESCO in 1947 identified as the two most significant developments since the eighteenth century, acceptance of the theory of evolution and the rise of Marxism. Evolution raised the question whether human rights too might be relative to conditions of time and place and subject to evolution. Marxism demonstrated a different approach to human rights, prioritising social and economic rights rather than the civil and political rights of the eighteenth-century declarations. The full realisation of social and economic rights in Marxist countries was predicated upon a strong central government and comprehensive planning, developments which cut across the eighteenth-century bias towards individual rights and freedom from government interference.

The consultation evidenced a large measure of agreement that formulations of human rights could not, and must not, remain static. An American political scientist described bills of rights as characteristically uncomprehensive, arguing that they 'take their cue from recent abuses'.[38] Another contributor agreed that ossifying human rights in the form of the eighteenth-century declarations would involve making a permanent virtue out of the needs of the rising commercial class of the eighteenth century.[39]

These observations focus upon the changing insights and needs of different times and conditions, but it is also possible, within any given time or place, for approaches to differ on the basis of culture or belief. The French philosopher Jacques Maritain observed that this need not inhibit the development of common lists of human rights, but their justification and exercise would differ within cultures in accordance with their beliefs and values. He reported an exchange at a UNESCO meeting at which some astonishment had been expressed at the measure of agreement reached between parties adhering to opposing ideologies, to which one such party had responded:

> Yes, we agree about the rights *but on condition that no one asks us why.*

That 'why', according to Maritain, 'is where the argument begins'.[40]

This understanding found support in a contribution by Richard McKeon, an American philosopher, who argued that agreement could be obtained only where a certain ambiguity remained. This did not undermine the effectiveness of the formulations, however, but rather provided a framework within which participants might move towards a shared practice and understanding.[41]

In 1947, the possibility of universalism was discussed largely within the context of the communist/capitalist polarisation. Some brief reference was made to the divergent philosophies of Asia and Africa, but these did not feature largely in the debate. A Chinese writer commented that, while the concept of human rights had not developed independently in China, the idea and practice of human rights was in fact present, manifesting mainly in the established right of the people to rebel against an oppressive ruler.[42] A writer on the Islamic tradition claimed the superiority of the early Islamic tradition of human rights over the subsequent flawed Western model. Disappointingly, no information was submitted to substantiate that claim or to identify the particular characteristics of the Islamic approach.[43] The Hindu concept of human rights was presented by S. V. Puntambekar, who expressed a preference for the concept of virtue over that of rights and laid emphasis on humankind's spiritual nature.[44]

On the basis of this consultation, the UNESCO Committee observed that:

> The philosophic problem involved in a declaration of human rights is not to achieve doctrinal consensus but rather to

achieve agreement concerning rights, and also concerning action in the realisation and defence of rights, which may be justified on highly divergent doctrinal grounds. [45]

It concluded that:

> Human rights have become, and must remain, universal ... Not only because there are no fundamental differences among men, but also because the great society and the community of all men has become a real and effective power, and the inter-dependent nature of that community is beginning at last to be recognised. [46]

4.6.2 From 1948 to 1986

1968 marked the twentieth anniversary of the Universal Declaration of Human Rights and was identified as the International Year for Human Rights. It was celebrated by the holding of a major international conference in Teheran, with a good representation of non-Western states, at which the Universal Declaration was affirmed as a common understanding of the peoples of the world. [47]

4.6.3 The 1986 Consultation

While the 1947 consultation discussed the possibility of universal human rights largely against the backdrop of European and American history and the capitalist/communist divide, the 1986 consultation extended the debate to take greater account of the philosophies, beliefs and experiences of Asian, African and Islamic cultures with divergent views of the nature and destiny of humankind. Voices emanating from those countries that had experienced colonial subjection spoke of an intent to resist the replacement of political imperialism with one of a philosophical or cultural nature. These tendencies, which might have lessened the influence of international human rights instruments, were balanced by perceptions that it might nevertheless be possible to reach a practical consensus, as the 1947 document had envisaged, and by a reclamation of the idea of human rights as a universal concept on the basis that the West had not so much invented the idea as the formal discourse about it.[48]

4.6.4 The Fiftieth Anniversary of the Universal Declaration – 1998

The fiftieth anniversary of the Universal Declaration in 1998 provided a further opportunity for review and reflection. The decade preceding the anniversary had been marked by radical political changes; in particular, the demise of many communist regimes reinforced the move away from the communist/capitalist divide within Europe that had coloured the earlier discussions about human rights. At the same time, the clamour to take greater account of non-Western voices increased. These non-Western nations took on the role of advocates for social and economic rights, which had earlier been exercised by the communist regimes.

In 1990, the General Assembly of the United Nations had decided to hold a World Conference on Human Rights to review and assess progress in implementation of the Declaration and make recommendations for the achievement of greater effectiveness.[49] Three preparatory regional meetings were held for Africa, Asia, and Latin America and the Caribbean, resulting in statements known respectively as the Tunis, Bangkok and San José Declarations.[50] These reaffirmed the regions' commitments to the Universal Declaration and the concept of universal human rights, sometimes with qualifications about their interpretation and application. In particular, they emphasised the need to respect different cultural and religious backgrounds. They also criticised the international community for its failure to give adequate development aid, emphasising that civil and political rights and social and economic rights were inseparable.

The World Conference, held in Vienna in June 1993, culminated in the adoption, by acclamation, of the Vienna Declaration and Programme of Action.[51] This reaffirmed the commitment to the 'purposes and principles contained in the Charter of the United Nations and the Universal Declaration of Human Rights', observing that 'The universal nature of these rights and freedoms is beyond question.' It added:

> While the significance of national and regional particularities and various historical, cultural and religious backgrounds must be borne in mind, it is the duty of States, regardless of their political, economic and cultural systems, to promote and protect all human rights and fundamental freedoms.

It affirmed the interdependence of democracy, development and respect for human rights, reaffirmed the right to development, and observed:

> While development facilitates the enjoyment of all human rights, the lack of development may not be invoked to justify the abridgement of internationally recognised human rights.

While the Vienna Declaration appears to resist the conclusions of the regional meetings insofar as they imply cultural relativism and propose the separation of development aid from human rights criteria, it has been observed that the West's acceptance of the *right* to development and the role of economic, social and cultural rights in promoting respect for civil and political rights was a major achievement. Consensus was furthered by the willingness of some previously resistant governments to acknowledge the contribution of democratic development towards sustainable economic growth.[52]

The final paragraph of the Vienna Declaration asked the Secretary-General of the UN to mark the forthcoming fiftieth anniversary of the Universal Declaration by a report on progress in achieving the goals set out in the Vienna Declaration. This report, building upon consultations with states and relevant agencies, proclaimed that:

Since the World Conference, the international community has continuously reiterated the validity of the universality of human rights, recognizing that although the significance of national and regional particularities, as well as various historical, cultural and religious backgrounds, must be borne in mind, it is the duty of States, regardless of their political, economic and cultural systems, to promote and protect all human rights and fundamental freedoms.[53]

The fiftieth anniversary itself was marked by a General Assembly resolution reaffirming that 'all human rights are universal, indivisible, interdependent and interrelated' and declaring a solemn commitment to fulfilment of the promise of the Universal Declaration.[54]

The fiftieth anniversary was also marked by a special seminar, organised by the UN High Commissioner for Human Rights in cooperation with the organisation of the Islamic Conference to provide Islamic perspectives on the Universal Declaration. Mary Robinson noted that, in the course of the seminar, 'no one expressed doubts about the Universal Declaration of Human Rights nor denied the legitimacy or universality of international human rights standards'.[55]

The Catholic view was expressed by the Pontifical Council for the Family, when it said of the Declaration:

[I]t is good to stress the convergence between this Declaration and Christian anthropology and ethics, despite the fact that the document makes no reference to God. There is also a conceptual proximity regarding the points admitted as being natural in that they are based on the common conscience of humanity. For this reason, it is certainly not a question of rights created by the Declaration, but rather of rights which it recognises and codifies. 'The Universal Declaration is very clear: it recognises the rights it proclaims, it does not grant them.'[56]

It would appear from the above that the concept of universal human rights is now widely accepted. However, a note of doubt appears in a comment by the High Commissioner that:

> The concept of universal and indivisible human rights has attained legitimacy, *officially at least*.[57]

This qualification may reflect the political realities rather than philosophical doubts, an appropriate comment in the context of what was a political rather than a philosophical review.

4.6.5 Conclusion on Universality

How is it possible to reconcile the assertion of universality with the insight that the form and content of human rights must evolve over time? One can do this only by accepting the possibility of changes in the formulations of rights, and any ranking within them, without changing their basic substance. Moreover, there must be sufficient communion of interest between different social and political cultures in any given time to allow common formulations that are meaningful and potentially effective for all parties. The UN Charter and the Universal Declaration of Human Rights affirm that that communion of interest lies in the increasing inter-dependence of nations and the universal desire for peace.

4.7 The Relevance of Natural Law and Implications for Belief in 'Inherent' Rights

4.7.1 The 1947 Consultation

While the UNESCO Committee identified the communist/capitalist philosophies as the significant opposing ideologies, both Lewis (an opponent of natural law) and Maritain (a supporter) perceived the two main 'antagonistic groups' in the debate as comprising those who accepted and those who rejected 'natural law' as the basis of human rights.[58] The natural law debate is related to the possibility of universalism in respect that supporters of natural law are more likely to view human rights as substantially unalterable, given that the authority of such rights is attributed to an external and unchanging source. According to Maritain, acceptance of natural law involves a belief that human nature is endowed with certain 'fundamental and inalienable rights' which are prior to society and are the source of societal development; rejection of natural law makes human rights relative to the historical development of society, and therefore 'constantly variable and in a state of flux'. [59]

Whilst both Lewis and Maritain acknowledged these approaches as ultimately irreconcilable, Maritain considered a rapprochement to be possible on the basis of mutual concessions. Natural law adherents could acknowledge that, while natural law was itself immutable and eternal, our knowledge and understanding of both its primary and secondary precepts increased over time. Opponents of natural law might be persuaded to acknowledge the existence of certain 'primitive,' fundamental rights, transcending time and socio-cultural conditions.

Maritain lamented the discredit that had fallen upon natural law because of its defacement by eighteenth-century rationalism which had dared to reduce it to a written code and to draw from it very detailed rules of human conduct. These claimed to be dictated by nature and reason, but were in fact 'arbitrary and artificial'. Such an approach tended to 'deify' the individual and equate his perceived rights with 'the absolute and unlimited rights of a god'. [60] Rather, we needed to understand that natural law had to be supplemented by human law if it was to serve the needs of particular times and circumstances. [61]

The document setting out UNESCO's conclusions from the consultation did not address the issue of natural law directly. It acknowledged, as some contributors had done, the possibility of parties agreeing upon a list of rights while basing them upon different and even divergent philosophies.

It appeared to align itself with the opponents of natural law in its 'working definition' of 'a right' as:

> A condition of living, without which, in any given historical stage of a society, men cannot give the best of themselves as active members of the community because they are deprived of the means to fulfil themselves as human beings. [62]

At the same time, it concluded that the 'rights of man':

> May be seen to be implicit in man's nature as an individual and as a member of society and to follow from the fundamental right to live. [63]

In this respect, the UNESCO Committee faced the problem of all those who wish to entrench fundamental rights in a context averse to any concept or standard of absolute truth.

4.7.2 The 1986 Consultation

The debate about natural law and natural rights continued in the 1986 consultation. Some considered the availability of an external standard of 'right' to be a necessary corrective to positive law, which would otherwise degenerate into a reflection of the interests of the ruling elite. At the same time, there was a concern to disentangle 'natural rights' from any religious basis. 'Deep-rooted moral beliefs' and human needs were suggested as alternatives, with needs being defined as the historically conditioned, necessary conditions of survival and development. [64] However, the very concept of 'natural right' was rejected by an Indian contributor, on the basis that, in his philosophy, every right was 'acquired' as the result of one's actions or one's status. [65]

4.8 Whether Rights are Based upon Needs

As suggested above, an alternative approach to justifying and identifying human rights is to found them in human needs. This raises the question whether all human needs are the same, or whether they can, and do, come into conflict. One contributor to the 1947 consultation argued that the true origin of the eighteenth-century rights was the need of the rising bourgeoisie for political and economic freedom from the aristocracy. These rights in turn had to be curtailed to meet the needs of the rising working classes. The identification of rights depended upon the needs of the class rising to power. [66]

When rights are based on needs, it becomes necessary to identify the ends which the 'needs' are meant to serve. One contributor identified common biological, psychological or spiritual characteristics that persisted in spite of cultural differences: the desire for life, food, sex and dominance; for home territory, personal freedom, movement and society; possibly linked with a common sentiment of religion and capacity for abstract thought (although it was acknowledged that some might regard these as culturally conditioned rather than innate). [67]

This is not too far in content from the primary natural law precepts identified by St Thomas Aquinas although these were classified as 'inclinations' rather than needs. Thus Aquinas identified inclinations which humankind shared in common with all substances ('being'), and in common with all animals (procreation and nurture/education). Unique to humankind was the inclination to know the truth about God and to live in society. [68] For Aquinas, however, these were all specifications of the primary precept that 'good is to be done and pursued and evil is to be avoided'. As regards humankind, 'good' was specified in relation both to God and to society. His specification was set within a much wider analysis of the human condition, within a belief system that identified a particular destiny to which humankind was directed.

The criterion of need might be seen as implicit in the 1947 conclusions of the UNESCO Committee set out above with regard to the identification of a right as a 'condition of living'. The end it served was the ability of a person to fulfil himself as an active member of the community. This, however, evades the question of an individual trying to lead a moral life within a community whose norms may be considered to breach human rights. Communities too have goals and ends, whether or not they are explicit.[69] In the 1986 consultation (as discussed above) one contributor proposed human needs as a secular grounding for a concept of natural rights, with needs being defined as the historically conditioned, necessary conditions of survival and development.[70] The teleological question is again left unanswered: development into what? In the absence of a teleology, the content of 'needs' is difficult to pin down.

4.9 The Meaning of 'Inalienability'

The word 'inalienable' (or 'unalienable') appears in many human rights documents. The American Declaration of Independence identified the endowment of 'unalienable rights' by the Creator as a 'self-evident truth'. The rights specified were to 'life, liberty and the pursuit of happiness'. The 1789 French Declaration of the Rights of Man and Citizen listed seventeen 'rights of man' described as 'natural, unalienable and sacred'. The 1948 Universal Declaration of Human Rights referred, in its first preambular paragraph, to 'the equal and inalienable rights of all members of the human family'. What does 'inalienable' mean?

In its natural meaning, it means a right that cannot be given away or taken away. An earlier formulation of the American concept is to be found in the 1776 Virginia Declaration of Rights, which stated:

> That all men are by nature equally free and independent, and have certain inherent rights, of which, when they enter into a state of society, they cannot, by any compact, deprive or divest their posterity ...

The later formulations would seem to clarify that neither can they deprive or divest *themselves*. The concept of inalienability was used to oppose those arguments of slave-owners that were based upon the rationality of a person selling himself into slavery in a time of destitution.[71] Inalienable rights are not property that can be traded; they are held in trust. While one might consent to specific incursions upon them, one cannot give them up.

One contributor told the UNESCO Committee that the rights of man were inalienable because 'rooted in the very nature of man'.[72] Another said that declarations of human rights had separated out those inalienable rights, which are to be protected from government interference, from alienable ones which were delegated to the government in return for just and effective government.[73]

The question arises whether our society actually does, or even can, operate effectively and fairly in a way that truly respects the inalienability of certain rights. Particularly in the sphere of criminal law, society does appear to be prepared to take away or qualify the rights of convicts and detained suspects to liberty and even life. How can this be justified if such rights are 'inalienable'? Maritain addressed this by distinguishing between the possession and exercise of inalienable rights:

> If a criminal can justly be condemned to lose his life, it is because he has, by his crime, deprived himself, not of his right to existence, but rather of the possibility of demanding that right with justice.[74]

This kind of approach found support in Kurt Riezler, an American philosopher, who identified a duty of each person to recognise the rights of fellow citizens:

> This would mean, in practice, that whoever advocates the disregarding or abolishing of these rights loses the moral claim to, and the legal protection of, his own human rights.[75]

This might seem a possible, though highly problematic, solution to the problem, but the question of inalienability will recur within the more specific context of the rights of parents.[76]

4.10 The Relationship between Rights and Duties or Responsibilities

One of the issues most consistently raised in the responses to the consultations was the relationship between rights and duties, responsibilities or obligations. At paragraph 3.8 above, we identified two different kinds of rights/duties correlation:

1. Between the rights of A and the duties of B – on the understanding that there can be no real right unless there is some correlative obligation on the part of someone else to fulfil it; and

2. Between the rights of A and the duties or responsibilities of A – on the understanding that a just and effective society must be based upon a network of *mutual* obligations.

The debate in this section focuses on the second kind of correlation.

4.10.1 The 1947 Consultation

In 1947, Jacques Maritain observed that:

> [A] declaration of rights should normally be rounded off by a declaration of man's obligations and responsibilities towards the communities of which he is a part, notably the family group, the civil society and the international community.[77]

E. H. Carr, a British diplomat, considered any declaration of rights to be *ipso facto* also a declaration of obligations. He said that the classical declarations appeared to have had a one-sided focus on rights, because of the historical conditions in which they were formulated. Obligations had been so all-pervading, and even dominant, in those societies struggling to free themselves from rigid social systems exhibiting the legacy of feudalism, that they had been taken for granted.[78] What are these correlative obligations? Carr says that the obligation correlative to political and civil rights is the mainly passive one of 'loyalty to the political order under which those rights are enjoyed'. There is a more active obligation correlative to social and economic rights in the sense that no society can guarantee them to its members unless that society 'has the right to call upon and direct the productive capacities of the individuals enjoying them'.[79]

What then is the relationship between rights and obligations? Should one concept be regarded as prior to, and the source of, the other? Is there a difference between historical and philosophical priority?

As regards history, Sergius Hessen (a Polish professor of the History of Education) described the early stage of political development as characterised by the Absolute State, which, while it laid the foundations of justice, did not recognise rights, but concerned itself with the duties of subjects.[80] This is the kind of political structure described as traditional in China, where society was built upon the Confucian concept of mutual obligations. The ruler had 'a duty towards heaven to take care of the interests of the people'. As indicated at 4.6.1 above, the people did have one right: the traditional right to rebel against an oppressive ruler. The weakness of the system lay in the tendency of the powerful to fail in their duties and to exploit their subjects. The lack of any rights other than rebellion explained the 'constant revolutions in Chinese history'.[81]

As regards philosophy, reference is often made to the view of Mahatma Gandhi that duties are the true source of rights, a traditional Indian view which he expressed in the following words:

> I learnt from my illiterate but wise mother that all rights to be deserved and preserved came from duty well done. Thus the

very right to live accrues to us only when we do the duty of citizenship of the world. From this one fundamental statement, perhaps it is easy enough to define the duties of Man and Woman and correlate every right to some corresponding duty to be first performed. Every other right can be shown to be a usurpation hardly worth fighting for. [82]

The difficulty posed by this approach is that if one truly believed that even the right to life had to be earned, there could be no concept of the rights of infants, or unproductive children, or the disabled, and it would be too easy for those in power to set and raise the price of life and liberty.

Concern about rooting rights in duties was expressed by Jean Haesaerts, a Belgian sociologist and political scientist. He was far from averse to the inclusion of duties and, in fact, criticised the UNESCO proposals for failing to balance the rights with corresponding duties, a practice which, he said, had resulted in 'disorder' and 'the discredit which has overtaken the vaunted individualism in these declarations'. Nevertheless, he also criticised the approach of a National Catholic Welfare Conference which 'began by defining man's duties, to fulfil which, it was said, he receives certain rights'. 'This,' said Professor Haesaerts, was 'pushing matters too far'. [83]

Unease about the matter was further articulated by Riezler who, while he observed that the natural law roots of rights also embraced duties, expressed concern at any tendency to make rights *conditional* on duties, considering that this opened the door to abuse of power. In his view, the only obligation that should receive legal recognition was the duty of each person to recognise the rights of fellow citizens. If further duties towards the state were specified as the condition of rights, 'the duties will uproot the rights. The rights will wither away.' [84] His conclusion was that a bill of rights would be weakened by the inclusion of duties.

Having surveyed the responses to its consultation, the UNESCO Committee concluded:

This universality of the rights of man, finally, has led to the translation into political instrumentalities of that close interdependence of rights and duties which has long been apparent in moral analysis. But the enjoyment of rights involves, not only the acceptance by the individual of corresponding obligations to society but is conditioned by the material resources of the society to which he belongs. Thus, the right to work implies the obligation to engage in work useful to the society; the right to maintenance, education, etc, can be enjoyed by each man only in so far as the society by productive work creates the resources out of which these rights can be assured.[85]

It would seem that the Committee wished to acknowledge the essential complement of obligations, while avoiding a possibly unhelpful emphasis upon them in any written declaration. The resultant formal declaration of 1948, as indicated above, has only one article qualifying the rights proclaimed, and that only to the extent necessary:

For the purpose of securing due recognition and respect for the rights and freedoms of others and of meeting the just requirements of morality, public order and the general welfare in a democratic society.[86]

In this respect, the Committee and the drafters of the Declaration appear to have taken account of the kind of concerns expressed by Riezler about the dangers of too great a specification of duties. Their approach also sends a message that, whereas rights may historically have their roots in duties or obligations, it is more conducive to human dignity to regard rights as inherent in humanity and either prior to duties or, at least, as inseparable from them as the two sides of a coin.

4.10.2 From 1948 to 1986

This period demonstrated a lingering concern from some quarters to emphasise the recognition and acceptance of human duties. As well as the Universal Declaration of Human Rights, 1948 had seen the passing of the American Declaration of the Rights and Duties of Man. The preamble sets the tone:

> All men are born free and equal, in dignity and in rights, and, being endowed by nature with reason and conscience, they should conduct themselves as brothers one to another.
>
> The fulfilment of duty by each individual is a prerequisite to the rights of all. Rights and duties are interrelated in every social and political activity of man. While rights exalt individual liberty, duties express the dignity of that liberty.
>
> Duties of a juridical nature presuppose others of a moral nature which support them in principle and constitute their basis.
>
> Inasmuch as spiritual development is the supreme end of human existence and the highest expression thereof, it is the duty of man to serve that end with all his strength and resources.
>
> Since culture is the highest social and historical expression of that spiritual development, it is the duty of man to preserve, practice and foster culture by every means within his power.
>
> And, since moral conduct constitutes the noblest flowering of culture, it is the duty of every man always to hold it in high respect.

This document was specifically referred to in a 1988 protocol to the 1969 American Convention on Human Rights. [87]

In 1981 the African Charter on Human and Peoples' Rights, demonstrating the perspective of countries emerging from colonial domination, was also notable for its equal emphasis on duties as correlative to rights. It provided that, 'the promotion and protection of morals and traditional values recognized by the community shall be the duty of the State'. [88] The Charter's separate chapter on duties states:

Article 27

Every individual shall have duties towards his family and society, the State and other legally recognized communities and the international community.

The rights and freedoms of each individual shall be exercised with due regard to the rights of others, collective security, morality and common interest.

Article 28

Every individual shall have the duty to respect and consider his fellow beings without discrimination, and to maintain relations aimed at promoting, safeguarding and reinforcing mutual respect and tolerance.

Article 29

The individual shall also have the duty:

1. To preserve the harmonious development of the family and to work for the cohesion and respect of the family; to respect his parents at all times, to maintain them in case of need;

2. To serve his national community by placing his physical and intellectual abilities at its service;

3. Not to compromise the security of the State whose national or resident he is;

4. To preserve and strengthen social and national solidarity, particularly when the latter is threatened;

5. To preserve and strengthen the national independence and the territorial integrity of his country and to contribute to its defence in accordance with the law;

6. To work to the best of his abilities and competence, and to pay taxes imposed by law in the interest of the society;

7. To preserve and strengthen positive African cultural values in his relations with other members of the society, in the spirit of tolerance, dialogue and consultation and, in general, to contribute to the promotion of the moral well-being of society;

8. To contribute to the best of his abilities, at all times and at all levels, to the promotion and achievement of African unity.

4.10.3 The 1986 Consultation

The debate about the relationship between rights and duties continued into the 1986 consultation, heightened by the higher profile given to the perspectives of cultures other than those descending from Western liberalism. Tensions were identified where 'rights' had been embraced by the political leaders of cultures with a different orientation. As regards Japan, Inagaki commented upon the emergence of rights as the primary concept in the 1946 Japanese constitution. While this had been supported by the Japanese people, it was largely an innovation in a society whose political structure had been modelled upon family loyalty and obligation.[89] Despite the openness to abuse and injustice presented by the family obligation model, its lingering influence had made the Japanese reluctant to claim their rights through institutional procedures, a behaviour that was considered by them not virtuous, possibly indecent.[90]

As regards India, Pandeya affirmed the priority of duties over rights espoused by Gandhi in 1947, and derided the reversal of priorities implicit in the Constitution enacted by Nehru, which echoed the concepts of the constitution of the United States. The result had been that the rights framework had been used more by the powerful to vindicate their privileges than by the vulnerable members of society who still followed the traditional ways.[91]

Writing about the Islamic states, Taylor observed that, while they had a concept of public welfare and limits which the State must not transgress, the lack of any individual power to challenge such transgressions meant that there was no real concept of personal rights.[92]

Zakaria, an Egyptian philosopher, pointed out that, for Muslims, the Koran was the basic source of human rights.

Respect for human rights was an integral part of the Islamic system. Those who breached such rights would be subject to divine punishment in the afterlife. There was, however, no traditional mode of redress in this world for those whose rights had been violated. Islam acknowledged that, since the Golden Age of the Prophet and the four Rightful Caliphs, leaders had often failed in their responsibilities. Respect for human rights fluctuated according to the piety of the ruler.[93]

Even in the West, there were indications of some resistance. Tay and Kamenka, writing from an Australian perspective, noted a reaction against the apparent stridency of 'rights' claims, and the neglect of duties, in a culture where the discourse was (unhelpfully it seems) dominated by lawyers rather than philosophers.[94] This is an example of the 'confrontational' objection to 'rights' discussed at 3.7.2 above.

4.10.4 The Fiftieth Anniversary of the Universal Declaration – 1998

In the run-up to the fiftieth Anniversary, groups of politicians and religious leaders worked to give a higher profile to the concept of human responsibility or duty. The political initiative came from a group of former government leaders, called the InterAction Council, who drafted a 'Universal Declaration of Human Responsibilities' in the hope that it would be adopted as a complement to the Declaration of Human Rights.[95] The basic premise of this project is evident from the Preamble to the Declaration, published in September 1997, which observed:

> *whereas* the exclusive insistence on rights can result in conflict, division, and endless dispute, and the neglect of human responsibilities can lead to lawlessness and chaos ... [96]

The Declaration's nineteen articles required every person to treat every other in 'a humane way'. Everyone had a responsibility 'to promote good and to avoid evil in all things'. It repeated what is known as the Golden Rule: 'What you do not wish to be done to yourself, do not do to others.'

Every person had a responsibility to behave with integrity, honesty and fairness, and to 'develop their talents through diligent endeavour'. Wealth and power must be used responsibly and in the service of economic justice and of the social order. Religious freedom must be guaranteed, but balanced with tolerance and respect for other beliefs. The relationships between sexual or marriage partners, and between parents and children, should be respectful and non-exploitative. The final article stated:

> Nothing in this Declaration may be interpreted as implying for any state, group or person any right to engage in any activity or to perform any act aimed at the destruction of any of the responsibilities, rights and freedoms set forth in this declaration and in the Universal Declaration of Human Rights in 1948.

Helmut Schmidt, former Chancellor of the Federal Republic of Germany, and a subscriber to the Declaration, outlined his reasons for supporting it. He echoed the concern expressed by some developing countries when he condemned the selective use of 'human rights' by Western governments in furthering their foreign policy objectives. He identified an over-emphasis on rights to the detriment of responsibilities as a Western approach that failed to take proper account of the Asian focus on virtue or obligations.[97]

The InterAction Council had a number of advisers in this work, including Hans Küng, a theologian from Tübingen University, who had, since 1993, been working with the Parliament of the World's Religions, to develop a 'global ethic', a basic, human, moral attitude concerned with 'the inner realm of the person, the sphere of conscience, of the heart'.[98] Küng's commentary on the Declaration of Human Responsibilities is keen to emphasise that there is no suggestion that rights have to be earned by the performance of duties, but insists that the human person 'is always at the same time one who has rights and responsibilities', a perspective which we have already criticised at 4.10.1 above.[99]

The Declaration of Human Responsibilities was forwarded to the Secretary-General and received a polite acknowledgement and expression of willingness to discuss the matter. It was not approved as part of the fiftieth anniversary celebrations. Whatever its expressed intent, it was viewed by some as a potential threat to the concept of universal human rights, and as an unjustified, if implicit, criticism of the 1948 Declaration for fostering an 'unbridled emphasis on human rights and freedoms',[100] without sufficient acknowledgement of the contribution of other factors such as the global economic forces that increasingly shaped our world and our attitudes.

Nevertheless, the High Commissioner for Human Rights marked the fiftieth anniversary by re-emphasising the importance of Article 29's commitment to responsibilities. She identified profound changes in society since the Declaration's promulgation in 1948. In addition to technological, environmental and economic changes, she observed:

> Beliefs and values are everywhere challenged. It is no exaggeration to speak of a moral and ethical vacuum in many societies. At the same time, some religious proponents seek to impose their beliefs by force on their fellow human beings.[101]

She reminded her audience of the responsibilities of individuals in terms of Article 29 of the Universal Declaration:

> The message of Article 29 is clear. It tells us, at a time of moral and ethical confusion, that we are members of one human family with rights in common and duties towards each other. As we look to the future, the sense of humankind 'being in this together' could be a potent force for strengthening and protecting human rights.

It would appear that the UN is committed to promoting the correlativity of human rights and responsibilities, but remains wary of too great a specification of, or emphasis on, them.

4.11 The Relative Attractions of Approaches based upon Rights and Virtues

In 1947, S. V. Puntambekar considered the language of human rights to be desirable, but inappropriate for the troubled contemporary situation in India.[102] He reframed the debate from rights and duties to the 'freedoms' or 'assurances', and 'virtues' or 'controls' taught by great thinkers like Manu and Buddha. This was allied with an understanding of the human person as embracing a deeper self, benign in nature, which must be discovered and protected so that it could be used for the welfare both of that person and the whole of humanity. Just as many other correspondents viewed duties as the necessary correlative of rights, so Puntambekar pointed to the need to balance any notion of freedoms with a corresponding commitment to virtue. What he appears to be arguing for is a reformation of society working from the inside out, rather than from the regulation of human conduct by means of the external controls provided by rights and duties. This raises the question whether a reformation proceeding uniquely from either external regulation or internal renewal is likely to be successful. This question, and the concept of 'virtue', will be discussed more extensively in 5.3.1 and 7.2.1 below.

4.12 The Relevance of Spiritual Considerations

Spiritual considerations frame a person's understanding of the nature and destiny of humankind, and therefore of the needs or conditions that will promote human fulfilment. This brief section merely sets out references to this consideration within the consultations. Theological and spiritual matters will be the main focus of chapters 5, 7 and 8.

As regards the *nature* of humankind, an Indian contributor to the 1947 consultation referred to the duality of humankind as body and soul.[103] There was a need to 'develop our idea of the good human life', by transcending material values and including spiritual values.[104] Mainstream Christian anthropology would view a person as a unity comprising physical and spiritual dimensions rather than a duality as such,[105] but that spiritual dimension would colour the identification of human need. A secular perception of duality was presented by American physiologist, A. W. Gerard, who categorised it in terms of the individual being both an entity in his own right and part of a social unit.[106]

As regards the *destiny* of humankind, religious views of the conditions for attaining any life after death or happy reincarnation will inevitably colour the conditions identified for favourable progress towards that goal. However, ideas of destiny are not restricted to the religious sphere. Hessen noted that the early years of the Bolshevik revolution had an 'eschatological character'.[107] Those involved expected to see, in their lifetimes, the realisation of the communist ideal, involving the abolition of law, 'rights' and economy in favour of a society of 'sympathy, equity and mutual aid' based upon the necessity of nature or the inner voice of conscience.[108] Therefore, it is not that secular or materialist philosophies necessarily have no 'end' in mind, but that, according to Maritain, they may be more susceptible than religious philosophies to the sanctification of an end at the cost of the means required to achieve it.[109]

The conclusions drawn by the UNESCO Committee from its 1947 consultation start with an expression of 'faith' and end with a reference to 'the enrichment of the human spirit'. Thus, an international declaration of human rights is described as: 'the expression of a faith to be maintained no less than a programme of actions to be carried out'.[110] Human rights are said to be: 'of fundamental importance not only to the enrichment of the human spirit but to the development of all forms of human association'.[111] There is no explicit reference to religion. Faith in human rights is presented as one faith underpinning divergent philosophies, in language that is capable of either a secular or religious interpretation.

Faith relates to that which is unseen. It points ahead to a fulfilment. It has an eschatological dimension. [112] So this statement, whether read from a religious or from a secularist standpoint, links up with the questions of human destiny taken up in Chapter 8.

4.13 Individualism versus Community

A recurring theme of the above discussions has been the relative weight to be given to civil and political rights, and economic and social rights. It was noted that:

the classical human rights documents of the seventeenth and eighteenth centuries focused on civil and political rights (para. 4.6.1);

the first twenty-one articles of the 1948 Universal Declaration of 1948 addressed civil and political rights, with the following seven addressing social and economic rights (para. 4.3);

the promulgation in 1966 of two International Covenants placed equal emphasis on the different classes of rights (para. 4.5);

the 1986 consultation was concerned to enquire into the implications of this increased emphasis on social and economic rights (para. 4.5); and

there was – and remains – a concern about achieving the correct balance, evident in the discussions centring on the fiftieth anniversary of the 1948 Declaration (paras 4.5 and 4.6.4).

In particular, a tension was noted between the emphasis of the civil and political rights on freedom from government interference, and the perceived need for social and economic rights to be supported by a strong central government (para.

4.6.1) and the right of that government to 'call upon and direct the productive capacities' of the persons enjoying such rights (para. 4.10.1).

At the 1968 Teheran Conference (referred to at para. 4.6.2 above), the influence of the developing countries had shaped a statement emphasising the indivisibility of the different classes of human rights, and expressing the view that civil and political rights could be empty trophies in situations where basic social and economic rights were not recognised or respected.[113]

All of this raises questions about the status of the 'individual' in relation to the community of which he or she is a member. Indeed, while 'rights' in general are derided by some as too individualistic (an objection addressed at 3.7.4 above), such concerns about ultra-individualism have been matched in recent times by a contrary concern that the rights of the community – and the State – which have now also been embraced as 'human rights' are once again gaining too much prominence at the expense of the individual. The following paragraphs explore some of the philosophical discussions and reflections on this theme.

4.13.1 The 1947 Consultation

In terms of the historical evolution of law, the social contract theory prevalent at the time of the eighteenth-century declarations hypothesised that the origins of a regulated society lay in the surrender of individual freedoms in order to obtain the benefits of law and order. Margery Fry, former Secretary-General of the Howard League for Penal Reform, argued that the evidence actually pointed in the other direction, towards the growth of early law as a gradual restriction of the rights of the community over the individual member. Individuals in primitive societies had, in fact, 'an extremely small range of free action'.[114]

Whatever the historical truth, or truths, the question of the relationship between the individual and the community was a recurring subject of comment in the responses to the consultation, with some considering the focus on individual rights to act against the interests of the community and its members, and others regarding these interests as having the potential to be more complementary.

The former camp was represented by a Spanish scholar, who considered the concept of rights 'too narrow' to express the basic relationship between human persons. The relationship between an individual and society was much more complex. Indeed, he said, there was no such thing as an absolute individual.[115] He described the concept of rights as 'combative, biased and therefore limited in outlook', deriving this character from historical roots in the era of the French Revolution, and he urged less emphasis on 'the rights of man' and more on 'proper relations between man, nation and the world community'.[116] The identification of those 'proper relations' would be coloured by a person's religious, philosophical or political outlook.

The latter camp was represented by two contributors, one religious and one secular, who identified the living organism as the paradigm for a community. The religious perspective was given by Pierre Teilhard de Chardin, a Jesuit philosopher and palaeontologist. In his view, the eighteenth-century declarations were an assertion of the desire for individual independence. Society was now 'collectivising' or 'totalising' at a metaphysical level, requiring a modification of our understanding of rights. The rights of the individual and the society around him were complementary rather than conflicting. The individual found his greatest fulfilment within the group, which should seek to provide the conditions for his favourable development. The corollary was that 'the individual is no longer entitled to remain inactive',[117] but had an 'absolute duty' to work, and a 'relative right' to be supported in his personal development, along with an 'absolute right' not to be coerced. Societal pressure should rather be exerted through 'inward persuasion'.[118]

The secular perspective was provided by R. W. Gerard, an American physiologist who presented the example of a living organism in which the interests of both part and whole were promoted by supporting an appropriate 'differentiation'. Society was evolving in the direction of greater dependence of the individual on the group. A human person was a 'duality', and it was a mistake to regard him or her as *either* an isolated individual *or* a mere part of a group.[119]

Having surveyed the responses to its consultation, UNESCO concluded:

> These rights ... are claims which all men and women may legitimately make, in their search, not only to fulfil themselves at their best, but to be so placed in life that they are capable, at their best, of becoming in the highest sense citizens of the various communities to which they belong and of the world community, and in those communities of seeking to respect the rights of others, just as they are resolute to protect their own.[120]

The concern about community is also reflected in the 'working definition' of rights adopted by UNESCO, and already referred to at 4.7 above.

4.13.2 *The 1986 Consultation*

In the course of the 1986 consultation, Alwin Diemer (a German philosopher) identified, as main influences on the developments since 1948, a shift in emphasis towards Marxist and Third World priorities and concepts of human nature, culminating in the 1966 Covenant on Economic, Social and Cultural Rights, and the prominence of 'peoples' as the subject of rights in the Covenant on Civil and Political Rights.[121]

Whereas the debate in 1947 about the individual and the community had focused on whether the language of rights could adequately and appropriately express the relationship between the individual and the community in which he was rooted, the contributors to the 1986 consultation reflected upon the emergence of group or community rights as a qualifier of individual rights. Consultees had different views on the legitimacy or helpfulness of this development. Hersch took a very pessimistic view. She observed that the rights set out in 1948 had been directed to individuals. As former colonial countries were admitted to the UN, however, rights were increasingly ascribed to human communities and national state entities. This move was motivated by the vulnerability of the new states as they searched for an identity, and was supported by the communist states. It was allied with the increasing emphasis on social and cultural, as compared with civil and political rights. The Universal Declaration had been enacted to defend the individual against the power of the State. In Hersch's view, these new developments had made the State the 'privileged favourite' of human rights.[122]

Humphrey also feared the rise of collective rights at the expense of individuals, but was less pessimistic about the extent of their inroad. He pointed out that the 1966 Covenants, which were the cause of some of the concern, still largely identified the subject of rights as the individual.[123]

Taylor regarded the development of the community focus as a legitimate and healthy departure from the purely atomistic conception of the individual prevalent in the seventeenth-century philosophies. It acknowledged the cultural and collective dimension of human development. The right to education, for example, made sense only in the context of a society with the potential for taking positive action to respect it. The right to full development within one's own culture was an individual right, but one that was granted to a nation. Its fulfilment was dependent upon collective action. Taylor did not therefore deny the legitimacy of individual rights but presented them as achievable only within a system in which the rights of communities were also recognised. This made our conception of rights 'far more complex and difficult to apply'.[124]

4.13.3 *The Fiftieth Anniversary – 1998*

As indicated at 4.6.4 above, the preparations for the fiftieth anniversary of the 1948 Declaration involved much discussion about the relative importance of social and economic rights, and civil and political rights, culminating in a General Assembly resolution reaffirming that 'all human rights are universal, indivisible, interdependent and interrelated'.[125]

4.13.4 *Conclusion on Individualism versus Community*

This exploration shows that there remains a concern about how to recognise the social character of the human person and the reality of human interdependence, without opening the door to the kind of state oppression of the individual which the Universal Declaration had sought to counteract.

4.14 Summary of Conclusions on Philosophic Themes

This broad sweep of discussions centring on the 1948 Declaration shows:

a consistent reaffirmation by the international community of the universality of human rights, even in the face of challenges based on changes in focus over time, and differences in justification;

ambivalence about the existence of a 'natural law', combined with recognition of the need for some stable and external source of critique of positive law;

some suggestions about founding rights in needs, and the need to root this in a teleology;

a continuing contradiction between assertions of 'inalienability' and actual legal practice in authorising the deprivation of rights in certain circumstances;

an enduring concern about the exaltation of rights at the expense of duties, competing with a fear of diluting rights by exalting duties;

voices that speak of the spiritual nature of humankind and the role of virtue in shaping the fulfilment of one's personal destiny; and

a growing debate about how to achieve an appropriate balance between the rights of the individual and the complementary or competing rights of the communities of which he or she is a member.

4.15 The Ongoing Debate

At the beginning of this chapter we identified as current trends:

wariness about positing rights as the framework for human relationships;

concern to place an equal or correlative emphasis on duties;

a desire to return to the pursuit of virtue as more conducive to a humane society than the pursuit of rights; and

a sceptical attitude to the very concept of human rights.

These are, in particular, themes of the new communitarian movement,[126] which seeks a moratorium on 'new' rights and a greater emphasis on responsibilities,[127] allied with a careful balance of the interests of individuals and community.[128] Its most vocal exponent, Amitai Etzioni, wants to:

Restore civic virtues, for people to live up to their responsibilities and not merely focus on their entitlements, and to shore up the moral foundations of society.[129]

A communitarian society would be one based largely on moral commitment rather than on law. There is a *place* for law within it, as an expression of society's values and as a deterrent to wrongdoing, but this should not be overplayed.[130] Etzioni acknowledges that community forces have, in the past, been oppressive, and that they have the potential to be self-centred, also that there are extreme voices speaking under the banner of Communitarianism with which more moderate adherents would disagree; however, he says, just as extreme examples of dangerous driving are not regarded as a good reason for banning cars, neither should hard cases of community oppression be cited in opposition to the exercise of moral authority by communities.[131]

All of this sounds reasonable enough. However, the argument about dangerous driving could equally be applied to the much-cited abuse of rights; if the hard cases do not undermine the communitarian cause neither can they be presented as undermining the case for rights.[132]

A more positive approach to rights is presented by Alan Gewirth, whose 1996 *Community of Rights* sought to demonstrate how rights and community were complementary rather than antithetical. When rights were properly understood, he said, they 'entail a communitarian conception of human relations',[133] with the community as a network of mutual rights and responsibilities, consistent with the picture presented at 3.7.4 above.

Gewirth places great emphasis on social and economic rights; and it is the lack of this dimension in the UK's Human Rights Act 1998 that evokes some of the scepticism of the authors of *Sceptical Essays on Human Rights*. The Act, they say, gives precedence to civil and political rights. Moreover, it detracts from the normal political processes by giving too much power to an unelected and unrepresentative judiciary. Some of the authors also put forward the recurring complaint that a rights culture encourages antagonistic litigation (a matter we addressed at 3.7.2 above).[134]

What emerges from the exposition above is a growing awareness of the need for an appropriate balance between the rights of the community and the individuals that comprise it. Since 1948, the cost of maintaining a worldwide commitment to the universality of human rights has been the positive embrace of social and economic rights as of equal value. These rights have a cost in terms of some erosion of the individual 'freedom from' government or community control that lay at the heart of the classic declarations of civil and political rights. There has been an evolving appreciation of the interdependence of: the individual and the community; individual rights and community rights; and civil/political and social/economic rights.

Interdependence demands equilibrium and a continuing awareness, monitoring and process of adjustment to maintain it. This is a much more demanding task than the proclamation and pursuit of absolute, individual rights, and a situation that renders individual rights potentially more vulnerable, given that this monitoring and readjustment is likely to be a function of the State – one of the very parties whose 'rights' are in the balance. It demonstrates the need for the establishment of independent bodies such as human rights commissions, and also an independent judiciary. While some of the sceptical authors question the perceived shift in power from politicians to judges, one might argue that such power-sharing is not in itself a bad thing, and that the concerns expressed by sceptics might be better addressed by reviewing the calibre, qualifications and appointment of the judiciary.

An aversion to 'rights talk' and a preference for 'virtue' is also evident in the work of Alasdair MacIntyre, whose views have already been referred to at para. 4.2 above. Human rights were, he said, a fictional product of a liberal individualism that existed in a state of deep opposition to the virtue-based ethic inherited from Aristotle. In his view, a restated Aristotelianism, a new virtue-based ethic oriented towards an explicit teleology, offered the best hope for humanity.[135] It should be remembered that the target of MacIntyre's opposition was human rights as an ontological category rather than as a product of positive law. There is a danger that this qualification will be forgotten. It is possible to accept the validity of human rights declarations as a statement of agreed standards, without agreeing on justification for them; to accept them as a useful contribution of positive law, even while rejecting any particular philosophical justification.

It is our view that religion, morality and virtue offer an alternative and complementary route to human fulfilment rather than one existing in opposition to a rights perspective. The 'inner realm of the person', the sphere of conscience, of the 'heart' identified by Hans Küng as the proper realm of 'ethic',[136] and the 'virtue' espoused by philosophers such as MacIntyre, are essential to the fullest implementation of human rights. However, it might be argued that, if people were truly virtuous, human rights and the apparatus of the law would not be necessary at all. The fact is that people are *not* all virtuous. Education and encouragement to virtue must be important, but we will never be in the position where we do not need law and rights. One might conclude that rights allow the vulnerable to present their claims against the suffering caused by lack of virtue in the powerful. The danger in proposing virtue as opposed to rights is that today's cutting–edge philosophy, with all of its subtle nuances, will degenerate into tomorrow's debased commonplace. We will have undermined or sidelined human rights at our own peril and that of future generations.

4.16 Resistance to the Development of Human Rights

It remains to look at some of the more political or pragmatic sources of resistance to the development of human rights, which recur in only slightly different incarnations in the resistance found today to the rights of the child. Lauren notes that:

> [A]ll ... visions of human rights confronted powerful opposition and forces of resistance every step of the way. The reason can be simply stated: they all raised profoundly disturbing issues about what it means to be human, thereby directly threatening traditional patterns of authority and privilege, vested interests and prerogatives, and the claims of national sovereignty.[137]

Opposition was justified with reference to a number of arguments, which will be discussed briefly in turn:

authoritarianism;
protection of national sovereignty;
justified discrimination;
intervention might make things worse;
developments moving beyond the original intent;
political sensitivity;
religious sensitivity; and
cultural relativism.[138]

4.16.1 Authoritarianism

While Thomas Paine's *The Rights of Man* had been a best-seller on its publication in 1791, it had also provoked public and political outrage. In England, effigies of the author had been hanged and burned by crowds singing 'God save the King'. A royal proclamation had called for Paine's arrest for sedition.[139] Such apparently extreme reactions might be explained by their proximity to the chaos and bloodshed resulting from the French Revolution. More generally, however, there was a fear that the attribution of rights for all, as opposed to duties, might undermine the authority of divinely-sanctioned hereditary rulers, the order of society, and thus the common good.[140]

The communist countries that had abstained from the vote on the Universal Declaration in 1948 were concerned, among other things, about its potential to restrict their authority.[141]

4.16.2 Protection of National Sovereignty

The international dimension of human rights was viewed with great suspicion by those who feared that any comment, monitoring or judgement upon them would erode their national sovereignty.[142] As a result, early international law concerned itself solely with relations between states. The debate, and the resistance to the recognition of the rights of individuals under international law, continued right up to the drafting of the Universal Declaration. The ultimately unacceptable implications of too great a deference to national sovereignty were manifest in the course of the post-World War II international military trials at Nuremberg, when Hitler's deputy, Hermann Goering, defended himself against charges of gross violation of human rights by declaring, 'But that was our right! We were a sovereign State and that was strictly our business'.[143]

4.16.3 Justified Discrimination

Some argued that there existed fundamental differences between human persons, which justified their differential treatment. Age, education, language, religion, class or caste, possession of property, gender and race, all were advanced as justifying discriminatory treatment.[144] One way to exempt a particular group from the benefits of human rights is to define them out of the category of persons deserving such dignity. Thus, in the case of race and gender, the arguments went as far as questioning the human status of particular peoples and of women in general.[145] In 1879, a judge in the USA is reported to have 'broken new ground' by ruling that:

> An Indian is a 'person' within the meaning of the laws of the United States, and has therefore the inalienable right to 'life, liberty and the pursuit of happiness'.[146]

In the run-up to the finalisation of the Charter of the United Nations, American and Chinese women had felt it necessary to emphasise that:

> Women should be regarded as human beings.[147]

4.16.4 Intervention Might Make Things Worse

It has been observed that, 'Humanitarian intervention always carried the risk that it could provoke even worse reactions against the very people that it wanted to protect'.[148] For example, political correspondence relating to a situation in Syria in 1860 demonstrates a fear about the potential adverse consequences of such intervention. Moreover, those intervening could be intimidated by a fear that the spotlight might be turned back upon them, showing up their own inadequacies or failure to live up to ideals.

4.16.5 Developments Moving Beyond the Original Intent

One approach to resisting developments in human rights was to argue that they went beyond the original intent of their founding proclamations. This was the basis for some resistance, for example, to the work of the International Labor Organisation.[149]

South Africa, which abstained from the vote on the Universal Declaration, complained that it went 'far beyond' the rights contemplated in the Charter of the United Nations.[150]

Commentators consider that there may be some truth in the suggestion that important statements and declarations tend to take on a life of their own, and evolve into something more substantial. Some of this can be justified in legal terms through their gradual acceptance as 'customary law' with legal force.[151]

4.16.6 Political Sensitivity

Opposition might also be based upon the political sensitivity of an issue, a justification often given for failure to respond appropriately to issues affecting racial, linguistic and religious minorities.[152]

4.16.7 Religious Sensitivity

Despite the leading role of its own First Lady in drafting the Universal Declaration, opposition to it was particularly strong within the United States of America. There was fear of a communist influence within the UN promoting an agenda of social and economic rights. The perceived threat to national sovereignty was closely linked to religious sensitivity. A Republican Senator described the draft Declaration as a 'UN Blueprint for Tyranny', which was 'completely foreign to American law and tradition'. On the floor of the Senate, he announced:

> I do not want any of the international groups, and especially the group headed by Mrs. Eleanor Roosevelt, which has drafted the covenant of Human Rights, to betray the fundamental, inalienable, and God-given rights of American citizens enjoyed under the Constitution.[153]

4.16.8 Cultural Relativism

The Soviet Union, which abstained in the vote on the Universal Declaration, condemned the civil and political rights within it as representing nothing more than 'bourgeois values'.[154]

There was no explicit resistance from what are now known as 'developing countries', many of which were still under colonial domination. The charge of 'cultural imperialism' was to grow in volume with the passing of time.[155]

4.16.9 Conclusion

Some of these objections now sound strange to our ears. We will see in Chapter 6 how they have re-emerged, however, with only slightly different packaging, in resistance to the articulation and development of the rights of the child.

4.17 General Conclusion

The discussions in this chapter evidence much support for the concept of universal human rights, from all parts of the globe, even in the face of philosophical disagreement about their justification and content, and political and pragmatic resistance to their development and implementation.

Critics have questioned the impact on human relationships of viewing them within a rights-based framework, commenting correctly that human life is richer than that. However, the rights framework is not presented here as the only, or even most basic way, of speaking about human relationships, but rather as one that is appropriate and effective for the kind of dialogue necessary to achieve the ends set out in the UN Charter. These ends – the promotion of human dignity, justice and peace – are as valid today as they were in 1945, even if their achievement remains elusive. It is perhaps *because* of the difficulties in maintaining our course towards them that we need, more than ever today, a common language that will help different cultures, and different groupings within the emerging multi-cultural societies, discuss their differences in the light of the impact their disagreement may have on what all hold dear. The world today seems smaller than ever, with developments that ease mobility and aid communication of ideas; and yet that very smallness and ease of communication brings home to us more than ever the reality and implications of diverse and divergent philosophies. These philosophies provide the primary framework for the cultures that adhere to them. We should not underestimate the momentous significance of the remarkable measure of acceptance of the international human rights framework. Proposing their character as a secondary framework is not a demotion, but a recognition of their actual status in many cultures as well as their ability to underwrite the divergent philosophies that otherwise divide our world.

Of course, this agreement has been achieved at the cost of a certain amount of 'ambiguity', and this will translate into different ideas about implementation. But the important thing is that we keep on talking about human dignity, and that we have a language that allows us to do so.

In terms of their efficacy in achieving the aims of the UN Charter, some have argued that the rights proclaimed by the Universal Declaration as an antidote to the power of the State and a contribution towards world peace are sometimes used by the powerful as weapons *against* the weak. Powerful individuals will be more able to vindicate their individual positions through assertion of their rights, as will powerful states. The question is whether the situation would be improved by a return to a primary focus on responsibilities or virtue. One might argue that rights are the power to insist on the implementation of responsibilities and to counteract the worst consequences of lack of virtue. The fact that that power may sometimes be one-sided because of inequities within our society suggests a need for more support for the vulnerable rather than dilution of the concept of rights. The powerful and determined will manage to manipulate any system that is in place; but some systems are potentially more equitable than others.

Notes

1. In the UK, for example, the Human Rights Act 1998 incorporated the major part of the European Convention on Human Rights into UK law.

2. As an aspect of postmodernism, for example, or of a communitarian approach that sees 'rights' talk as too individualistic. See, for example, A. Etzioni, *The Spirit of Community: Rights, Responsibilities and the Communitarian Agenda*, London: Fontana Press, 1995, and L. R. Meyer, 'Unruly Rights', *Cardozo Law Review*, 22:1 (2000), pp. 9–12.

3. R. Traer, *Faith in Human Rights: Support in Religious Traditions for a Global Struggle*, Washington, DC: Georgetown University Press, 1991, p. 21, quotes Erich Weingärtner, *Human Rights on the Ecumenical Agenda: Report and Assessment*, Geneva: Commission of the Churches on International Affairs, World

Council of Churches, 1983, p. 11: 'Human rights are not ends in themselves, but the conditions for the realization of human dignity.'

4. P. G. Lauren, *The Evolution of International Human Rights: Visions Seen*, Philadelphia: University of Pennsylvania Press, 1998, p. 15.

5. Lauren, *Evolution of International Human Rights*, p. 22.

6. MacIntyre, *After Virtue*, pp. 66–8.

7. MacIntyre, *After Virtue*, p. 67.

8. MacIntyre, *After Virtue*, p. 69.

9. MacIntyre, *After Virtue*, pp. 68–9.

10. M. Dixon, M., *Textbook on International Law* (2nd edn), London: Blackstone Press, 1990, p. 279.

11. There were legal/political documents before that date, such as the English *Magna Carta* of 1215, or the *Magnus Lagaboters Landslov* issued by King Magnus of Norway in 1275, but these were more limited in scope. See Lauren, *Evolution of International Human Rights*, p. 13.

12. Lauren, *Evolution of International Human Rights*, p. 12.

13. There is some debate about whether the *ius gentium* and the *ius naturale* were separate or identical. J. Muirhead, *Historical Introduction to the Private Law of Rome* (2nd edn, revised and edited by H. Goudy), London: Adam and Charles Black, 1899, pp. 280–3, argues for separation, citing aspects of slavery as consistent with the *ius gentium* in terms of being common to all known nations at that time, but inconsistent with the *ius naturale* to the extent that it classified a slave as a mere chattel.

14. For example, Thomas Aquinas, *Summa Theologica* (ST) II-I.95.2, citing Augustine, *De Lib. Arb.* I,5.

15. J. Lewis, 'On Human Rights', in UNESCO, *Human Rights: Comments and Interpretations*, London and New York, Allan Wingate, 1949, pp. 54–71, and B. Croce, 'The Rights of Man and the Present Historical Situation', in UNESCO, *Human Rights*, pp. 93–5.

16. Romans 2:14 – 'When gentiles who have not the law do by nature what the law requires, they are a law to themselves, even though they do not have the law. They show that what the law requires is written on their hearts.'

17. Bertrand Russell, *A History of Western Philosophy*, London: Unwin Paperbacks, 1984, p. 275.

18. Lauren, *Evolution of International Human Rights*, p. 15.

19. Lauren, *Evolution of International Human Rights*, p. 13.

20. UNESCO, *Human Rights*, Memorandum, Appendix I, 'Memorandum and Questionnaire Circulated by UNESCO on the Theoretical Bases of the Rights of Man', pp. 251–7; H. J. Laski, 'Towards a Universal Declaration of Human Rights', in UNESCO, *Human Rights*, pp. 78–92.
21. Lauren, *Evolution of International Human Rights*, p. 13.
22. UNESCO, *Human Rights*, Appendix 1.
23. Quoted in Croce, 'Rights of Man', p. 93.
24. Lauren, *Evolution of International Human Rights*, p. 54.
25. E. H. Carr, 'The Rights of Man', in UNESCO, *Human Rights*, p. 19–23.
26. Quote referred to in Lauren, *Evolution of International Human Rights*, p. 206.
27. Lauren, *Evolution of International Human Rights*, p. 214.
28. Preamble to the Universal Declaration of Human Rights (1948).
29. Lauren, *Evolution of International Human Rights*, p. 237.
30. P. B. Baehr, *Human Rights: Universality in Practice*, London: Macmillan, p. 9.
31. This is a selective and simplified list of the rights proclaimed, designed merely to give an idea of their scope.
32. Universal Declaration of Human Rights, Article 29.2.
33. Universal Declaration of Human Rights, Article 29.1.
34. UNESCO, *Human Rights*, Appendix II, 'The Grounds of an International Declaration of Human Rights', pp. 258–72 (262).
35. The book: *Human Rights: Comments and Interpretations*, sets out a selection of the replies received. The editors comment: 'In selecting the texts of the replies which are included in the volume, an attempt has been made to offer a representative sample of the whole range of opinions expressed. In addition, it was thought desirable to give publicity to the opinions of certain thinkers which differed from the final conclusions of UNESCO, but which were, nevertheless, stimulating in their originality of thought' (p. 7).
36. UN Documents: *Convention on the Political Rights of Women* (1952); *Supplementary Convention on the Abolition of Slavery, the Slave Trade, and Institutions and Practices Similar to Slavery* (1956); *Convention concerning the Abolition of Forced Labour* (1957); *Declaration of the Rights of the Child* (1959); *Declaration on the Elimination of All Forms of Racial Discrimination* (1963); *The International Convention on the Elimination of All Forms of Racial Discrimination* (1966); *Declaration on the Elimination of Discrimination against*

Women (1967); *Declaration on the Elimination of All Forms of Intolerance and of Discrimination based on Religion or Belief* (1981); *Convention against Torture and Other Cruel, Inhuman or Degrading Treatment or Punishment* (1984). Regional Documents: *The European Convention for the Protection of Human Rights and Fundamental Freedoms* (1950, plus later protocols); *The American Convention on Human Rights* (1969); *The Inter-American Convention to Prevent and Punish Torture* (1985); *The African Charter on Human and Peoples' Rights* (1981).

37. The consultation was carried out by the International Institute of Philosophy, and its conclusions were set out in a book of essays entitled, *Philosophical Foundations of Human Rights*, Paris: UNESCO, 1986.

38. A. J. Lien, 'A Fragment of Thought concerning the Nature and Fulfilment of Human Rights', in UNESCO, *Human Rights*, pp. 24–30.

39. Lewis, 'On Human Rights', p. 59.

40. J. Maritain, 'Introduction', in UNESCO, *Human Rights*, pp. 9–17.

41. R. McKeon, 'The Philosophic Bases and Material Circustances of the Rights of Man', in UNESCO, *Human Rights*, pp. 35–46 (46).

42. Chung-Shu Lo, 'Human Rights in the Chinese Tradition', in UNESCO, *Human Rights*, pp. 186–90. He points out that the Chinese language had no word for 'rights' until it adopted a word 'Chuan Li', meaning 'power and interest', first coined by a Japanese writer on Western Public Law in 1868.

43. H. Kabir, 'Human Rights: The Islamic Tradition and the Problems of the World Today', in UNESCO, *Human Rights*, pp. 191–4.

44. S. V. Puntambekar, 'The Hindu Concept of Human Rights', in UNESCO, *Human Rights*, pp. 195–8.

45. UNESCO, *Human Rights*, Appendix II, p. 263.

46. UNESCO, *Human Rights*, Appendix II, p. 267.

47. Lauren, *Evolution of International Human Rights*, 270, quoting from the 'Proclamation of Teheran on Human Rights', 13 May 1968, in UN Document A/CONF.32/41, *Final Act of the International Conference on Human Rights*, pp. 2–5; and UN Archives/Geneva, SO, Box 218, File 218(1), *International Conference on Human Rights*.

48. P. J. Hountondji, 'The Master's Voice: Remarks on the Problem of Human Rights in Africa', in UNESCO, *Philosophical Foundations of Human Rights*, p. 323.

49. UN General Assembly Resolution 45/155, of 18 December 1990.
50. Tunis: UN Document, A/CONF.157/AFRM/14, A/CONF.157/ PC/57; Bangkok: UN Document, A/Conf.157/ASRM/8, A/Conf.157/PC/59; San José: UN Document, A/CONF.157/ LACRM/15, A/CONF.157/PC/58.
51. UN Document, A/CONF.157/23 of 12 July 1993.
52. Amnesty International, *Reviewing the Vienna Declaration and Programme of Action and the 50th Anniversary of the Universal Declaration of Human Rights*, www.amnesty.org/ ailib/intcam/unchr50 /review.htm.
53. Report of the High Commissioner for Human Rights to the fifty-third Session of the UN General Assembly, *Human Rights Questions: Comprehensive Implementation of and Follow-up to the Vienna Declaration and Programme of Action*, UN Document A/53/372, 11 September 1998.
54. UN Document A/RES/53/168, of 11 February 1999.
55. Office of the High Commissioner for Human Rights, Enriching the Universality of Human Rights: Islamic Perspectives on the Universal Declaration of Human Rights, and Personal Impressions of the Seminar by Mary Robinson, High Commissioner for Human Rights, November 1998. The latter document expressed a commitment to publication of the proceedings, but this does not appear to be available.
56. Pontifical Council for the Family, *Family and Human Rights*, para. 2, quoting Pope John Paul II.
57. Mary Robinson, High Commissioner for Human Rights, *Human Rights: 'On the Eve of the Twenty-First Century',* The Paris Meeting, 7 December 1998 (author's emphasis).
58. Maritain, 'Introduction', p. 13. Lewis, 'On Human Rights', pp. 58–9.
59. Maritain, 'Introduction', p. 13.
60. J. Maritain, 'On the Philosophy of Human Rights', in UNESCO, *Human Rights*, pp. 72–7 (73).
61. Ibid.
62. UNESCO, *Human Rights*, Appendix II, p. 263.
63. Ibid., p. 268.
64. M. Markovic, 'Differing Conceptions of Human Rights in Europe – towards a Resolution', in UNESCO, *Philosophical Foundations of Human Rights*, p. 119.
65. R. C. Pandeya, 'Human Rights: An Indian Perspective', in UNESCO, *Philosophical Foundations of Human Rights*, p. 267.

66. Lewis, 'On Human Rights', pp. 58–9.
67. Q. Wright, 'Relationship between Different Categories of Human Rights', in UNESCO, *Human Rights*, pp. 143–51.
68. Aquinas, ST II-I. 94.2.
69. See para. 4.12 below in relation to the 'ends' of a communist society.
70. Markovic, 'Differing Conceptions of Human Rights in Europe', p. 119.
71. Example taken from Jeremy Waldron, 'Inalienable Rights', *The Boston Review* (April/May 1999).
72. S. Hessen, 'The Rights of Man in Liberalism, Socialism and Communism', in UNESCO, *Human Rights*, pp. 108–41 (110).
73. McKeon, 'Philosophic Bases', p. 37.
74. Maritain, 'Introduction', p. 15.
75. K. Riezler, 'Reflections on Human Rights', in UNESCO, *Human Rights*, pp. 156–7.
76. See discussion at 6.2.3 below.
77. Maritain, 'On the Philosophy of Human Rights', p. 76.
78. Carr, 'Rights of Man', p. 21.
79. Carr, 'Rights of Man', p. 22. The necessary correlation of rights and responsibilities was also upheld by other contributors, including Lien, 'Fragment' (p. 28), and Lewis, 'On Human Rights' (p. 56).
80. Hessen, 'Rights of Man in Liberalism', pp. 108–10. The alternative hypotheses of the 'social contract' is referred to at 4.13.1 below.
81. Chung-Shu Lo, 'Chinese Tradition', pp. 187–8.
82. M. Gandhi, 'Letter to the Director-General of UNESCO', in UNESCO, *Human Rights*, p. 18.
83. J. Haesaerts, 'Reflections on Some Declarations in the Rights of Man', in UNESCO. *Human Rights*, pp. 96–104 (100).
84. Riezler, 'Reflections on Human Rights', p. 156.
85. UNESCO, *Human Rights*, Appendix II, p. 267.
86. Universal Declaration of Human Rights (1948), Article 29.
87. The American Convention has been ratified by a large number of Latin American States. The USA signed it in 1977 but has not, at the time of writing, proceeded to ratification.
88. Article 17.3.
89. The groundwork for the change had, however, been laid by a nineteenth-century French jurist who had introduced ideas of natural law, and also by subsequent Christian influence.

90. R. Inagaki, 'Some Aspects of Human Rights in Japan', in UNESCO, *Philosophical Foundations of Human Rights*, pp. 179ff.

91. Pandeya, 'Human Rights', p. 274.

92. C. Taylor, 'Human Rights: The Legal Culture', in UNESCO, *Philosophical Foundations of Human Rights*, p. 52.

93. Zakaria, F., Human Rights in the Arab World: the Islamic Context, in UNESCO 1986, pp. 227–41, at pp. 228, 230.

94. A. E. Tay and E. Kamenka, 'Human Rights: Perspectives from Australia', in UNESCO, *Philosophical Foundations of Human Rights*, p. 159.

95. The Interaction Council was formed in 1983 by the Prime Minister of Japan as a 'loose association of former heads of state and of government'. See H. Küng and H. Schmidt (eds), *A Global Ethic and Global Responsibilities: Two Declarations*, London: SCM Press, 1998, p. 85. Its Declaration of Human Responsibilities was endorsed by members from: Germany, Australia, The Netherlands, Thailand, Costa Rica, the UK, the USA, Mexico, Switzerland, France, Spain, the USSR, Zambia, Singapore, Japan, Colombia, Israel, Portugal, Brazil, Korea, Finland, Canada, Sweden, Cyprus and Austria.

96. Küng and Schmidt, *Global Ethic*, p. 6.

97. Ibid., p. 76.

98. Ibid., p. 57.

99. Ibid., pp. 109–10.

100. Theo van Boven, Dutch human rights expert, quoted in Baehr, *Human Rights*, p. 17.

101. Robinson, *Human Rights*.

102. Puntambekar, 'Hindu Concept', pp. 196–7.

103. Ibid., p. 195.

104. Ibid., p. 197.

105. See Vatican Council II, *Gaudium et Spes: Pastoral Constitution on the Church in the Modern World*, para. 14, in A. Flannery (ed.), *Vatican Council II: The Conciliar and Post-conciliar Documents*, Leominster, Hereford: Fowler Wright Books, 1981, pp. 903–1014.

106. R. W. Gerard, 'The Rights of Man: A Biological Approach', in UNESCO, *Human Rights*, pp. 205–9.

107. Interestingly, some of both the secular and religious respondents are dismissive of the alternative approach as based upon prejudice or superstition. While 'superstition' is a standard criticism of religion by secularists, Puntambekar referred to

the 'superstitions of material science and limited reason'. See Puntambekar, 'Hindu Concept', p. 197.

108. Hessen, 'Rights of Man in Liberalism', pp. 128–32.

109. Maritain, 'On the Philosophy of Human Rights', p. 76.

110. UNESCO, *Human Rights*, Appendix II, p. 258.

111. UNESCO, *Human Rights*, Appendix II, p. 271.

112. See Aquinas, ST II-IIae.4.1, quoting Hebrews 11:1.

113. Lauren, *Evolution of International Human Rights*, p. 270.

114. M. Fry, 'Human Rights and the Law-Breaker', in UNESCO, *Human Rights*, p. 246–9. This coheres with the view expressed by Hessen, 'Rights of Man in Liberalism', and discussed at 4.10.1 above in the context of rights and duties.

115. Don S. de Madariaga, 'The Rights of Man or Human Relations?', in UNESCO, *Human Rights*, pp. 47–53.

116. Ibid., p. 48. This is an example of the 'confrontational' objection to rights in general that was explored at 3.7.2 above.

117. P. T. de Chardin, 'Some Reflections on the Rights of Man', in UNESCO, *Human Rights*, pp. 105–7 (106).

118. Ibid., p. 107.

119. Gerard, 'Rights of Man: A Biological Approach', pp. 205–8. A different perspective has been put on the individual/social unit relationship by Richard Dawkins's book, *The Selfish Gene*, Oxford: Oxford University Press, 1989, first published in 1976. This illustrates how precarious it is to derive rights or any sort of normative ethics from a biological base; a point with some relevance also to theories of natural law. The significance of Gerard's contribution is therefore not so much in its substantial conclusions as its place in a succession of perspectives on the contribution of perceived biological truths to moral and legal issues.

120. UNESCO, *Human Rights*, Appendix II, p. 260.

121. A. Diemer, 'The 1948 Declaration: An Analysis of Meanings', in UNESCO, *Philosophical Foundations of Human Rights*, pp. 99–101.

122. J. Hersch, 'Human Rights in Western Thought: Conflicting Dimensions', in UNESCO, *Philosophical Foundations of Human Rights*, pp. 141–2.

123. J. Humphrey and R. Tuck, 'The International Bill of Rights', in UNESCO, *Philosophical Foundations of Human Rights*, p. 62.

124. Taylor, 'Human Rights: The Legal Culture', pp. 55–7.

125. UN Document A/RES/53/168, of 11 February 1999.

126. 'New' in the sense of resurgence. It claims to have roots in ancient Greece as well as the Old and New Testaments. In modern times, the term 'Communitarianism' was coined by Goodwyn Barmby to promote communistic or socialist theories. Its twentieth-century usage focuses on what pertains to or is characteristic of a community. The movement's current incarnation emerged from a 1980s group of political philosophers committed to a concept of the 'common good'. In the 1990s, Etzioni was associated with the launch of a quarterly journal, *The Responsive Community: Rights and Responsibilities*, which took these ideas into the wider society. See Etzioni's Introduction to *The Essential Communitarian Reader*, New York: Rowman & Littlefield Publishers, Inc., 1998, and his preface to the 1995 British edition of *Spirit of Community*.

127. Etzioni, *Spirit of Community*, p. 5, and D. H. Oaks, in 'Rights and Responsibilities', in Etzioni (ed.), *Essential Communitarian Reader*, pp. 98–9.

128. Etzioni, Preface to the 1995 British edition of *Spirit of Community*, p. x.

129. Etzioni, Preface to the 1995 British edition of *Spirit of Community*.

130. Etzioni, *Spirit of Community*, pp. 47–8.

131. Etzioni, *Spirit of Community*, pp. xii and 36–7.

132. This argument arises again in Chapter 6 in connection with the more extreme libertarian views on children's rights.

133. A. Gewirth, *The Community of Rights*, Chicago and London: University of Chicago Press, 1996, p. 6.

134. See A. Tomkins, 'Introduction: On Being Sceptical about Human Rights', in Campbell, Ewing and Tomkins (eds), *Sceptical Essays on Human Rights*, pp. 1–11.

135. MacIntyre, *After Virtue*, Ch. 18.

136. See 4.10.4 above.

137. Lauren, *Evolution of International Human Rights*, p. 2.

138. These headings represent the authors' own classification of kinds of resistance, drawing largely on the history set out by Lauren in *Evolution of International Human Rights*.

139. Lauren, *Evolution of International Human Rights*, p. 21.

140. Ibid., p. 23.

141. Ibid., p. 238.

142. Ibid., pp. 26–8.

143. Ibid., p. 210.

144. Ibid., p. 23.

145. Ibid., pp. 24–6.

146. Ibid., pp. 48.
147. Ibid., p. 190.
148. Ibid., p. 70.
149. Ibid., p. 126.
150. Ibid., p. 239.
151. Ibid., p. 239.
152. Ibid., pp. 126–9.
153. Ibid., p. 246, quoting Senator John Bricker in: 'UN Blueprint for Tyranny', *The Freeman*, 2 (28 January 1952), p. 265; and US Congress, *Congressional Record 1952*, 98, pt 1, p. 912.
154. Lauren, *Evolution of International Human Rights*, p. 245.
155. Baehr, *Human Rights*, p. 10.

5

Human Rights
and the Churches

5.1 Introduction

In the last chapter we looked at the concept of human
rights as it has come to expression within the framework
of international agreement and at the philosophical and
ethical reflections which underlie that expression. We will
now try to see how all that fits into the evolving Christian
theological tradition. That means that we will be looking
at the use of rights language within the churches and trying
to say something about its theological justification. In the
process, we will respond to two widely held anxieties about
the place of rights language within the Christian tradition, and we will suggest that talking about rights gives
the churches an effective way in our world of putting some
of the things that the Christian tradition has been broadly
concerned with from the beginning.

So this chapter is – and is not – a fresh start. We will be
thinking about the same areas of human and ethical concern
that we dealt with in the last chapter, but this time we will
be looking at them from another – explicitly Christian
– perspective. And yet the legal and moral considerations of
the last chapter are in fact themselves integrally connected
with the Christian tradition. And that is true in at least two
ways.

In the first place, the specifically Christian input into the
developments we were looking at in the last chapter was, as
we have seen, far from negligible. To take but one example,

we had occasion to note the important contributions made to the 1947 philosophical consultation by the neo-Thomist theologian Jacques Maritain.[1]

But there is a second factor of even greater importance. The mutuality of ethical insight – the possibility of achieving a shared vision of the appropriate response to the needs and demands of other human beings – is and for many centuries has been a central problem in *Christian* theology and *Christian* ethics. That problem, or cluster of problems, has much to say about our understanding of the human person and of the world in which we live – what is it that we all have in common, and how far does the created order succeed in manifesting the purposes of the one who made it? And therefore that problem, or cluster of problems, has much to say as well about our understanding of the God who creates and redeems.

That is a modern problem, very much debated in contemporary ethics, but it is also an old problem, reaching back to the very beginnings of Christian theology.[2] Theologians of the Middle Ages reflected on natural law, which they saw as a pattern of basic ethical insight which should be accessible to all men and women in virtue of their common humanity and their capacity for rational ethical choice. And they also spoke of a law of nations which partially manifested the natural law and which comprised a collection of basic principles of fairness and forbearance which was manifested in the positive codes of virtually all societies. That line of thinking is very much related to our concerns here, since, as Jean Porter has observed,

> The moral and legal agreements and conventions that today serve as a framework for international relations are our contemporary equivalent of the ancient and medieval law of nations and, like the law of nations, they can themselves be considered as a kind of natural law.[3]

But first we should say something about our choice of words. We have just referred to 'the place of rights *language* within the Christian tradition', and we will often find ourselves speaking about rights *language* rather than about rights. Why?

As we saw in 4.2 the existence of rights is a complicated question, but it is one that – for our purposes – we do not need to get bogged down in. Broadly speaking, it is possible to say that rights are there because somebody put them there or because they have some kind of objectively real and independent existence. The former view – the positivist position – holds that rights exist because they have been enacted as law by some competent authority, so they 'exist' in the same sense that the highway code exists. That is clear and straightforward, but leaves unresolved any question of the universality of rights.

The latter view – that we might call an ontological position – asserts that human rights exist because they are in some way built into the structure of reality. This has usually been expressed in terms of *natural* rights.[4] And if we want to hold that there are natural rights, we might say that they are there because God deemed that it should be so, or we might want to say that they are simply self-evident, like logical truths. Those two ideas can of course be combined, as they are, for example, in the American Declaration of Independence: 'we hold these truths to be *self-evident* ... that all men are created equal; that they are endowed by their *Creator* with certain inalienable rights'.[5]

There are two points we would like to make. The first is that these two views – what we have called the positivist position and what we have called an ontological position – need not be in contradiction. It is perfectly possible to hold that there are natural rights, accessible to reason, which are partially and imperfectly embodied in various legal systems. That is, in fact, more or less the idea that the classical Roman jurists and many medievals had of what they called the law of nations.

The second point we would like to make is that there is a distinction to be drawn between the existence of rights and their justification. An argument for the existence of rights also justifies us in talking about them. But there may be justifications that have no direct bearing on the objective existence of the rights we are talking about. There may, for example, be a significant but overlapping consensus in society that finds it helpful to talk about rights but does not at all represent a common mind as to their nature and origin. And this may represent more than give-and-take compromise or the establishment of a liberal modus vivendi.[6] It may represent an as yet unarticulated reaching out by and from the traditions that constitute our pluralistic society – a reaching out towards some sort of common value that can help to underpin the authority of that society itself.[7]

In any event, our concern here is not so much with the philosophical (and theological) question of the origin and objective existence of rights as it is with the theological (and philosophical) question of how they fit into the Christian scheme of things. It is our contention throughout this book that rights *language* gives us a helpful and coherent way of talking about our fundamental obligations toward each other; it helps us understand and express things of central importance in the Christian tradition. Its justification is that it works.

So rights exist, we want to say, at least in the sense that we can talk about them intelligibly and usefully.[8] More than that we need not at present say.

On this view of things the fact that a broad measure of consensus has been achieved among the churches on the fundamental importance of rights language is in itself a significant moral datum. We now turn to that process, and we begin – as the previous chapter did – in the aftermath of World War II.

5.2 Accepting the Language of Rights

At the same time that the United Nations was conducting the consultation which shaped the Universal Declaration of Human Rights, major Christian denominations were forming the World Council of Churches (WCC).[9] There was, of course, a background. A provisional structure, The World Council of Churches in Process of Formation, had been established on the eve of the War – at Utrecht in 1938. And behind that in turn lay the Faith and Order Conferences and the Life and Work Conferences of the 20s and 30s. But it was a moment of great significance when the first Assembly of the World Council convened in Amsterdam in 1948.

The declarations of the first Assembly spoke vigorously of rights that belonged to all human beings. In a chapter bearing what would have been in 1948 the highly evocative title 'The Church and the International Disorder', the Assembly declared:

> The Church has always demanded freedom to obey God rather than men. We affirm that all men are equal in the sight of God and that the rights of men derive directly from their status as the children of God. It is presumptuous for the State to assume that it can grant or deny fundamental rights.

The Assembly added that 'at the present time, churches should support every endeavour to secure within an international bill of rights adequate safeguards for freedom of religion and conscience',[10] and resolved:

> Whereas the World Council of Churches notes with satisfaction that the United Nations has accepted as one of its major purposes the promotion of respect for and observance of human rights and fundamental freedoms for all without distinction as to race, sex, language or religion, ... be it resolved that the Assembly calls upon its constituent members to press for the adoption of an International Bill of Human Rights making provision for the recognition, and national and international enforcement, of all the essential freedoms of man, whether personal, political or social.[11]

This commitment to the idea of human rights has been reaffirmed at every subsequent Assembly of the WCC

– Evanston (1954), New Delhi (1961), Uppsala (1968), Nairobi (1975), Vancouver (1983), Canberra (1991) and Harare (1998).

The renewed interest in human rights after the War, manifested both in the UN and in the WC – this passionate concern to say 'never again' – actually marked something of a new direction in human rights thinking. The classic proclamations of human rights in the eighteenth century – such as the Virginia Bill of Rights of 1776 or the French Declaration of the Rights of Man and of the Citizen of 1789 – were shaped by the thought world of Enlightenment individualism.[12] Human beings were rational creatures, and that rationality was the ground of a unique dignity, a dignity that was in turn itself accessible by reason. So the rights of human beings were both prescribed by and deducible by the law of reason.

But, broadly speaking, by the second half of the nineteenth century, there was something of a crisis of confidence in the power of reason. There had been in much European thinking a shift away from reason as the basis of human rights and a move toward positivism. That is, there was a tendency to trace rights no farther back than the foundational documents of any particular legal or political system. They were positively set forth in a constitution or a bill of rights, and that was that. Rights could not be universalised.

The Second World War changed that. In the aftermath of the war, there was a desire to build institutions that would shape a new future for the whole human family – hence the United Nations and the World Council of Churches. And there was a renewed concern to affirm that the dignity of the human person had a basis which transcended the positive provisions that might be made for it in any particular legal code. Rights were universal. That is the sort of issue that was being thrashed out in the carefully measured responses to the UN consultation on human rights that we looked at in Chapter 4.

The great human rights declarations of the eighteenth century arose in part from the desire of individuals to secure their claim to liberties in the face of the absolutism of the post-Reformation state. And it was the new totalitarianism of twentieth-century states which led in no small measure to the desire after the Second World War to reaffirm the universality of human rights. So reason-based rights made a comeback.

From the beginning the World Council of Churches spoke in the name of the major Protestant and Orthodox communions, though not, of course, in that of the Catholic Church. (Accredited Catholic observers have been present at WC Assemblies since 1961.) But since the 60s the Catholic Church, too, has come to adopt the vocabulary of human rights.[13]

Nineteenth-century Catholicism was suspicious of rights language. Pius IX, for example, in 1864 affirmed that

> civil liberty for all forms of worship and the attribution to everyone of the full power of making plain openly and publicly any opinions and thoughts they please contribute more readily to the corruption of the morals and minds of a people and to the spread of the pestilence of indifferentism.[14]

As the reference to 'the pestilence of indifferentism' indicates, Pius IX – and much of the suspicion of the nineteenth-century Vatican – was driven by the fear that modern social and intellectual movements were sliding into a denial of any absolute value or objective truth.

But the nineteenth-century papacy could also speak of the equality of all human beings, who, 'endowed with the same nature, are called to the same dignity and ... must be judged by the same law'. Those are in fact the words of Pius IX's successor, Leo XIII,[15] with whom papal teaching began to show a renewed concern with social justice. Thus, Leo's encyclical *Rerum novarum*, issued on 15 May 1891, proclaims the right (*jus*) of a worker to a just wage.[16]

In 1939, at the beginning both of his own pontificate and of the War, Pius XII reaffirmed the existence of a natural law, accessible by reason, which could not be infringed by the absolutist claims of the State.[17] In thus insisting on the existence of an objective natural law, accessible to and binding on all human beings, Pius was, of course, following in the wake of a centuries' long theological tradition, a tradition that reaches all the way back to Paul's appeal in Romans 2:14–15 to the Gentiles who 'do by nature the requirements of the law'. But when he defends this tradition against the 'pernicious error' which 'attributes almost unlimited power to the state' and which asserts that the rights of the State are 'quite absolute and answerable to no one at all',[18] he is responding to the tragic developments of the decade in which he was writing. After all, throughout the 30s, the future Pope, as Eugenio Cardinal Pacelli, had been Papal Secretary of State. He held that office when the concordat with Nazi Germany was negotiated in 1933, and he held it when Pius XI finally denounced Nazi beliefs in the encyclical *With Burning Concern* (Mit brennender Sorge), which was smuggled into Germany and ordered to be read from every pulpit on Palm Sunday 1937.

But the idea of natural law is not the same thing as the idea of human rights. And that is true even if the list of moral demands thought to be derivable from the former were identical with the list of moral demands proclaimed by the latter. Even if the content of the two were in that sense identical, they would still be different sorts of moral tools. A concept of natural law lacks the primary focus on claim-rights and the insistence on the strict correlativity of claims and duties that we saw in Chapter 3 to be essential to the concept of rights.

So even if all the elements needed to build a theory of human rights were in place in the line of papal social teaching that runs from Leo XIII to Pius XII, the decisive step had yet to be taken. It was taken by Pius XII's successor, John XXIII.

John's great encyclical *Peace on earth* (Pacem in terris) was intended to support and to provide a Christian justification for the principles of the United Nations Universal Declaration of Human Rights. It is dated 11 April 1963 and is addressed to all men and women of good will; copies were officially presented to the members of the United Nations. In it John affirmed,

> In any human society that we want to be well ordered and beneficial, this principle is to be regarded as fundamental: that every human being is identified as a person. That is, every human being is a nature endowed with intelligence and with free will. And he therefore has, in and of himself, rights and duties which are governed by his nature and which together flow from it and which, inasmuch as they are general and inviolable, can in no way be alienated.[19]

Pacem in terris was issued less than two months before John's death. That was during the Second Vatican Council, which he had decided to call shortly after he was elected Pope. His teaching on human rights is echoed in the last authoritative document to emanate from the Council, the *Pastoral Constitution on the Church in Today's World*, proclaimed on 7 December 1965.[20] The constitution goes on to declare, 'In the power of the Gospel that has been entrusted to her, the Church therefore proclaims the rights of human beings and acknowledges and esteems the dynamic of the modern world whereby these rights are everywhere promoted.'[21]

So in the two decades after the war, the churches, both Catholic and Protestant, began to incorporate the language of human rights into their formal discourse. In one sense this was something new. In another it was as old as the gospel itself. This gives rise to two objections which we will consider in the next section.

5.3 Something Old, Something New? Two Objections

5.3.1 A false start?

While the last fifty years have seen the formal adoption of rights language by the churches, they have also seen continuing and – if anything – increasing currents of philosophical and theological dissatisfaction with the whole project. These currents of dissatisfaction come from very varied quarters, and coming to grips with the problem is not made easier by the fact that quite similar sounding objections can in fact be coming from opposite directions and can mean very different things within the context of the systems to which they belong. In particular, the idea of rights is attacked on the one hand by those who think that it undermines communal values of human solidarity and on the other by those who think that it is a secular and humanist idea (and that that is a bad thing). The social visions of these two groups are poles apart, and yet they feel a common unease at the (historical) connection between human rights language and the ideals of eighteenth-century individualism which helped define the concept of rights as well as those of nineteenth-century liberalism which did so much to develop and apply it.

In this first section we will look at two sorts of objections which spring from a similar source but which tend to point in quite different directions.

5.3.1.1 The It's-too-individualistic Objection

It is often said, on both the left and the right, that the language of human rights – so confidently adopted by the churches in the course of the twentieth century – is inherently confrontational and self-regarding. It is used to assert *my* rights and pays scant regard to the Christian duty of love of neighbour. It fragments society and promotes the individual, and so has no place in the life of a Christian or of a Christian community. Thus the influential American ethicist

Stanley Hauerwas can say succinctly that 'the language of rights is of recent origin and presupposes an individualistic understanding of the person in society'.[22]

We will look at Hauerwas' views in more detail in a later chapter (7.2.1). Here we want to draw attention to the connection he implies between the 'recent origin' of rights language and the 'individualistic understanding of the person in society' which it is said to presuppose. We saw in the last section that the classical statements of human rights from the eighteenth century breathe the air of Enlightenment individualism. Is the very idea of human rights somehow tainted by that fact?

The *individualism* of the Enlightenment has come in for quite a bad press in recent years. We might well want to say that we need to get back behind the view of a fragmented humanity that characterized so much eighteenth- and nineteenth-century thought and try to recover something of the sense of corporate solidarity – something of the sense of community – that is found, for example, in the social and ethical thought of the scholastic tradition, or something of the sense of the organic nature of society, of the correspondence between the microcosm of the human person and the macrocosm of human social structures, that characterizes so much of the thought of both the classical and Renaissance worlds. In contemporary discussion, that sort of view is often connected with the programme to recover a virtue-based ethic, the sort of line that is associated with a moral philosopher like Alasdair MacIntyre, whose brilliant book *After Virtue*, first published in 1981, set the agenda for so much subsequent discussion.[23] That book tells the story of the different stories that have been told throughout the history of ethical reflection to describe what it means to be a good human being.

The sort of objection we are dealing with now might argue that until, say, the eighteenth century, a good human life would normally have been described in terms of the possession of virtues – which are skills of living well, those acquired patterns of behaviour that make a human being truly human, that let him flourish in the exercise of his humanity.

We can then finger the Enlightenment as the time when that picture of humankind as social animals, flourishing through interaction with their fellows, fell apart, to be replaced in Western thinking by a picture of the isolated self, banding together with others only for the purpose of establishing a self-protective social compact. The full-frontal version of this picture is found, for example, in the thought of Jean-Jacques Rousseau.

Thereafter, the theory would continue, the story of the ideal human life is all too often told simply in terms of the keeping of rules. A *descriptive* account of what it means to be a good human being is, as it were, replaced by a *prescriptive* account.

And, on this view, talk of human rights does not and cannot escape its eighteenth-century parentage. A bill of rights, we might conclude, is most at home in the hands of a querulous, litigious individual, looking to keep society at bay.[24]

Now, there is much in that picture of human life that is actually quite persuasive. But as an objection to speaking about human rights, and in particular about the rights of children as we will go on to do, it misses the mark in two quite important ways.

In the first place, the model of human rights it is operating with is a civil libertarian one. It assumes that rights are – as they were in their eighteenth-century origins – designed to protect the freedom and property of the individual. But the understanding of rights at least since the Second World War has laid stress not just on protection *from*, but also on protection *for*. That can be illustrated by the way in which the Universal Declaration of Human Rights was implemented in 1966 by two separate but parallel conventions, the International Covenant on Civil and Political Rights and the International Covenant on Economic, Social, and

Cultural Rights. This was, to be sure, a compromise, designed to accommodate the preoccupation of the West with civil liberties and the preoccupation of the former Eastern bloc with social and economic rights, but that does not obviate the symbolic importance of the fact that the two documents were given equal standing.

The second point to be made is that to object to talk of human rights on this score is to treat them as an artifact – as a product of the age in which such thinking arose, like a Chippendale chair or a Capability Brown garden. But, as we saw in Section 3.1, rights are not *things*. They are a way of talking about human relationships. They are a tool, a tool to be used when things have gone wrong. We may deplore an individualism that fractures society and still feel that individuals need protection.

An appeal to human rights can undoubtedly be used to make confrontational and self-regarding claims. The question is whether the availability of the concept *causes* people to become confrontational and self-regarding. Lifeboats do not cause ships to sink.

We live in a post-medieval, post-Enlightenment world, whether we like it or not, and bits of the mental furniture of both those worlds stock – or litter – our minds. You can use a hammer to drive a nail without worrying unduly about when hammers were invented. Or, as Kieran Cronin has said, 'Ask not whether rights exist, but how the language of rights is used'.[25]

One consequence of this way of looking at things is that we do not need to say that the use of rights language is the end of the story. That's not all there is to say about society and our place in it.

We can see the force of that if we look at the reflections of Rowan Williams on 'a rights-based order'.[26] The Archbishop starts from a distinction made by the Canadian philosopher Charles Taylor between those he calls 'liberals' and those he calls 'communitarians'. The former '(very broadly) begin with a basic conviction about societies as composed of individuals endowed with intrinsic rights and liberties that require both protection and room for fair and balanced negotiation', while the latter 'see persons as constituted by personal and communal belonging and as finding their value or dignity, perhaps even their sense of "rights", through identification with the values of the community'.[27]

In this engagement, 'the language of right and claim, when it becomes the dominant form of moral discourse in a society', is not enough; there is 'a morally thin atmosphere in the discourse of rights'.[28] But the appeal to rights language cannot simply be jettisoned.

> The concentration on rights as the primary focus of political action is a response to the long and appalling history of inequity, the denial to certain groups of a voice of their own, a freedom of self-determination or self-definition. To stand against the pursuit of such freedom is to collude with oppression.[29]

At the same time, 'a society whose values were established by an unspoken (and unaccountable) community consensus'[30] is not the answer either.

Instead, there is a need to go beyond mere debate between 'liberals' and 'communitarians'. There is a need for 'a true conversational relation' in society, in which we are really morally present to each other.

> We need to understand the sense in which the robust, primitive, individual self, seeking its fortune in a hostile world and fighting off its competitors, is a naive fiction. What lies beyond that understanding is a commitment to the charitable conversation that has in fact always and already included me.[31]

We find that vision very attractive. And it is important to see that it largely coheres with what we want to say about rights.

We make no claim in the abstract for the superiority of a 'right-based' moral theory over other models of the moral life,[32] and a society in which – in Rowan Williams' phrase – 'the language of right and claim ... becomes the dominant form of moral discourse' would not be a society in particularly good moral health.

But in the world in which we live, rights are useful – indeed, indispensable. Williams has a vision of the 'moral-than-liberal society'[33] that might emerge from the great conversation. But that is in the future. It lies at the end of a long road and is accessible now only through the virtue of hope.

A world of caring and belonging, a world of common values and shared responsibilities, would be better than a world dependent on a mechanism of rights and claims.[34] But for the present that is the kind of world in which we live. Perhaps – just perhaps – in the providence of God, the need to exercise that mechanism of rights and claims will in time wither away in the face of Williams's 'charitable conversation'. But that time is not yet.

If those who propound the objection we have just been considering feel some unease at the use of rights language because of a yearning for a 'more-than-liberal society', others feel unease because of a nostalgia for what we might (unkindly perhaps) call a less-than-liberal society. To the other side of the objection to the Enlightenment origins of so much of rights language we now turn.

5.3.1.2 The It's-just-secular/humanist Objection

So far we have been dealing with what we might call a polite version of an objection based on the idea that the very concept of human rights, in our sense of the term, arose within the philosophical culture of the eighteenth century. But there is a harder and more radical version. In that version it is argued that the idea of human rights is an invention of secular humanism and as such has no place in Christian discourse. The polite version convicts the language of human rights of retaining too many of the preoccupations of the age in which it arose. The hard version assumes that there are Christian or biblical words and ideas and there are secular or humanist words and ideas and that rights language was born and brought up on the wrong side of the tracks.

Both the historical premise and the theological conclusion need to be carefully examined. We spoke earlier of the way in which the classical statements of the doctrine of human rights in the eighteenth century were shaped by the ideology of Enlightenment individualism. That is, broadly speaking, true, but to say that the whole idea of human rights was *invented* in that context would be a gross oversimplification.

The idea of human rights has roots that go deep. We could point to the concern of the Old Testament with justice for the poor. Thus, the Lord is a God who 'hears the needy', who 'maintains the cause of the afflicted', who 'delivers the needy when he calls, the poor and him who has no helper' (Ps. 69:33; 140:12; 72:12 (RSV)). Or we could point to the rich natural law tradition of medieval theology, which in turn has roots both in the tradition of Greek philosophy – especially Stoicism – and in the thought of the Roman jurists who affirmed the existence for all humankind of a universal and rational law. And after the Reformation, there was in some quarters, and particularly in the work of Calvinist theologians, a concern to protect the freedom of the individual conscience and the freedom of religion.

There has been quite a bit of important work done in recent years on the historical origins of the ideas of natural law and natural rights in the classical[35] and medieval[36] worlds. In part, of course, when and where we pinpoint the origin of these ideas depends on the way we define them. But it does seem clear that scholastics of the thirteenth century could use the word *jus* ('law', 'that which is lawful') in a way that corresponds to our notion of a 'right'.[37] They were, for example, able to 'speak of a right on the part of the poor to the superfluities of the rich' and to 'assert the existence of an individual right, explicitly referred to as a *jus*, which is grounded in the law rather than in specific social conventions, and which gives rise to claims that can be legally enforced'.[38]

But even when that has been said – even when we have made every allowance for similarity of idea and congruence of concern – it remains true that the language of the thirteenth century was not that of the eighteenth. Aquinas, for example, in the words of Jean Porter, 'has a concept of the natural right, or *jus*, as an objective order of equity established by nature, but he does not speak in terms of rights inhering in individuals, which give rise to duties in others' (*Summa Theologiae* II–II 57.1,2).[39] If he had had the chance, he might well have found himself in agreement with much in the Declaration of the Rights of Man or the UN's Universal Declaration of Human Rights. But self-evidently he did not have that chance, and their words are not his words.

So ideas flowing from ancient and medieval sources fused together in the new social and ideological climate of the eighteenth century to produce classical statements of human rights. And what emerged was indeed something new.

The German theologian Wolfgang Huber – who himself vigorously defends the validity of human rights discourse – could summarize the historical development by saying quite baldly, 'The human rights movement is a worldly, secular phenomenon'.[40] That is, I think, rather too dismissive of the roots within the Judaeo-Christian tradition of the idea of human rights and too dismissive of the gradual adumbration of its component parts. But let us, for the sake of argument, agree with Huber. Would it follow that rights language should be eschewed by those who desire to speak from within the Christian tradition? Clearly not.

Throughout the history of Christian thought terminology and ideas have been imported from outside that have enriched the Church's conceptual vocabulary and facilitated the articulation of its faith. The Church has grown – theologically as well as numerically – by conversion.

A prime example can be traced back to the New Testament itself. The Prologue of John's Gospel describes Christ as the *Logos* or Word of God. Logos was a term with heavy resonance. In ordinary Greek it meant, not normally 'word' in the sense of something you look up in the dictionary, but meaningful discourse. It suggested rational structure, order, coherence. In the philosophical tradition of the Stoics it meant the force that gave an articulated structure to inchoate matter, the rational impulse that organized the world. It would have reminded John of the word of the Lord that came to the prophets (though that was in fact expressed by a different term in his Greek Bible) and of the creative role of the Wisdom of God in some of the later books of the Old Testament.

The idea of Christ as Logos was developed by the Christian Apologists of the second century and became one of the central concepts in much of the theology of the third, above all in the thought of the highly influential Alexandrian theologian Origen. The use of the term enabled Christians in the second and third centuries to build bridges to the surrounding pagan culture. But there was much more to it than that. It enabled them to talk about the cosmic Christ and to say that in the historical figure of Jesus was to be found the meaning of things.

Theological ideas often come with a sell-by date. By the middle of the fourth century, there had been massive changes in Church and society and in the thought-world in which men and women lived. The Logos idea had helped Christians deal with the relationship between Christ and the *world*. But by the middle of the fourth century they were focusing more on his relationship to the Father. So the idea of Logos was not shelved, but it ceased to be the central organizing concept around which a whole theology could be built.

An idea had been imported from the pagan world. For two centuries and more it proved to be a useful tool that helped Christians say what they wanted to say about the centrality of the person of Christ. Eventually the time came when the idea had done its job, and theology moved on. But the Logos concept *had* done its job. It had helped Christian thought to grow and mature, and its legacy remains with us.[41]

For another example of the creative impact of 'alien' ideas on Christian thought, we could look to the influence of Aristotelianism on the theology of the thirteenth century. The rediscovery of Aristotle by the Latin West – in no small part mediated through Islamic philosophy – led to a great theological efflorescence. Central Aristotelian concepts like matter/form, substance/accident, act/potency gave the Scholastics a conceptual structure within which they could organize their theological vision with clarity and coherence.

Once again, changes in the intellectual climate meant that the borrowed philosophical framework eventually came to be rethought, and by, say, the eve of the Reformation the Aristotelian consensus had collapsed. But the legacy of the Scholastic synthesis remained. And the renewed interest within the past decade or so in the thought of Thomas Aquinas – among philosophers and theologians, Catholics and Protestants alike – bears witness to the continuing power of the fruit of that synthesis within the Christian tradition.

As a final example of the role of borrowing from the outside on the development of Christian thought we could look to a very different corner of the Christian tradition. John Calvin was deeply influenced by the new humanism of the sixteenth century. His first published work was a commentary on Seneca's tract *De Clementia*. The privileging of the classical past that characterized the new humanism helped structure his approach to the Christian tradition: he often cites the Fathers but seldom medievals.[42] And the skills of the new learning contributed to the freshness and depth of the biblical commentaries that were so central a part of his theological programme.

The classical learning of the sixteenth century is – for good or ill – no longer central to our education and our culture. But flourishing church communities of the Reformed tradition throughout the world – who may never have heard nor want to hear of Seneca's *De Clementia* – bear witness to Calvin's continuing legacy.

We have, then, looked at three (among many) examples of the formative influence on Christian thought of imports from the non-Christian world. The first was a concept; the second, a philosophy; and the third, a skill. Each helped shape the thought of an age, and each had a lasting impact on the development of the Christian tradition in all its richness and diversity.

So even if we were to grant that human rights language was an invention of secular humanism – even if we were to grant that overly simplistic distortion of the truth, it would not follow that rights language had no place in Christian discourse. It could still be a useful tool for helping us articulate sharply and clearly the age-old affirmation that the Lord maintains the cause of the afflicted and delivers the needy when he calls.

In the Preface to *Saint Joan*, George Bernard Shaw said that the test of sanity is not whether you hear voices but whether what the voices say makes sense. Perhaps the test of the sanity of Christian discourse is not whether you hear non-Christian voices but whether they help you make sense – to yourself and to others – of the faith you hold.

5.3.2 Unbiblical?

The anxiety that the language of rights is somehow non-Christian is often expressed in the specific claim that it is non-biblical or unbiblical. In this section we will attempt to respond to that objection.

In one sense of the word, rights language *is* obviously non-biblical. The concept does not appear in either the

Old or New Testament for the simple reason that it had not been invented yet. The same is true of many of the problems that a moral theologian must deal with today, such as genetic engineering or global warming or Third World debt. The biblical theologian will hope that he can address those modern problems on the basis of principles that *are* biblical or on the basis of the scriptural approach to ancient dilemmas that are in some ways analogous to his modern ones.

Similarly, it is the contention of this whole discussion that rights language provides a way of responding to perennial problems, an efficacious conceptual vocabulary in which to express at the present time insights that the Christian tradition has been concerned with all along. In Chapter 7 we shall try to flesh that contention out with particular reference to the needs of children.

Here we want to look at the stronger claim that rights language is not just *non-biblical*, but that it is actually *unbiblical*. The discussion is obviously complicated by the very different approaches taken to the interpretation of Scripture within different sections of the Christian tradition. So first we have to say something about that.

The interpretation of Scripture is one of those areas in which a certain circularity of method can actually be quite productive. It is possible to move from theoretical reflection on how you should read Scripture to a particular text and then, in the light of what you have found, move back to the theory again. So we do not necessarily need to achieve a prior consensus on the theory before we look at some of the relevant texts. We hope that the studies of particular texts offered both here and in sections 7.2.2 and 8.1 below will have something to say to Christians who approach the Bible from different angles and with different presuppositions in mind.

Here we will simply say that some of the key polarities that are often assumed to divide Christians as they approach the Bible seem to us to be misplaced. In the first place, it is sometimes thought that the fundamental divide is between those who take the text literally and those who do not. But no-one in fact takes the entire text of the Bible *absolutely* literally. When Deuteronomy 4:24, for example, says that God 'is a consuming fire', that is clearly a metaphor. [43] So already we can see from that simple example that we have to look at the function of the text as well as at its straightforward meaning. What is simple narrative and what is poetic imagery? What is rhetorical or ironic, humorous or deadly serious? And that means that we have to ask how the text was intended to be taken.

Intended by whom? Divine authorship and human – inspiration and human instrumentality – are not incompatible. But we do not need to get involved in theories of inspiration to suggest that, if God spoke at a particular time and in a particular place, the text must have been intelligible – in the first instance, at least – to those to whom it was addressed and who wrote it down. And so, whatever else we might want to go on to say about a deepening understanding of the text over time, we cannot avoid asking what *they* thought it meant.

Again, it might be thought that the fundamental divide is between those – of a Catholic tradition, perhaps – who think that a text must be read within the context of its reception and use by the Church down the centuries and those who – in accord with a Protestant *sola Scriptura* principle – think that the text speaks directly and immediately to us.

But this is once again, in part at least, a false divide. No major tradition, Catholic or Protestant, denies the ultimate authority of Scripture and its primacy in theological discourse. And no-one can avoid approaching the text from within the context of some sort of interpretative tradition. It may be an ecclesial tradition or a doctrinal tradition or a scholarly and academic one. But we are all accustomed to approaching the text in a certain way, with a certain set of questions in mind, and with some sort of provisional expectation as to what in the end we might find the text to be saying.

More fundamental than those two divides is, we think, a divide between those who approach the text piecemeal and those who want to see it whole – a divide, that is, between those who take particular phrases of verses[44] in isolation and those who think that they come to us as a part of a package. One might have thought that if God *meant* us to take individual verses in isolation, his revelation – consisting of a whole library of books, belonging to very different literary types and produced over a period in centuries – took a curiously roundabout form.

Be that as it may, in the studies that follow we will be trying to put the texts in context. That means, first and foremost, looking carefully at the *words* that are used and what they mean, a meaning that can best be approached by seeing how the same words are used elsewhere – in the same book, in other parts of the Hebrew and Greek Bibles, in related literature. Secondly, we have to look at the context within the biblical book to see what is going on in the passage in question and of what kind of a discussion it is a part. And finally, we have to look on occasion to the broader cultural context to try to see what a passage might have meant in the world for which it was first written and in which it was first heard – the worlds of the ancient Near East and of the Jewish and Hellenistic cultures of the Roman Empire.

Context, then, must be the key.

In Chapter 7 we shall draw attention to two pairs of texts that are very commonly cited in support of the claim that the language of *children's* rights in particular is unbiblical. Here we will look at some implications of two texts from the Gospels, the Golden Rule of Matthew 7:12 and the command to love your neighbour as yourself (Matt. 22: 39/Mark 12:31/Luke 10:27). Those two texts are of such fundamental importance that to deal with them properly would require nothing less than a full-scale treatment of the norms of Christian ethics. But that is part of the point we would like to make. It is not transparently clear how they are to be put into practice, and in particular the relationship of those texts to specific precepts is far from being self-evident. And that means that their bearing on the validity of rights language cannot be self-evident either, since the correlativity of rights and duties discussed above (in Chapter 3) means that a right possessed by one person can always be restated in the form of a precept that no-one else encroach upon it.

In any event, those texts – though they may be characteristic of Christian morality and may point to what is distinctive about it – did not emerge out of a vacuum. The Golden Rule ('Whatever you want people to do to you, so you also do to them', Matt. 7:12) has antecedents in Jewish ethics. A negative form is found in the book of Tobit ('What you hate, do not do to anyone', 4:15), which was probably written in Aramaic in the third century BCE.[45] A negative form is also found in a saying attributed to Rabbi Hillel in the Talmud (b. Shabbath 31a) and, in the New Testament itself, in some manuscripts[46] of Acts 15:20 and 29, again in a Jewish context – the instructions of the Council of Jerusalem for Gentile converts. The negative form also appears in Christian literature, beginning with the Didache (1.2), a manual of moral instruction and church discipline that may be as early as the end of the first century CE. Thereafter negative and positive forms continue to exist side by side. (We have already met one negative formulation of the Golden Rule – in the Universal Declaration on Human Responsibilities proposed in 1997.)[47]

The command to love your neighbour as yourself also has a prehistory. All three accounts – Matthew, Mark and Luke – are quoting Leviticus 19:18, and all three cite that text from the widely used Greek translation of the Old Testament known as the Septuagint. In other words, not only does this saying of Jesus draw upon the Law of the Old Testament, but the form in which the saying is reported in all three Gospel accounts reflects the reading and the study of the Law within the synagogues of Hellenistic Judaism.

The point is that both these texts come to us embedded in a tradition. And their subsequent use by Christians would give rise in turn to a further rich tradition of interpretation and reflection. So once again we are led to expect that their application might not be transparently clear. These texts may lie at the root of Christian ethical thinking, but they don't do all our work for us.

It might seem natural today to see a contrast between the self-regarding claiming of a right and an other-regarding Christian love. But it has not seemed so for much of the history of Christine ethics. Augustine, for example, regards the natural law as being more or less equivalent to the Golden Rule which encapsulates it, and he thinks that human beings should – ideally at least – be able to reason their way from that Rule to the basic principles of moral conduct. (It *should* be so, but in practice the ability to draw out those conclusions is impaired in fallen humanity, and so God has provided for us in the Decalogue a written compendium of these implications.)[48] And for Aquinas, Matthew 22:39 expresses the most fundamental principle of ethical behaviour that is ascertainable by reason and which should underlie specific norms and standards of morality.[49]

In that way of looking at things, the command to love is not in competition with specific precepts. And hence it is not, in principle at least, in competition with talk of human rights, since *my* right can be regarded as equivalent to a precept incumbent on *you*. If a good, happy pagan, say, has a right to freedom of religion, then you are bound by the precept not to baptize him by force. Rather, the command to love operates at a different level of analysis from more specific precepts, and so at a different level of analysis from rights-based claims. The two simply do not occupy the same moral space.

In saying that we are not necessarily trying to argue that Augustine and Aquinas have got it right on this point (though we happen to be quite sympathetic to their view).

We are rather trying to show that it is simplistic to say that there is a dichotomy between rights and love.

The same point can be made from another angle if we ask precisely *how* rights and love are deemed to be in tension. In the first place, Christian love – Christian *agape* – cannot be *simply* other-regarding. If it were, it would be self-defeating. That – to take a trivial instance – is apparent to anyone who has stood back to let another go through a door first, only to find that the other is stubbornly doing the same. And in any event, the command as expressed in Matthew 22:39, in Mark 12:31 and in Luke 10:27 is – in all three accounts – to love your neighbour *as yourself.* We are, then, presented with the question of the appropriate form of self-love. It is an intricate question and a basic problem in Christian ethics. Here we may simply note that it has to be taken into account when we try to work out the implications of neighbour love.

The same sort of problem is raised by the Golden Rule. It is certainly other-regarding, but it is not simply self-abnegating. It implies a parity of dignity and status and would, if observed on both sides, yield a relationship of reciprocity. In the concrete working out of my relationships, therefore, the way in which I want to be treated has to be taken into account.

Again, it is simply not the case that rights must always be in tension with an other-regarding love. We can, to be sure, imagine scenarios in which that is so. That would, for example, seem to be the case if we were to suppose that Mr Burns held the mortgage on Homer Simpson's house and decided to exercise his right to foreclose, so rendering the Simpson family homeless. But it need not be so. We saw when we introduced the language of rights (in Chapter 3) that some rights can be waived. This would be a case in point. Mr Burns *need* not foreclose. The fact that he has a legal right to do so does not preclude the possibility that he might have a Scrooge-like conversion experience and choose not to exercise that right. Homer's perilous plight is not necessarily an argument against the existence of Mr Burns's legal right, unless we were to say that whenever there is a possible conflict between neighbour love and claim rights, so much the worse for claim rights and draw the radical conclusion that we should live in a society in which there are no enforceable obligations at all.

But we also saw in Chapter 3 that rights can be claimed either by the right-holder or by someone else on their behalf. (And the latter will, in fact, very often be what has to happen in the case of children's rights in particular.) Suppose, then, that the mortgage is actually held by a trust fund that supports the poor orphans of Springfield and that Mr Burns is simply administering the charity's interests. Which neighbour must he love, Homer or the orphans?

And, finally, we might just imagine that Mr Burns might think that neighbour love for Homer involves treating him like a responsible moral agent, capable of undertaking and fulfilling contractual obligations, rather than a feckless, Duff-swilling layabout.

This last consideration is a more serious point than it might seem to be from our rather frivolous example. Injustice, like all vice, demeans the perpetrator and impedes the flourishing of his humanity. Aquinas says that 'since honour follows upon some excellence ... one dishonours another when he deprives him of an excellence because of which he had honour'.[50] The same could be said of *allowing* another to inflict such harm on yourself; that is also a way of dishonouring because it is a way of demeaning.

We can easily imagine more serious – and more plausible – cases than Mr Burns's touching concern for Homer's moral welfare. Suppose that an elderly and housebound parent is being neglected by her daughter who likes to go clubbing. Or, alternatively, suppose that the elderly parent demands constant attention and never lets her daughter leave the house. In either case, how is neighbour love best served (and the relationship best fostered) by the injured party?

We have, then, seen that in all sorts of specific contexts it is simply not the case that there is a straightforward conflict between an affirmation of rights and the practice of an other-regarding love. Some claims might appropriately be waived. Others are made to protect the interests of a third party and so are in and of themselves an expression of neighbour love. And there may be times when love is best served by confronting the neighbour and deflecting him from a wrongful course. There remain cases in which a right cannot, or cannot appropriately, be waived; in which the right is asserted by and in the interests of the claim-holder; and in which the claim-holder would only be deceiving themselves if they chose to believe that their primary concern was the moral welfare of the other.

Is it always a mistake to advance such self-regarding claims? It cannot be if both the Golden Rule and the commandment of neighbour love enjoin some form of self-love as well. Let us take a case that is rather more complex than Mr Burns foreclosing Homer's mortgage. Suppose that in a previous relationship a woman has been repeatedly and systematically humiliated and abused (physically, verbally or emotionally). And suppose further that her partner in a new relationship expects her to get on with the washing up while he goes off to see his mates in the pub. What should she do as he rummages through her purse looking for another fiver? Should she tell herself that Christian morality is based on other-regarding love? Or should she assert her dignity as a human being and her equality within the relationship by claiming a right to be treated with dignity and respect?

These problems arise because neighbour love has to be cashed. We may well agree that the command to love is the foundation of Christian ethics; we may well agree that it is what is distinctive about the demands of the Christian moral life. But we cannot leave it at that. As Augustine and Aquinas saw, there is no necessary conflict between the love command and more specific moral norms because they operate at different levels.

In this section we have looked at two major objections to use of the language of claim-rights. We looked first at the argument that the concept of human rights comes out of the Enlightenment world of individualism and humanism and, being ineluctably redolent of its roots, has no place in contemporary Christian discourse, and then we looked at the objection that two key scriptural texts pre-empt an appeal to rights. We tried to show that the conclusion to the former argument does not follow from the premise – even to the extent that that premise is allowed to be true, and we tried to show that the latter objection is not supported by a careful reading of the texts adduced.

But that still leaves the question why bother with human rights language in the first place; what gain is there in going down that road? That is the question to which we will try to propose an answer in the next section.

5.4 What's the Theological Payoff?

We saw in the first section of this chapter that in the last fifty years or so the churches have invested a considerable amount of theological energy in the language of human rights. But of course Christian morality managed quite well for centuries before that. What is the theological payoff? What is the advantage for us today in explicating the implications of Christian morality in those terms?

In this section we shall suggest three lines of approach. First, rights have a force and a focus that can sharpen and toughen up a general appeal to duties and obligations. Secondly, rights language shifts the focus from the stronger party in a relationship to the weaker. And, thirdly, rights language gives the Christian community at this point in time access to the wider world – a way of engaging with the secular society in which we live and a way of becoming involved in a global conversation and a global enterprise to extend protection to the needy and oppressed.

Some of these points have been adumbrated in the course of previous discussions, but here we shall draw the threads together. And some of our conclusions will turn out to apply with special force to the rights of those human beings who happen also to be children. Where that is the case we shall draw attention to the fact and so anticipate slightly the discussion of the next chapter, which will be devoted to children's rights in particular.

In Chapter 3 we saw that the idea of rights involves a correlativity of claims and duties, and, in considering the 'redundancy' objection, we asked what difference it would make if we simply talked about duties and left it at that, without turning the coin over to look at its other side – the language of rights – at all.[51]

A part of the answer is that starting from rights rather than from duties concentrates the mind. That is, it gives the discussion of duties and obligations a focus and a specificity it might otherwise lack.

What we mean can be illustrated from the classical treatment of a traditional problem in Christian ethics. In his treatise *On Christian Teaching* Augustine starts from the command to love your neighbour as yourself (Matt. 22:39) and then asks how that love is to be apportioned among various neighbours. His solution is to say that

> all are to be loved equally, but since you cannot be of benefit to all, you must take thought most especially for those who chance to be joined more closely to you by favourable circumstances of place or time or whatever.[52]

The idea is developed by Aquinas in a passage of the *Summa* that is dependent for its problematic and its structure, though not for its conclusions, on this passage of Augustine. Aquinas argues that we should love first God, then self, then others. And among others a distinction may be made between those who are close to us and those who are not. That leads on to a further set of questions. Should one love kinfolk more than other associates? Offspring more than father? Mother more than father? Wife more than father and mother?[53] The questions in the latter group are not fatuous. Raising them enables Thomas to make some quite nuanced points about different kinds of love and different ways of measuring love.

The picture one gets in both Augustine and Thomas is of concentric circles radiating outwards. But where duties are delineated, not as the consequence of the command to love but as the correlative to rights, the picture one gets is of an interlocking network of lines, forming a spider's web, a lattice – perhaps, we might say, a safety net.

The two pictures are not incompatible. Indeed, they are complementary. But the rights-based picture allows the needs of a specific other, who may be only a distant neighbour but who still has a claim on me, to come more sharply into focus.

That is all the more true in the case of those who cannot put their own claim, who can find no moral voice of their own. And that will often be the case when the rights at stake are those of children. The putting of the claim draws attention to the needs of those who are too young or too incapacitated or too frightened to speak up for themselves and who might otherwise get lost in the shuffle.

Another point in starting from rights rather than duties is that it facilitates discussion – it enriches a moral conversation with yourself or someone else. To appeal to my sense of moral duty *should* be enough to get me to do something, but in a messy and complicated world I may remain unmoved. To be told 'But he has a *right* ...' brings into play other moral factors such as my basic sense of justice and can have a strong, because focused, emotional force.

That is of course why charities, including Christian ones, that appeal on behalf of the starving do not expound the obligation of love of neighbour, but show us the face of a hungry child. There is a serious moral argument there, and not just an advertising ploy. Moral philosophers and theologians often make ethics sound like a purely abstract and cerebral matter, but anything which involves truly human action involves the whole person. And that includes imagination and sympathy.[54] The focused nature of claim-rights appeals to the whole self to respond.

This is connected with a second advantage which accrues to Christian ethics from the use of rights language. That is the way in which speaking of the rights of those in need shifts the centre of attention from the strong to the weak, from the giver to the receiver. The focus is no longer on *my* sense of duty or *my* altruism or *my* benevolence, but on the need of the claimant.[55]

And this is, again, particularly important for the rights of children. Here it will not infrequently be the case that claims have to be advanced on behalf of the child by someone else. The notion of rights gives that third party a standing; it empowers someone else to take up the case. And even if an appeal for the implementation of rights fails, something has still been gained by approaching things from that angle. The child is not appealing, directly or through a third party, to the charity of someone in a position of authority, but is putting forward a claim to a justified entitlement. And to be able to do so or to have that done for one is in itself an affirmation of human dignity.

This shifting of the focus from the strong to the weak, from the giver to the receiver, performs a service for the whole Church, for it helps preserve the radical character of Christian ethics. We can find an example of what we mean if we look to a very different church in a very different age – if we look to the homilies of John Chrysostom.

John preached in the great city of Antioch toward the end of the fourth century. He lived in a time of rapid social change. The gap between rich and poor was becoming wider, and he was deeply moved by the plight of the poor and homeless sleeping rough in the streets and porticoes of a resplendently wealthy city. But in an age which had virtually no concept of *structural* social change, there was little that Chrysostom could do other than appeal to the charity of the rich. They had a Christian duty to share their wealth; they should recognize Christ in the face of the poor. And the poor in turn had an obligation to be grateful to and pray for their benefactors.

John did what he could in the world in which he lived. But from our point of view, it often looks as if what he is doing in his homilies is simply reinforcing the social structures which had created the problem in the first place. Both rich and poor were called upon to accept – as a Christian duty – their place in a strongly hierarchical social order and a steep-sided economic pyramid.

Had it been possible for some sort of intellectual time-machine to have beamed the concept of rights back into the fourth century, we might fantasize that John could have come to see things in a new light. Perhaps he could have seen things less through the eyes of the prosperous and educated men of Antioch (for it was a patriarchal as well as hierarchical society) – men with whom he shared so many assumptions of class and culture and education – and come to see them more through the eyes of the poor whose *right* to life and shelter and sustenance could then have been advanced.

Of course that speculation is wildly anachronistic. There is no such thing as an intellectual time-machine. We all belong to a time and to a place. And that actually points to a third reason why it is useful for the churches today to speak the language of human and children's rights.

We live in a society in which there is in many ways no longer a Christian ethical consensus – or rather in which the Christian values that *have* helped shape our society and continue to influence it are by so many no longer held on consciously Christian grounds. Insofar as there is an ethical consensus in our society at all, it is perhaps held together by a kind of unreflective utilitarianism ('always act so as to promote the greatest happiness', in John Stuart Mill's catchphrase) or by some sort of residual sense of fairness and equality – in other words, by a sense that people have rights.

That means that using rights language helps us to communicate. It helps us to take our rightful place, we might say, in public debate. And if that is true of our post-Christian society, it is all the more true of our involvement with non-Christian societies around the world. The Saudi comments on the Universal Declaration of Human Rights, analysed above in Chapter 2, bear ample testimony to that. Whatever ambiguities and misunderstandings may be left in that conversation, conversation was at least possible. And it was possible only because of a framework of commonly professed assumptions.

There is nothing inherently odd about using a theory of human rights to support beliefs we as Christians happen to hold on other grounds as well. If we believe in the coherence of truth – which we as Christians must if God is the author of our world and Jesus Christ is himself the Truth – then different lines of argument can, and indeed must, converge to support the same conclusion.

A rather loopy example is provided by early Christian response to the exposure of unwanted infants – an accepted, if not particularly common, practice in the pagan world but one which was consistently rejected in the Jewish and Christian traditions. In an *Apology* for Christianity implying a pagan audience and written around the year 154 CE, Justin Martyr asserts that Christians do not do it. But he never mentions the fate of children who are left to die. Instead, he claims that most of those who are picked up by somebody are picked up by pimps who rear them for a life of prostitution. And that means, Justin says, that a man may unwittingly commit incest when he visits a brothel.[56] In a section which is full of sarcastic denunciations of pagan immorality, the argument makes a little bit of sense – but not much.

That is a somewhat extreme example, taken from a key text of the Early Church, to illustrate the somewhat melancholy fact that it is perfectly possible to support a sound conclusion with a weak argument. But there would have been nothing to stop Justin from saying that the exposure of infants is prohibited by the command to love or by the 'Thou shalt not kill' of the Decalogue *as well* – if he had thought of it.

A weightier but more problematic example is provided by arguments for the existence of God. We might all agree that the existence of God is a datum of revelation. But whether the same conclusion can *also* be reached purely by reason has been a matter of intense philosophical and theological debate. Scripture, or Scripture *and* philosophical argument? Let us, just for the moment, side with those who are committed to the latter view.[57] They would say that they have two, independent ways of talking about the same reality and that argument based on Scripture may be well and good within the Christian or Judaeo-Christian community, but philosophical engagement with the world outside is not thereby precluded.

A still more germane example is provided by John XXIII's encyclical *Pacem in terris*, that we looked at in the first section of this chapter. After the paragraph quoted above in which John affirms as a fundamental principle that every human person possesses inviolable rights,[58] he adds a further, Christian argument:

> But if we consider the dignity of the human person on the basis of truths that have been divinely handed down, then we cannot help but give to that dignity a far higher estimation. This is because human beings have been redeemed by the blood of Jesus Christ, have by celestial grace become children and friends of God, and have been made heirs of eternal glory.[59]

That sort of Christian argument can perfectly happily coexist with a philosophically based assertion of the existence of human rights, and both can lead to the same conclusion affirming the dignity of the human person.

The language of rights has become a sort of moral lingua franca in our world. The Church has nothing to lose and much to gain by using it when appropriate.

In this chapter we looked at the adoption of rights language by the Churches. We then tried to engage with two widely voiced objections – two sources of the suspicion that often surrounds this development. And in the final section we pointed to some of the advantages of learning to use the language of rights.

But the advantages we looked at were of a prudential order. That is, they were pragmatic gains, in the sense that they corresponded to ways in which rights language enabled the Christian community to do more efficaciously things it wanted to do anyway.

In the next two chapters we shall move on to look at children's rights in particular. But, in considering their theological justification, we will also try to move beyond pragmatic considerations of this sort and see if we can find a way of grounding rights language, and above all the language of children's rights, in central concerns of the Christian tradition. In Romans 11:17 Paul speaks of a wild-olive shoot grafted into a cultivated olive tree and coming 'to share in the richness of the root of the olive'. It may turn out to be the case that rights language is a bit like that.

Notes

1. Maritain's thought on these problems is expressed from a theological/philosophical point of view above all in his *Man and the State*, Chicago: University of Chicago Press, 1951. For an analysis of his thought, see Thomas A. Fay, 'Maritain on Rights and Natural Law', *The Thomist*, 55 (1991), pp. 439–48.

2. I am here thinking, for example, of the way in which the first Christian apologist, Justin Martyr, in the middle of the second century claimed that all who have at any time lived in accordance with right reason are Christians. His word for 'reason' is *logos*, and he, like the prologue of John's Gospel, believes that Jesus Christ *is* the *Logos* or Word of God. We will return to this line of thought below.

3. Jean Porter, *Natural and Divine Law, Reclaiming the Tradition for Christian Ethics*, Saint Paul University Series in Ethics, Grand Rapids: William B. Eerdmans, 1999, p. 312.

4. On the development of the idea, see Richard Tuck, *Natural Rights Theories, Their Origin and Development*, Cambridge: Cambridge University Press, 1979.

5. For a modern development of the idea that natural rights are self-evidently good, see John Finnis, *Natural Law and Natural Rights*, Oxford: Clarendon Press, 1980.

6. On the idea of overlapping consensus, see John Rawls, *Political Liberalism*, New York: Columbia University Press, 1996.

7. We are indebted here to very helpful comments by Andrew Morton of New College, Edinburgh. See William Storrar and Andrew Morton (eds), *Public Theology for the 21ˢᵗ Century*, Edinburgh: St Andrew Press, forthcoming.

8. So, from a different perspective, Jeremy Waldron speaks of a right which 'exists in the fairly straightforward sense that talk about it is made intelligible by referring to the terms' of the normative moral commitment which it formulates: Waldron (ed.), *Theories of Rights*, p. 5.

9. On the whole history of the appeal to human rights by the World Council of Churches, see Alf Tergel, *Human Rights in Cultural and Religious Traditions*, Uppsala Studies in Faiths and Ideologies, 8, Uppsala: Uppsala University, 1998, pp. 206–58.

10. World Council of Churches, *The Message and Reports of the First Assembly of the World Council of Churches*, London: World Council of Churches/SCM Press, 1948, p. 68.

11. Ibid., p. 71.

12. See the discussion in Waldron (ed.), '*Nonsense upon Stilts*', pp. 7–25, with the text of the 'Declaration of the Rights of Man and the Citizen 1789', pp. 26–8.

13. For human rights and the modern Catholic Church, see in general Tergel, *Human Rights*, pp. 107–202.

14. To be precise, in a round about fashion the Pope *condemned* the proposition, 'It is indeed false that civil liberty for all forms of worship …' (Pius IX, *Syllabus of Errors* (8 December 1864) 79 = Henricus Denzinger and Adolfus Schönmetzer (eds), *Enchiridion Symbolorum, Definitionum et Declarationum de Rebus Fidei et Morum* (24th edn), Barcelona: Herder, 1967, 2979). The *Syllabus* was a catalogue of liberal and secularist theses condemned in various papal pronouncements of varying weight and authority over a number of years. This particular proposition was extracted from a papal allocution (a relatively low-grade document) of 15 December 1856.

15. Leo XIII, *Quod apostolici muneris* (28 December 1878) = Denzinger and Schönmetzer (eds), *Enchiridion Symbolorum*, 3130.

16. For the text of *Rerum novarum*, see Denzinger and Schönmetzer (eds), *Enchiridion Symbolorum*, 3265–71. According to the encyclical, human beings have certain rights (the plural is used in 3266), which are given by nature and are anterior to any social compact or human law (3265, 3270, 3271). The prime example that is adduced is the right to private property (3265, 3266, 3267, 3271). That right or *jus* is something which every human being *has* (3265), but the term 'human right' is not in fact used. Leo's understanding of *jus* is certainly compatible with the idea that the worker has a claim-right to a just wage, but that step is not actually taken in the encyclical.

17. Pius XII, *Summi pontificatus* (20 October 1939) = Denzinger and Schönmetzer (eds), *Enchiridion Symbolorum*, 3780–6.

18. Denzinger and Schönmetzer (eds), *Enchiridion Symbolorum*, 3782 and 3785.

19. John XXIII, *Pacem in terris* (11 April 1963) = Denzinger and Schönmetzer (eds), *Enchiridion Symbolorum*, 3957.

20. See especially *Church in Today's World* (*Gaudium et spes*) 26: Norman P. Tanner (ed.), *Decrees of the Ecumenical Councils* (2 vols), London: Sheed & Ward, 1990, Vol. 2, 1085, lines 1–9. Tanner provides an English translation together with the original Latin text, but the translation we have used here is our own.

21. *Church in Today's World* (*Gaudium et spes*) 41 = Tanner (ed.), *Decrees of the Ecumenical Councils*, Vol. 2, 1095, lines 7–9.

22. Stanley Hauerwas, *Suffering Presence: Theological Reflections on Medicine, the Mentally Handicapped, and the Church* (Notre Dame: University of Notre Dame Press, 1986, pp. 127–8.

23. MacIntyre, *After Virtue* (2nd edn, 1985).

24. So this modern objection turns out, despite its very different foundation, to have quite a bit in common with the egoist objections of Bentham and Marx that we looked at in Chapter 2.

25. Cronin, *Rights and Christian Ethics*, p. 16. Essentially the same claim is made by Michael J. Perry, *The Idea of Human Rights: Four Inquiries*, New York: Oxford University Press, 1998, p. 56: 'What really matters – what we should take seriously – is not human rights talk but the claims such talk is meant to express: the claims about what ought not be done to or about what ought to be done for human beings.'

26. Rowan Williams, *Lost Icons: Reflections on Cultural Bereavement*, Edinburgh: T&T Clark, 2000, p. 86.

27. Ibid., p. 75.

28. Ibid., pp. 114 and 112.

29. Ibid., p. 85.

30. Ibid., p. 86.

31. Ibid., pp. 114 and 93.

32. The influential philosopher Ronald Dworkin makes an oft-repeated distinction between 'right-based', 'duty-based' and 'goal-based' moral theories: Dworkin, *Taking Rights Seriously*.

33. Williams, *Lost Icons*, p. 86.

34. In speaking of different models of democracy, Martin Loughlin considers a *'bourgeois liberal* position' which seeks 'to create a zone of private autonomy which prevents democratic decision-making authority from invading an individual's fundamental liberties' and contrasts it with a *'communitarian* position, one that strongly links democracy with an attachment to the traditions and practices of a distinctive community'. He goes on to note that 'communitarians do not dismiss the value of rights. But they do argue against their primacy ...': Martin Loughlin, 'Rights, Democracy and Law', in Campbell, Ewing and Tomkins (eds), *Sceptical Essays on Human Rights*, pp. 41–60, at pp. 47–8. The essays as a whole can be read as sounding a warning note – in both theory and legal practice – against what Sandra Fredman characterized as 'a liberal, individualist and property-oriented notion of human rights': Fredman, 'Scepticism under Scrutiny: Labour Law and Human Rights', in Campbell, Ewing and Tomkins (eds), *Sceptical Essays on Human Rights*, pp. 197–213, at p. 197.

35. For the classical sources of the idea of natural law, see in particular Helmut Koester, 'NOMOS PHYSEOS: The Concept of Natural Law in Greek Thought', in Jacob Neusner (ed.), *Religions in Antiquity*, Leiden: Brill, 1968, pp. 521–41: the importance of Philo stressed over against the common emphasis on Stoic influence; and Richard A. Horsley, 'The Law of Nature in Philo and Cicero', *Harvard Theological Review*, 71 (1978), pp. 35–59: the importance of Cicero as well as Philo, behind whom lies a Stoic tradition which 'has been reinterpreted by a revived and eclectic Platonism on which both Cicero and Philo drew' (p. 36).

36. See especially Tuck, *Natural Rights Theories*: a concept of human rights traced back to fourteenth-century discussions on Franciscan theories of poverty; and Annabel S. Brett, *Liberty,*

Right and Nature: Individual Rights in Later Scholastic Thought, Cambridge: Cambridge University Press, 1997: surveys critical reaction to Tuck's thesis (pp. 10–87). Brian Tierney, *The Idea of Natural Rights: Studies on Natural Rights, Natural Law and Church Law, 1150–1625*, Atlanta: Scholars Press, 1997, finds discussions of natural rights in texts of the very early thirteenth century.

37. So Tierney, *Idea of Natural Rights*, pp. 54–69, against MacIntyre, who claims that there was no word to express such a concept 'until near the close of the middle ages' (*After Virtue*, p. 69).

38. Porter, *Natural and Divine Law*, p. 275, citing and supporting Tierney's conclusions.

39. Ibid., p. 272.

40. Wolfgang Huber, 'Human Rights – A Concept and Its History', in Alois Müller and Norbert Greinacher (ed.), *The Church and the Rights of Man*, Concilium, New York: Seabury Press, 1979, pp. 1–10, at p. 5.

41. This could be compared with the use of the Convention on the Rights of the Child as a 'secondary framework' discussed at 2.5.1 above in relation to Saudi Arabia.

42. Anthony N. S. Lane, *John Calvin, Student of the Church Fathers*, Edinburgh: T&T Clark, 2000.

43. This verse was already cited in the first half of the third century by the great theologian Origen as a stock example in a discussion of the literal reading of Scripture: Origen, *On First Principles* 1.1.1.

44. It may be worth remembering that verse divisions were only introduced by sixteenth-century editors; the very first were those in the edition of the Greek New Testament published in Geneva in 1551 by the printer Robert Stephanus. (Our modern chapter divisions were created for purposes of study in the theology faculty of the University of Paris in the later twelfth and early thirteenth centuries.)

45. Both date and original language have been much discussed. See Emil Schürer, *The History of the Jewish People in the Age of Jesus Christ (175 B.C.–A.D. 135)*, revised edn by Geza Vermes et al. (3 vols in 4), Edinburgh: T&T Clark, 1973–87, Vol. 3.1, pp. 222–32.

46. The so-called Western text, including the great manuscript D (Codex Bezae), now in Cambridge.

47. See above, Chapter 4.10.4 (p. 124).

48. See Porter, *Natural and Divine Law*, pp. 125–7. Her whole discussion of the treatment of Scripture and natural law in

scholastic thought (pp. 121–85) is important for the present discussion.

49. ST I. II ae. 100.3.
50. ST II IIae 72.1. On the importance of this passage, see Jean Porter, *The Recovery of Virtue: The Relevance of Aquinas for Christian Ethics*, London: SPCK, 1994, p. 136, and Porter, *Natural and Divine Law*, p. 316.
51. See para. 3.7.1 above.
52. Augustine, *De Doctrina Christiana* I.xxvi.27–xxviii.29; the quoted passage is I.xxviii.29.
53. Thomas Aquinas, ST IIa IIae 26.2–11.
54. On the value of theological imagination, see Cronin, *Rights and Christian Ethics*, especially pp. 153–5.
55. Always acknowledging that 'rights' too can be abused by the powerful. See the comments by the Indian philosopher Pandeya at 4.10.3 above.
56. Justin Martyr, *First Apology* 27.1–3.
57. Thomas Aquinas would be a classical example.
58. See above, p. 161.
59. John XXIII, *Pacem in terris* (11 April 1963) = Denzinger and Schönmetzer (eds), *Enchiridion Symbolorum*, 3957.

6

The Human Rights of the Child

6.1 Introduction

This chapter proceeds on the premise that the 'rights' discourse, and in particular the concept of 'human rights', is valid and useful, and asks:

1. What does it mean to say children have human rights (developing the 'philosophic themes' from Chapter 4)?
2. What are the objections to such 'children's rights' (developing the areas of 'resistance' identified in Chapter 4)?
3. How do children's human rights differ from adult rights?
4. How are 'rights' important to the lives of children?

It then explores some particular issues from a children's rights perspective:[1]

freedom of thought, conscience and religion and the implications for education;

freedom of association;

protection of privacy;

physical punishment; and

obedience.

6.2 What does it Mean to Say Children have Human Rights?

In Chapter 3 we explored the meaning of children's rights in terms both of Hohfeld's categories and the 'will' and 'interest' theory debates. Here we are concerned in particular with what it means to say that children have 'human rights'.

In section 4.2 above, 'human rights' were defined as 'standards of human dignity justified with reference to moral, religious or legal authority or reasoning'. On that understanding children's rights are standards relating to the human dignity of the child. It is often forgotten that children, as 'humans,' are entitled to benefit equally from the universal standards of human rights set out in the documents discussed in this book. The child-focused declarations of the twentieth century represented recognition of the particular vulnerability of children, requiring special assistance, but did not detract from the status of children as humans with the same rights to human dignity as the adult population.

By 1989, when the Convention on the Rights of the Child was passed, children were already included within the ambit of approximately eighty international instruments.[2] However, the general proclamations of rights had not been drawn up with children particularly in mind, and the child-specific declarations had no legal force. Many of the general conventions had been fitfully ratified. It was felt that a convention focusing specifically on children, and setting their general rights within the context of their particular needs, would be more appropriate, more accessible, and more likely to attract the approval of states; an insight vindicated by the rapid and almost universal ratification of the Convention on the Rights of the Child.[3]

The 'meaning' of children's rights can be explored with reference to some of the 'philosophic themes' of human rights identified in Chapter 4.

6.2.1 *Universality*

The question of the universality of children's rights is significant because attitudes to children are central to family relationships and therefore arguably more intimate and more culturally conditioned than those relationships with the State that were the main focus of general human rights. At the same time, adherents of a universal 'natural law' are vociferous in their emphasis upon whatever that law is considered to say about children and their role in the family. The Holy See regards the family as a 'natural society' that exists prior to the State and possesses 'inherent rights which are inalienable'. Marriage and the family are part of 'the plan of God instilled in human nature'.[4] It will be recalled that, while cultural diversity was pleaded as a potential qualifier to universalism in the run-up to the fiftieth anniversary of the 1948 Declaration, the statements around the event itself reaffirmed the concept of universality, while taking account of some of the legitimate concerns of former colonial territories.[5]

Questions have also been posed about the universality of the Convention on the Rights of the Child. The Senegalese representative on the Working Group spoke about the importance of the Convention, but expressed the view that the drafting process had not taken appropriate account of the concerns of the developing nations. He cited as examples the definitions of terms such as 'guardianship', 'adoption', 'filiation', 'legal situation of legitimate and illegitimate children', 'protection of the child before birth' and 'custody of children'. This view was supported by Egypt and Morocco.[6] The editors of the *Traveaux Preparatoires* agree that representation on the Working Group was uneven, with severe under-representation of African, Asian and, to a lesser extent, Latin-American countries. This raised the question whether the text was geared more to the situation of children in affluent, industrialised countries. It was therefore encouraging that the Convention had received such rapid and widespread approval and ratification.[7]

Given that debates may persist about the universality of the *terminology* of the Convention on the Rights of the Child, in terms of its universal *application* it may be regarded as the kind of practical consensus referred to at 4.6.1 above, which inevitably leaves the degree of ambiguity (and consequent scope for differences in interpretation and application) which the American Richard McKeon had earlier identified as inevitable in statements of this kind.[8]

6.2.2 Rights and Needs

The contention that 'rights' are based upon 'needs' may seem to be even more weighty in its application to children than to adults. Children's needs are clearly important. The 1924 Declaration on the Rights of the Child proclaimed the right of the child to have certain needs met. This is significant, because implementation of the right should involve a mechanism for *ensuring* that the needs are met, that they can be pursued as a legitimate claim upon society. The needs of the child give substantial content to the rights of the child, and the rights give power to the needs.

The focus on needs links in to the 'best interests' test that appears both in the 1989 Convention and in our legal systems and, as discussed in 2.8 above, brings with it questions about: who should determine what a child needs are, or where the child's best interests lie; what checks, if any, there should be upon the person with the power of determination; and the standards upon which any such checks should themselves be based. This issue will be further discussed at 6.2.4.3 below in connection with the relationship between the child, the parents and the State.

This kind of assessment suffers from the same difficulty as discussed in relation to adults: 'needs' can be identified only in relation to 'ends,' involving perceptions of human life and destiny. Needs are also related to expectations about acceptable standards of fulfilment. Without a clear 'end' or agreed standards, the concept of needs is very open ended.⁹ To the extent that children are perceived as 'adults in the making', one can identify a very basic common 'end', related to survival and development. But this does not alleviate the problem of identifying the human characteristics towards which efforts at development should be directed. Parents and states will identify the needs of children in accordance with their perceptions or beliefs about human destiny, thus exploiting (often legitimately) the degree of ambiguity that allowed the Convention to achieve almost universal ratification. However, for the Convention to have any impact, there must be some limits on the degree of ambiguity and freedom of action. Both the Convention on the Rights of the Child and UK law identify the child's natural parents as the persons primarily vested with the 'right' to determine what the child's needs are and thereby shape the child's development. The parental rights to do this are often described as 'inalienable', a concept that requires further consideration.

6.2.3 Inalienable Rights

The 'inalienability' of rights is a concept already identified as requiring further elucidation in relation to the understanding of the Holy See.¹⁰ The question marks arising in relation to it can be better understood by consideration of a particular example. Pope John Paul II's 1981 Exhortation *Famialiaris consortio* states:

> The right of parents to choose an education in conformity with their religious faith must be absolutely guaranteed … Those in society who are in charge of schools must never forget that the parents have been appointed by God himself as the first and principal educators of their children and that their right is completely inalienable (para. 40).

The question arises whether the Holy See truly believes this to apply to all parents and to all 'religious faiths'. Would it be permissible for a parent to deny a female child any education on the grounds of religious faith? Would parental rights be inalienable where the parents were involved in Satanism or occult practices believed by others to be harmful? Should parents be free to inculcate in their children hatred for others who do not share their beliefs? How can the 'inalienable rights' of parents to direct and shape the lives and development of their children be reconciled with the inalienable rights of their children, set out in the Convention on the Rights of the Child?[11]

'Inalienability' appears here as a concept that can be defended only if accompanied by the qualification attached by Jacques Maritain that, while a person may not be deprived of his 'inalienable' right, he may, by his own actions, divest himself of 'the possibility of demanding that right with justice'.[12] The question is then whether this understanding of inalienability does not void it of any real meaning. Does it not mask an underlying reality, that might more accurately be described as a presumption in favour of the rights of parents to determine where the interests of their children lie, accompanied by an identifiable threshold for state or community intervention in pursuit of the rights of the child? If one accepts this analysis, the focus shifts away from the concept of 'inalienability' and towards the process and criteria for a proper determination of where to draw the line between family autonomy and state or community control.

It would be understandable were a resistance to be experienced to this conceptual shift, which might seem to assume too much power on behalf of the State. However, the issue cannot be avoided; those who wish to adhere to the concept of inalienability must articulate an understanding of it that more accurately reflects the reality of family life, the rights of the child and the (assumedly) universal commitment to the protection of children.

And in fact, while the law too has used the language of 'inalienability' as regards parental rights,[13] this has never been treated as an absolute. Courts have always exercised a power to intervene in whatever cases were regarded as appropriate to the times. Within Scotland, 'inalienability' can be said to exist only in respect that parents who have parental responsibilities and rights cannot voluntarily give them up or surrender them to someone else without the intervention of a court. Parents may arrange for someone else to carry out some responsibilities on their behalf;[14] they also have authority to nominate a guardian to assume full parental responsibilities and rights on the parent's death;[15] but parents cannot 'abdicate' their parental status.[16] Courts can, however, for good reason, remove parental rights in part or in whole.

One of the reasons our society has shifted towards growing recognition of children's rights is our increasing awareness of the extent of abuse of parental authority and its devastating implications for the children concerned. When *Familiaris consortio* was promulgated in 1981, there was no reference to child abuse or neglect. There was some acknowledgement of a need to find alternative homes for some children, but the document spoke only of children who were orphaned, or whose parents had abandoned them.[17] The Holy See's Initial Report to the UN Committee in 1994 did make reference to the reality of some forms of parental abuse, while retaining *Familiaris consortio*'s language of inalienable parental rights in a way that the Holy See representatives themselves had difficulty justifying. This developing understanding of the vulnerability and abuse of children inevitably raises questions about whether the concept of inalienability can be maintained. Consider, for example, the following scenario:

> Robin and Maria are addicted to heroin. Their lives are chaotic and they have spent several periods in prison for drug-related offences. Their three children, aged 2, 4 and 7, have suffered severe neglect and have now been made available for adoption, against their parents' wishes, after several periods

in foster care and children's homes, and many unsuccessful attempts at rehabilitation with their parents. Social services are optimistic about finding homes for the younger children, but the seven-year-old is now highly disturbed and will be difficult, and possibly impossible, to place with a family.

For whatever reason, social service and drug-related agencies have not been able to provide sufficient support to help Robin and Maria to become drug free or to cope with the demands of a young family. Provision of services may have been insufficient, or may have been resisted in the face of the addiction. It now comes to the attention of the authorities that Maria is pregnant again. They need to decide whether they can this time support Robin and Maria to look after the expected child, or whether to take action to remove the child from them at birth to give it a chance of a stable and caring family life.

From the point of view of advocates of the rights of the family or of parents, the problem is that, as soon as you breach the absolute and inalienable character of parental rights, you are faced with the problem of deciding where and how to draw the line between family autonomy and State intervention. However carefully rules and guidelines are framed, the issue will inevitably involve human judgement in any individual case.[18] Wherever there is discretion on matters as sensitive and open to subjective interpretation as 'the child's best interests', all interested and concerned people will, understandably, want to be vigilant about how it is being interpreted; and there will always be some disagreement about it. A major contribution of the Convention is that it provides a common starting point and language for dialogue, interpretation and application of its standards for the protection and welfare of children.[19]

6.2.4 Rights and Duties

The philosophic theme of the relationship between rights and duties is also relevant to any exploration of children's rights. It has three different focuses:

the relationship between the rights and duties of the child;

the relationship between the rights and duties of the parent; and

the consequences for the relationship between child, parent and State.

6.2.4.1 Child

Poland's Initial Report to the UN Committee pointed to the dangers of separating the child's rights from his or her duties.[20] The Holy See did not specifically identify the need for a greater focus on the duties of children, but its 1983 *Charter of the Rights of the Family* speaks of the need for all family members 'to harmonize the rights of individuals with other demands of social life'. More interestingly, its Initial Report to the UN identifies the correlative to the rights of the child as being the duties of society rather than the duties of the child.[21]

In addressing the question of rights and duties in relation to children, it is important to dismiss immediately the suggestion that rights must be earned by duties. As indicated at 4.10 above, if this were the paradigm, small children, incapable of performing duties, would have no rights at all, not even to survival. The inability of young children to perform duties highlights the fact that any necessary correlation between rights and duties is (as observed by the Holy See) a characteristic of a system rather than of an individual. No system can effectively protect rights unless someone within it has a corresponding duty to respect those rights. As regards an individual, one might more appropriately identify the correlation as being between power[22] and responsibility. Insofar as a system recognises and upholds the power of an individual, the person possessing that power has a correlative responsibility to exercise it with respect for the rights of others. This applies equally to children. Where recognition of the evolving maturity of a child is reflected in a power to act autonomously or to influence or make decisions, to that extent the child has a responsibility to respect the rights of others. The important conclusion for this context is that children *can* hold rights without the personal burden of correlative duties.

6.2.4.2 Parents

With parents it is somewhat different. Indeed it may seem paradoxical that, having concluded that rights do not flow from the performance of duties,[23] modern thought sees the relationship between parent and child as characterised by the *duties* of the parent, for the exercise of which the parent holds certain rights. Some scholars have concluded from the eighteenth-century *Commentaries on the Laws of England* by Sir William Blackstone that the commandment in Exodus 20:12 to honour one's parents implies that, 'The power of a parent over his children is derived from *their* [the children's] duty to him.'[24] However, Blackstone addressed the relations between parent and child in the following sequence:

1. the legal duties of parents to their legitimate children;
2. their power over them; and
3. the duties of such children to their parents.[25]

Blackstone specifically stated that the powers of parents arose from the *parents'* duties, and consisted principally of maintenance, protection and education.[26] In relation to the duties of *children*, he observed:

> The duties of children towards their parents arise from a principle of natural justice and retribution. For to those who gave us existence, we naturally owe subjection and obedience during our minority, and honour and reverence ever after; they, who protected the weakness of our infancy, are entitled to our protection in the infirmity of their age;

they who by sustenance and education have enabled their offspring to prosper, ought in return to be supported by that offspring, in case they stand in need of assistance. Upon this principle proceed all the duties of children to their parents.[27]

There is no reference to the commandment as a founding principle, and the child's duties are presented as a response to the parent's care, on the assumption that parents have in fact protected, supported and educated their child appropriately. This legal view is consistent with modern thought which sees the parental power as deriving from, and subsidiary to, the *parent's* duty to the child.

Within Scotland too, the common law historically viewed parental duty as the primary and founding concept. Erskine, an eighteenth-century writer whose work holds considerable authority in the Scottish legal system, observed:

Parents lie under the strongest obligations, from nature itself, to take care of their issue during their imperfect age, in consequence of which they are vested with all the powers over them which are necessary for the proper discharge of their duty.[28]

Both Blackstone and Erskine described the parental authority as a 'power'. While it would be anachronistic to understand this choice of language in terms of the Hohfeldian analysis discussed in Chapter 3 above, it is of interest that Wilkinson and Norrie's 1993 book observes that:

Though the term 'parental rights' is commonly used, and has statutory sanction, the term parental power or privilege is jurisprudentially more accurate. The rights of parents are not absolute ... Rather, parental power is more in the nature of entitlement or privilege, whereby the law will recognise the parent's abilities competently to perform certain acts in relation to and on behalf of the child, and will give legal force to these acts. Parental power is also limited by the requirement that its exercise must satisfy the welfare test ...[29]

This had also been observed by the Scottish Law Commission, whose 1992 *Report on Family Law* observed of parental 'rights':

> It has frequently been pointed out that 'rights' is here used in a loose sense. The right of guardianship, for example, is really a power to take legally effective action on behalf of a child.[30]

This natural recourse to the vocabulary of 'powers' rather than 'rights' in relation to parental authority reflects the fact that those liable to the exercise of that power are also human beings with human rights that must be respected. As seen in the story of Emily discussed at 3.4 above, parental 'rights' might be better classified in Hohfeldian terms as powers, liberties (or privileges) and immunities, whose scope of application is circumscribed by respect for the rights, powers, liberties and immunities of the child.

The result of this shift in terminology is that the law now characterises the relationship between parent and child primarily as one of 'parental responsibility', with ancillary parental rights flowing from, and dependent upon, an appropriate exercise of that responsibility. Thus, in Scotland, Section 1 of the Children (Scotland) Act 1995 defines 'parental responsibilities'.[31] Section 2 defines 'parental rights' and says that a parent holds them, 'in order to enable him to fulfil his parental responsibilities in relation to his child'.[32]

The extent to which public perception acknowledges this focus on parental responsibility can be seen in the almost universal approval of cases in which children have been removed from parents on the basis of their severe neglect or abuse of them; and also the media and public condemnation of cases where children have suffered because the child protection authorities failed to intervene appropriately to protect them. There are, however, greyer areas where there is less agreement about the appropriateness of intervention or removal of children. At these points, there is often recourse to the language of 'parental rights', 'family privacy' and 'family autonomy', by people who, one suspects, would not, if pushed, hold these rights as absolute. The real concern is the threshold for, and degree of, intervention.[33]

This may appear to diverge from the 'biblical' perspective adopted by some of the opponents of the Convention whose views were discussed at 2.7 above, and whose legitimacy will be further discussed below. However, it is difficult to imagine that many would wish to adopt an absolutist view of childhood duty and parental power, given what we know today about the extent of abuse of parental power. Indeed, one might argue further that the biblical commandment to honour one's parents cited by such commentators does not tell the full story. Pope John Paul II has noted that the 'honour' of parents required by the Fourth Commandment is not one sided: 'Indirectly, we can speak of the "honour" owed to children by their parents.'[34]

This issue will be explored further at 7.2.2 below.

We have identified a challenge to the concept of the 'inalienability' of parental rights and even to the identification of the parent as a 'right-holder' in the strict sense. We must now ask what this means for the relationship between the child, the parent and the State.

6.2.4.3 Child, Parent and State

Many of the explorations in this chapter have led to the same question: who should decide what is in a child's best interests? The Convention is clear that that right and responsibility to decide on the child's best interests belongs *primarily* to the child's parents. However, such determination cannot be left *exclusively* to parents. There must be some mechanism for the broader society of which the child is a member to intervene in the face of inappropriate parental behaviour such as that of Robin and Maria in the example cited at 6.2.3 above. This is consistent with the Holy See's acknowledgement of the necessity of State intervention in some circumstances, and with the ordinary meaning of 'primary' as 'firstly', rather than 'exclusively'. Accepting for the moment the identification of the parental power as a 'right', one might argue that the primacy of parental rights might be reconciled with the rights of the child by holding them to be 'primary' as against the State but 'secondary' as against the child.

Figure 1 shows the model proposed by the Convention on the Rights of the Child, in which the primary rights and responsibilities in relation to children belong to their parents, but change in character and degree in line with the child's evolving capacities (represented by the dotted line). The role of the State is to support parents in the exercise of their responsibilities and rights.[35]

Figure 1: State Support for the Primary Responsibilities and Rights of Parents

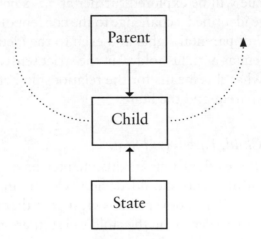

This relationship can break down in two ways:

1. A rogue State can try to assume too much power, thus setting up an opposition between the parent/child unit and the State:

Figure 2 : Conflict Precipitated by a Rogue State

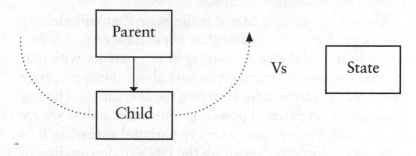

Within this conflict, the rights of the parents are primary in relation to the claims of the State. However, another type of conflict is possible:

2. Rogue parents can neglect their responsibilities or abuse their rights in relation to children, thus setting up an opposition between the child (supported by the State) and the parents:

Figure 3 : Conflict Precipitated by a Rogue Parent

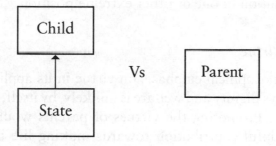

Within this conflict, because the rights of parents exist to allow them to fulfil their parental responsibilities, they are secondary to the rights of their children to the three Ps: provision, protection and participation.[36] It is therefore appropriate for the State to act as advocate or supporter of the rights of the child where these are being undermined by the parent. In the scenario above, the State may well intervene to remove the baby from the parents in order to respect the rights of the child.

The critical issue is that it is the State that will identify what constitutes abuse or neglect of parental responsibility and power, and therefore justifies its interference with that power. There will be disagreements about the appropriate threshold for intervention. However, the alternative, of having no controls on parental power, is untenable, unless we are willing to give free reign to every parental excess, lack of care, or eccentricity. Recalling the UN's understanding of its 1948 Declaration as a response to the abuses perpetrated by totalitarian governments, one can detect a tension within our recent experiences and the 'rights' asserted in response to them. On the one hand, the rights of parents provide the bulwark for the child and family against the kind of totalitarianism seen during the twentieth century. On the other hand, the rights of children are a bulwark against the reality of parental abuse and neglect of children, whose extent has become more evident in recent years.[37] The answer must be vigilance and acknowledgement of the difficulties of achieving a balance, rather than an attempt to find an easy solution in one or other extreme position.

6.2.5 Virtue

The philosophical emphasis on virtue in its application to children's dignity and welfare is unlikely, by itself, to secure its aims. Promoting the virtues of parents would indeed be a helpful contribution towards making life better for children. However, rights are needed to secure and advance the claims of children where virtue fails to shape parental behaviour.

6.2.6 Spiritual Considerations

Spiritual considerations are clearly relevant to one's attitude to the concept of children's' rights and to particular articulations of them. Questions of human nature and destiny, of divinely ordained structures of authority, of obedience and free will, all shape attitudes to the rights of the child. These issues are more fully explored in chapters 7 and 8 below.

6.2.7 Individualism

As discussed at 3.7.2 to 3.7.4 above, some of the resistance towards the 'rights' discourse comes from those who see it as a reflection of an unhelpful, and sometimes selfish, individualism. In relation to the rights of children, this can take the form of an aversion to anything that appears to isolate the child from his or her family setting. Thus, as indicated at 2.5.2 above, the Pontifical Council stated: 'The family is thus a whole which should not be divided up when it is being dealt with by isolating its members ...'[38]

Some of the reflection upon the community dimension of human life, referred to at 4.12 above, proposed an 'organic' model, a win/win situation in which the group provided the optimum environment for the flourishing of its members. The 1986 consultation demonstrated concern by some, and relief from others, that the newer human rights documents were moving back to a greater emphasis on the group. Those who felt relieved had considered the 1948 focus too individualistic. Those who were concerned pointed out that it was the dominance of groups, culminating in totalitarianism, that had allowed the horrors from which the Universal Declaration was trying to protect later generations. Similarly, with children, our current emphasis on the vulnerability of the individual child in the power of irresponsible or abusive parents, who fail to provide an acceptable environment for their children, can lead to articulations of rights which some feel are liable to undermine the family, the very environment that the child needs for optimum development. The search is always for the elusive balance that will monitor and intervene enough to prevent and address violations of the rights of the child without undermining the stability of the family environment that is valuable for most.

A recurring theme in chapters 3, 4 and 5 has been the objection or concern that a rights-based approach either creates or supports an individualism that runs counter to the sense of community that is more conducive to human welfare and fulfilment. We have made the point that rights help to address the consequences of fragmentation within a society rather than create it. This is nowhere more true than with regard to the rights of the child. The one thing that the protagonists in the debate seem to agree on is that society today (in the West at least) is fundamentally individualistic. *If* it is true that adults today place greater emphasis than before upon their own personal fulfilment at the expense of responsibilities towards the family and the wider community, and to the *extent* that it is true that our society expects parents to serve the needs of the economy before those of their children, then children within our society, deprived of the traditional and enduring support of the family or community, need also to have their individual rights recognised and supported if they are to have a stake in that society and a claim on its goods. In that respect, recognition and promotion of the rights of children is a necessary consequence of recognition and promotion of the rights of adults, and of the kind of society in which we live.

6.2.8 Conclusion

The application of these philosophic themes to the rights of the child shows that, to some extent, the 'macrocosm' of the general human rights considerations is reflected in the 'microcosm' of child and family. The difference is that general human rights issues focus on the relationship between the individual and the State, whereas issues about individuals who are children involve third parties: the children's parents or guardians.

Given the particular developmental potential and susceptibility to influence of childhood, what is at stake is not only the good of the child (including, some would say, his or her eternal destiny) but the good of the concentric circles of community of which that child is a member and with whom the child exists in a symbiotic relationship. Even if children were to be regarded as 'property', they could not be purely private property. Their enhanced status as the possessors of dignity and the incarnation of particular gifts which should be developed for the good both of themselves and their communities, legitimates the attribution of 'rights' where this involves a system for pressing their legitimate claims against all, family or State, who have authority over them and can help or hinder their appropriate development. It must be a system of checks and balances, where each extension of the circle is vigilant about the excesses of any other.

6.3 What are the Objections to Children's Rights?

The 'macrocosm/microcosm' analogy can also be applied to objections to the rights of the child. Section 4.16 above explored the resistance to the development of human rights. With some slight alterations (and here some slight re-ordering), the sub-headings under which this was discussed can be applied to the resistance to children's rights. The point of the comparison is to facilitate reflection upon the validity of the objections to the rights of the child. Anyone proposing to sustain any of the objections to children's rights that will be considered below must consider whether such objection cannot also be applied to human rights in general, and must re-evaluate his or her stance on human rights on that basis. The objections to children's rights are discussed under the headings of:

authoritarianism;
protection of family privacy and autonomy (compared with national sovereignty);

the assertion that intervention might make things worse;

the claim that developments have moved beyond their original intent;

political sensitivity;

religious sensitivity;

cultural relativism; and

justified discrimination.

6.3.1 Authoritarianism

Just as the early advocates of human rights were charged with undermining the authority of divinely sanctioned hereditary rulers and the good order of society so, in our day, advocates of the rights of the child are sometimes accused of undermining the divinely sanctioned authority of parents and the good order of society effected through family control of the child. We repeat here the comment by the Center for Reclaiming America, cited at 2.7.1 above:

> Scripture is clear on the rights and responsibilities of parents and children. The Fifth Commandment, 'honour your father and mother', is God's standard for domestic order. For that reason, those who seek to elevate the rights of children at the expense of parents are at war with God's original design and, therefore, with God himself.[39]

In the nineteenth century, the now widely accepted restrictions on child labour and insistence on compulsory education were opposed on the grounds that they interfered with parental rights and family responsibility.[40]

6.3.2 Family Privacy and Autonomy

The protection of national sovereignty argued in opposition to the development of human rights has an equivalent in the protection of family privacy and autonomy argued in opposition to the rights of the child. This is the argument often put forward in the face of State intervention in family life in order to protect a child.[41]

Within the United Kingdom, it has been observed that, even acknowledging that parents are in the best position both to protect and to tyrannise children, 'social policy, strongly influenced by common assumptions about family privacy and parental autonomy, reflects a distinct lack of sympathy for the view that the law should attempt to interfere with family life'.[42]

UK legislation has been criticised for adopting the laissez-faire approach advocated by Goldstein, Freud and Solnit in *Before the Best Interests of the Child*, a philosophy described as 'much criticised'.[43] These authors, in a trilogy of related books, advocated 'minimum state intervention' and, in cases of difficulty, a search for the 'least detrimental alternative' for the child rather than the unrealistic ideal.[44] The authors argue that it is not in the interests of children to have the decisions and wisdom of parents constantly second-guessed by the State.[45] The significance of this debate is that it is not about absolutes (the authors acknowledge the need for intervention in some cases) but about the threshold for intervention and the relative weight to be given to the right of the child to the benefits of family autonomy and the right to be protected according to external criteria. It is possible to sympathise with the concern about any 'constant second-guessing' of parental decisions while, at the same time, disagreeing with the very high threshold for intervention set by the authors. This discussion is therefore about the very identification of a threshold that has, in this chapter, been proposed as a truer reflection of the reality of life in our communities than adherence to absolutist concepts.

One of the criticisms of Goldstein, Solnit and Goldstein's approach is that it leaves children very vulnerable in some significant areas of their lives. In the area of medical treatment, they say the State should intervene only where parents refuse to authorise life-saving medical care which is likely to result in 'a chance for normal, healthy growth, or a life worth living'.[46] Where reasonable persons disagree about whether the child's life is likely to be 'worth living', they say that the State must respect the decision of the parents. The practical implications of this approach were described by Bernard Dickens:

> Implications of this philosophy appear to include that the State should not intervene if parents decide to submit their children to non-therapeutic, irreversible surgical procedures, such as contraceptive sterilisation of mentally retarded adolescents ...[47]

In particular, he cites a 1979 California case in which the court followed 'the thrust of Goldstein's reasoning' when it supported the right of the parents of an 11-year-old Downs syndrome boy (cared for since birth in a residential institution) to refuse potentially life-saving surgical treatment on the grounds that:

1. since the boy's life was not a 'life worth living', he should not have his life prolonged by surgery;
2. he would outlive his parents if the life-extending surgery was performed, and they would be unable to supervise his placement and care; and
3. the operation was too risky and might result in his death.

Dickens notes that medical experts had been in agreement about the benefits of the proposed surgery, and the application to overrule the parents' refusal of consent had been made by the child's actual carers.[48]

Dickens acknowledges the value in the work of these authors. The real issue is identifying the point at which parents' decision-making in relation to a child is so potentially harmful that the state ought to intervene to override them. In his view, Goldstein, Solnit and Goldstein place the threshold at so high a level that children are likely to suffer unnecessarily as a result. Dickens argues that parental rights 'exist to preserve and to prepare children for adulthood and emerging autonomy'.[49] Adopting this as a measure would, he says, allow State intervention in life-threatening situations, or when parents authorised contraceptive or eugenic sterilisation, organ donation between siblings, or committal of a child to 'voluntary' detention in a psychiatric facility. Such detention can present as an attractive option to the parents of troubled children, who are likely to receive sympathy if their delinquent adolescent is identified as 'mad' rather than disgrace if they are seen as 'bad'.[50] In these circumstances, there is a clear conflict of interest between parent and child.

It should be noted that criticism of absolute (or near absolute) parental autonomy does not necessarily imply criticism of the subjective motives of parents. Some may have selfish or vengeful motives; others may be 'parents whose well-meaning and conscientious initiatives are misguided or insensitive in ways denying children future rights'.[51] Dickens concludes:

> Without questioning parental good intentions, one can see that cases exist which show that the latest [i.e., 1979] proposals of Goldstein, Freud and Solnit, strongly favouring parental autonomy, should not drown other and opposing views giving emphasis to the rights of children themselves.[52]

6.3.3 Intervention Might Make Things Worse

The concern about family privacy shades into the argument that 'intervention might make things worse'. Michael Freeman (writing in 1983) cites Goldstein, Freud and Solnit among proponents of this view which, he says, is difficult to contradict, given the research indications about the failure of many interventions to make life better for children.[53]

Nevertheless, not even the trilogy authors deny the need for *some* intervention. Freeman acknowledges the dilemma in drawing a line between helpful and unhelpful interventions, while arguing that Goldstein, Freud and Solnit's criteria for intervention are too narrow.

It has been argued that, while UK law promotes the concept of parental responsibility over that of parental rights, at the same time, it 'deliberately adopts what has been described as the 'hands-off approach' of the trilogy authors, on the basis that lawyers and litigation often do more harm than good'.[54]

This may well, sadly, be the truth in some cases. The question is whether the proper approach is to acknowledge the system's deficiencies and leave children unprotected, or to seek to make the system more sensitive and effective. There are echoes of this concern in the Scottish legislation's insistence that no court order should be made in relation to a child unless it can be shown that making the order will be better for the child than not making an order.[55]

6.3.4 Developments Moving beyond the Original Intent

The argument about developments moving beyond the original intent has also been applied to the Convention on the Rights of the Child. The final shape of the Convention, with its emphasis on participation, moved beyond the intent of the initiating Polish delegation to the UN. The interpretation of some its provisions, for example, as regards physical punishment of children (discussed further below), is sometimes proffered as an example of over-interpretation of a particular provision.

The question is whether the original intent of the authors of a provision is always determinative, or whether interpretation and application is legitimately subject to evolution. The principles of international law allow recourse to the *Traveaux Preparatoires*, or preliminary papers, of the drafting body to aid interpretation where the matter is unclear. Going further than that, the European Court of Human Rights has explicitly adopted a principle of 'evolutive interpretation' in its approach to the European Convention on Human Rights. Similar debates surround the interpretation of religious texts, where the intention of the author may be considered as one among a number of considerations to be taken into account in assessing its application for a different time and circumstance.[56] As regards the Convention on the Rights of the Child, each issue needs to be decided upon its merits and in line with those basic principles of the Convention which permeate all others. So, for example, if evidence comes to light that a particular course of action is likely to breach the child's right to have his or her best interests taken as a primary consideration (in accordance with Article 3), then that is relevant to the formulation of new interpretations of other provisions of the Convention.

6.3.5 Political Sensitivity, Religious Sensitivity and Cultural Relativism

Political sensitivity, religious sensitivity and cultural relativism can all be proposed as arguments for a 'softly, softly' approach to children's rights, just as they are for human rights generally. The Convention on the Rights of the Child is arguably in a stronger position than other international treaties to withstand such qualifiers, having been almost universally ratified. Such sensitivities may be relevant to the manner of, and timescale for, implementation, but cannot be proposed as a justification for undermining the rights themselves.

Many articles of the Convention seek to respect and safeguard the riches of a child's culture, but the Convention also sets fundamental principles and standards which must be respected even at the expense of custom. The need to override even very deep-rooted customs out of respect for the rights of the child is often recognised by the national and regional authorities of the areas in which the traditions exist. The African Charter on the Rights and Welfare of the Child, while recognizing in its preamble that 'the child occupies a unique and privileged position in the African society', also takes a firm stance in its opening paragraph about unhelpful cultural and other practices:

> 1.3 Any custom, tradition, cultural or religious practice that is inconsistent with the rights, duties and obligations contained in the present Charter shall to the extent of such inconsistency be discouraged.

Article 21 of the Charter states:

> 1. States Parties to the present Charter shall take all appropriate measures to eliminate harmful social and cultural practices affecting the welfare, dignity, normal growth and development of the child and in particular:
>   (a) those customs and practices prejudicial to the health or life of the child; and
>   (b) those customs and practices discriminatory to the child on the grounds of sex or other status.
> 2. Child marriage and the betrothal of girls and boys shall be prohibited and effective action, including legislation, shall be taken to specify the minimum age of marriage to be 18 years and make registration of all marriages in an official registry compulsory.

Given the criticism sometimes made that the Convention is largely a 'Western' or 'Northern' document,[57] it is important that developing nations feel they are heard in the deliberations of the UN Committee about what constitutes an appropriate interpretation. As recalled at 4.6.3 above, former colonial countries are understandably determined to resist the substitution of a cultural imperialism for a political one. It is humbling to reflect on some aspects of past Western arrogance in forcing a particular perspective on subject nations which most would now recognise as harmful.[58] However, neither should Western guilt be used to justify an uncritical approach to non-Western cultural practices where these are harmful to children. It is a difficult balance.

Religious sensitivities are important qualifiers, particularly where states have entered reservations to the Convention out of regard for religious beliefs. The task here is to analyse the customs and practices proposed as 'religious' in order to identify those aspects that are truly required by religious belief and those that have attracted a religious mask. This was the task the UN Committee on the Rights of the Child set for Islamic scholars in Saudi Arabia, but it is equally important for other faiths.[59]

6.3.6 Justified Discrimination

Resistance on the basis of 'justified discrimination' has been held back to the end of this list because this perhaps requires the most detailed exploration in relation to the rights of the child, and leads into the next section, addressing the question: how do children's rights differ from adult rights?

At 4.16.3 above, it was observed that the differences between human persons were sometimes used to justify excluding them from basic human rights. Lauren observes of international discussions between the two world wars:

> When dealing with issues of women or watching the evolution of the Declaration of the Rights of the Child, some delegates expressed dismay over the involvement of women in the first place, protested that children either had no rights at all or that if they did they had no place in the important discussions of an international organization, or that all matters of family relationships remained exclusively within the domestic jurisdiction of member nation-states.[60]

Thankfully, the 1947 UNESCO consultation concluded that: 'Democratic liberty is a liberty that does not distinguish by age or sex.'[61]

'Children are people too' is a common plea for recognition of the humanity and dignity of the child. Nevertheless, it cannot be denied that some discrimination *is* justified in the treatment of children and adults. It will be recalled that the Preamble to the Convention on the Rights of the Child refers back to the Universal Declaration's claim that 'childhood is entitled to special care and assistance' and that ' the child, by reason of his physical and mental immaturity, needs special safeguards and care, including appropriate legal protection, before as well as after birth'. This may be an argument for justifying *positive* discrimination in favour of children, of giving them additional rights or additional assistance in enforcing their rights, rather than a justification for opposing the concept of the rights of the child.

In assessing the scope of 'justified discrimination' in relation to children, it is important to bear in mind the long and varied scope of 'childhood', from pre-birth to 18 years of age. One might well argue that discrimination is more justified between an infant and an adolescent than between an adolescent and an adult.

The special character of children should therefore not be proposed in opposition to the concept of the rights of the child; it may be a legitimate consideration in relation to the identification and mode of implementation of the rights of the child, but account must also be taken of the varying capacities and needs of the whole range of humans falling within the definition of 'child'.

6.3.7 *Conclusion*

None of the listed objections can be upheld as a bar to children's rights. Some of the issues raised might legitimately be taken into account in the mode and pace of implementation of the Convention on the Rights of the Child, and the identification of thresholds for intervention in family life. The danger is that this legitimate need can be presented as an excuse for non-compliance rather than a spur to more effective compliance. This underlines the critical role of the UN Committee on the Rights of the Child in monitoring implementation of the Convention.

6.4 How do Children's Rights Differ from Adult Rights?

6.4.1 *How do Children Differ from Adults?*

In assessing the extent to which it is justified to differentiate between adult and child rights, one must first ask, what is different about children? Commentators give conflicting answers to that question. Goldstein, Solnit and Freud point to: the changing developmental needs and capacities of children; the tendency of young children to experience all events solely with reference to their own persons; and the predominance of the irrational part of children's minds – primitive wishes and impulses that lead to unhelpful reactions to threats to their emotional security.[62]

This view is contested by 'child libertarians', the proponents of an approach that emerged in the 1960s and 70s. Holt and Farson argued that the restriction of the rights of children represented an oppressive and unwarranted restriction of their freedom. Children were much more capable of rational decision-making and self-determination than most adults would be prepared to acknowledge. According to Fortin:

> Holt argued that children of any age should have, amongst other things, the right to vote, to work for money, to own and sell property, to travel, to be paid a guaranteed minimum state income, to direct their own education, to use drugs and to control their own private sexual lives. The fact that children might be too young to wish to exercise any of these rights was merely part of their freedom of choice; they could exercise them, when and if they chose, in precisely the same way as adults do.[63]

This approach was supported by the work of Philip Ariès and others which purported to show that childhood was a relatively recent Western, social invention, a theory which, some say, has been refuted by later research.[64]

The more extreme propositions of the child liberationists have been largely rejected. A negative consequence of this work has been a mistrust of the concept of 'children's rights' where these are perceived as the indiscriminate extension of 'adult' rights to children.[65] A positive consequence is that the debate catalysed by the liberationists generated a reassessment of the actual capacities of children. Thus Bainham, in 1988, proposed a balance between liberation and paternalism, acknowledging the actual capacities of children and young people, which had possibly been under rated, while drawing back from the kind of autonomy that might prejudice the maturation of the child towards meaningful independence.[66] The balance between 'now and future freedoms' will be further explored below in relation to children and education.

The debate has now centred upon a narrower spectrum of views, but a spectrum nevertheless in which professionals from a variety of backgrounds seek to identify the range of capacities one might expect of children at different developmental stages in relation to different situations.[67] The law has followed by identifying some broad parameters for childhood, sometimes hedged about with specific age limits, but emphasising the need to identify the actual capacity of particular children in relation to particular matters, an approach that is consistent with the perspective of the Convention on the Rights of the Child.

Much of the opposition, not just to liberationist theories but sometimes to the very concept of 'children's rights', resolves into a clarion call that children should 'be allowed to be children' and not forced prematurely into the world of adult responsibilities.[68] This neglects the fact that many of the rights of children set out in the Convention are about protection and support rather than participation or autonomy. The importance of articulating them as rights is that this stakes a claim for children, and allows a focus for calling to account those who have promised to acknowledge them, lest they be smothered by the priorities of more vocal, visible and influential groups. Moreover, as will be discussed further below (at section 6.5), it fails to acknowledge the importance of the participation right in securing protection of children and appropriate resources for their development.

6.4.2 *Thresholds for Rights*

The differentiation between child and adult rights is based on an assumption that at some stage this development becomes complete enough for the person to be identified as capable of assuming the whole range of human rights and responsibilities. We do not generally allow any detraction on the basis of low intelligence or psychological immaturity; nor do we lend greater weight to high intelligence, the wisdom of individuals, or the cumulative experience of old age. This constitutes a presumption in favour of real and equal human rights for adults. Given the diversity of childhood and of children, it is important that this positive presumption is not mirrored by a negative one that presumes that children under a certain age have no rights. The Convention on the Rights of the Child seeks to pre-empt any such presumption.

It is undeniable that the span of childhood covers massive and very visible developmental changes, physical, mental and behavioural, the result of natural maturation coloured and shaped by experience. However, the actual designation of childhood as a dependent status is more culturally, and sometimes arbitrarily, determined. Societies display a variety of approaches, with consequent differences in attribution of rights and responsibilities. For some, 'childhood' is largely a relational term; a person is always legally or morally a 'child' during the lifetime of his or her parents.[69] For others, it is a dependent status that can be brought to an end only through a specific initiation process or an event like marriage or parenthood.[70] Where age limits are identified as definitive, different ages have been regarded as appropriate. Thus, for example, Scottish law adopted the Roman Law division of children into infants (under 7), pupils (7 to puberty) and minors (puberty to whatever was the legal age of majority), with different capacities and rights attributed at each stage.[71] Clearly, perceptions of childhood affect perceptions of the rights of children and the character of their differentiation from adult rights.

The Convention on the Rights of the Child defines a child as anyone under the age of 18, with some concessions for countries where the age of majority is lower. It recognises no distinct sub-categories, but does acknowledge the need to set lower ages for some purposes in order to safeguard the rights of the child. States are required to set minimum ages: for employment, by Article 32; for criminal responsibility, by Article 40; and, implicitly, for compulsory primary education, by Article 28. The Reporting Guidelines issued by the Committee on the Rights of the Child also seek information from States on any legal minimum ages for: legal or medical counselling without parental consent; the end of compulsory education; part-time, full-time and hazardous employment; sexual consent, marriage, voluntary enlistment or conscription into the armed forces; criminal liability, choice of religion and attendance at religious school teaching, and other matters.[72] The Committee has consistently promoted high minimum ages for employment, criminal responsibility and sexual consent.[73]

Moreover, the Convention recognises the need for a gradualist approach to the exercise of particular rights by children, and their need for guidance by responsible adults, with a presumption that parents will fulfil this role. This is most explicit in Article 5, which says:

States Parties shall respect the responsibilities, rights and duties of parents or, where applicable, the members of the extended family or community as provided for by local custom, legal guardians or other persons responsible for the child, to provide, in a manner consistent with the evolving capacities of the child, appropriate direction and guidance in the exercise by the child of the rights recognised in the present Convention.

In its dialogue with States, the UN Committee on the Rights of the Child has repeatedly emphasised that Article 5 must not be used to undermine the rights of the child. Parents have an important role to play, and the character of their support to the child will vary according to the child's age, maturity and 'evolving capacities'. However, it is not open to parents to use this provision to direct that the child's rights shall not be respected.[74] Reference to the growing maturity of the child is also found within the texts of articles 12.1 (concerning the weight to be given to the child's views), 14.2 (freedom of thought, conscience and religion), 31.1 (the right to engage in play and recreational activities appropriate to the age of the child), 32 (the right to protection from economic exploitation or work that is hazardous or harmful to the child's development), 37(c) (conditions of detention) and 40 (administration of juvenile justice).

6.4.3 Content of Rights

A number of conclusions might follow from identification of characteristics specific to childhood. One might argue that:

1. children do not therefore have some of the rights held by adults;
2. they have the same rights, but they may require assistance in enforcing them; or
3. they have the same rights, plus additional rights arising out of their special circumstances.

The following paragraphs explore the extent to which each of these perspectives is reflected in the 1948 Universal Declaration of Human Rights and the 1989 Convention on the Rights of the Child.

The Universal Declaration of Human Rights makes little special reference to children. The articles on: equal dignity; protection from torture, inhuman or degrading treatment; from slavery; from arbitrary detention; to a fair hearing when charged with an offence; to privacy of family life; to reputation, etc., can reasonably be understood as applying equally to children (although one might question the extent to which equal dignity and reputation, for example, are truly reflected in practice). Some discrimination is evident where childhood is referred to as a status requiring 'special care and assistance' (acknowledging point 2 above) and where the right to marry and found a family is restricted to 'men and women of full age', a right intrinsically related to human development (apparently supporting point 1 above).[75] There are no age or maturity restrictions upon other 'freedoms': of movement; of thought, conscience and religion; of opinion and expression; of peaceful assembly and association; of participation in government; of the right to work. Some restrictions might be justified, both for children and adults, with reference to Article 29.2:

> In the exercise of his rights and freedoms, everyone shall be subject only to such limitations as are determined by law solely for the purpose of securing due recognition and respect for the rights and freedoms of others and of meeting the just requirements of morality, public order and the general welfare in a democratic society.

The presumption is in favour of the extension of such rights to humans of all ages.

The Convention on the Rights of the Child does not derogate from any of the rights set out in the Universal Declaration. It restates many of them, with greater specificity in relation to the balance between the freedom of children and the responsibility of parents or other legitimate authorities to provide direction and guidance to the child. Direction will be appropriate for young children, as regards their safety and education, for example, with guidance being more appropriate for those at the upper end of the age scale as regards most matters. The Convention too asserts the rights of the child to 'freedoms' of expression, of thought, conscience and religion, and of association. There are carefully worded qualifications to all such 'freedoms'. All are also subject to the guidance of parents referred to in Article 5; but the rights are real, and restrictions have to be justified.

There are also new rights specifically addressed to children (supporting point 3 above): to have their best interests taken as a 'primary consideration' in all actions concerning them; to protection from abuse and neglect; to live with their families and to be protected when they are without families. The Convention does not derogate from the child's right to work, but requires the identification of a minimum age for employment (Article 32) and gives an additional right to protection from work that is hazardous or exploitative or is likely to affect the child's development adversely. The child is to be protected also from other forms of exploitation, including sexual exploitation.

To sum up, point 1 applies in respect that children are specifically excluded from the right to marry and found a family. The Universal Declaration explicitly supports point 2, about special care and assistance for children. This concept is threaded throughout the Convention on the Rights of the Child, with parents identified as the primary providers of that assistance. Point 3 is also true in respect that the additional rights of children, to protection and development, lead to many situations requiring a balancing act, where the different rights accruing to children are put on the scale, and adjusted by weights representing the primacy of the child's interests (Article 3) and the child's opinion (assessed in conformity with Article 12), as also the right and responsibility of parents to direct or guide the child, weighted in accordance with the child's 'evolving capacities'. The purpose of the exercise is not to determine whether the child actually possesses the right in question – clearly he or she does – but to resolve any disputes about its exercise in any particular situation by any particular child.

6.5 How are 'Rights' Important to the Lives of Children?

This book has several times made the point that being a possessor of rights is important because it facilitates pursuit of acknowledged claims in a way not open to those who are merely the intended beneficiaries of duties or objects of the exercise of virtue. Children may well need assistance to pursue those claims. In most cases, their advocates will be their parents, who are recognised by most systems of law, whether secular or religious, as the presumptive guardians of their children's interests.

Where parents fail, a state that acknowledges the rights of the child must provide mechanisms for others to identify and pursue the child's claims insofar as the child is unable to do so him or herself, or prefers to have such assistance.

Section 2.2 above noted the practice of identifying within the Convention on the Rights of the Child three categories of rights, commonly referred to as the three Ps: provision, protection and participation. This section of the book demonstrates the importance of rights for the lives of children by exploring the relationship of these different classes of rights, both in general, and with reference to case examples.[76]

Franklin observed that: 'Children's claims to protection rights have rarely been contested. Their claims for liberty rights invariably are.'[77]

Similarly, few would oppose the claims of children to the provision of services to promote their survival and development. The three Ps are, however, interrelated and cannot be separated. It may be helpful to analyse their relationships as three 'pairs':

provision–protection;

provision–participation; and

protection–participation.

6.5.1 Provision–Protection

Children need the *provision* of assistance to promote their survival, development and *protection*. Article 18 of the Convention on the Rights of the Child sets out the basic principle that responsibility for the upbringing and development of the child lies primarily with the parents. Where parents cannot perform this function, this article obliges the State to support parents by rendering assistance to them and providing institutions, facilities and services for the care of children. Article 19 focuses more specifically on the protection of children from abuse and neglect by their parents or other carers, and obliges the State to provide support for the child and his or her carers, as well as services aimed at prevention of abuse and neglect, identification, reporting, referral, investigation, treatment and follow-up.

Scenario A

Margaret, a single mother, is encouraged to seek employment to support her children. She finds a job as a cleaner, requiring her to leave home in the morning before her children, Eddie, aged 7, and Sarah, aged 9, leave for school. A neighbour tells social services that the children are left unattended and therefore 'at risk'. The authorities are sensitive about unattended children because a local child died recently as a result of a house fire caused by her attempt to make toast while her parents were out of the house. They interview Margaret who explains that: she has no support from relatives or neighbours; she cannot afford child care services; and she feels her children are well trained and responsible, and safer at home for that hour than if she put them out early to hang around the streets or the school playground.

In this situation, Margaret needs to be provided either with financial support to remain at home with her children, or services or assistance to help her protect Eddie and Sarah.

Scenario B

Jennifer is 13 and has been placed in public care because she is beyond parental control. While at home, she had been staying out all night without permission and seemed to be involved in indiscriminate sexual activity. She is removed from home and placed in a residential facility which also houses three unruly and sexually active teenage boys. Staff at the residential unit say they cannot guarantee protection for Jennifer, but there are no other residential places available.

In this situation, the provision of an inappropriate service, masked by the term 'care,' may be exposing Jennifer to more risk than remaining at home. Her protection requires the provision of appropriate services and support.

6.5.2 Provision–Participation

Scenario B, above, also demonstrates the link between *provision and participation*. As children grow older, it becomes more difficult for any authority, parental or state, to impose its will upon them. If Jennifer's cooperation is not secured, the only 'safe' option will be to lock her up, which may be a disproportionate reaction causing more long-term harm than trying to manage the risk of keeping her at home. It may be more effective to engage Jennifer's cooperation through her participation in the process of assessing options for support and service provision.

Scenario C

A local authority decides to invest in a well-equipped youth centre for a deprived part of the city. They consult a local committee of adults and identify a site. After a time, it becomes clear that the resource is not being used by the target group of young people. A youth worker is deputed to find out the reason. It emerges that, while it is located at the centre of the adult-defined 'community', the resource is at the border of the 'gang areas' identified by young people. Most of the target group live on the other side of the boundary from the youth centre and will not cross the line to use it. Had the local authority consulted young people beforehand, they might have targeted their efforts more appropriately. Participation of young people would have resulted in provision of a resource that might actually have been used.

6.5.3 Protection–Participation

The right to *participation* is also important in securing the *protection* of children and young people.

Scenario D

In response to recent tragedies in schools, a secondary school tightens its security systems for controlling entry and making the school a safer environment for pupils.

Subsequent consultation with pupils discloses their perspective on 'feeling safe'. They are able to identify areas both within the school grounds and on the routes to and from their homes where they feel unsafe because of the activities of bullies, or environmental conditions such as bad lighting, unsafe pathways, or overcrowded and inadequately supervised transport.

In this case, listening to the pupils helps identify what they need to promote their protection.

Scenario E

Mary is 11 years old. Her grandfather, a prominent lawyer, has been sexually abusing her since she was 8. He warns her that, if she tries to tell anyone, she will not be believed and will be put in a home. Mary is aware from watching the television news that many adults think children make up stories about abuse, and that the children are called 'liars' when the court does not believe them.

This is a classic case study. Many children do not tell about abuse, in families or institutions, because of an often justified fear of not being believed. Inquiries into the abuse of children in many circumstances, including residential institutions, have concluded that children do not tell of their fears or experiences when they are in an environment that does not listen to them.[78] It is important to note that the general responsive character of the environment is important, not just the institution's explicit strategy for responding to allegations of abuse. Thus, for example, a primary school that used the principles of the Convention on the Rights of the Child as a basis for involving children in planning school activities by seeking their views and valuing their opinions discovered that, even apart from the advantages to the ethos and achievements of the school, this resulted in a greater willingness of children to tell someone in the school about abuse at home or other concerns for their own safety.[79] Thus, the general 'participatory' ethos of the school promoted and facilitated the protection of the children attending it.

There is also an important link between more general child welfare issues, not involving 'abuse,' and the right of the child to contribute to decisions. Many legal systems now identify the 'best interests of the child' as the criterion for decision-making about children's issues. This approach begs the question: how can anyone claim to be acting in the interests of a child or young person, if that child or

young person has views on the matter under consideration and the adult involved does not know what they are?
Ascertainment of the views of a child, if the child wishes
to express them, is an essential part of identifying where
the child's interests lie.

The qualification, 'if the child wishes to express them',
emphasises the fact that participation is a 'right' of the
child rather than a duty. Research on children affected
by divorce has shown that, while children often want to
influence decisions,[80] they frequently make it clear that
they do not wish to be given the actual responsibility for
making painful choices, and wish to be protected from
that burden.[81] Those children in the research who insisted
on their right actually to make the decision were those
who were frightened of, or had a strong dislike for, one
parent.[82] This indicates that the law needs to take great
care about how this right of participation is translated
into practice, particularly in sensitive areas such as family
break-up. Children and young people will often have a
perspective which they wish to contribute, sometimes
forcefully; but the processes for involving them must not
be such as to impose on them the responsibility for the
actual decisions; their right in terms of the Convention is
to participate and influence in accordance with age and
maturity, not to control.[83] Having said that, Scenario F
(below) shows circumstances in which it makes sense for
the views of a mature young person to be decisive, even
where others think his decision is not conducive to his
best interests.

Scenario F
Kevin is 14 and has lived with his father since his parents'
separation a year previously. He says he does not wish to
see his mother ever again. At the court hearing, the mother's
request for contact is nevertheless granted, a psychologist
having advised that this would be in Kevin's long-term
interest. Each Saturday, Kevin's father drives him to the

block of flats where his mother lives and deposits him at the front door of her fifteenth-floor apartment. By the time his father has returned to his car, Kevin is waiting for him, having run down the fire escape.

In legal terms, it would be possible for officers of the court to be authorised to manhandle Kevin to ensure that the order for contact is enforced. This is unlikely to be successful in the long term or to improve Kevin's relationship with his mother. It makes more sense for the court to go along with Kevin's wishes and make no order for contact but, if appropriate, to pave the way for access to supportive services that may help Kevin work through this difficult period and possibly move towards a reconciliation with his mother.

6.5.4 Conclusion

These scenarios show some of the ways in which the three Ps interrelate in children's lives. The importance of identifying them as rights rather than just good practice is that it makes it less likely that the needs and voices of children and young people will be drowned by adults eagerly proclaiming their own rights, or rushing to meet timescales or budgets for which they will be called to account by other adults. Rights give children a stake in our society. The content of these rights is significant for the actual lives of children and for the well-being of society in general.

The rest of this chapter explores some specific aspects of children's lives where religious considerations meet the human rights of children. These are:

freedom of thought, conscience and religion, and the implications for education;

freedom of association;

protection of privacy;

physical punishment; and

obedience.

6.6 Freedom of Thought, Conscience and Religion, and the Implications for Education

In Western society today, we take it for granted that each individual is entitled to freedom of thought, conscience and religion. We may find it difficult to accept, or even understand, the approach of those Islamic states that refuse to recognise the right of Muslims to change their religion. [84] The question becomes more complex when the subject of the right is a 'child', a status extending from nought to eighteen years. The texts of the Universal Declaration and subsequent documents reflect the tension between recognition of the human rights and freedoms of the child, and the potential for manipulation of such 'freedom' by regimes intent on indoctrinating children with their own philosophy against the wishes of their parents.

The right to freedom of thought, conscience and religion is intimately related to the question of education. The rights of parents to direct the education of the child can protect the child against manipulation for political or religious purposes. At the same time, as discussed at 6.2.4.3 above, the rights of the child must also be protected by the imposition of some limits on parental power.

From the point of view of the rights of the child, the question arises: if education aims to equip a child with the knowledge, skills and values to make decisions, at what point does the child become sufficiently equipped to make decisions about that education itself? At what point can the child's judgement be regarded as informed enough to reject the value content of its education as being in conflict with his or her conscience and religion? At what point is the child insightful enough to reject the religious or ethical formation and direction provided by her or his parents?

Of the states which were the subject of case studies in Chapter 2 above, the Holy See entered reservations to Article 14 (freedom of religion) and Article 28 (education), insofar as they might be interpreted as diminishing the 'primary and inalienable rights of parents'. Poland 'declared' that the right under Article 14 was to be 'exercised with respect for parental authority'. These matters might also fall within the embrace of the general reservation made by Saudi Arabia, although they are not specified.

The following paragraphs explore what the international community has to say about the overlapping and interweaving rights: of parents and children to freedom of thought, conscience and religion; of parents to direct the education of their children; of children to be educated and have their best interests taken account of; and of the State to act as arbiter. This takes account, not just of the Universal Declaration of Human Rights and the Convention on the Rights of the Child, but also other documents of international law.

When the 1948 Universal Declaration proclaimed freedom of thought, conscience and religion for all, along with the 'prior right of parents to choose the kind of education that shall be given to their children', it introduced the tension between the rights of parents and children that remains to this day. The following list of statements is based upon those set out in a number of international documents. The relevant sources can be found by consulting Appendix 2.

> Children have a right to spiritual development.
>
> Every child has a right to freedom of thought, conscience and religion. No child should be coerced in matters of religion or belief.
>
> Parents have both a right and duty to direct the child in the exercise of their right to freedom of thought, conscience and religion, in a manner consistent with the evolving capacities of the child. They should take account of the views of their children.
>
> Practices of religion or belief in which a child is brought up must not be injurious to the physical or mental health or full development of the child.
>
> The religious, moral or philosophical character of a child's education should be determined primarily by the parents,

but guided by the child's best interests. Parents and educators should take account of the views of children.

Parents have the right to organise their family life in accordance with their religion and belief. They should take account of the views of their children.

The religious character of any alternative care (including adoption) should take due account of any expressed wishes of the parents, and the need for continuity in the life of a child. The best interests of the child should be 'the guiding principle' and 'a primary consideration'. In adoption it should be the 'paramount consideration'.

Account should also be taken of the views of the child.

There is potential for tension between the child's right to freedom of thought, conscience and religion, and the right of parents to arrange for their education and to organise family life in accordance with their own religious and philosophical convictions. The Guidelines for Reporting issued by the UN Committee on the Rights of the Child ask governments in general about the legal protection of children's civil rights and, in particular, about 'measures to ensure respect for the child's rights in relation to any religious teaching in public schools or institutions'. However, there has been little information or discussion on this subject. Hodgkin and Newell note that, 'The Committee has as yet made little comment on the effective implementation of article 14'.[85] This may be because it is an issue that is hidden due to ignorance or inability to pursue a claim, or because it is one that causes fewer problems in practice than in theory. It may be that parents and children manage to negotiate such issues or to respond on the basis of an acknowledgement of practical considerations. It is difficult to force a young person physically to attend religious services or participate meaningfully in religious education if he or she is disinclined to do so. It may also be difficult for a young person to practise an alternative religion of his or her choice without the cooperation of parents.[86]

The kind of practical problem that can arise is shown by an example set out in the Initial Report of Belgium to the Committee on the Rights of the Child:

> A balance of rights and duties in the family cell is vital in order to ensure the stability that is essential for the harmonious development of the young person. However, what is to be done by a school principal who is told by a child that he wants to attend the course in Catholic religion while his parents say that he is to follow the course of non-denominational ethics? There are nowadays signs of a willingness, in some isolated decisions, to authorize minors to act of their own accord when their request relates to a personal right and they are sufficiently old to be assumed capable of judgement.[87]

Application of the principles of the Convention on the Rights of the Child would require that the young person's freedom be respected, subject to the parents' right and duty to provide direction to the child, in a manner consistent with the child's evolving capacity. The 'direction' appropriate for a four year old who expresses a desire to attend a religious meeting after hearing a brass band in the street and being given a lollipop will be quite different from that appropriate for a fourteen year old who is seriously exploring issues of faith. Given the natural prejudice in favour of one's own beliefs when so much is at stake, it may be helpful to consider one's response to the Belgian scenario with the child's preferences reversed, or other belief systems substituted.

The position of the Roman Catholic Church on conscience is set out in the Second Vatican Council's *Constitution on the Church in the Modern World*, para. 16 of which upholds the 'dignity of moral conscience', which a person is bound to obey. It makes reference to a 1952 radio message of Pope Pius XII on rightly forming the Christian conscience of youth, in which parents are reminded of their duty to respect the consciences of their children. More specifically, Pope John Paul II's 1979 Apostolic Exhortation *Catechesi Tradendae*:

On Catechesis in Our Time, addressed a scenario similar to that described by the Belgian report:

> My thoughts turn next to the ever increasing number of children and young people born and brought up in a non-Christian or at least non-practising home but who wish to know the Christian faith. They must be ensured a catechesis attuned to them, so that they will be able to grow in faith and live by it more and more, in spite of the lack of support or even the opposition they meet in their surroundings.[88]

This argues in favour of allowing a sincere young person to choose his or her religious education where that tends towards Christianity. The same document also supports the rights of children in Catholic establishments to follow their consciences while, at the same time, insisting upon the right and duty of Catholic schools to proclaim the gospel:

> While Catholic establishments should respect freedom of conscience, that is to say, avoid burdening consciences from without by exerting physical or moral pressure, especially in the case of the religious activity of adolescents, they still have a grave duty to offer a religious training suited to the often widely varying situations of the pupils.[89]

The Holy See's Reservation to Article 14 of the Convention should be placed in the context of this broader understanding.

Those holding deep religious beliefs sincerely believe that what they want to pass on is the best, or even the only, road to salvation, the route to eternal life, possibly the avoidance of a terrible eternal fate, and the real fulfilment of human destiny. This can result in an unbalanced approach to the rights of the child; one might respect the child's right to adopt one's own religion, on the basis that the child should not be denied what is true and good, while rejecting or resisting the child's choice of a religion other than one's own, where that is regarded as the road to ruin or shame. Where the power of the State is allied to a particular belief (religious or not), decisions can be made which later generations might regard as completely unjust. Thus, in 1665, the Scotch Privy Council, in exercise of its power to supervise the morals and education of the community, removed the children of Scott of Raeburn and his wife, on the grounds that the parents were 'infected with the error of Quakerism'. In the same year they also removed the young Marquis of Huntly from the care of his mother and guardians:

> they being popishly inclined; and ordanes him to be educat in the family of the Lord Archbishop of St Andrews (Sharp), to whose tender care they recommend him, and that no person popishly inclined have liberty to serve or attend him.[90]

It is difficult here to extricate the elements of social control for political reasons from those of a genuine religious concern for the child's fate. More explicitly political is the policy of atheist states where this inculcates secular values and attempts to alienate children from religion. Much of the resistance to the United Nations of the particular groups referred to earlier is based upon the suspicion that it is seeking to control the education and upbringing of children on the basis of secular humanist values. And indeed, Article 29 does espouse explicit values in its identification of the aims of education. It says:

Article 29

1. States Parties agree that the education of the child shall be directed to:

   a) The development of the child's personality, talents and mental and physical abilities to their fullest potential;

   b) The development of respect for human rights and fundamental freedoms, and for the principles enshrined in the Charter of the United Nations;

   c) The development of respect for the child's parents, his or her own cultural identity, language and values, for the national values of the country in which the child is living, the country from which he or she may originate, and for civilisations different from his or her own;

d) The preparation of the child for responsible life in a free society, in the spirit of understanding, peace, tolerance, equality of sexes, and friendship among all peoples, ethnic, national and religious groups and persons of indigenous origin;

e) The development of respect for the natural environment.

2. No part of the present article or article 28 shall be construed so as to interfere with the liberty of individuals and bodies to establish and direct educational institutions, subject always to the observance of the principles set forth in paragraph 1 of the present article and to the requirements that the education given in such institutions shall conform to such minimum standards as may be laid down by the State.

Reservations or declarations to Article 29 were submitted by only three countries (Indonesia, Thailand and Turkey) and were in very general terms, referring to a preference for their own constitutions or existing practices. This virtually universal support is encouraging, if somewhat surprising given the potential impact on the child of the values imparted through education. This impact was recognised as far back as the fourth century BCE by Plato, whose *Laws* recommended state regulation of both the education and games of children. Freedom to change games, he said, would lead them to believe that, when they were grown up, they could alter the immutable laws.[91]

The world today can never be subject to the kind of strict environmental control envisaged by Plato. Nor do we generally subscribe to the same static vision of the universe. We are more aware of the radical changes that have taken place throughout human history and even prehistory, and of the need to prepare our children for life in a multicultural, highly diverse and ever-changing society, coloured by a kaleidoscope of conflicting value systems presented to them with the enthusiasm of the professional publicist. In such a context children need to learn the art of discrimination and the skill of choice. This does not mean that such education is, or can be, value free. Some proponents of a secular society argue that religious indoctrination by parents or their agents can be as detrimental to a child, and as restrictive of freedom of thought, as indoctrination by the State. This assumes that it is possible to educate a child in a purely rational way, and also that this is something that should be desired; or that it is possible to discriminate at least between 'harmful and restrictive' and unharmful and non-restrictive religious education, a value-decision in itself.

This notion of 'freedom of thought' draws attention to the variant understandings of the meaning of 'freedom'. Where secular individualism has traditionally focused on 'freedom from' restraint, religious adherents have tended to promote 'freedom for' fulfilment of one's supernatural destiny. This might involve forming the child's character through the cultivation of 'virtue' that will orient him towards human fulfilment and engender respect for the similar freedom of others. Article 29, which sets out some goals of human development, is arguably closer to the religious than the secular understanding. Questions then arise about the extent to which the aims of Article 29 are reconcilable with those of the religious faiths, and the extent to which there is any merit in the allegation that the UN is poised to supplant religion with secular humanism.

The fact that Article 29 has been almost universally accepted does not mean that religious bodies must jettison their own conceptual frameworks in favour of the Convention. One might recall here the concluding comments (at section 2.5 above) of the authors of this book with regard to the dialogue between Saudi Arabia and the Committee on the Rights of the Child concerning the former's adherence to the Koran as its primary conceptual framework, accompanied by their acknowledgement that the Convention was consistent with it. Similarly, in a resource relating to the rights of the child in education, the headmaster of a Roman Catholic Secondary School observed that the ethos of the school was shaped by Christian values of love and tolerance, but that the Convention on the Rights of the Child provided a useful resource to back that up.[92] The value of Article 29 is that it provides a common language for dialogue about what is or is not acceptable. The primary value and belief frameworks remain, but their translation into the terms of Article 29 facilitates self-scrutiny, dialogue and external critique.

6.7 Freedom of Association

Article 15 of the Convention on the Rights of the Child acknowledges the child's right to freedom of association and peaceful assembly. Article 16 (discussed below) reflects the right of the child to privacy. As indicated at 2.3 above, some states entered reservations to these articles out of concern for their impact on parental authority. And indeed, baldly stated in their application to children under 18, one might well question the extent to which these rights are consistent with children's right to protection from themselves as well as from predatory others.

Hodgkin and Newell note that the Convention on the Rights of the Child is here merely rearticulating rights children already have by virtue of their humanity under a number of other international instruments.

The Convention places only limited restrictions on the right to association, related to public safety, public order, the protection of public health or morals or the protection of the rights and freedoms of others. Like all rights of children, it is subject to the appropriate direction and guidance of parents, taking account of the evolving capacities of the child (Article 5). Direction might be appropriate for a five year old wishing to stay out playing with friends after dark; whereas guidance would be appropriate for a fourteen year old wishing to join an association. Naturally, there are many 'grey areas' in between which could be the subject of extended debate, for which the Convention helpfully provides a framework. A balance must also be struck between this article and those protecting children from various forms of exploitation; for example, articles 32 (child labour), 33 (drug abuse), 34 (sexual exploitation) and 36 (a catch-all relating to 'other' forms of exploitation). Scottish law, which was revised to take account of the Convention, lists a number of 'danger thresholds' justifying a consideration of whether compulsory measures of supervision are necessary in relation to a child. These include the receipt of information suggesting that a child 'is beyond the control of any relevant person' (normally a parent) or 'is falling into bad associations or is exposed to moral danger'.[93] These provisions are open to subjective interpretations that might breach children's rights under the Convention, but might also be used appropriately to protect immature children from the consequences of their bad judgement or all children from exploitation. One might argue that the Convention challenges would be to particular applications of the provisions rather than to the provisions themselves. On the other hand, it is more difficult to reconcile the Convention with the action of some local authorities in Scotland in imposing blanket curfews on children being out in public after certain hours.[94]

In their consideration of States Parties' reports, the UN Committee on the Rights of the Child has focused on student organisations in schools and children's organisations in their local area. One might well argue that promotion of proactive involvement on the part of children, even apart from its status as a fundamental human right, is a valuable part of the currently popular push for 'citizenship education'.

6.8 Protection of Privacy

Article 16 protects the child from 'arbitrary or unlawful interference with his or her privacy, family, home or correspondence'. 'Privacy' embraces confidentiality, but is wider than it. It should include protection from media intrusion as well as the right to privacy within residential institutions where the child is living. It requires that any monitoring or interception of the child's mail or other communications be in accordance with the law and not 'arbitrary'. This means that, while there might be justification in some cases, the scope of legitimate interference should be set out in law and be consistent with other articles of the Convention.

Many of the contentious issues focus on confidentiality. The Working Group drafting this article was careful to note the balance with Article 5, the parental right of appropriate direction and guidance.[95] This would apply, for example, to matters relating to medical confidentiality. The UN Committee asked Sweden to reconsider a provision allowing children to seek legal and medical consent from the age of 7 without parental consent.[96] It seems clear that the Committee thought this too young an age for such a blanket freedom. The situation might be quite different as regards, for example, a sixteen year old, or even a fourteen year old, seeking contraceptive or other medical advice. Discussion of the latter scenario within a religious context is complicated where there is religious opposition to contraception as such, and the issues of the rights of the young person are difficult to extricate from the contentious subject matter.

The child's right to privacy can be important where, for example, children seek advice on a subject that they are not yet ready to share with their parents. Confidential child counselling systems such as ChildLine in the UK are tremendously popular with children precisely because confidentiality is (practically) guaranteed. The alternative is generally that children will not seek help and their problems will remain, or possibly get worse. Having said that, within the secular field, no confidentiality is ever absolute;[97] there are always qualifications based upon significant risk to persons, especially vulnerable persons. This applies to adults as well as to children; for example, where a doctor knows that an adult who proposes to drive will be a danger to others, he or she is entitled to breach confidentiality by notifying the appropriate authorities.[98]

The value of the article on privacy is that it acknowledges the child's human dignity as the starting point, while leaving room for appropriate and justified interference.

6.9 Physical Punishment

The most public debate about Christian approaches to the rights of the child focuses on the legitimacy of physical punishment. Physical punishment represents a mode of disciplining children advocated by some on a pragmatic basis and by others on a religious basis. As indicated at 6.3.4 above, this is an area in which some accuse the Committee on the Rights of the Child of moving beyond the original intent of the Convention by its explicit opposition to physical punishment. The Committee's approach is based upon Article 19, which says:

1. States Parties shall take all appropriate legislative, administrative, social and educational measures to protect the child from all forms of physical or mental violence, injury or abuse, neglect or negligent treatment, maltreatment or exploitation, including sexual abuse, while in the care of parent(s), legal guardian(s) or any other person who has the care of the child.

2. Such protective measures should, as appropriate, include effective procedures for the establishment of social programmes to provide necessary support for the child and for those who have the care of the child, as well as for other forms of prevention and for identification, reporting, referral, investigation, treatment and follow-up of instances of child maltreatment described heretofore, and, as appropriate, for judicial involvement.

As indicated at 2.2.3 above, all articles of the Convention must be considered within the broader context of the basic principles that permeate it. These include Article 6, which proclaims the child's inherent right to life and the State's duty to ensure 'to the maximum extent possible the survival and development of the child', and Article 3, which identifies the child's 'best interests' as the primary consideration where any matter is being decided about a child. These principles legitimise an evolving understanding of the implications of Article 19 in line with developing understanding and experience. There is much research today about the ineffective and often harmful effects of physical punishment on children.[99] However, there is also a question of basic rights, turning on the human dignity of children and the legitimacy of allowing adults to perpetrate upon them violent measures that would not be allowed in relation to another adult. In 2001, the UN Committee on the Rights of the Child made the following recommendation arising out of a General Discussion on 'Violence against children, within the family and in schools':

> The Committee urges State Parties, as a matter of urgency, to enact or repeal their legislation in order to prohibit all forms of violence, however light, within the family and in schools, including as a form of discipline, as required by the provisions of the Convention and in particular articles 19, 28 and 37(a) and taking into account article 2, 3, 6 and 12 as well as 4, 5, 9, 18, 24, 27, 29 and 39.[100]

The Committee favours both legislative and educational matters to change attitudes and practice, stressing that the purpose is educational rather than punitive. It has criticised those states (including the United Kingdom) whose law attempts to distinguish between the physical correction of children and excessive violence through the concept of 'reasonable chastisement'. A member of the Committee commented:

> In reality the dividing line between the two is artificial. It is very easy to pass from one stage to the other. It is also a question of principle. If it is not permissible to beat an adult, why should it be permissible to beat a child? One of

the contributions of the Convention is to call attention to
the contradictions in our attitudes and cultures.[101]

It is important to note that the concept of discipline is broader
than that of punishment. The many child welfare organisations that advocate the banning of physical punishment and
other forms of humiliating treatment of children nevertheless
support discipline in the form of 'positive parenting'.[102]

Historically, it has often been regarded as permissible
for those in authority to administer physical punishment
to persons subject to them. In the past, this has extended
to servants, seamen and wives, practices now thankfully
forbidden in many countries.[103] A growing number of
countries has prohibited physical punishment of children,
thus extending to them the same rights as adults to freedom
from assault.[104] It is still, however, legally permissible to
administer physical punishment to children in the UK,
provided it is 'reasonable', an elastic concept open to much
subjective interpretation.

Physical punishment is often mentioned in the Bible and
cited in support of the continuing physical punishment of
children. However, while in Matthew 18:34, the torture of
an unforgiving servant is referred to without any adverse
comment, and even as an example of how God will treat
those who fail to forgive others, this has not prevented legal
reform protecting adults from such pain and degradation. As
regards children, the religious problem lies in the fact that
the Christian Scriptures appear not only to tolerate physical
chastisement but to demand it. Chapter 7 below includes
a theological critique of some of the passages most often
cited in support of physical punishment. At this point we
will merely note that the Gospels are silent on the question
of physical chastisement of children who, by all accounts,
Jesus treated kindly.[105]

As indicated at 2.5.2 above, the Holy See's delegate to
the UN Committee on the Rights of the Child identified no
specific religious doctrine on physical punishment:

Corporal punishment ... was a matter of considerable controversy ... [H]is comments did not constitute the set doctrine of the Holy See. In his view, corporal punishment should not be banned until such time as psychoanalysts, sociologists, jurists, doctors and educators agreed.[106]

This ambivalence can only be justified by a definition of 'violence' that excludes the physical punishment of children. The Roman Catholic Church has often spoken out against violence. For example, in 1975, Pope Paul VI's exhortation on *Evangelisation in the Modern World* stated:

The church cannot accept any form of violence, and especially of armed violence – for this cannot be restrained when once it is unleashed – nor the death of any man as a method of liberation. She knows that violence always provokes violence and inevitably gives rise to new forms of oppression, new forms of servitude even more grievous than those from which men were supposed to be emancipated.[107]

The text addresses *in particular* the question of armed violence, but the commitment to non-violence is expressed in a more general way. Turning towards the specific situation of the family, it is difficult to reconcile approval of physical punishment with the message delivered by Pope John Paul II for the World Day of Peace, 1 January 1996:

Let us give children a future of peace! This is the confident appeal which I make to men and women of good will, and I invite everyone to help children grow up in an environment of authentic peace. This is their right, and it is our duty ...

Little children very soon learn about life. They watch and imitate the behaviour of adults. They rapidly learn love and respect for others, but they also quickly absorb the poison of violence and hatred. Family experiences strongly condition the attitudes which children will assume as adults. Consequently, if the family is the place where children first encounter the world, *the family must be for children the first school of peace* ...

Let us show them examples of peace and not just examples of violence![108]

Further, it is difficult to reconcile toleration of physical punishment with the need to give clear guidance to children about their rights to protection. Thus the *Independent Review on Child Protection in the Catholic Church in England and Wales* (known as the Nolan Report) acknowledges the importance of 'Raising children's own awareness of appropriate and inappropriate behaviour', and commends as an example of good practice a diocesan Declaration of Children's Rights which includes the statement: 'God gives you the right not to be hurt in your body by grown-ups.'[109]

The World Council of Churches has also taken a strong stance on non-violence, having initiated a Decade to Overcome Violence (2001–10).[110]

Within Scotland, a public consultation in 1992 on proposals to restrict the scope of legitimate physical punishment by parents produced some religious comment. A number of reformed churches and individuals supported the retention of physical punishment on the basis that it was validated by Scripture. There was no contribution to the debate at that time from either the Church of Scotland (the mainstream Protestant church) or the Roman Catholic Church.[111]

A further consultation in 2000 attracted a wider range of religious responses. The mainstream Protestant churches were generally not in favour of physical punishment as a method of child-rearing, but expressed concern about the impact on family life of bringing minor parental assaults upon children within the scope of the criminal law. The Catholic Bishops Conference supported retention of a limited right of physical chastisement, basing its stance upon concern about State intrusion into family life.[112]

The issue is an evolving one, with indications of further developments in the ongoing reflection encouraged, for example, by the Churches Network for Non-violence, an ecumenical body in the UK, aiming to:

> promote respect for children in churches and the wider community;

promote positive non-violent discipline;

inform, resource and support Christians working towards legal reform to end physical punishment;

find ways to effectively challenge the view that corporal punishment is a biblical doctrine; and

make wider connections with individuals and organisations for the benefit of children. [113]

What is significant is that, for mainstream Christianity, the debate has moved on from a simple reliance upon scriptural texts considered in isolation. There are Christians who argue forcefully *against* physical punishment on the basis of a thoughtful and comprehensive consideration of Christian Scripture, centred on a fuller understanding of the Old Testament and a focus on the attitudes of Jesus in the New Testament.[114] It would be overstating the case to claim that mainstream Christian opinion currently regards physical chastisement as inherently unchristian; what is clear is that the view that physical chastisement is a Christian *duty* is becoming restricted to a vociferous few.

Further, the legitimacy of physical punishment as a means of discipline is being increasingly challenged within mainstream churches. Where those churches resist legal reform to give children the same protection from assault as adults, this is based upon a fear that, given how widespread the practice is, such reform would bring many ordinary parents within the ambit of the criminal law and would increase the potential for State interference in family life. However, as the literature on physical punishment shows, such reforms have already taken place in many countries and have *not* resulted in widespread criminalisation and over-intrusion. Law-breaking does not lead inevitably to prosecution. Official documents of the prosecution authorities already set out the criteria to be taken into account in deciding whether to prosecute, to drop the matter or to move towards diversionary, and possibly supportive, measures. One criterion is the extent to which the public interest would be served by such a prosecution.[115] Most minor assaults are not prosecuted, and there is no reason why the approach to assaults upon children should be any different. As responsible adults, we must take on the task of devising a system that achieves the balance we seek between the protection of children and support for family life. We cannot avoid it by redefining violence to exclude that perpetrated upon the most vulnerable members of our society.

The challenge to the churches is to follow through their principles, which argue against physical punishment, with measures of public education, especially of their own congregations, and cooperation with others in moving towards a method of dealing with parental transgression that does not entail the draconian consequences that they fear. This must be achievable.

6.10 Obedience

The Convention on the Rights of the Child does not mention the word 'obedience'. Its respect for the legitimate exercise of parental and other authority is evident in several provisions:

> Article 5, which acknowledges the rights of parents, guardians and others 'to provide, in a manner consistent with the evolving capacities of the child, appropriate direction and guidance in the exercise by the child of the rights recognized in the present Convention';

> Article 14, which uses similar wording in relation to the child's right to freedom of thought, conscience and religion;

> Article 12, which requires the views of the child to be given 'due weight in accordance with the age and maturity of the child';

Article 28, which acknowledges the need for discipline in schools, while insisting that it be applied in a way that respects the child's dignity;

Article 29, which includes engendering respect for parents among the aims of education; and

Article 40, which acknowledges the need for systems of juvenile justice.

The words are carefully chosen. There may be a need to 'direct' a child of a certain age or level of maturity in certain matters. There may be a need to discipline a child. But children should always be listened to and any such measures administered with due respect for the child's rights.

The negative connotations of an unqualified commitment to obedience are manifest in the literature surrounding child abuse, where this is a result of physical chastisement aiming to instil obedience. For example, a submission to the Committee on the Rights of the Child by the NGO's Coalition on Child Rights, Pakistan commented:

> A second level of causation of child abuse may be intrinsic to the social construction of childhood in society. How does a society view its children and how does it define their rights? How much obedience, submission and conformity does it expect of children? Failure on the part of children or parents/caregivers to meet these standards is a major direct cause of many forms of child abuse at family level.[116]

The literature on child soldiers also points out that the very susceptibility of children to obey authority figures makes them attractive as 'cheap and expendable troops', being 'easier to condition into fearless killing and unthinking obedience'.[117]

Given that Christian suspicion of the Convention often focuses on its potential to undermine parental authority,[118] it is necessary to explore what the Christian tradition has to say about obedience. This will be a central concern of the next chapter.

6.11 Conclusion

Because children are human too, and because children's rights are human rights, it should be no surprise that many of the debates that took place in earlier decades about the legitimacy and utility of human rights should arise again in relation to the rights of the child. The point of comparing them is to stimulate reflection upon the legitimacy of the different stances we might take in such debates, given whatever position we take about significant differences in any relevant characteristics of adults and children.

Some of the debates about human rights in general (in particular about the relationship between rights and responsibilities, and between the individual and the community) have never gone away, but have merely shifted focus with the changing configurations of our society and the challenges thrown up by them. This is as it should be, because they are about the achievement of balance between competing tendencies, and the need to maintain that balance by appropriate and thoughtful readjustments is a continuing one.

The discussions in this chapter have included reference to some of the contributions of religious thinkers to the understanding of children's rights, and some specific objections to them. In the next chapter we shall embark upon a more positive and creative exploration of the potential for grounding the human rights of the child in Christian theology.

Notes

1. In 1999, the UN Committee on the Rights of the Child recommended that children's rights be viewed as 'the human rights of children', noting that, 'The experience of general human rights activities over recent decades should be analysed and used to promote respect for the rights of the child ...' See Hodgkin and Newell, *Implementation Handbook for the Convention on the Rights of the Child*, p. 161. While the general concept of the human rights of the child provides the framework for

this book, the term, 'children's rights' is also used at times for reasons of brevity.

2. Detrick, *Traveaux Preparatoires*, p. 20.

3. Detrick, *Traveaux Preparatoires*, pp. 29–30.

4. See 2.5.2 above.

5. See 4.6.4 above.

6. Detrick, *Traveaux Preparatoires*, pp. 623–4.

7. Detrick, *Traveaux Preparatoires*, pp. 632–3.

8. See 4.6 above.

9. See V. Mathieu, 'Prologomena to a Study of Human Rights from the Standpoint of the International Community', in UNESCO, *Philosophical Foundations of Human Rights*, pp. 33–46.

10. See 2.5.2 above.

11. It will be recalled here that the Committee on the Rights of the Child noted, in its concluding observations on the Holy See's Initial Report, that, while Article 5 acknowledges the rights of parents and guardians to give direction and guidance to the child as regards the exercise of rights, this does not give parents the right to use their power to undermine the rights of the child.

12. See 4.9 above.

13. Particularly, within Scotland, focused upon the ancient Roman *patria potestas* of the father. See A. B. Wilkinson and K. McK. Norrie, *The Law relating to Parent and Child in Scotland*, Edinburgh: W. Green/Sweet & Maxwell, 1993, p. 166.

14. Children Act 1989, Section 2 (9); Children (Scotland) Act 1995, Section 3 (5).

15. Children Act 1989, Section 5 (3); Children (Scotland) Act 1995, Section 7.

16. This is specifically stated in the relevant provisions within the 1989 and 1995 Acts. See also the discussion in Wilkinson and Norrie, *Law relating to Parent and Child in Scotland*, p. 166. Mothers can also agree to the child's unmarried father having parental responsibilities and rights by entering into a written and registered agreement; but this does not divest the mother of her own responsibilities and rights. See Children Act 1989, Section 4 and Children (Scotland) Act 1995, Section 4.

17. Pope John Paul II, *Familiaris Consortio: The Christian Family in the Modern World 22 November, 1981*, n. 41, in A. Flannery (ed.), *Vatican Council II: More Post-conciliar Documents*, Leominster, Hereford: Fowler Wright Books, 1982.

18. Scenarios similar to Robin and Maria's have been the subject of decision in the European Court of Human Rights. The Court requires 'extraordinarily compelling reasons' before sanctioning

the removal of a newborn child. In the case of *K. and T. v Finland*, 12 July 2001, 25702/94, this standard was not met and the Court ruled in favour of the parents. In the case of *N. V. and A. P. v Finland*, 13 September 2001, No. 29899/96, the standard *was* met, and the Court ruled in favour of the state. In this latter case, the parents suffered from alcohol and drug abuse and had a history of violence.

19. The question of the interface of children's rights and family values is more specifically addressed in a small leaflet: K. Marshall, *Children's Rights and Family Values: Complement or Conflict*, Glasgow: Blackfriars, 2002.

20. See 2.5.3 above.

21. See 2.5.2 above.

22. 'Power' is used here in a general sense, rather than as a Hohfeldian category.

23. See the UNESCO conclusion at 4.10 above.

24. B. M. Dickens, 'The Modern Function and Limits of Parental Rights', *The Law Quarterly Review*, 97 (July 1981), pp. 462–85 (462), attributes this view to the common law in general and to a nineteenth-century commentator in particular; Robert M. Kerr. *The Student's Blackstone: Commentaries on the Laws of England by Sir William Blackstone: Abridged and Adapted to the Present State of the Law* (1880), p. 100.

25. W. Blackstone, *Commentaries on the Laws of England*, accessed at www.yale.edu/lawweb/avalon/blackstone/, Book 1, Ch. 16.

26. Ibid.

27. Ibid.

28. Erskine (1773), *An Institute of the Law of Scotland*, I, vi, 53, quoted in Wilkinson and Norrie, *Law relating to Parent and Child in Scotland*, p. 163.

29. Wilkinson and Norrie, *Law relating to Parent and Child in Scotland*, p. 165.

30. Scottish Law Commission, *Report on Family Law* (Scot Law Com No 135), Edinburgh: HMSO, 1992, p. 6, n. 4.

31. Section 1 says parental responsibilities are: (a) to safeguard and promote the child's health, development and welfare; (b) to provide direction and guidance in a manner appropriate to the stage of development of the child; (c) if the child is not living with the parent, to maintain personal relations and direct contact with the child on a regular basis; (d) to act as the child's legal representative.

32. Section 2 says parental rights are: (a) to have the child living with him or otherwise regulate the child's residence; (b) to control, direct or guide, in a manner appropriate to the stage of development of the child, the child's upbringing; (c) if the child is not living with him, to maintain personal relations and direct contact with the child on a regular basis; (d) to act as the child's legal representative.

33. The passing of the Human Rights Act 1998 has led to much use of this language in relation to child protection concerns. The case law of the European Court of Human Rights shows how it seeks to reconcile the rights of both parents and children to privacy of family, home and correspondence, with the right of the child to life, dignity and freedom from want, fear or abuse. See U. Kilkelly, *The Child and the European Convention on Human Rights*, Aldershot (England): Ashgate and Brookfield (USA): Dartmouth, 1999.

34. Pope John Paul II, *Letter to Families*, 1994, accessed via Vatican website, n. 15.

35. This analysis first appeared in Marshall, *Children's Rights and Family Values*.

36. See 2.2 above regarding the three Ps.

37. Detrick, *Traveaux Preparatoires*, p. 158, reports an intervention by the Canadian delegation to the effect that, 'in protecting the family from the State, the family must not be given arbitrary control over the child. Any protection from the State given to the family must be equally balanced with the protection of the child within the family.'

38. Pontifical Council for the Family, *Family and Human Rights*, para. 2.9.

39. The Center for Reclaiming America www.leaderu.com/issues/fabric/chap16.html.

40. Jane Fortin, *Children's Rights and the Developing Law*, London: Butterworths, 1998, p. 9, quoting Lorraine Fox Harding, *Perspectives in Child Care Policy*, London: Longman, 1991, at p. 35.

41. For example, The Center for Reclaiming America observed in relation to an executive order by President Clinton in 1997 requiring child impact statements by federal agencies: 'The risk is not that the Clinton Administration isn't concerned with child welfare, but that the White House has demonstrated from the beginning a very different view from most Americans of "the rights of the child." The President's order, which establishes an inter-agency task force on children's health and safety, is precisely

the kind of bureaucratic and regulatory vehicle government liberals have used before to challenge parental rights and turn the government into a national nanny'. www.leaderu.com/issues/fabric/chap16.html.

42. Fortin, *Children's Rights*, p. 225.
43. Fortin, *Children's Rights*, p. 228, referring to J. Goldstein, A. Freud and A. Solnit, *Before the Best Interests of the Child*, London: Burnett Books, 1980.
44. J. Goldstein, A. Solnit, S. Goldstein and A. Freud, *The Best Interests of the Child: The Least Detrimental Alternative*, New York: The Free Press, 1998.
45. Ibid., p. 90.
46. Ibid., p. 128.
47. Dickens, 'Modern Function', p. 468.
48. *Re Philip B* (1979) 156 Cal.Rptr. 48, *cert denied* (1980) 100 S.Ct. 1597. Discussed by Dickens, 'Modern Function', pp. 480–3. This case is not presented as typical but as an example of the uncomfortable consequences of placing too much weight on parental autonomy.
49. Dickens, 'Modern Function', p. 472.
50. Ibid., p. 478. See also V. Coppock, 'Medicalising Children's Behaviour', in B. Franklin (ed.), *The New Handbook of Children's Rights*, London and New York, Routledge, 2002, pp. 139–54.
51. Dickens, 'Modern Function', p. 474.
52. Ibid., p. 485.
53. M. D. A. Freeman, *The Rights and Wrongs of Children*, London and Dover, NH: Frances Pinter (Publishers), 1983, pp. 248–50.
54. Fortin, *Children's Rights*, p. 227, referring to B. Hoggett, *Joint Parenting Systems: The English Experiment* [1994] 6 JCL 8, at p. 10.
55. Children (Scotland) Act 1995, Sections 11(7)(a), 16(3) and 96.
56. The Roman Catholic view is set out in the Second Vatican Council's *Dei Verbum: Dogmatic Constitution on Divine Revelation*, 1965, in Flannery (ed.), *Vatican Council II*; in particular in para. 12.
57. Detrick, *Traveaux Preparatoires*, p. 23 re the drafting process: 'The industrialised countries were significantly over-represented at all stages. Fear that the outcome would be a heavily Northern-oriented text were widespread and justified. They were attenuated only by particularly active participation on

the part of certain developing countries (Algeria, Argentina, Senegal and Venezuela were remarkable in this respect) as well as, in 1988, a sudden last-minute surge of delegates from the South, many from States with Islamic law.'

58. For example, Clarissa W. Atkinson writes (in Bunge (ed.), *Child*, p. 237) of the efforts of seventeenth-century Ursuline and Jesuit missionaries to 'New France' to accustom the Huron Indians to the practice of physical chastisement of children.

59. See 2.5 above.

60. Lauren, *Evolution of International Human Rights*, p. 130.

61. UNESCO 1947, p. 263.

62. This is a selection of the criteria set out in Goldstein, Solnit, Goldstein and Freud, *Best Interests of the Child*, p. 9.

63. Fortin, *Children's Rights*, p. 5, citing J. Holt, *Escape from Childhood: The Needs and Rights of Children*, London: E. P. Dutton, 1974. Also R. Farson, *Birthrights*, Harmondsworth: Penguin, 1978.

64. Fortin, *Children's Rights*, p. 5, cites P. Ariès, *Centuries of Childhood*, London: Jonathan Cape, 1962, which she claims is contradicted by L. Pollock, *Forgotten Children: Parent-Child Relations from 1500–1900*, Cambridge: Cambridge University Press, 1983. It is beyond the scope of this book to survey and assess these theories, which are likely to be the subject of ongoing academic debate. The purpose here is to show that there is a variety of understandings of children and childhood. The religious dimension over the centuries is well documented by Bunge.

65. Farson, *Birthrights*, p. 5.

66. A. Bainham, *Children, Parents and the State*, London: Sweet & Maxwell, 1988, p. 6, where he refers to Freeman's theory of 'liberal paternalism' in *Rights and Wrongs of Children*, pp. 54–60.

67. Fortin, *Children's Rights*, cites J. Harris and B. Franklin as modern, less radical child liberationists. She refers to Franklin's 1995 *Handbook of Children's Rights*, which has since been updated as *The New Handbook of Children's Rights*.

68. See Fortin, *Children's Rights*, pp. 5–8.

69. This can be presented as a religious perspective, founding on the application of the commandment to 'honour your father and your mother' to adults (Matt. 15:3–6; Mark 7:6–13). Before the commandments, Genesis 6–9 shows the obligations of Noah's sons to their father. Genesis 24:6 shows Abraham giving a servant authority over his 'adult' son, Isaac. Genesis

26:18 shows how this requirement to 'honour' persisted after death.

70. See, for example, C. K. Omari and D. A. S. Mbilinyi, *African Values and Child Rights: Some Cases from Tanzania*, Dar es Salaam: DUP (1996) Ltd, 1997, p. 2.

71. The divisions were not watertight. Children approaching puberty were regarded slightly differently from those at the infant end of the scale. The canon law of the Roman Catholic Church also adopted Roman law categories (see c. 97 of the 1983 Code of Canon Law). In both systems, puberty now has little legal relevance.

72. Hodgkin and Newell, *Implementation Handbook for the Convention on the Rights of the Child*, p. 2, quoting Guidelines for Initial and Periodic Reports.

73. Ibid., pp. 1–2.

74. See Marshall, *Children's Rights in the Balance*, p. 31, and the Committee's recommendations to the Holy See, at 2.5.2 above.

75. The Universal Declaration leaves it up to nation states to identify what 'full age' means. In systems based upon Roman Law, marriage was permissible from the age of puberty, and was thus related to an identifiable stage of physical maturity.

76. The case examples are drawn from the legal author's own practice and experience. Identifying details have, where relevant, been changed to protect confidentiality.

77. Franklin (ed.), *New Handbook of Children's Rights*, p. 21.

78. See, for example, K. Marshall, C. Jamieson and A. Finlayson, *Edinburgh's Children: The Report of the Edinburgh Inquiry into Abuse and Protection of Children in Care*, Edinburgh: City of Edinburgh Council, 1999, Lesson 19.

79. See R. Maguire and K. Marshall, *Education and the Rights of the Child*, Glasgow: University of Glasgow Centre for the Child & Society, 2001, Document 22.

80. See R. Gallagher, *Children and Young People's Voices: The Law, Legal Services, Systems and Processes in Scotland*, Edinburgh: The Stationery Office, 1999, p. 30.

81. Discussed by Franklin (ed.), *New Handbook of Children's Rights*, p. 72, and Fortin, *Children's Rights*, p. 30.

82. Franklin (ed.), *New Handbook of Children's Rights*, p. 72.

83. See K. Marshall, E. K. M. Tisdall and A. Cleland, *Voice of the Child under the Children (Scotland) Act 1995: Giving Due Regard to Children's Views in Matters that Affect Them*, Edinburgh: Scottish Executive Research Unit, 2002.

84. See 2.1 above regarding the impact of this view on the wording of Article 14 of the Convention on the Rights of the Child; and 4.14 above regarding Saudi Arabia's abstention on the vote approving the Universal Declaration because of its opposition to the right to 'adopt' a religion. We should of course remember that European history too has witnessed periods when those who renounced their religion were vulnerable to severe penalties for heresy or schism. The practical exercise of any theoretical freedom was also restricted by the philosophy of *cuius regio eius religio*, the formula adopted by the Peace of Augsburg in 1555, which decreed that the religion of the prince should determine that of the people.

85. Hodgkin and Newell, *Implementation Handbook for the Convention on the Rights of the Child*, p. 193. Neither does the case law of the European Court of Human Rights give much guidance on how any conflicts ought to be resolved.

86. K. E. McKenna, in *A Concise Guide to Canon Law*, Notre Dame, Indiana: Ave Maria Press, 2000, p. 34, suggests that, while the law of the Roman Catholic Church might permit a minor to enrol in the pre-baptismal programme (RCIA) without the permission of parents (the search for salvation being mandated by divine law), 'Practically, however, one would question the wisdom of such an admission, given the lack of support the minor would have in the practice of the faith from the parents.'

87. Belgium Initial Report, para. 140, quoted in Hodgkin and Newell, *Implementation Handbook for the Convention on the Rights of the Child*, p. 200.

88. Pope John Paul II, *Catechesi Tradendae: On Catechesis in Our Time*, para. 42, in Flannery (ed.), *Vatican Council II: More Post-conciliar Documents*, pp. 762–814.

89. Ibid., para. 69. See also the Congregation for Catholic Education, *The Religious Dimension of Education in a Catholic School*, 1988, n. 6: 'The religious freedom and the personal conscience of individual students and their families must be respected, and this freedom is explicitly recognised by the Church. On the other hand, a Catholic school cannot relinquish its own freedom to proclaim the Gospel and to offer a formation based on the values to be found in a Christian education; this is its right and duty. To proclaim or to offer is not to impose, however; the latter suggests a moral violence which is strictly forbidden both by the Gospel and by Church law.'

90. P. Fraser, *A Treatise on the Law of Parent and Child* (3rd edn, by J. Clark), Edinburgh: W. Green & Sons, 1906, pp. 90–1.

91. J. M. Zane, *The Story of Law* (2nd edn), Indianapolis: Liberty Fund, 1998, p. 143.

92. Maguire and Marshall, *Education and the Rights of the Child*, video component.

93. Sections 52(2)(a) and (b), Children (Scotland) Act 1995.

94. See Scottish Office, *Evaluation of the Hamilton Child Safety Initiative* (known as the Hamilton Curfew), Edinburgh: Scottish Office Central Research Unit, 1999.

95. See Hodgkin and Newell, *Implementation Handbook for the Convention on the Rights of the Child*, p. 214.

96. UN Paper CRC/C/SR. 56, para. 33, quoted in Marshall, *Children's Rights in the Balance*, pp. 26, 27 and 30.

97. In Roman Catholicism, there is absolute confidentiality within the confines of the Sacrament of Reconciliation.

98. Mason and McCall Smith, *Law and Medical Ethics*, p. 173.

99. See the website of Children Are Unbeatable at: www.childre nareunbeatable.org.uk/.

100. Report on the twenty-eighth session, September/October 2001, CRC/C/111, para. 715, cited in Hodgkin and Newell, *Implementation Handbook for the Convention on the Rights of the Child*, p. 265.

101. UN Committee on the Rights of the Child, CRC/C/SR.176, 10 October 1994, para. 46, quoted in Hodgkin and Newell, *Implementation Handbook for the Convention on the Rights of the Child*, p. 267.

102. For example, the April 2002 briefing on physical punishment by the Children Are Unbeatable! Alliance in Scotland advises, 'All children need boundaries, a clear framework that helps them to understand what is acceptable and unacceptable behaviour, but this does not need to include physical punishment. Positive discipline aims to encourage and reward good behaviour rather than simply reacting to bad behaviour.' See also the guidance produced by voluntary organisations, such as Barnardo's, *Getting Positive about Discipline*.

103. See P. Newell, *Children Are People Too: The Case against Physical Punishment*, London: APPROACH, 1992, pp. 98–9, for the history of English law. More generally, see George Ryley Scott, *The History of Corporal Punishment*, London: Senate, 1996 (first published as *Flagellation*, by Tallis Press Ltd, in 1968).

104. At the time of writing, physical punishment of children is completely banned in 10 states: Austria (1989), Croatia (1999), Cyprus (1994), Denmark (1997), Finland (1983), Germany

(2000), Israel (2000), Latvia (1998), Norway (1987) and Sweden (1979).

105. See Matthew 18:1–6, 10–11, 14.

106. UN Committee on the Rights of the Child, Summary Record CRC/C/SR.256, para. 23.

107. Pope Paul VI in *Evangelii Nuntiandi: Evangelisation in the Modern World*, 1975, n. 37, in Flannery (ed.), *Vatican Council II: More Post-conciliar Documents*, pp. 711–61.

108. Pope John Paul II, *Let Us Give Children a Future of Peace: Message of His Holiness Pope John Paul II for the XXIX World Day of Peace*, 1 January 1996, accessed via Vatican website: www.vatican.va/holy_father/.

109. Catholic Bishops Conference of England and Wales, *A Programme for Action: Final Report of the Independent Review on Child Protection in the Catholic Church in England and Wales*, London: Catholic Media Office, 2001, para. 2.9.3.

110. See the World Council of Churches website for details.

111. Scottish Law Commission, *Report on Family Law*, para. 2.80.

112. The Responses to the consultation were published on the Scottish Executive Website.

113. Other religious support for banning physical punishment is available at www.stophitting.com/religion/.

114. Ibid.

115. See the Prosecution Code of the Scottish Crown Office at: www.crownoffice.gov.uk/publications/CO_Pcode.pdf.

116. NGOs Coalition on Child Rights – Pakistan (no. 1), Submission to the Committee on the Rights of the Child Day of General Discussion on *Violence against Children within the Family and in Schools*, Geneva, 28 September 2001, UN website.

117. CBS News, *Cheap and Expendable Troops*, London, 12 June 2001, www.cbsnews.com, accessed 6 March 2003.

118. See discussion at 2.7 above.

7

A Theological Look at Children's Rights

In Chapter 5, when we were considering human rights and the churches, we had occasion to look at the way in which rights language has come to be adopted in specifically Christian discourse, and we tried to respond to two widely held theological objections to the use of that language. At the end of the chapter we compared the development to Paul's image of the grafting of a wild-olive shoot into the richness of the cultivated olive tree. In this chapter we shall, as it were, look at the point of insertion, but with a shift of focus from human rights in general to children's rights in particular.

But first we shall clear the ground by mapping out some of the ways in which questions raised by the notion of children's rights have been handled historically within the Christian tradition and then by examining two theological objections to talk of children's rights. That will help us finally to move on to the more positive work which is the goal of this chapter – to explore some of the ways in which the concept of children's rights can be grounded within the Christian theological tradition. So there are three sections to this chapter: the history of the problem; two objections; and the theological foundation for a doctrine of children's rights.

7.1 The Resources and Concerns of the Theological Tradition

The Christian tradition of thinking theologically about children has been the object of renewed interest in recent years – not all of it, by any means, favourable.[1] The incorporation of the language of children's rights within this tradition is of course a recent development. But the concerns which that language is meant to express have been around from the beginning. In this section, then, we want to sketch out the contours of that tradition. Doing so will help us to identify points that are capable of sustaining new growth and to pinpoint some problems and areas of confusion that need to be addressed.

The history of theological thinking about children is a vast area of research. In this sketch we draw above all on the very valuable collection of essays edited by Marcia Bunge in 2001 under the title *The Child in Christian Thought*, which provides us with a sort of snapshot of recent work.[2]

7.1.1 *Duties and Obligations*

The tradition[3] naturally contains no talk of children's rights till quite modern times, but much has been said about the more amorphous notion of obligations. Parents in particular are commonly regarded as having strong obligations for the care and nurture of their children. This almost universal view is, for example, strongly expressed by John Chrysostom[4] in the fourth century; Thomas Aquinas[5] in the thirteenth; Luther,[6] Calvin,[7] and the Anabaptist Menno Simons[8] in the sixteenth; and Schleiermacher[9] in the early nineteenth. The obligation may be grounded simply in the natural order of things as well as in reason or revelation.[10]

This obligation is embodied in a God-given authority which makes its discharge possible. Descriptions of this authority sometimes take extreme form. Aquinas, for example, says that in relation to the power and authority of his parents a young child 'differs not from an irrational animal' and is to be raised according to the parents' desires.[11] And Luther proclaims that 'there is no greater or nobler authority on earth than that of parents over their children, for this authority is both spiritual and temporal'.[12]

Correlative with this parental authority is the obligation of filial obedience, often grounded on the Fourth Commandment.[13] Again, the language is often strong. In the Massachusetts Bay Colony, for example, it was a capital offence for children over 16 to strike or curse their parents,[14] and even Schleiermacher believed in the virtue of absolute obedience.[15] Moreover, the Fourth Commandment receives privileged treatment; thus, in the discussion of the Ten Commandments in Luther's Large Catechism, it is the Fourth that receives by far the most ample consideration.[16]

But it is important to note that neither of these obligations – the parent's obligation to nurture and the child's obligation to obey – is really absolute, despite the force of the rhetoric that is often employed. The tradition not infrequently recognises limitations. The parent's obligation – or the power it implies – may be overridden by the wider claims of Church or State, and the child's obligation may, under certain circumstances, be dissolved.

Thus, on the one hand, Luther recognises the overarching authority of the State in education and even the propriety of its intervention in cases in which parents are trying to force children into unwelcome marriages.[17] A somewhat bizarre example – which yet illustrates an important principle – is Calvin's insistence that pastors in Geneva could vet the names parents proposed to give their children at baptism and reject any that savoured of superstition.[18] For Menno Simons, a Church 'ban' could separate children from parents.[19] And, among modern theologians, Karl Barth sees the authority of parents as being conditioned both by the authority of God and by the call which others have to exercise a share in the bringing up of their children.[20]

On the other hand, the duty of obedience is often said to be conditional. It is superseded if obedience would lead children to act in ways which would be in conflict with the law of God or the will of God. That is the position of John Calvin,[21] Menno Simons,[22] and the eighteenth-century Pietist

August Hermann Francke.[23] And obedience to parents is relativised even by the Fourth Commandment itself: for Luther, that Commandment enjoins obedience to 'fathers' in Church and State, as well as to biological fathers.[24]

7.1.2 Pluses and Minuses

The tradition as outlined here has of course both strengths and weaknesses. There are resources that can be carried forward in our attempts to deal with the needs of children today, and there are problems that need to be addressed.

The obligations to nurture and to obey prescribed by the tradition – in this case, in particular, the Reformation tradition of Luther and Calvin – are ambiguous. The limitations imposed on the duty of obedience – to do nothing that would contradict the law or will of God – are so general that they cannot serve as guides without further elucidation. But they are still there. So the tradition leaves room for the incorporation of a conceptual framework that would allow those conditions to be tidied up and tightened up. But it is possible to say more than that.

One strength, one resource of the tradition is its thorough-going commitment to care and nurture. But on the whole the tradition has been more interested in discussing authority and obedience than in discussing care and nurture. And that leaves a problem in need of attention.

The obligation of filial obedience – so strongly stressed in the tradition – is correlative with parental authority. Logically, that makes sense: the parent has a right to exercise authority, and the child has a duty to obey. But that is just the problem. Filial obedience is *not* correlative with the parental obligation to nurture and to care. That obligation has no correlative. There is no flip side – no conjugate member of the pair – unless we are to say in a somewhat Pickwickian sense that the child has an obligation to be nurtured or to allow himself to be nurtured.

And yet parental authority is not primary. It does not exist for itself. It exists in order to enable the obligation to nurture and to care. But, while the existence of some limitations on that authority is recognised, the obligation itself is left largely undefined and its operation is left largely untrammelled.

That can be seen from an analogy of which Chrysostom is fond. Parents, he thinks, are like artisans in relation to their child. They have an obligation to mould, to sculpt, and to paint, while the child is an artefact of their nurturing labour.[25]

Perhaps some clarity could be gained by trying to pin down that obligation to nurture and to care rather than shifting the focus so quickly to authority and obedience. That would mean seeing the obligation to nurture and to care as correlative with a right to be nurtured and cared for. And defining that would have to start with the child. There would then be a tight nexus between the duty (incumbent on parents and others as appropriate) to meet the needs of the child and the right of the child to have those needs met.

Perhaps there the dynamic of the tradition points beyond itself.

Another strength of the tradition – as outlined here – is its emphasis on human solidarity, an emphasis that can be seen as a counterweight to a post-Enlightenment liberal individualism. But perhaps more needs to be said about the way in which that solidarity can be grounded.

In particular, more could perhaps be made of the notion of the image of God, to which we shall return later at the end of this chapter. And where that notion has been allowed to come into play, it has often been as something to be revealed or recovered rather than as a simple given of human existence. Thus, in Chrysostom's analogy which we looked at a moment ago, the object of the parents' artistic activity is to reveal the image of God within.[26] And for John Wesley, with his doctrine of human perfectibility, the ultimate goal of education is nothing less than the recovery of the image of God.[27]

A significant mechanism for underpinning human solidarity turns out to be a doctrine of original sin. And there is a certain irony in that in view of the influential theory of 'poisonous pedagogy' put forward by the historian Philip Greven and the psychiatrist Alice Miller.[28] The Greven–Miller thesis points to a theory of the radical depravity of children maintained in certain Pietist circles and in some related brands of American Protestantism. This theory of radical depravity led to an ethos of strict control and strong discipline – including the generous use of force – and to an emphasis on the breaking of the will of the child. All of that – so the thesis runs – had a baleful legacy and is one of the major roots of child abuse.

But paradoxically, a strong sense of original sin – as in Calvin[29] – underlines the unity of humankind in the face of the commonality of human failure. And so, far from running counter to any notion of children's rights – as the 'poisonous pedagogy' thesis might suggest – a doctrine of original sin actually reinforces the inclusivity and universality of application required by any theory of rights. As Margaret Bendroth says, 'Depravity is, at least, a thoroughly democratic principle'.[30]

But on the whole the issue of Christian exclusivity is one of the problems which must be faced by any attempt to build on the tradition outlined here in a discussion of children's rights. Almost all of the thinkers analysed in Bunge's collection approach the question of obligations *to* children and obligations *of* children from the perspective of those who are within the community of faith. Thus, Barbara Pitkin, in a careful study of children in the theology of John Calvin, admits that she simply does not know what Calvin would have said about the obligations of society to a child who did not have even one believing parent.[31]

There are some attempts within the tradition to stretch the categories. Thus, Menno Simons thought that all children

– even those of unbelieving parents – are covered by God's grace.[32] And among modern theologians, who are on the whole more aware of what is at stake here, Karl Barth thinks that children are bearers of a promise and recipients of a prevenient grace,[33] while humanity, for Rahner, is itself graced.[34]

But if we are to talk of rights in the proper sense, we have to make sure that we are not just addressing Christian children or the children of Christians and then thinking of some way of letting others slip in under the wire. That is one of the tasks we will have to address when we come to try to find a secure grounding for talk of children's rights somewhere within central concerns of the Christian theological tradition.

But first we want to look, in the second section of this chapter, at two major objections to the use of the language of children's rights. Doing so will help us see more clearly where that language must fit into the ongoing history of Christian reflection on the child.

7.2 Two Objections

In Chapter 5 we looked at two clusters of objections that can be raised from a theological point of view against the use of human rights language. They were, first, the objection that human rights language is inherently individualistic, adversarial and self-regarding and bears on its forehead the mark of its historical origins within the matrix of a secularist ideology and, secondly, the objection that human rights language is unbiblical. Here we want to consider two parallel objections that are raised against the idea of children's rights in particular.

7.2.1 The Fragmentation-of-family-and-society Objection

We can pose the problem something like this: the notion of children's rights permits or encourages an attitude of self-seeking confrontation between child and parent and so reflects or even encourages the fragmentation of the family and of society. So once again the problem is that rights language is seen as being too individualistic in its presuppositions and in the aims of its application, but here that problem is given greater poignancy by the fact that it sees rights language as driving a wedge not just between fellow members of society, but between fellow members of the most intimate and basic unit of society, the family.

By now it will be apparent how we might respond to a general objection along those lines. Rights are there as a safety net or a backstop. They come into play when things go wrong, as in our world they all too often do. It is perfectly possible for a loving, well-functioning family to function without any need to advert to the category of children's rights at all.

It seems odd to claim that a recognition of the existence of children's rights *encourages* confrontational and adversarial relationships within the family or a breakdown in the cohesion of family and society. Surely that is an example of a *post hoc ergo propter hoc* ('if A comes after B, B must be the cause of A') fallacy. Surely the causal connection – if there is one – works in the opposite direction. That is, adversarial relationships may find expression in an appeal to one's rights. Fragmentation of family and society may encourage the development – well meaning or not – of mechanisms for invoking and enforcing them. Self-evidently the existence of a concept of children's rights *enables* an appeal to be made to those rights – it makes it possible for a confrontational attitude to find expression in that way. But that is quite a different thing from causing or promoting such a confrontational attitude in the first place.

So it is along those lines that we could in general reply to the fragmentation-of-family-and-society objection. But that objection can be put in a more sharply focused way – a way that raises important questions about the nature of human community and, indeed, about the very nature of the moral life.

One important voice in contemporary Christian ethics that is highly sceptical of the notion of children's rights is that of Stanley Hauerwas. 'I think it is extremely doubtful', he says, 'if rights are appropriately attributed to children (or anyone else for that matter).'[35] Why?

Hauerwas argues that it only makes sense to talk about the roles and obligations of parents and children – indeed, that we only know what we are talking about when we speak of a 'child' at all – within the context of the historically given presuppositions of some community. 'In other words, to speak of family and child is exactly to speak of the duties of parents and children toward one another that are grounded in the concrete expectations of particular communities.'

He attacks:

> The pretension of modern ethical theory that it could free itself from such historical presuppositions and ground moral judgments in man's 'rational' nature *qua* man – i.e., as if we were strangers to one another in the sense that we share no history or common purposes. That is to isolate the family from any context in which it morally can make sense.[36]

This means that Hauerwas entertains grave reservations about the desirability of rights language in general and denies its applicability to the family in particular. In the place of an abstract and supposedly universalisable account of rights and duties within the family, he paints a rather idealised picture of nurture within a conservative religious community, taking Orthodox Judaism as a model.[37] If you are a parent in such a community, he claims,

> you must care for children in a manner appropriate to making them full participants in your community ... The child does not have 'rights' *qua* human being, but the child does have a standing as an independent agent in relation to its parents because both parents and child are subject to the community's expectations.[38]

And so, on this view, an appeal to the concept of rights, including children's rights, is a symptom of social and personal fragmentation.

> The language of 'rights', especially as it is displayed by liberal political theory, encourages us to live as if we had no common interests or beliefs. We are thus trained to regard even our children as potential strangers from whom we need protection. But this is a formula for the disintegration of society as well as the disintegration of the moral self, as it trains us to pursue our interests as ends in themselves.[39]

It is tempting to see Hauerwas's appeal to the expectations of a conservative religious community as nostalgia for a lost world of moral consensus and to ask what happens if, even within such a stable environment, a young child is abused or an older child comes to reject the values of the community and wants to embark on a different style of life. But there is more at stake here than a sort of Huckleberry Finn morality, for Hauerwas's appeal to the community is a part of a whole moral programme.

As we saw in Chapter 5, there has, for the last twenty years or so, been a strong move to recover a virtue-based ethic.[40] Virtue was a central concept for thinking about human flourishing – for talking about what it was that made a human being truly human – in Aristotle and in the scholastics after him. Thus, Thomas Aquinas organises his consideration of the demands and possibilities of the Christian life as an analysis of the virtues.[41] The idea tended to be eclipsed in Western ethical thinking after Kant, but has now come into play once again. One of the thinkers to be so influenced is Stanley Hauerwas.

A virtue in the Aristotelian or scholastic sense is essentially a skill – an acquired skill of living well an authentically human life. Because it is a *skill*, it is a facility or a habit or a knack of acting and reacting freely and spontaneously in a manner appropriate to the particular virtue – acting honestly or justly or temperately, or whatever it might be.

Because it is an *acquired* skill, it is something you get better
at with practice, but something you can gradually lose if you
let it slip. In that way, it is a bit like the skill of playing the
bagpipes or sinking a putt. But because the skills involved
are the skills of living well, what they describe – and what
they produce – is not just a good piper or a good golfer, but
a good man or woman.

Thus, 'virtue' is one of those words that has undergone a
shift in meaning in modern usage, and *that* is something we
have to be wary of here. Suppose I really want to stop in the
pub after work and have a drink with my mates but force
myself to go home instead because it's my turn to make dinner
tonight. You might tell me, as I boast of my achievement,
'That was very *virtuous* of you.' The trouble is that now the
word 'virtue' – when it does not call up associations of prim
self-righteousness – is all too often connected with doing
something after a struggle and out of a sense of duty.

But for someone like Aquinas, my conduct in not heeding
the siren call of my friends in the pub and going home instead
would not have displayed much virtue at all. My *decision*
was the morally appropriate one; I did the right thing in
going home. But I am still deficient in the virtues of temperance – which is an appropriate moderation of appetites[42]
– and fidelity to my commitments. If I had acquired those
virtues to the requisite degree, they would have enabled me
to act easily and almost without thinking about it; the right
course of action would have become second nature to me.
Still, in forcing myself to pursue the right course of action
in the end, I am getting in some practice at those virtues.
I have gone a little bit farther along the road to becoming
a virtuous person.

Now, an account of the virtues taken together produces a
picture of a virtuous human being. It tells a story of what a
good life is like. And different stories will be told in different
historical contexts.

Hauerwas claims that the story only makes sense within the
context of a particular community. The virtues are 'specific

skills required to live faithful to a tradition's understanding of the moral project in which its adherents participate'[43] and 'there is no other basis of moral convictions than the historic and narrative-related experience of a community'.[44]

And the community in which Hauerwas is interested is the community of the Church. Thus, the important work in which he pioneered this vision of Christian ethics is called *A Community of Character* and is subtitled *Toward a Constructive Christian Social Ethic*. For Hauerwas, there is no other way in which Christian ethics can be approached than from the story of Jesus which the Church community recounts in a narrative that 'claims and shapes our lives'.[45]

We can now see where Hauerwas's opposition to the idea of children's rights is coming from. He sees a radical opposition between the historically shaped narrative of a particular community and the Enlightenment ideal of universal moral norms derivable by reason. And he sees a strong – though not total – opposition between a virtue-based ethic that tells a truthful and coherent story of human life and a rule-based ethic that is adapted only to dealing with specific and often abnormal problems in a rigid and inflexible way. So on both counts rights lose out to virtues since they claim to be universalisable and are associated with rules.

This is a powerful attack, precisely because of the attractiveness of the campaign for the recovery of a sense of virtue. Let us look at each of the points of opposition that we have just indicated.

First, is it true that virtues and rights must be opposed because any account of the former is culturally bound while the latter are generalisable? Only if the story of human life which the virtues delineate is indeed so radically determined by culture that there are no overarching narratives.

But if there is some broader vision of a good human life that enfolds and encompasses the specific narratives of particular communities, then there is no reason why there should not be generally applicable safeguards to protect the goods that are an integral part of that vision. Such safeguards would protect the conditions prerequisite for human flourishing anywhere, in any community, and help to ensure that the specific narratives of specific communities did not become too aberrant.

Is there some such broader vision of the good human life, some overarching narrative? That is of course a huge question. We shall offer two considerations that suggest that it *might* at least be so.

The first is a simple analogy. We have been speaking of pictures and stories. It is obviously the case in the plastic and narrative arts that there are culturally bound conventions and ideals. And yet it is also the case that we can respond to and be moved by the artefacts of another time and place. There is *some* common element that links us to the vision of human life articulated in the *Iliad* or the *Divine Comedy*. We recognise *something* ideal embodied in the sculptures of the Parthenon or the temples of Angkor. Why should the same not be true of that most precious and evanescent of cultural artefacts, a fully human life?

The second consideration is that, as a matter of empirical fact, a considerable measure of agreement is attainable on what we have just referred to as safeguards that protect the conditions requisite for human flourishing. That is attested by the simple fact that all but two states in the world have accepted the Convention which is the subject of this book. This suggests that even if there is great diversity in the specific narratives which are then constructed, there is a broad measure of consensus concerning the central human values which need safeguarding. Perhaps we should think of a number of narratives constructed at different levels with different degrees of specificity. The most specific and detailed ones are of course the most diverse and the most strongly culturally bound. But other, more general narratives can also be constructed. Broad brushstrokes can still paint a picture.

Second, is it true that there is a tension and opposition between a virtue-based ethic and a rule-based ethic? It depends where you think the rules come from, and why you think they are there. They can be thought of as a more-or-less arbitrary code. This would be the view, maintained in the Middle Ages by Duns Scotus, that God does not command things because they are good; they are good because he commands them.

There is an important difference between two possible answers to the moral 'why': why should I do this or not do that? One possible answer is 'because it's the rule or the law or the commandment (and that's all there is to it)'. But another possible answer is 'because it will contribute to my human flourishing and so make me happy in the proper sense of the word "happy"'. Rules – whether we think they are deduced by reason or given by revelation or some combination of both – are there to point us in the direction of concrete applications of the virtues. They help us know what we should do and what we should avoid in order to grow in virtue. And they help keep the less virtuous among us from going off the rails.

The relationship between virtues and rules is like that between the skills of being a good driver and the highway code. They are quite different things, but it seems odd to suggest that they are opposed.[46]

The point is that virtues and rules or virtues and rights are not competing for space. They inhabit different floors within the structure of morality. We can see that by looking at something we might want to say lives between them. According to Aquinas, the first principle of morality is the commandment to love God and your neighbour as yourself.[47] Let us – at least for the moment – accept that formulation. It is then possible to imagine moving upward, as it were, from that principle to an account of the virtues that would tell the story of what a loving life looks life. And it would also be possible to move downward from it to a set of rules that would cash some of the implications of acting lovingly

– that would tell you, for example, that you should help little old ladies across the street and that you should not practise the bagpipes late at night.

Our look at Hauerwas's attack on the notion of children's rights has been complex because his case is complex. It is made up of a number of different strands woven together. Taken as a whole, it has a strong emotional and rhetorical appeal, with on the one hand its invocation of the values of community and on the other its raising of the spectre of 'the disintegration of society' and 'our children as potential strangers from whom we need protection'.[48] But to go down that road is, in the end, to give up the claim not just to shared norms but to shared discourse. You have your community and your narrative and I have mine, and that's all there is to it.

Whatever we may want to say about that view on other grounds, what Hauerwas would call the foundational narrative of our community will not let us stop there. The story of Jesus of Nazareth, as it has been understood in Christian tradition, is the story of the Word of God – the *Logos*, the one who is the meaning of all things – coming into our world of time and space to live an authentically human life, a life that has significance for the whole of humankind.

And the story of Jesus of Nazareth fits into the broader story of the history of humankind. Indeed, it is a fundamental Christian conviction that the history of humankind is a story – that it has coherence and a plot with a beginning and a middle and an end. But that end is not yet. The end of the story is the vision of which John speaks in the Revelation of the New Jerusalem coming down from heaven prepared as a bride adorned for her husband. 'And the city has no need of sun or moon to shine upon it, for the glory of God has illumined it and its lamp is the lamb. And the pagans will walk in its light' (Rev. 21:2 and 23–4).

It is that city and nothing smaller that is the community whose narrative must determine our ethic. And it lies at the end of the journey of the whole of humankind. That is a vision from which we cannot retreat.

7.2.2 The Unbiblical Objection

In Chapter 5 we looked at the claim that the idea of human rights is unbiblical. The same complaint is often lodged against the notion of children's rights in particular. So here we will examine two sets of texts that are often cited in support of that claim and see what they do say and what they do not say.

7.2.2.1 Honouring and Obeying

The first set of texts to which we wish to draw attention falls into two pairs: the commandment to honour father and mother (in Exod. 20:12 and Deut. 5:16) and the injunction to children in Ephesians 6:1 and Colossians 3:20 to obey their parents. The argument is that children in claiming rights against their parents would contravene the biblical demand for submission. So we will look at these texts to see what they have to say about the nature of obedience and about what it means to honour.

We begin with the Fourth Commandment of the Decalogue – or the Fifth, depending on how you number them. (Catholic and Lutheran practice normally counts the injunctions against the worship of false gods and graven images (Exod. 20:3–6/Deut. 5:7–10) as the First Commandment, so making the honouring of parents the Fourth, while Orthodox, Anglican and Reformed usage normally splits the former in two, so making the latter the Fifth.)[49]

The essential wording of the precept is the same in both versions of the Decalogue – that in Exodus (20:12) and that in Deuteronomy (5:16), though the latter is reinforced by a clause supplying an additional promise or motivation, 'in order that it will be well for you'.[50] The Hebrew verb is the same in both versions – *kabbedh*, an imperative of a verb the root meaning of which is 'to be heavy'. The form used here means 'to treat (someone or something) as being of weight' and so 'to honour' or 'glorify'. It does not, then, primarily at least, mean 'submit' or 'obey'.

Is obedience implied in the kind of honour that is commanded? In order to answer that question, we have to see how this form of the verb is used elsewhere in the Hebrew Bible.

Sometimes obedience would indeed fit as a part of the connotation. Malachi 1:6, for example, speaks of a son *honouring* his father and a slave his lord. Again, the verb is used a number of times of honouring the Lord, and sometimes the mode of honouring him that is described is also the fulfilling of a precept. Thus, he is *honoured* by one who offers a thanksgiving sacrifice (Ps. 50:23) or by one who shows favour to the poor (Prov. 14:31).

But there are other passages in which obedience or submission is clearly *not* what is in mind. In the book of Numbers, for example, Balak king of Moab promises to *honour* Balaam if he will curse the people of Israel (Num. 22:17, 37; 24:11). It is clear from the context that this means giving Balaam presents, not to say a bribe (see 22:18 and 24:13). Indeed, it is Balak who is trying to persuade Balaam to obey his wishes (by cursing Israel), rather than the other way round.

Again, Wisdom will *honour* the one who embraces her (Prov. 4:8). Clearly, this does *not* mean that Wisdom will obey him. What it does mean is depicted in the next verse in the imagery of a banquet or a celebration: she will put a 'graceful wreath', a 'glorious crown', on his head (Prov. 4:9).

If it would make little sense to say that Wisdom is obedient to a human being, it clearly makes even less sense to say that God is. And yet in 1 Samuel 2:30 the Lord says that he will *honour* those who *honour* him.[51] That this is not just a metaphor for acceding to their wishes is confirmed by Isaiah 60:13, in which the Lord declares that he will *honour* Zion, 'the resting place of my feet'.

From all that, we can, I think, conclude that 'honour' is in fact quite a good translation of *kabbedh* in the Fourth (or Fifth, if you prefer) Commandment. It means that parents should be treated as figures of weight. They should be treated with respect and consideration and deference. They should be pumped up rather than put down.

Treating people with deference will, of course, often involve deferring to their wishes. But that notion is not, as it were, built into the word that is used in the text of Exodus and Deuteronomy. Submission may, in certain circumstances, be the appropriate way to put the Commandment into practice – indeed, it very often will be the appropriate response. But it is the application of a principle, not its straightforward meaning, and it has no more integral a connection with the Commandment than does building a granny flat or sending flowers on Mother's Day.

Indeed, the whole wording of the Decalogue implies that the Commandments are, in the first instance, addressed to adults rather than to minors – addressed to those who have menservants and maidservants, sons and daughters, and who can covet their neighbours' wives. We in our society might be better employed in considering the honour such people owe to (elderly) parents than in using the texts as a device for controlling children.

Moreover, it is possible to imagine circumstances in which obedience would *not* be the appropriate response of a child to her parent. We can take an extreme scenario to make the point. Suppose that a father ordered his son or daughter to support him by prostitution. In such a case we would surely want to say that the general presumption that one should be submissive to those to whom deference is owed must give way in the face of a specific moral prohibition. Or, in terms of children's rights, we could say that the general duty of obedience is here 'trumped' by the child's right to protection from sexual abuse and exploitation.[52]

But that is not all that can be said, for here the Commandment itself would enjoin disobedience. What is commanded is to honour. But to obey would in this case be to demean both father and child and further to degrade what would obviously be an already broken relationship. For a child to obey in such circumstances would be precisely to dishonour rather than to honour the parent.

In dealing with the next pair of texts, we will have to return to this question of exceptive clauses – that is, to a consideration of what happens when a general duty of obedience collides with contravening and overriding moral norms.

The other pair of texts is Ephesians 6:1 and Colossians 3:20. Both texts say, 'Children, be obedient to your parents'. Colossians adds 'in all respects', while Ephesians *may* add 'in the Lord' (the manuscript tradition is fairly evenly divided on whether the phrase is to be included or omitted). And the two epistles differ in the explanation that is then adduced. Ephesians says simply, 'for this is just', while Colossians has 'for this is well-pleasing in the Lord'.

What are we to make of these texts? In order to understand them, we first have to set them in context. They come from very closely related sections of very closely related letters. The precise relationship between the letters – whether either used the other or each drew on some sort of common source – and the question of their authorship – whether Paul wrote either, neither, both, or a now lost letter which the existing texts have reworked – are very actively debated questions.[53] Those complex problems are not our immediate concern. What we are concerned with here is the texts as they exist and as they have been incorporated in the canon of the New Testament.

Both Ephesians and Colossians contain a list of household duties, describing the behaviour that is appropriate on each side in a series of two-way relationships: wife and husband, child and parent, slave and master (Eph. 5:22–6:9 and Col. 3:18–4:1). This household code is often referred to by

New Testament scholars as the *Haustafel* (a term which in this context goes back to Luther).[54] Roughly similar lists of reciprocal duties can be found in both Jewish and pagan literature.

What Paul – or whoever actually wrote Ephesians and Colossians in his name – is doing is to prescribe the relationships that should exist in a household that has become Christian. He simply presupposes the normal social structure of a prosperous household in the Graeco-Roman world. The *familia* includes slaves as well as the members of the immediate, biological family. All are addressed directly, with a second person ('you') form, and it is assumed that all are Christian. Hence all the admonitions can be grounded by an appeal to Christian values or by the citation of an Old Testament text.

The household codes have often been regarded – particularly within the tradition of Lutheran interpretation – as a watering down of the original, radical demands of the gospel and as a sell-out to the conventional standards of Hellenistic morality.[55] Be that as it may, the codes were, no doubt, in part meant as an antidote to the widely held suspicion in the pagan world that Christianity was subversive of family values.

But the codes actually have a rather more radical character than might at first appear. We can see that, for example, in the injunction of Colossians that children are to obey their parents *in all things* (Col. 3:20). The rabbinic tradition was familiar with discussions of possible limitations on the duty of obedience (if, for example, a father should command his son to make himself ritually unclean or to refuse to return a deposit).[56] And so was Hellenistic philosophy.

A younger contemporary of Paul, the Roman Stoic, Musonius Rufus, produced a discussion on the question 'Whether Parents Are to Be Obeyed in All Things', and the second-century writer Aulus Gellius noted that the topic was a commonplace in philosophical debates.[57]

Musonius argued that a father should not be obeyed if he commanded that which was bad or hindered that which was good. His argument is, first, that a son who pursues the good is *really* doing what his father wants – whatever the father thinks he wants – since (1) all parents are well-disposed toward their children, (2) he who is well-disposed toward someone wants what is beneficial for him, but (3) doing the good is what is really beneficial.[58] And Musonius' second argument is that, even if the father forbids his son to practise the life of virtue, yet Zeus, the father of gods and men, commands it and in such a case it is necessary to obey Zeus rather than a human being.[59]

In the last section, as an example of a situation in which disobeying a command would actually be honouring one's parents, we cited the hypothetical case of a father who orders his child to prostitute himself. Musonius actually produces an identical scenario as an example of a situation in which disobedience is virtuous, and he claims to have known of such a case personally.[60]

We have looked at this discussion in some detail because it shows clearly that when the writer of Colossians admonishes children to obey their parents *in all things*, he was taking sides in a current debate. The first readers of the letter would have realised that it was addressing a problem they were familiar with and that it was taking a pretty uncompromising line.

Does that mean that Colossians and Ephesians preclude any idea of the child's moral autonomy? Does their demand for obedience totally exclude the exercise of claim-rights by a child on his parents and militate against the possession of claim-rights by a child at all? Three observations may be advanced in reply – concerning the nature of the *Haustafel*, its limited range and the need for exceptive clauses.

We have seen that in using the *Haustafel* form, the letters to the Ephesians and Colossians are taking a Graeco-Roman convention and giving it a Christian spin. They presuppose a conventional social structure and ask how the various members of the household must behave within that structure. Hence the practice of slavery is simply taken for granted.

It would be mad to say that the household codes legitimate slavery. They offer no comment on the institution one way or the other. What they do is tell slaves how they should relate to their masters and masters how they should relate to their slaves within the existing social parameters.

But that society, which accepted slavery as a fact of everyday life, also accepted as a fact of everyday life a heavily patriarchal family structure. What the texts give us is not a timeless blueprint of familial relationships, but norms to be observed within particular structures. From that it may be possible for the biblical theologian to deduce certain generalisable patterns of response, but that is another matter.

The second observation we would like to make concerns a limitation built into the household codes, a limitation in the range of those to whom they are meant to apply. The *Haustafel* assumes, as we have seen, that both partners in each relationship are Christian. And the children – like all the partners in the various relationships – are addressed directly: in both Ephesians and Colossians, 'children' in the vocative is followed by a second person plural imperative. So it is assumed that the children in question are of an age to understand and to respond.[61] It is also assumed, of course, that the children being addressed are not precluded from responding by incapacity or disability.

And the only relationship dealt with in the household codes which involves children is the relationship between child and parent. Nothing is said about how children are meant to respond to other figures of authority, to other relatives, or to adults in general.

So even if we were to think that the household codes debar any appeal to claim-rights by Christian children against Christian parents, an awful lot of questions are still left unanswered. There is an awful lot of moral territory left uncharted.

The household codes were written up in a way that in the first century CE, at the very beginning of the spread of the gospel, would apply to only a tiny fraction of the population of the empire – indeed, a tiny fraction of the population of the cities to which they were first written. [62] It is again true in our society that only a minority of parents and children would meet all the conditions presupposed by the *Haustafel*. But our situation differs radically from that of the small, isolated communities that first heard these letters read.

Those communities could (at first) exert but small influence on the norms of the society around them and were in no position to help effect legal change. An example is the Christian attitude to the exposure of unwanted newly-borns. Christian writers were consistently opposed to the practice, [63] but were of course in no position to stop it. Legislative intervention came with the first Christian emperor, Constantine, who discouraged exposure, though even he did not forbid it.

We are in rather a different position. Even if we were to think that within the walls of the Christian community, the household codes leave no room for appeal to children's rights, there remains a world outside. Abuse and exploitation and oppression exist in our society and in our world, and our society and the global community of which we are a part simply have to face that fact.

The third observation we would like to make concerning the relationship between the *Haustafel* and rights language is that the household codes leave many things deliberately unsaid. The norms which they prescribe are quite general, and there is no attempt to construct a casuistic system to deal with various sorts of possible problems. In part at least that is because the *Haustafel* is interested in painting a picture of how the household as a whole should operate.

All of the relationships listed in the *Haustafel* are reciprocal – husband/wife, child/parent, slave/master. For each pair we are told first how that partner in the relationship who is, in terms of the norms of the ancient world, the weaker should respond to the partner who is in the stronger position, and then how the stronger should treat the weaker. And the two halves of that relationship cannot be severed.

We are shown how the *relationship* should work. We are told that children should obey their parents and that fathers should not provoke their children to anger (Eph. 6:4) or irritation (Col. 3:21). But we are not told what happens when the relationship breaks down, and we are not told what is the appropriate response to various situations that do not quite fit the pattern.

The New Testament itself sends out mixed signals on the question – or rather, shows that different situations impose different demands. On the one hand, Mark 7:10–13 and its parallel in Matthew 15:4–6 can be read as supporting the obligation to parents. There Jesus sets the force of the Commandment over the force of the voluntarily contracted obligation of an offering to the Temple: 'honour your father and your mother' takes precedence over 'whatever benefit you would have received from me is *corban* – that is, gift'.

In contrast, in Luke 14:26 Jesus says, 'If anyone comes to me and does not hate his own father and mother and wife and children and brothers and sisters and even his own life, he is not able to be my disciple.' And what it might mean to say that the demands of the gospel have priority over family ties is fleshed out at Mark 1:20/Matthew 4:22 when James and John are called to leave their father Zebedee in the boat to follow Jesus. Again, at Matthew 8:21–2/Luke 9:59–60 an anonymous disciple is told to follow Jesus without first going to bury his father – a basic religious duty of fundamental importance in the Jewish world which would certainly have fallen under the commandment to honour father and mother. And there is the general precept of Acts 5:29, 'It is necessary to obey God rather than human beings.'

It is of course possible in various ways to harmonise these seemingly disparate points of view, and centuries of Christian ethical reflection bear witness to that fact. But that is just the point: the household codes still leave us with work to do.

So throughout the centuries commentators faced with the task of interpreting the command to obedience in Ephesians and Colossians have had recourse to some sort of exceptive clause. Indeed, it is difficult to see how it can be denied, once the question has been raised, that there are at the very least certain theoretically possible parental commands which must *not* be obeyed.

We can take a few examples. The most influential commentator on Paul in the Greek Church was John Chrysostom. The homilies in which he expounded the Epistle to the Ephesians were delivered sometime before he left Antioch for Constantinople in 397. Chrysostom, like most ancient writers, extols a strongly hierarchical family structure and tends on the whole to regard children as being the passive recipients of the process of education. He can, as we have seen, compare the work of parents in the bringing up of their child to the work of sculptors or painters. As the artists are honoured for producing an image of the emperor, so much the more should parents be honoured for beautifying the truly royal image which is their child – a human being who is the image of God.[64]

But even with this tendency to stress the role of parents – primarily the father – and the passivity of the child, Chrysostom still allows for exceptions to the obligation of obedience.

'Children', he says, 'obey your parents *in the Lord*'[65] – that is, in accordance with the Lord. He says that's what God commanded. So, what if what *they* command is out of kilter? Of course [in delivering the homily from the pulpit, John would no doubt have indicated by tone of voice that he is being ironic here] a father never commands anything that out of kilter, even if he's out of kilter himself. But nonetheless – even so – he took precautions by saying 'in the Lord' – that is, in those matters in which you don't collide with God. So if he's a pagan or a heretic, it's not necessary to obey him, for then his command isn't 'in the Lord'.[66]

John Chrysostom, then, recognises, as we did above, that the *Haustafel* is only meant to apply to cases in which both partners in the relationship are Christian ('if he's a pagan or a heretic, it's not necessary to obey him'). But he also makes an exception – which he leaves without further attempt at specification – for cases in which what is commanded would cause the child to 'collide with God'.

Thomas Aquinas's commentary on Paul was delivered as a series of lectures around 1270. He takes the same line on Ephesians 6:1 that John Chrysostom does. 'It says "in the Lord" because neither parents nor anyone else is to be obeyed in things that are contrary to God. Thus Acts 5 says, "It is necessary to obey God rather than human beings".'[67]

John Calvin's commentaries on Ephesians and Colossians were first published in 1548. At Ephesians 6:1 he notes sadly that 'experience teaches how rare is the virtue' of obedience, and he adds as a comment on the phrase 'in the Lord':

> He [Paul] teaches that, apart from the law of nature, which is received among all nations, the obedience of children is also sanctioned by the authority of God. Yet it follows from that that parents are to be obeyed to the extent that piety toward God is not damaged. For if the norm for the subjection of children is that it is to be required on the basis of the fact that it was established by God, it would be preposterous through subjection to be led away from that same God.[68]

At Ephesians 3:20, 'Children, obey your parents', Calvin explains:

> He enjoins on children that they obey their parents without exception. But what if the parents should wish to incite them to something illicit? Will they obey without distinction even then? But it would be most unworthy for human authority to prevail and for God to come second. My answer is that here too we have to understand what he actually expresses elsewhere, namely, 'in the Lord'.[69]

John Wesley's attitude to children cannot be described as overly protective or overly sentimental. His advice to

parents was 'Break their will, that you may save their soul.'
'Why did you not break their will from their infancy?' he
asked. 'It should have been done before they were two years
old: It may be done at eight or ten, though with far more
difficulty.'[70]

Wesley's *Notes* on the New Testament were first published
in 1754. At Ephesians 6:1, his gloss on 'children, obey your
parents' is 'In all things lawful the will of the parent is a
law to the child.'[71]

The great Anglican scholar J. B. Lightfoot published his
commentary on Colossians in 1875, the year he became
Lady Margaret Professor of Divinity in the University of
Cambridge. On the phrase '(be obedient) *in everything*' (Col.
3:20), he observes, 'The rule is stated absolutely, because
the exceptions are so few that they may be disregarded'[72] – a
comment which, with true Victorian primness, acknowledges
that exceptions must be made while providing absolutely
no help in identifying them.

Finally, the new *Catechism of the Catholic Church*,
issued by John Paul II in 1992, provides an alternative to
the traditional sort of exceptive clause. It first affirms that
a child has an obligation of obedience to his parents 'in all
that they ask of him *when it is for his good or that of the
family*'. The *Haustafel* admonition of Colossians 3:20 is
then cited, and the obligation is extended by the observation that children also owe obedience – by proxy, as it were
– to 'the *reasonable* directions of their teachers and all to
whom their parents have entrusted them'. But finally it is
observed that 'if a child is *convinced in conscience* that
it would be morally wrong to obey a particular order, he
must not do so'.[73]

The *Catechism* has, then, broadened the basis for
exceptions to the duty of obedience. A child is under
a general obligation to obey his parents (and authority
figures nominated by them) provided that the command
is (1) beneficial, (2) reasonable and (3) not contrary to the
child's conscience.

The *content* of these provisions is now much closer to a statement of the rights of the child. Thus, the UN Convention specifies that 'in all actions concerning children ... the best interests of the child shall be a primary consideration' (Art. 3.1) and that the child's right 'to freedom of thought, conscience and religion' shall be respected (Art. 14.1).[74] But the *form* resembles that of the exceptive clauses employed by commentators since John Chrysostom.

That means that the exceptive provisions continue to be vague and ill defined and the relationship continues to be looked at primarily from the perspective of the empowered adult. We will have more to say on that point in the next section.

7.2.2.2 *Punishing*

The other set of texts we want to consider here is a group of texts in the book of Proverbs that permit – indeed, enjoin – the beating of children. If the protection of children from physical abuse is deemed to include protection from corporal punishment, at least in its heavier and more enthusiastic forms, then Proverbs might be thought to provide clear scriptural warrant for rejecting the idea of children's rights altogether.

The texts in question are

13:24	The one who withholds his rod is one who hates his son, and the one who loves him is the one who seeks him early[75] with discipline.
22:15	Foolishness is bound up with the heart of a boy; the rod of discipline removes it far away from him.
23:13–14	Do not withhold discipline from a boy; when you beat him with a rod, he will not die. You will beat him with a rod, and you will deliver his life from Sheol.
29:15	A rod and rebuke bestow wisdom, and a boy sent away is putting his mother to shame.

To these passages we should add the admonition in 19:18 to 'discipline your son', where the verb is obviously being used in the same sense as the related noun in the first three texts above.

What are we to make of these passages? They clearly condone the beating of children – or, to be more precise, they countenance and encourage a liberal use of force as a part of the educational process.

There are four points we would like briefly to make. The first concerns the words that are actually used in the Hebrew text. The words we have translated as 'discipline' are a verb and a noun from the same root that have a wide range of meaning – a range that is difficult to capture in English simply because we have a different concept of education. The verb can mean 'punish' – as it does, for example, in Leviticus 26:18 and 28 or Deuteronmy 22:18 – but it can also mean simply 'instruct' or 'train' – as it clearly does in, say, Hosea 7:15, Isaiah 28:26, or Proverbs 31:1. The word can have that range of meaning because the primary model of education in the ancient Near East was coercive.

The 'rod' is regularly used for punishment (or protection: the word is used of 'your *rod* and your staff' with which the Lord comforts his sheep in Ps. 23:4). But it is also used of a ruler's sceptre, the mark of his authority – clearly because of the connection between the authority to govern and the power to coerce. It is so used, for example, in Genesis 49:10, Psalms 47:5 (twice) and Amos 1:5 and 8.

This means that while the picture is first and foremost one of a child being beaten with a stick, the image shades over into a picture of authoritative teaching. The Hebrew words carry a resonance that their English counterparts do not.

Secondly, the moral quality of an act is not necessarily the same in all cultures. The ancient world was a world in which physical punishment was commonplace and severe. The beating of a child in such circumstances would have a different social significance and perhaps a different psychological effect from the one it would have in a society where such actions are much rarer. That, of course, in and of itself, neither condones beating in the ancient world nor condemns it in the modern, but it does mean that the position is not in all respects the same.

Thirdly, if we *did* think that these texts were directly applicable to our world and justified parents in beating their children, we might note that they would *not* cover something like spanking a little girl with a hairbrush – and that on two counts. In the first place, the texts apply to 'sons' and 'boys'. Both words are in Hebrew gendered words, and there is in each case a related feminine form which exists but which is not used here. That of course is because of the contingent fact that in the ancient Near Eastern culture for which the book of Proverbs was written, education was an exclusively male preserve, or very nearly so. That may be a historical accident, but it is a fact, and if we take the texts literally, it limits their scope. Again, all these passages – apart from Proverbs 19:18, which contains no *explicit* mention of physical punishment at all – refer to a 'rod', a stick, as the instrument of 'instruction'. So presumably hairbrushes and belts and slaps with the palm of the hand are out.

Now, those who are keen to apply these texts directly in the education of their sons and daughters no doubt assume that an extension to children of either sex is legitimate, and that the instrument of punishment is irrelevant to the point of the texts. And that no doubt is true, as far as it goes. But if we extend the literal meaning of the texts in those ways in order to apply them to our world, why not extend them in other ways as well? If the instrument of punishment is irrelevant, why not the notion of physical punishment itself?

That brings us to our last and most important point. If we are to apply scriptural passages like these, we have to look at how they functioned in their original context. We have to reason by analogy. We have to construct a sort of proportion and say

> the beating of children: education in ancient Near Eastern culture::
> what?: education in modern Western society.

The book of Proverbs continues to puzzle modern scholarship. Its date remains elusive.[76] It is clearly a compilation of various collections. That is not only a conclusion arrived at by the methods of modern critical scholarship; it is explicitly indicated in the headings of various sections of the book.[77]

There are close connections with other collections of wise sayings from other cultures in the ancient Near East. For example, Proverbs 23:13-14 that we have just looked at has a close parallel in the highly popular tale of Ahiqar, the original form of which may date from around 600 BCE.[78] These parallels led scholars for most of the twentieth century to think that the sayings collected in Proverbs originated in court circles – that it was a sort of handbook for yuppies, advising them on etiquette and matters of practical wisdom. But in recent years there has been more of a tendency to trace the sayings to the folk wisdom of ordinary people in a pre-urban society.[79]

Be that as it may, what we have in the book is a stress on the importance of education and the pursuit of wisdom. Indeed, that pursuit is of such fundamental importance that it can be regarded as a matter of life and death (23:13-14). And so a father has a primary duty to seek to inculcate wisdom in his son. In a world in which the basic model of education was coercive, that of course involved a generous application of the rod. Can we seriously claim that it should be so for us?

7.3 Children's Rights and the Theological Tradition

In this section we want to look for a solid foundation within the central traditions of Christian theology for the notion of children's rights. From within the particular perspectives of Christian theology, we want to find an answer to the question why is it that *all* children have certain claims on us, and indeed on all human beings. We have, then, a fairly good idea of what we want to construct. Where can we build it?

We note first of all that such a foundation within the Christian tradition for *children's* rights will turn out to provide a foundation for the more general notion of *human* rights as well. But we think that it is a good idea to do things this way around. We think that it is important to make children's rights in particular the paradigm case.

In their Enlightenment origins, affirmations of human rights were connected with affirmations of human rationality. The same was, broadly speaking, true of the antecedents of the idea in the natural law theories of the scholastics.[80] The answer to the question why do humans have rights is in that way of looking at things connected with the fact that humans are rational.

But that means that the paradigm case – the model for understanding what rights are all about – is a fully functioning adult.[81] And that in turn means that those who do not fit the paradigm, because of age or disability, have to be somehow tacked on. The mentally ill and the simple-minded, being members of the human species, *would* be fully rational, other things being equal, and the very young *will* be so. On this model, those who do not fit *have* human rights to be sure, but in a real sense human rights are not *for* them.

Now, human rights, if they are genuinely *human* rights, must apply to children as well. And we do not want to end up saying that children's rights are something completely different. They are rather a further specification of human rights. They are the particular form of human rights that is appropriate for those whose particular form of being human is to be children.

So we want to construct a foundation that will make the particular rights of children and all their human rights truly *for* them and that will give them a full entitlement, in and of themselves, in virtue of what they are and not in virtue of what they are in the process of becoming – except insofar as we might decide to include some reference to what all humankind is in the process of becoming. But that is something we will look at in Chapter 8 when we consider the model of the kingdom.

If we can succeed in laying such a foundation, children will be performing a service for others as well. We would like to think that in our society the aim of rights is not so much to guarantee the social and economic security of those best able to function, but rather to protect and to promote the weak – the poor and the vulnerable, the disabled and disempowered and disadvantaged. Whether that is so in our society or not, it must be our aim as we reflect on the matter from within the context of the Christian theological tradition.

So if we take children as the paradigm case, we may be able to build a model of rights that is more truly and comprehensively human. Our first requirement, then, as we try to decide where to build is that the space must be big enough to hold everybody. The starting point must be inclusive.

The second requirement is that our starting point must have an evocative power and a richness of resonance. Human rights are a relatively modern idea, and children's rights are a very modern one, but they have organic connections with things that are deep rooted in the Christian theological tradition. And so here we find that we have to move beyond the analogy with building sites and construction work and appeal to a more organic theme. We are back with Paul's image of the wild-olive shoot grafted into the old olive tree and sharing in the richness of its root (Rom. 11:17).

Theology works by making connections. The theological imagination of some thinkers – like Augustine, say – gives free play to a handful of themes and images rich in association which are invoked over and over again in a variety of different contexts. In Augustine's case that would be themes such as the two cities – the city of God and the human city – or the Pauline triad of faith, hope and love, which became ever more central to his thought as he grew older, and images like that of the wayfarer singing on his journey – singing a new song to the Lord. Those ideas are like haunting melodies that keep recurring in Augustine's writing – like a theme in a film score or like the new song itself.

What we are looking for here, then, is a theme or an image which is capable of doing two things. It must be robust enough to support the idea of rights and to make sense of the claim that children and other human beings have them. And it must, at the same time, be rich enough to help us make connections to other theological concerns.

The associations and resonances evoked by different themes will affect readers in different ways. We shall try out some concepts which may prove useful.

The ideas we shall look at are person, covenant, image and (in the next chapter) kingdom.

7.3.1 Person?

The word 'person' might seem the most natural of bridges between the Christian tradition and the concerns of children's and human rights. It was indeed so used in one of the key phases in the development of rights language within the churches that we looked at in an earlier chapter – John XXIII's encyclical *Pacem in terris*.[82]

What makes the word so attractive in this context is, on the one hand, its association with ideas of human dignity, integrity and equality and, on the other, the fact that it is so deeply rooted in Christian discourse. Indeed, much of the meaning with which we invest the word when we use it today is in fact a Christian development.[83] But person turns out to be a slippery word, and some of its associations are ones we might want to avoid.

To see why that is so, it will be necessary to look briefly at the history of the word. In both Greek and Latin, the word (*prosopon* in Greek, *persona* in Latin) could mean the mask an actor wore on the stage and so came to mean a character in a drama. It was in that sense that it began to be used for what we would call the persons of the Trinity.

If you were studying a poem or a play in the schools of the ancient world, you would ask who was meant to be speaking which lines. (And since ancient manuscripts had but sporadic punctuation and were often careless or inconsistent in indicating a change of dramatic speaker, the question was not always easy to answer.) One way of doing that was to ask *from whose person* – that is, by which character – a line was said.

By the middle of the second century, Christian theologians were anxious to prove that it was not always the same 'I' speaking in the prophetic texts of the Old Testament. Thus, Justin Martyr thinks that when the text of Isaiah says, 'What sort of a house will you build for *me*, says the Lord? Heaven is *my* throne, and the earth the footstool of *my* feet', the words are spoken 'from the *person* of the Father'.[84] But in the same book the passage 'I became manifest to those who were not asking after *me*; I was found by those not seeking *me*' is spoken 'as from the *person* of Christ himself'.[85] So the word 'person' was first used in Christian discourse to refer to the actors in the drama of salvation.

By the fourth century, it was commonly used as a label for what there were three of in the Trinity.[86]

By the middle of the fifth century, it had become established as orthodox doctrine that Christ was one *person* in two natures. 'Person' could be used when you were talking about *who* he was – Jesus Christ or the Word made flesh or Emmanuel, for example – and 'nature' could be used when you were talking about *what* he was – divine and human.

The Trinitarian and even more the Christological debates of the fourth and fifth centuries meant that the word 'person'

shifted a bit in meaning. The actor-in-a-drama sense tended
to be displaced by an emphasis on individuality. The word
came to suggest above all discrete existence, a separate
subsistent entity.

But not just any old separate subsistent entity would qualify.
As the word had originally meant a character in a drama,
so it continued to be used to refer to someone capable of
meaningful interaction. The Christian philosopher Boethius,
writing about 520, expressed what became the classical
definition in the Latin-speaking Church. A person, according
to Boethius, was 'an individual substance of rational nature'[87]
– that is, a particular specimen of something that possesses
rationality. So the word could be applied to human beings,
to angels and to the three who are the Trinity.

This connection with rationality has tended to stick to
the word. At the beginning of this section we referred to
John XXIII's encyclical *Pacem in terris*. We saw in an earlier
chapter that he there characterised a person as 'a nature
endowed with understanding and free will'.[88]

To construct a concept of rights around such an idea of
person is tempting. Each person is created by God, and each
person receives a call from God to live with him forever.
On that fact can be built notions of personal dignity and
personal equality.

And we could then give an explanation of where rights
come from. We could say that they flow from our inherent
dignity as rational creatures.

And if that is where rights come from, we could say that
that explains why some animals have them and others do
not. All human beings would have them, as would any other
intelligent animals, if there are any, while 'lower' animals
would not. So Mr Spock – we might think – has rights,
but not my cat.

That last conclusion is one not everybody would want
to agree with. There are vigorous defenders of the idea of
animal rights, such as the Oxford philosopher Andrew
Linzey.[89] Whether it makes sense to say that there are such

things as animal rights is not our concern here, but there are two points we would like to make.

In the first place, we noted in the last chapter that, while we have tended to speak here of a correlativity between *my* rights and *your* duties, it is also possible to think in terms of the connection that exists between *my* rights and *my* duties. If I have a right to vote, you have an obligation not to try to stop me – by tearing up my poll card, for example, or lying when I ask you where the polling station is. But I have an obligation in turn not to tear up your polling card or misdirect you. So my rights (normally) go hand in hand with a corresponding set of duties to others. Now, it does not make any sense to say that Rudi the cat has a set of duties she has to perform. I can try to dissuade her from scratching the upholstery to shreds, but I cannot call her a moral failure if she does. So if we think that that connection – between my rights and my duties – is an important part of what it means to have rights, it becomes quite odd to say that 'lower' animals have them.

And the second point we want to make is that even if we are reluctant to say that animals have *rights*, it does not follow that I have a *right* to treat the cat any way I want. In order to say that it is wrong to inflict pain on the cat, I do not need to claim that she has rights in the same sense that I do; I can simply say that it is wrong to inflict pain.

In any event, the problem of whether Mr Spock has rights and Rudi does not is a complex one, and it is not our business to try to solve it here. Our concern here is simply to say that tying rights to the idea of *person* and defining person as 'an individual substance of *rational* nature' would give us a tidy way of answering questions like that. And that would seem to be an advantage. It would seem to be another thing that that approach to the idea of rights has going for it.

Despite all that, we feel a certain reluctance to make the idea of person as we have just been using it the platform on which to erect the notion of rights. The problem is that it seems to do less than justice to the status and dignity of those who are not fully rational. That would be of concern in any discussion, but it is a particular concern in a consideration of children's rights.

Children's rights have to apply to infants, whose rational powers have not developed; to the very young, whose powers are developing; and, of course, to the handicapped, whose powers are impaired. If you take the kind of line we have just been floating – that rationality is central to the idea of person and person is central to the idea of rights – you end up saying that rights belong to persons who will be rational (someday) or who would be rational (other things being equal).[90]

The very young and the handicapped, on that sort of approach, end up being thought of as honorary members of the club of those who possess rights. And that is not something that we want to end up saying.

To try to get around that problem, we could abandon the traditional, Boethius-style understanding of person and decide to adopt a more flexible, psychologically determined one. That is, we could understand person in relational terms and say that a person is someone capable of significant interaction with others.[91] (Though Rudi the cat might then end up with rights after all, and we would have to think carefully through what we were saying in order to make sure that Lara Croft – of the computer game – did not have them as well.)

That kind of relational approach to the idea of person actually recovers some of the original meaning of the word. After all, as we have seen, 'person' entered the theological vocabulary to refer to characters playing their parts in a drama – the drama of salvation.

And it has a pleasing emotional resonance. To define a person as someone capable of significant interaction with others might seem an appropriate way of expressing the ultimate significance of the developing and expanding patterns of interaction of the child.

But again there is a problem, and it is hidden in the phrase 'developing and expanding patterns of interaction' that we have just used. A newly born infant is of course capable of deeply significant patterns of interaction – with the mother who feeds her, for example. But the stress that this approach places on relationship and interaction might suggest that fully developed personhood is somehow connected with fully developed patterns of interaction.

But we most emphatically do *not* want to end up saying that an infant or young child is only an apprentice at the job of being a person. The child is not 'a creature in search of humanity',[92] much less 'a brute having the shape of a man'.[93] The child is not on the way to being human, but is human.[94]

And so we are nervous of asking the word 'person' to do too much work.

7.3.2 *Covenant?*

Another tack we might take in our search for a theological foundation for human and children's rights is to explore the rich biblical theme of *covenant*. It could be said that the whole of scripture is the story of the working out of God's covenant with his people. God establishes a covenant with Abraham and his descendants forever and renews it in the covenant he makes with Moses at Horeb. And the New 'Testament' – the relationship between the words 'covenant' and 'testament' will occupy us in a moment – is the story of the 'new covenant in my blood' (Luke 22:20; 1 Cor. 11:25) which Jesus proclaims and establishes.

A covenant is essentially a bilateral agreement. In the ancient Near East it could refer to agreements between equals, like marriage contracts or treaties between states. But in the case of both the covenant with Abraham and the covenant with Moses, it is God and God alone who takes the initiative. The Lord appears to Abraham and says, 'I will *grant* my covenant between me and you' (Gen. 17:2) and 'I will *set up* my covenant between me and you and your posterity' (Gen. 17:7). And when Israel is afflicted in Egypt, he '*remembers*' his covenant (Exod. 2:24 and 6:5) and speaks to Moses on the mountain.

God's initiative calls a people into being. And that people is called upon collectively to accept covenant obligations in response to God's initiative and God's promise. Though it is to Abraham and Moses alone that God is speaking, a 'you' plural is in each case summoned to 'keep' the covenant (Gen. 17:10 and Exod. 19:5). And so in Deuteronomy when Moses presents the Ten Commandments to the children of Israel, he says,

> Israel, hear the decrees and judgements which I am speaking in your ears today. Learn them and keep them so as to do them. With us did the Lord our God seal a covenant on Horeb. It was not with our Fathers that the Lord sealed the covenant, but with us ourselves, the very ones who are here. (Deut 5:1–3)

And the Commandments which follow could be said to define a mutually binding set of claims and obligations. A son, a daughter, a manservant, a maidservant has a right not to work on the sabbath (Deut. 5:12–15). You have an obligation not to covet your neighbour's property (Deut. 5:21).

So it is tempting to use the covenant idea as a foundation if we want to say that God has called into being a human community bound together by a network of rights and duties. It would explain where our obligation comes from, how it is that we all share it, and how it is fundamentally God's gift.

A problem comes, though, from the fact that, as we have seen, a covenant was, in ordinary usage, a *bilateral* agreement. So *as a model* the idea of covenant – borrowed from the ordinary contractual language of the ancient Near East – captured the element of response that was an essential part of Israelite theology: 'learn them and keep them so as to do them'. But the model was less successful in bringing out God's sovereign freedom in choosing Israel and his gracious initiative in establishing the covenant.

That fact clearly bothered the Greek-speaking Jews who produced what became the standard translation of the Hebrew Bible into Greek – the Septuagint – in the third and second centuries BCE. So to translate 'covenant' they did *not* use the most natural Greek word for a bilateral agreement. Instead, almost without exception, they represented the Hebrew word *berith* (which occurs 284 times) by the Greek word *diatheke*. Now, *diatheke* comes from the same root as the most natural Greek word for a bilateral agreement (*syntheke*), but it means something that one person sets up or establishes. Its normal meaning in everyday Greek is 'will' – as in 'last will and testament'.

It is because of this special use of *diatheke* in the Septuagint that *diatheke* is also the normal word for 'covenant' in the New Testament – as in 'new covenant in my blood'. And it came to be translated into Latin as *testamentum*. That of course is why we speak of an Old *Testament* and a New.

For both the translators of the Greek Old Testament and the writers of the Greek New Testament, *diatheke* was a distinctly odd word to choose. After all, a will only comes into force at the death of the one who has made it, whereas the God who makes covenant lives forever, and it is precisely an abiding relationship with that God that the idea of covenant is meant to express. But the translators were willing to put up with that anomaly[95] in order to underline the untrammelled freedom that God enjoys in inaugurating the covenant.

Now, it turns out to be the case that the same problem that confronted the Alexandrian Jews who began the translation of the Septuagint in the third century BCE confronts us, in a particularly acute form, if we want to use the idea of covenant as a basis for a theology of human and children's rights. That is because rights of that sort – if they exist at all – have to be universal. We have to be able to say that *every* human being is the subject of human rights and *every* child possesses the rights of a child.

But that means that we have to have a *universal* covenant to start from. A special covenant, a partial covenant could be used as a model for exploring a child's position within a particular community, such as the Church. One theologian who in fact uses the idea of covenant in this way is John Calvin.

Calvin accounts for the practice of infant baptism – on which he insisted – by appealing to the notion of covenant. Infants are presented for baptism in order 'to confirm and ratify the covenant made with them by the Lord'. Parents also benefit, for in offering their children for baptism they 'arouse themselves to a surer confidence, because they see with their very eyes the covenant of the Lord engraved upon the bodies of their children'.[96]

The covenant so confirmed and ratified is, for Calvin, 'in substance and reality ... actually one and the same' as 'the covenant made with all the patriarchs'.[97] But it is still a partial covenant, a result of God's intervention within the course of human history. So Muslim parents, for example, clearly have no obligation to present their children for baptism. And yet we need to be able to say that, if children's rights are based on some sort of covenant, all children have rights and all parents – Christian, Muslim, whatever – have obligations.

Where can we find such a universal covenant? In the Old Testament the only plausible candidate is the one that God makes with Noah after the flood (Gen. 6:8–17). But that is in some ways a very odd covenant.

For one thing, God establishes his covenant not only with Noah and his posterity but also 'with every living beast of the earth with you – flying things, cattle, and every beast of the earth with you, of all that comes forth from the ark, every beast of the earth' (Gen. 9:9–10). Now, when we were thinking about animal rights, we said that it makes no sense to say that Rudi the cat has obligations: she just is. And similarly, it makes no sense to say that the covenant with Noah imposes covenant obligations in the ordinary sense if it includes all the beasts of the earth.[98]

And in fact the account of the covenant in Genesis 9 includes no response from Noah and no demand for a response. The preceding verses contain a prohibition on eating 'flesh with its life, the blood' and a general injunction against the shedding of human blood, backed up by the threat that God will 'exact' it from every beast or human that sheds it (Gen. 9:4–6). But even here no response is asked for or obtained.

Rabbinic tradition expands the list by speaking of seven Noachic commandments: prohibitions of the eating of living flesh, murder, idolatry, blasphemy, incest and theft, and the positive command to establish judicial authority.[99] These seven commandments are connected with the covenant of Genesis 9 and thought to be binding on every human being, Jew and non-Jew alike. Again, though, there is no room for response. Noah and his sons are not asked to accept or reject the seven commandments; they are simply given.

We have, then, noted three features of the covenant with Noah that set it apart from the normal sense of covenant in the Old Testament. It is universal; it includes both human and non-human animals; and it is established by God with no indication that it is accepted, or needs to be, by those with whom it is made.

Now, those three features are all interconnected. A *bilateral* covenant establishes a special relationship between God and his covenant partners and so sets them apart from others. But this covenant – the one with Noah – is more like a unilateral gift. It is in fact quite like God's blessing on creation. Indeed, the blessing on Noah and his sons in Genesis 9:1–3 corresponds quite closely in both theme and wording to the original blessing given at the creation of humankind in Genesis 1:28–9.

Can we, then, talk about a covenant with Adam or a covenant with creation? Those phrases are occasionally found. Irenaeus – the great theologian of the second century at whom we shall look more closely in the next section – speaks at one point of four covenants – the covenants of Adam, of Noah, of Moses and of the gospel.[100] But that is unusual. The word 'covenant' in fact appears for the first time in the book of Genesis in connection with God's promise to Noah.[101]

One contemporary ethicist who does make use of the idea of a creation covenant is Kieran Cronin. For Cronin, it is an important part of the theological foundation for rights language.

> The notion of an inclusive covenant which is framed at creation and constantly renewed throughout history, is the most basic doctrine of Christian ethics. It draws attention to God's loving initiative which is further expressed in special covenants with individuals and groups.[102]

From these various covenants it is, he argues, possible to derive networks of mutual rights and obligations. Of such covenants in which the emphasis is on promise – like that with Noah – and covenants in which the emphasis is on the demand of response – like that associated with the giving of the Law at Horeb – he writes:

> Together [they]underline God's transcendence as well as his respect for his creatures. He initiates and gives backing to human covenants by refusing the paternalistic option and respecting our dignity by demanding our participation in the right–duty relationship. God entrusts persons to one another in these normative relationships. By means of these covenants and rights he creates situations where human freedom and power are both constrained and extended. Through them he exercises his own 'power with' people to further his Kingdom. Above all God waits for humanity to recognise the challenge implicit in the concept of inclusive covenant.[103]

That is in many ways a very attractive picture. The danger is that it will end up stretching the idea of covenant so far that it snaps.

What makes the covenant model so attractive in the first place as a foundation for an explanation of rights is the picture of a *responsible* community called into being by God – a community responsible both in the sense of responding to the God who forms it as a community and in the sense of bearing responsibility to and for each other. 'Covenant' was, for Israel, an ideal way of expressing that – precisely because in everyday use it meant a bilateral agreement.

But there can be no bilateral agreement with creation. 'He spoke and it came to be; he commanded and it was present' (Ps. 33:9).

So we would like to look for a concept that will let us talk about the *relationship* between God and creation – or, to be precise, a concept that will let us talk about the relationship between God and the whole human creation. For it is only if we have a way of talking specifically about the human part of creation and of including all human beings that we can talk about a theological foundation for *human* rights and for the rights of that particular class of human beings who are also children.

We shall try to do that with the idea of *image*.

7.3.3 Image!

According to Genesis 1:26, 'God said, 'Let us make humankind in our image and according to our likeness'.' Few verses of Scripture have been the object of more theological reflection. Clearly, we cannot hope here to solve the problem of the text. Indeed, we might think that there is no 'solution', at least in any straightforward sense.

What we will try to do is, first, clarify the question we are asking. What *sort* of help can the text give us in our attempt to build a theological foundation for the concept of children's (and human) rights? Then we shall indicate something of the range of possible answers by looking briefly at different ways in which the image of God has been understood in the Church's reading of this text down the centuries. And finally we shall explore one possible answer, one model which can, we think, enrich our understanding of rights.

7.3.3.1 *The Image Question*

At least until the development of critical methods for the study of the Old Testament in the middle of the nineteenth century, the meaning of Genesis 1:26 was normally explored within the context of doctrinal or dogmatic discussion. That is, interpreters were not in the first instance asking the question what *did* the text mean (in the world in which it was written), but rather the question what *does* the text mean (for those who read it now). And so they were less interested in asking what it had to say about the thought and belief of ancient Israel and more interested in asking what it had to say about the Christian doctrine of creation. In the course of the last century, the study of comparative material from the ancient Near East made a substantial contribution to the debate,[104] but theological rather than more narrowly exegetical concerns often continued to set the agenda; examples would be the way in which reflection on Genesis 1:26 enriched the theological treatment of creation in the work of Dietrich Bonhoeffer and Karl Barth.

That means that down the centuries the interpretation of Genesis 1:26 has been shaped much more by theologians exploring problems of human existence than by commentators approaching the text without any theological axes to grind (or at least any they would advert to). So in looking at Genesis 1:26 the 'image' the theologian has seen has often been his or her own face reflected back from the text.

And that in turn means that down the centuries it has normally been an element of human existence that was felt to be particularly precious that has shaped the understanding of what it means to say that humankind is made in the image and according to the likeness of God. And sometimes this particularly precious characteristic of human existence has been thought of as something that was under threat – something that seemed in a particular time and a particular place to be in need of safeguarding.

A concrete example would be the way in which 'image' was interpreted by the second-century theologian Irenaeus of Lyons. At the end of this section we shall return to Irenaeus and suggest that he has much to contribute to our quest for a theological foundation for the language of rights. But here we would like to draw attention to the connection between the problem he faced and the theology of image which he developed: the question he asked shaped the answer he found.

As we will see later in this section, human beings are, for Irenaeus, said to be in the image of God primarily through their *bodies*. How did that idea fit into his thinking?

Irenaeus' great work *Against the Heresies* is an attack on different types of *Gnostic* thinking. Gnosticism was a widespread phenomenon in and on the edges of the second-century Church. Various Gnostic groups wanted to say – in different ways – that the material world we live in could not be the good creation of a good God. It was either a disastrous mistake or the product of an incompetent or malevolent maker who was a lesser being than the true God who lay somewhere beyond. So the real 'me' is something spiritual, something that has to be liberated from the dark, intractable unreality of the human body.

Irenaeus, by contrast, wants to insist that the glory of God is manifested in the material/spiritual creature he has made. Gnostics felt alienated from the material world and from their own bodies, reacting with loathing and revulsion to the meaninglessness of the material order and the evils of the world. For Irenaeus, the human body was the focal point of a world in process of transformation. Human beings in their materiality were bearers of the divine – supremely so in Christ and destined to be so in us at the resurrection.

How Irenaeus worked that out in terms of a theology of image, we shall see later in this section. The point we want to make now is that, in the second-century context, it was the physicality, the materiality of the human person that needed to be affirmed, and, as Irenaeus meditated on the meaning of Genesis 1:26, that is precisely what he saw.

So it is hardly surprising that different insights into what it is that makes a human being human have been reflected in different readings of what it means to be made in the image and according to the likeness of God. What *we* are looking for is a model that seems to do justice to the biblical text, on the one hand, and that resonates with the theological concerns we bring to it, on the other. In particular, that means one that will let us affirm the God-given dignity of all human beings in a way that will apply directly and forcefully even to the smallest and weakest.

7.3.3.2 Models of Image

What, then, does it mean to say that humankind is made in the image of God? We can look at some of the models that have been offered down the centuries in explanation of Genesis 1:26.

Historically, some of these theories – like that of Irenaeus – have distinguished sharply between image and likeness, while others – Calvin's, for example – identify the two and regard the whole phrase as an instance of the parallelism that is so characteristic of biblical Hebrew. The tendency of contemporary Old Testament scholarship is to make no distinction between the two prepositions ('in' and 'according to') and to regard the two nouns ('image' and 'likeness') as having the same referent.[105] Be that as it may, we shall focus here on image.

The answers that have at different times been proposed to the image question can be grouped in different ways.[106] It might be most helpful for our purposes to note that the image can be thought of as something intellectual, something moral, something relational, or something physical.

1. The human attribute that has most often been identified as the content of the image is rationality. Thus, the Alexandrian Jew Philo, early in the first century CE, thought that 'image' was used in Genesis 1:26 'with reference to the mind which governs the soul'.[107] That proved the most common answer in antiquity and is, for example, the view of Athanasius in the fourth century.[108]

   Augustine sometimes makes the same move of locating the content of the image in rationality,[109] but far more influential was to be the move he made in his monumental work *On the Trinity,* where he tentatively pointed to the triad of the faculties of memory, intellect and will as an analogy, an image of the Trinity within each of us.

   So the privileging of reason as the essential mark of true humanity begins to give way before Augustine's new interest in interiority, in inner psychological process. But it is still a set of *mental* attributes – something that goes on in your head – that characterises humanity.

   The identification of image with rationality appears also in the thought of the scholastics such as Thomas Aquinas in the thirteenth century,[110] though here the emphasis is less on rationality as an abstract quality and more on what it lets us do. In keeping with Thomas's concern with the fundamental orientation of the human person toward the good, it is, he thinks, above all in virtue of a 'capacity for rational self-direction' that we are said to have been made in the image of God.[111]

2. So there is in the later Middle Ages a partial shift in emphasis toward moral capacity, and with the Reformers this is the perspective that becomes dominant. Image is now understood less in terms of mental faculties (reason or the triad of memory, intellect and will) and more in terms of uprightness, mental and moral. It is as if the sixteenth-century world bears more dimly the imprint of the divine, and the response is a longing for

the restoration of a lost integrity. There is – on both sides of the religious divide – less optimism over the power of reason. And there is – on the Protestant side in particular – a need to affirm the radical fallenness of our broken and sinful world.

The Reformers, then, want to say that the image is lost or at least badly mangled at the Fall. The faculty of reason may become distorted and even perverted, but it is not actually lost. So it is not enough to say that the image resides there.

Luther knew that discussion of the image raised 'a sea of questions'. The views of his predecessors like Augustine involved 'not unpleasant speculations', but were 'not very useful'. For Luther himself, the image encompassed the whole being of Adam, physical, moral and intellectual.

> The image of God, in which Adam was created, was something by far the most illustrious and most noble, since no infection clung either to his reason or his will. But his interior and exterior senses were all spotless as well. His intellect was most pure, his memory most excellent , and his will most sound in splendid security with no fear of death or any anxiety. To these interior qualities there was added also a most beautiful and most excellent efficacy in his body and all his members … Adam had that image in his very being because not only did he know God and believe that he was good, but he even lived a fully divine life – that is, he was without fear of death or of any danger, satisfied with the grace of God.

But through sin that image was 'lost', 'obscured', 'vitiated', and replaced by 'the image of the devil'.[112]

For Calvin, also, the image touched the whole person. It described 'the integrity with which Adam was endowed' and 'was visible in the light of the mind, in the uprightness of the heart, and in the soundness of all the parts'. The Fall did not mean that 'God's image was totally annihilated and destroyed in him, yet it is so corrupted that whatever remains is frightful deformity'.[113]

It is not without implications for our project of exploring the connection between the concept of image and the language of rights to observe that Calvin points to the image of God as a foundation for our moral duties toward all human beings. Scripture teaches us, he says, that 'we are not to consider that men merit of themselves but to look upon the image of God in all men, to which we owe all honor and love'. It is, admittedly, 'among members of the household of faith that this same image is more carefully to be noted', but it can still be discerned in all humankind. We must 'look upon the image of God in them, which cancels and effaces their transgressions, and with its beauty and dignity allures us to love and embrace them'.[114]

We shall have occasion to return to Calvin on the image in the next section.

3. The twentieth century saw attempts to link the concept of image with a more holistic, more unified view of the human person. Thus, for Karl Barth, the 'God-likeness' the text speaks of 'is not a quality of man ... It does not consist in anything that man is or does.' Instead, 'he is the image of God in the fact that he is man.'[115]

Barth acknowledges his debt here to Dietrich Bonhoeffer, the Evangelical theologian who was hanged by the Nazis just a month before the end of the Second World War. Bonhoeffer was concerned with the shape of Christianity in a secular world and with a theology of and for 'man come of age'.

The image is for Bonhoeffer made manifest in the freedom to relate – to God and to each other. On the one hand,

> man differs from the other creatures in that God himself is in him, in that he is God's image in which the

free Creator views himself ... In the free creature the
Holy Spirit worships the Creator; uncreated freedom
praises itself in created freedom.

And, on the other hand, 'man is free by the fact that
creature is related to creature. Man is free for man
...'[116] And, for Bonhoeffer, the primal and paradigmatic
instance of this relatedness is the relationship of male
and female. After all, the text of Genesis goes on in
the next verse to say, 'And God made the human
being. According to his image he made him. Male
and female he made them' (1:27).

That idea is developed by Barth. As he expresses
it, God 'wills and creates man as a partner who is
capable of entering into covenant-relationship with
himself'.[117] Thus, God 'as Creator is free for man, and
the corresponding being is the man who as a creature
is free for God'.[118] This freedom finds expression in
an I–Thou relationship, both vertically – between
humankind and God – and horizontally – among
human beings. Humankind is

> created as a Thou that can be addressed by God but
> also as an I responsible to God; in the relationship
> of man and woman in which man is a Thou to his
> fellow and therefore himself an I in responsibility
> to this claim.[119]

Now, each of those three approaches to the problem,
each of those three clusters of answers, privileges one
aspect of human life, one dimension of human experience
– an aspect which was felt in a particular time and a
particular place to be most characteristic of truly *human*
life. And in each case, that in which the content of the
image is understood above all to consist not only gives
a picture of the ideal human life but also is the place
in human life where things have gone wrong.

Thus, in the prevalent psychology of the ancient
world, the human person – left to himself or herself

– is out of control. That was often expressed, in the writings of the Early Church, in terms of the model of the charioteer, borrowed from Plato's dialogue *Phaedrus*. The soul is like a chariot pulled by two feisty and high-spirited horses. The charioteer is the mind, the rational faculty of the soul. The horses are the appetitive and aggressive faculties that make us want things and assert ourselves to get them. The charioteer should be in charge, but he is in fact not, and the horses are running away with the chariot. The reaffirmation of reason, then, looks to the restoration of right order within the human person.

For Aquinas, men and women are so constituted that they naturally seek the good, but our priorities are so twisted and distorted that we seek lower goods at the expense of higher ones. Truly 'rational self-direction' here would not only enable the leading of a rightly ordered life but also would open us up to the appropriation of that friendship with God which is the gift of grace and which is the true good that is the real goal of human life.

Much of the thought of the Reformers is concerned with the radical depravity into which humankind has fallen as a result of Adam's baleful choice. So the problem is not just inverted priorities, but a desperate perversion of the will and the disintegration of true humanity.

Bonhoeffer's *Creation and Fall* was published in 1933 – the year that Hitler came to power. It is no coincidence that reflection on the proper modality of human relatedness should feature so prominently on the theological agenda.

In all these cases, then, the perception of a problem – a radical human problem – helped shape the identification of that in which the image was said to consist. Where does that leave us?

If our concern here is with the rights of the child, we want to start by affirming the basic human dignity of all children. And that means that we want to be able to talk about the way in which God is imaged forth even by those who are too young to exercise the power of reason or to make moral choices or consciously to shape their patterns of relationship.

7.3.3.3 Irenaeus and the Bodily Image of God

Let us return to Irenaeus of Lyons, the most powerful theological voice of the second century. He came from the Eastern Mediterranean – probably from Smyrna on the coast of Asia Minor[120] – and he thought and wrote in Greek. But around the year 177 CE he became bishop of Lyons in southern Gaul. His congregation would have been primarily an immigrant community, Greek- and perhaps some Aramaic-speakers in a Latin-speaking city that dominated a Celtic-speaking countryside. And just before he became bishop the church in Lyons suffered a vicious local persecution in which the pagan mob turned savagely against their Christian neighbours.[121]

But despite this context of social and cultural alienation, Irenaeus's theology is marked by an optimism and a confidence that God's plan of salvation is being worked out in the history of the good world that the good God has made. This vision is expressed in two surviving works – a massive refutation of various forms of Gnosticism which was written in the 180s and is known as *Against the Heresies* and a much shorter exposition of basic Christian teaching, no doubt for catechetical purposes, called the *Demonstration of the Apostolic Preaching*.

We start with the creation of Adam. 'Humankind was,' Irenaeus says, 'made through the hands of the Father – that is, through the Son and the Spirit' and was 'in the image and likeness of God'.[122] What he means above all when he says that is that it is the *flesh* which is formed in the image of God, while God-likeness is an extra gift, a gift of incorruptibility and immortality conferred through the Spirit. 'If the Spirit is absent from the soul, the one who is left in that condition is truly a creature of soul and flesh and will be imperfect since he has the image in his body but has not received likeness through the Spirit.'[123]

But humankind as it exists now – after Adam and before the appropriation of that gift of immortality which has been conferred on us in Christ but will not finally be ours until the resurrection – is no longer *like* God. It is, however, still in his *image*. Why that should be so can only be understood within the context of the whole story of God's plan of salvation as it is worked out in the course of God's dealings with his children.

For Irenaeus, the story of humankind is not just a story of Fall and redemption – of reversal and restoration. It is above all a story of growing up. Adam 'was a little one; for he was a child and had need to grow so as to come to his full perfection'.[124] And he was given Eve, who was also a child – which is why they did not have sex in the Garden. Though they were naked, 'their thoughts were innocent and childlike' and so '*they were not ashamed* [Gen. 2:25], as they kissed each other and embraced with the innocence of childhood'.[125]

But Adam 'was only a little one, and his discretion still undeveloped, wherefore also he was easily misled by the deceiver'.[126] And so Adam and Eve disobeyed God.

One consequence of this deception is that they were deprived of the gift of being in the likeness of God according to which 'the primal nature of humankind' had been made.[127] But, though Irenaeus says a number of times – as he does here – that Adam was made in *both* the image *and* the likeness, he is not totally consistent on the point. His 'most characteristic understanding of Genesis 1:26, and the one that most coheres with the rest of his theological scheme' is – in the words of Denis Minns – 'the notion that Adam was not created perfect, but rather created in the image of

God and intended to come to be in the likeness of God at the end of a process of development'.[128]

The whole history of humankind is the story of that 'process of development'. Through successive dispensations, God has been at work 'accustoming' humankind to God and God to humankind.[129] The decisive chapter of that history is the coming of the Word of God into our world as Jesus Christ. His humanity makes God visible in our world of time and space and is the paradigm, the pattern, of what humanity is meant to be. That means that it is in his flesh that Christ is the true image of God – for that is how he makes God visible. And because his humanity is the pattern of what ours should be, it is in virtue of our flesh that we can be said to have been made in accordance with that image.

> For in past times it was said that humankind was made in accordance with the image of God, but it was not shown to be the case, for the Word – in accordance with whose image humankind had been made – was still invisible. And that is why the likeness was lost so easily. But when the Word of God became flesh, he confirmed both, for he showed forth the true image – when he became that which was actually *his* image – and he restored the likeness securely, so making humankind like the invisible Father through the Word who had become visible. [130]

In his humanity Christ sums up all of human history and draws all of humankind to himself. Irenaeus's word for that summing up is 'recapitulation'. Christ 'summed up/recapitulated all humankind in himself – the invisible made visible, the one who cannot be comprehended made accessible, the one who cannot suffer made to receive suffering, the Word made human, recapitulating all things in himself'.[131] In this process he enfolds 'all the races of humankind dispersed from the time of Adam and all tongues and generations together with Adam himself'[132] and gathers up all the stages of human life.

Therefore he passed through every age, becoming an infant for infants, to sanctify them; becoming a child among children, sanctifying those of this age as well and becoming for them also an example of piety and righteousness and submissiveness; among young people a young person ... so too an old man[133] among the elderly, that he might be a perfect teacher for all ... Finally he came even to death that he might be 'first-born among the dead and hold the primacy in all things' [Col. 1:18] – he who is the prince of life and who was before all and preceded all.[134]

[And so] when he became incarnate and was made human, he recapitulated in himself the long history of humankind, giving us salvation in a concentrated dose, that what we had lost in Adam – that is, being in the image and likeness of God – this we might recover in Christ.[135]

And even now God is still at work, through his Spirit, to bring this process to its fulfilment and to bring humankind to its goal – a goal for which, in the childhood of human history – men and women were not yet ready.

For just as a mother can, of course, serve her baby grown-up food, but he is not yet able to receive food that is too much for him, so also God for his part could have supplied humankind with perfection from the beginning, but they were unable to receive it, for they were in their infancy ... And so, as you would do for infants, he who was the strong bread of the Father presented himself to us as milk – and that was his coming in flesh – so that we might, as it were, be nourished through the breast of his flesh and through that milk become accustomed to eat and drink the Word of God and so become able to receive within ourselves that bread of immortality which is the Spirit of the Father.[136]

God does all this so that 'the Church might be fitted out in the shape of the image of his Son and humankind might at last grow up – growing enough to see and to comprehend God'.[137]

So for Irenaeus the image is (1) something bodily and physical in which all human beings share. It is (2) not lost at the Fall but rather remains as a locus of God's saving activity in the world. It is (3) modelled after the flesh of Jesus Christ, in which God became visible in the world he had made. And it is (4) the subject of a process of growth and transformation that will reach its culmination only when our human God-likeness is restored and we come to see God as he is, face to face.

It is that idea of image that we would like to adopt and make our own. It is that that we would like to put forward as a theological basis of the concept of children's rights.

At the end of the day children have rights because they have human bodies. And that means, from a Christian point of view, that they are made in the image of the Word who took flesh and came into the world. To be precise, they are made in the image of the Word who took flesh in the womb of his mother and came into the world as a child himself.

Indeed, this concept of image could give us a basis for the idea of human rights in general. It would bring to that task three major advantages. It is inclusive; it sees things from the side of the most vulnerable; and it points ahead.

First, inclusivity: embodiment is irreducibly the lowest common denominator of human existence. Perhaps that is why the Prologue to John's Gospel does not say that the Word became an individual substance of rational nature or a moral decision-maker or a 'Thou' to somebody else's 'I': it says simply that the Word became flesh. It is the whole of human history and all of humankind that is 'recapitulated' in Christ.

The very young, the very poor, the weak, the handicapped and the dispossessed are all, at least, embodied. The only human beings who are not embodied are the dead, and they do not possess rights. Their heirs might possess rights on their behalf. The heir of a dead author might, for example, sue for infringement of copyright, but the dead author cannot do so himself. Nor do they have obligations. They simply are what they are in the hands of God.

A second advantage that this Irenaean understanding of image has is that it gives priority to the most vulnerable. It lets us take as our paradigm, not those best capable of functioning in society, but those most at risk. We can look at humankind from their side. The suffering and the needy do not need to say 'we are rational' or 'we are capable of moral decision' or 'we are free' – or we would be or should be, other things being equal. All they need to do is say 'we are here'. And if they cannot even say that, here they still are. And when we are considering the handicapped or disabled, there is an added poignancy in the fact that it is precisely their physicality – the physicality of a crippled body or a twisted limb – that is here taken as the marker of their humanity.

There is a further advantage to this Irenaean notion of image: it has a dynamism that looks beyond our world as it is to what it will become. Some models of image have a static quality and point to an abstract element of the human person, such as rationality. Others lay stress on what we have lost, such as original righteousness. But this Irenaean model appeals to a process of growth and looks to a fulfilment that still lies ahead. The image in the pattern of which all humankind is made is the flesh of Jesus Christ – that flesh in which the Word became visible within our world and which now reigns in glory at the right hand of the Father. And at the resurrection, all God's children will reflect the glory and incorruptibility of that flesh in their own bodies. 'All of us are', in Paul's words, 'being transformed in the same image, from glory into glory' (1 Cor. 4:18).

Now, all these advantages apply with special force to the special case of those human beings who happen also to be children. Those who are too young to lay claim to rationality or to make moral choices or to relate with a relatedness that reaches beyond those who care for them and nurture them are still embodied and so enjoy the dignity that comes from being made in the image of the incarnate Son whose flesh they share.

And this Irenaean model lets us start – as the UN Convention wants us to – from the point of view of the child, whose rights flow, not from what he or she will be, but from what he or she is. We can, perhaps, avoid the trap of defining children's needs from an adult perspective, because we have avoided the trap of thinking of children as apprentice adults.[138]

But despite this insistence on the fact that the rights of children must be grounded in what they are rather they what they will become, the Irenaean model also lets us look ahead – not just to the future of the individual child, but to the future of the whole human family of which he or she is a part.

This means that our view of the needs of the child can be shaped by a vision that is as wide as our view of human destiny and as strong as our yearning for the kingdom. More of that in the next chapter.

But first, let us try to put Irenaeus in some sort of context. How far is the vision we have been building on uniquely Irenaean? How far can it be taken as a pointer to a rich and deep vein within the wider Christian tradition?

The answer is a bit of both. Irenaeus has a strong and evocative theological imagination. He has the gift of making connections and hearing echoes. And he has the ability to *see* – to see an image in vivid and concrete terms and not get lost in abstractions. He also had the advantage of living and thinking in a richly creative period in the history of Christian theology.

We have been using Irenaeus's understanding of the image and his poignant picture of Adam and Eve as children as a paradigm, a model. We hope that it lets us *see* as Irenaeus saw – that it lets us make connections we had not made before. If it does so, that is its justification.

Irenaeus does have a distinctive vision, and yet he is not alone: his vision can be tied in to major strands of the Christian tradition. We will take two examples, one from the Early Church and one from the Reformation.

The Christian doctrine of the relation of Jesus Christ to his Father – what we affirm in the creed when we say that the Son is 'God from God, light from light, true God from true God, of one being with the Father' – that doctrine was hammered out in the two decades or so after the Council of Nicaea of 325 CE. The key players in those years on what came to be regarded as the orthodox side were Marcellus of Ancyra and Athanasius of Alexandria.

For Marcellus, the image in which or in accordance with which Adam was created was the incarnate humanity of Jesus Christ. The whole point of an image is that it is supposed to make the invisible visible. The flesh of Jesus Christ makes God visible in our world of time and space, and it is after that pattern that Adam was fashioned.[139] So in Marcellus there is the same stress we found in Irenaeus on the physicality of the image and on the body as that in which and through which we find our place in God's plan of salvation.

Marcellus eventually came to be labelled a heretic, for views he supposedly held on the temporal end of Christ's kingdom, when he would in the fullness of time hand over all things to his Father. But the theological line that flows from Athanasius was developed by his great fifth-century successor, Cyril of Alexandria, and came to dominate the thought and the piety of the whole of Eastern Christendom.

The theological vision of Athanasius and Cyril is of a world transformed by the incarnation. For Athanasius – as for most of the Early Church – the image resides in the mind. But it is through the body that we experience human solidarity and through the body that we are joined to Christ. In the incarnation he takes our flesh – the corruptible, decaying flesh of perishing, mortal humanity – and fills it with his life and goodness. Our flesh is transformed because it is the same as his flesh; it becomes incorruptible – immune from decay – and ready for the stability and glory of the resurrection life.

This line of thought – which had such an influence on subsequent centuries – differs from Irenaeus in that it does not understand the image in bodily terms. But it does stress the bodiliness of our existence. We are one because we all share the same flesh, and all human flesh is, in principle at least, transformed in Christ.[140]

Finally, we shall look at a branch of the Christian tradition that seems to start from a very different view of the image and its corruption at the Fall. The classical Reformed tradition entertains a deep pessimism as to the radical effects of the Fall and stresses the loss of the image and the consequent alienation and estrangement of humankind in its present state. All that seems far removed from the optimism of Irenaeus's picture of the human family growing towards maturity. And yet even here bridges can be built.

Just above we identified four elements in Irenaeus's understanding of the image.[141] All find some sort of correspondence in the thought of John Calvin. We said, first of all, that the image is for Irenaeus something bodily and physical in which all human beings share. While for Calvin 'the primary seat of the divine image was in the mind and heart' of Adam, yet 'there was no part in which some sparks did not shine'. And, in particular, the senses and the body itself were well ordered to obeying the call of reason.[142]

Secondly, we said that for Irenaeus the image is not lost at the Fall but rather remains as the locus of God's saving activity in the world. Calvin's thought is of course more negative here. He can say that the image is 'destroyed'[143] or 'erased'.[144] But he can also say that 'certain faint outlines of that image remain behind in us'. A concrete example of what remains is dominion over the rest of the animal creation, which 'is indeed some part of the image of God' and which is handed down to Adam's posterity and in part at least is still found there. Indeed, even in his present, corrupt state, 'if you consider everything rightly, the human being is, among the other creatures, a remarkable specimen of divine wisdom, righteousness, and goodness'.[145]

In the third place, the image is, for Irenaeus, modelled after the flesh of Jesus Christ in which God was made visible in our world. Calvin specifically denies a thesis very like that in polemic against the Lutheran scholar Osiander.[146] But, in commenting on 2 Corinthians 3:18, he says that it is through contemplating the revelation of God in the gospel that 'we are transformed into the image of God'.[147] And he repeatedly argues backwards, from our transformation in Christ to the nature of the image that was lost in Adam. It is only through our experience of the former that we can come to understand the latter.[148]

And finally – and perhaps most significantly – there is also a correspondence with our observation that in Irenaeus the image is the subject of a process of growth and transformation that will reach its perfection only when we come to see God as he is, face to face. For Calvin,

> there must be a continual process of growth both in knowledge of and in conformity to the image of God ... The end of the Gospel is that the image of God ... be repaired in us, and this restoration progresses continually for the whole of our lives, because God makes his glory shine forth in us little by little.

There is 'daily progress', but 'perfection lies ahead'.[149]

Calvin's theology is very different from Irenaeus's, but there are significant points of contact. There are resources within Calvin's theology for developing the idea of image in a more Irenaean direction. And we may remember that Calvin himself uses the doctrine of the image to underpin our moral responsibilities toward each other.[150]

Irenaeus is distinctive, but he is not alone. His thought can help us see something that lies inchoate in other parts of the Christian tradition.

We shall conclude this section by drawing attention to one further consequence of the Irenaean model. If the whole of human history is a story of growing up, from the childhood of Adam and Eve in the Garden to the fullness of the vision and the knowledge of God at the end, the growing child turns out to be, not just a part of the human family, but the paradigm of the life of that family. In that sense the child is herself the model of what it means to be human. The dignity that entails gives us, we think, a theological foundation for our understanding of the origin and nature of children's rights.

Notes

1. See below on Greven and Miller's 'poisonous pedagogy' thesis.
2. Bunge (ed.), *Child*. We should note one of the constraints on the collection. The standpoint of the essays in Bunge's book largely reflects the concerns of contemporary American academic interest in the problem. That means among other things that there is a certain foreshortening of historical perspective: over half the essays in the volume deal with the last three centuries. And that in turn means that the shadows of post-Enlightenment individualism and consumerist economics hang heavily over many of the authors of these essays and many of the thinkers about whom they write. Social solidarity becomes, then, an item on an agenda rather than being a presupposition of discussion of the needs of children – as it was for thinkers like Augustine or Aquinas, who are discussed here. But if this foreshortening is a limitation in a historical sense, it is one which accurately reflects the social and academic context of much of the recent discussion. In that sense it is a limitation which we too inevitably face.
3. To speak in this context of *the* tradition in the singular is of course problematic. But that is to a large extent true of any theological tradition – even rather more narrowly defined ones, like 'the Reformed tradition' or 'the Thomist tradition'. The writers whose views we shall be considering in this section speak from a wide range of quite diverse ecclesial and dogmatic traditions and speak to a whole variety of social and historical

concerns. In using the singular we do not imply a denial of that diversity. But yet there are recurrent themes. And the history of attempts to grapple with the central problem of Christian nurture is *one* history, as the whole history of theology is one history.

4. See Vigen Guroian, 'The Ecclesial Family: John Chrysostom on Parenthood and Children', in Bunge (ed.), *Child*, pp. 61–77, at p. 74.

5. See Cristina L. H. Traina, 'A Person in the Making: Thomas Aquinas on Children and Childhood', in Bunge (ed.), *Child*, pp. 103–33, at pp. 121–2.

6. See Jane E. Strohl, 'The Child in Luther's Theology: "For What Purpose Do We Older Folks Exist, Other Than to Care for ... the Young?"', in Bunge (ed.), *Child*, pp. 134–59, at pp. 147–8, 150.

7. See Barbara Pitkin, '"The Heritage of the Lord": Children in the Theology of John Calvin', in Bunge (ed.), *Child*, pp. 160–93, at pp. 170–1.

8. See Keith Graber Miller, 'Complex Innocence, Obligatory Nurturance, and Parental Vigilance: "The Child" in the Work of Menno Simons', in Bunge (ed.), *Child*, pp. 194–226, at p. 194.

9. See Dawn DeVries, '"Be Converted and Become as Little Children": Friedrich Schleiermacher on the Religious Significance of Childhood', in Bunge (ed.), *Child*, pp. 329–49, at p. 342.

10. Guroian, 'Ecclesial Family', p. 74 (Chrysostom) and Traina, 'Person in the Making', pp. 121–2 and 125 (Aquinas).

11. Traina, 'Person in the Making', p. 126, citing ST II IIae 10.12.

12. Strohl, 'Child in Luther's Theology', p. 140, citing *Luther's Works*, ed. Jaroslav Pelikan and Helmut Lehmann, vol. 45, p. 46.

13. Or Fifth, depending on how one counts. The Commandment and its interpretation is discussed below, in 7.2.2.

14. See Catherine A. Brekus, 'Children of Wrath, Children of Grace: Jonathan Edwards and the Puritan Culture of Child Rearing', in Bunge (ed.), *Child*, pp. 300–28, at p. 307.

15. DeVries, 'Be Converted'. pp. 343–4.

16. Strohl, 'Child in Luther's Theology', p. 147.

17. Ibid., pp. 146, 155–6.

18. Pitkin, 'Heritage', pp. 177–8; see also pp. 174 and 186–7.

19. Miller, 'Complex Innocence', pp. 217–19.

20. William Werpehowski, 'Reading Karl Barth on Children', in Bunge (ed.), *Child*, pp. 386–405, at pp. 395–7.

21. Pitkin, 'Heritage', p. 172.

22. Miller, 'Complex Innocence', p. 212.

23. Marcia J. Bunge, 'Education and the Child in Eighteenth-Century German Pietism: Perspectives from the Work of A. H. Franke', in Bunge (ed.), *Child*, pp. 247–78, at p. 266.

24. Strohl, 'Child in Luther's Theology', p. 147.

25. Guroian, 'Ecclesial Family', pp. 66 and 69; see also p. 76 (a seal leaving an impression in wax).

26. *Homily on Eph 6:1–4*, cited by Guroian, 'Ecclesial Family', p. 66.

27. Richard P. Heitzenrater, 'John Wesley and Children', in Bunge (ed.), *Child*, pp. 279–99, at p. 293.

28. See Philip Greven, *The Protestant Temperament, Patterns of Child-Rearing, Religious Experience, and the Self in Early America*, New York: Alfred A. Knopf, 1977, and *Spare the Child*; Alice Miller, *For Your Own Good: Hidden Cruelty in Child-Rearing and the Roots of Violence*, tr. Hildegarde and Hunter Hannum, New York: Farrar, Straus & Giroux, 1983.

29. On the ambiguities in Calvin's discussion of infants, see Pitkin, 'Heritage', pp. 166–9.

30. Margaret Bendroth, 'Horace Bushnell's *Christian Nurture*', in Bunge (ed.), *Child*, pp. 350–64, at p. 363.

31. Pitkin, 'Heritage', pp. 190–1.

32. Miller, 'Complex Innocence', pp. 195 and 202–3.

33. Werpehowski, 'Reading Karl Barth on Children', pp. 389 and 391–2.

34. Mary Ann Hinsdale, '"Infinite Openness to the Divine": Karl Rahner's Contribution to Modern Catholic Thought on the Child', in Bunge (ed.), *Child*, pp. 406–45, at pp. 421 and 424.

35. Hauerwas, *Suffering Presence*, p. 125.

36. Ibid., p. 129.

37. This seems to echo the approach of Saudi Arabia and the Holy See referred to at 2.5.1 and 2.5.2 above.

38. Hauerwas, *Suffering Presence*, p. 129.

39. Ibid., p. 130.

40. Particularly since the publication of MacIntyre's *After Virtue*, the first edition of which appeared in 1981.

41. An excellent introduction to and analysis of Thomas's thought on the question is Porter, *Recovery of Virtue*.

42. Thus, 'temperance' is another of those items in the moral vocabulary that has shifted its meaning. For someone like Aquinas, teetotalism would have been *intemperate*, because it is an extreme and

temperance involves keeping the right balance. Another example of a word that has shifted meaning is prudence. For someone like Aquinas, prudence is one of the four cardinal virtues (along with temperance, fortitude and justice). It enables us to choose and to put into practice that course of action which is best suited in a particular context to realise that which is truly good. What prudence all too often means in contemporary parlance would for Aquinas be the vice of parsimony.

43. Stanley Hauerwas, *A Community of Character, Toward a Constructive Christian Social Ethic*, Notre Dame: University of Notre Dame Press, 1981, p. 115.

44. Ibid., p. 99.

45. Ibid., p. 97.

46. Hauerwas does acknowledge that 'neither the language of duty nor of virtue excludes the other on principle' (ibid., p. 114), but normally speaks as if there is a strong tension between virtues and rules.

47. ST Ia IIae 100.3 *ad* 1: 'those two precepts are the first and common precepts of the law of nature, which are known in and of themselves to human reason, either through nature or through faith'; Ia IIae 100.4 *ad* 1; Ia IIae 100.11.

48. Hauerwas, *Suffering Presence*, p. 130.

49. The opposite is done with the injunctions against covetousness at the end of the list (Exod. 20:14/Deut. 5:18), so ensuring on either reckoning that the Ten Commandments are in fact ten in number.

50. Some medieval rabbinic commentators saw in that clause a promise of the life of the world to come. See the citation of Abraham Ibn Ezra in A. Cohen (ed.), *The Soncino Chumash: The Five Books of Moses with Haphtaroth*, Soncino Books of the Bible, London: Soncino Press, 1947, p. 1018.

51. The previous verse has accused Eli of *honouring* (same word) his sons more than the Lord by letting them take the best bits of sacrificial meat.

52. For this use of the idea of trumps, see above, 3.3.3.

53. For a recent and very useful discussion of the relationship between Colossians and Ephesians and of the authorship of the letters, see John Muddiman, *A Commentary on the Epistle to the Ephesians*, Black's New Testament Commentaries, London: Continuum, 2001, pp. 2–47.

54. For the *Haustafel* as a conventional literary device and for the interrelationship of the various New Testament examples, see Ernest Best, *A Critical and Exegetical Commentary on Ephesians*,

International Critical Commentary, Edinburgh: T&T Clark, 1998, pp. 519–27, and Muddiman, *Ephesians*, pp. 250–5.

55. This was essentially the view of Martin Dibelius, whose pioneering discussion of the *Haustafel* form underlies all subsequent critical study. He thought that 'their existence in early Christian writings bears witness to the need primitive Christianity had to settle down in everyday life'. The radically eschatological message of early Christianity meant that it 'was scarcely prepared to satisfy that need and could, at any rate, not do justice to it in terms of the thought of the Gospel of Jesus': Martin Dibelius, *Die Briefe des Apostels Paulus* II, *Die neun kleinen Briefe*, Handbuch zum neuen Testament III, Tübingen: J.C.B. Mohr (Paul Siebeck), 1913, p. 91.

56. See the texts cited in Hermann L. Strack and Paul Billerbeck, *Kommentar zum neuen Testament aus Talmud und Midrasch*, III, *Die Briefe des neuen Testaments und die Offenbarung Johannis*, München: C. H. Beck, 1926, p. 614.

57. Musonius, *Oration* 16 (ed. Hense (1905), pp. 81–8); Aulus Gellius, *Attic Nights* II.7.

58. Musonius, *Or.* XVI (p. 84.2–14 Hense).

59. Musonius, *Or.* XVI (p. 86.15–p. 97.11 Hense).

60. Musonius, *Or.* XVI (p. 83.4–8 Hense).

61. No upper age is specified. Commentators point out that in both Judaism and Graeco-Roman society, adults were assumed still to have a duty of obedience toward their parents (see Best, *Ephesians*, p. 563). That is true, but the whole picture of the concentric circles that make up the *familia* – parents, children, household slaves – presupposes that the children have not yet established their own families.

62. It is not self-evidently the case that Ephesians and Colossians were first addressed to Ephesus and Colossae. The problem is that (1) both letters lack the specificity of detail, the local colouring of people and problems, that are found in other Pauline letters and (2) a small but very significant group of manuscripts omits 'in Ephesus' from the address of Ephesians (Eph. 1:1), leaving, as it were, a blank where the identification of the recipients should be.

63. See, for example, *Didache* 2:2 (perhaps from the end of the first century) and Justin Martyr, *First Apology* 27:1 (from the middle of the second).

64. John Chrysostom, *Homily XXI on Ephesians* (p. 164 B-C Montfaucon). For Chrysostom's attitude to children, see the slightly gushing appreciation by Guroian, 'Ecclesial Family'.

65. Whether this phrase was part of the original or not, it eventually became the standard reading in the Greek Church and was already firmly established in the so-called Syrian text type which John Chrysostom used.

66. John Chrysostom, *Homily XXI on Ephesians* (p. 158F–p. 159A Montfaucon).

67. Thomas Aquinas, *Super Epistolam ad Ephesios Lectura*, chapter 6, lectio 1.

68. John Calvin, *Opera Exegetica*, vol. XVI, *Commentarii in Pauli Epistolas ad Galatas, ad Ephesios, ad Philippenses, ad Colossenses*, ed. Helmut Feld, Geneva: Librarie Droz, 1992, p. 275.

69. Ibid., p. 455.

70. Both quotations are from Wesley's Sermon 96 (= *The Bicentennial Edition of the Works of John Wesley*, Nashville: Abingdon, 1975–), 3, 367 and 370. The passages are quoted in Heitzenrater, 'John Wesley and Children', at pp. 279 and 285.

71. John Wesley, *Explanatory Notes upon the New Testament*, London: Epworth Press, 1950.

72. J. B. Lightfoot, *Saint Paul's Epistles to the Colossians and to Philemon* (3rd edn), London: Macmillan and Co., 1879, p. 225.

73. *Catechism of the Catholic Church*, no. 2217 (p. 478): our italics.

74. The duty to follow one's conscience, even if it is in fact (objectively) mistaken, is a traditional part of Catholic moral teaching. See, for example, Thomas Aquinas, ST Ia IIae 19.5.

75. The word here translated 'seeks him early' is difficult, and its meaning is in fact uncertain.

76. See the discussion in R. N. Whybray, *The Book of Proverbs: A Survey of Modern Study*, History of Biblical Interpretation Series 1, Leiden: E. J. Brill, 1995, pp. 150–7.

77. See the headings at Proverbs 1:1; 10:1; 22:17; 24:23; 25:1; 30:1; and 31:1.

78. *Ahiqar* 81–2, in James H. Charlesworth (ed.), *The Old Testament Pseudepigrapha* (2 vols), London: Darton, Longman & Todd, 1983–5, vol. 2, p. 498. For the date, see vol. 2, p. 482.

79. See Whybray, *Proverbs*, pp. 6–33.

80. A difference is that scholastic natural law theory was – as Jean Porter well shows in her admirable study *Natural and Divine Law* – more specifically linked to human capacity for rational self-determination and moral choice.

81. Perhaps we should say a fully functioning adult *man* since it can be claimed, from one point of view, that the aim of rights

language was to underpin the freedom of action and guarantee the political and economic security of those in the best position to function well in eighteenth-century society.

82. See above, p. 161.
83. See, for example, Loren E. Lomasky, 'Person, Concept of', in Lawrence C. Becker (ed.), *Encyclopedia of Ethics* (2 vols), Chicago: St James Press, 1992), vol. 2, pp. 950–6.
84. Justin Martyr, *First Apology* 37:1–4, citing Isaiah 66:1 (and inverting the order of the clauses).
85. Justin Martyr, *First Apology* 49:1–4, citing Isa. 65:1–3.
86. 'Person' was far from being the only word in use to refer to what there were three of in the Trinity. Athanasius – the great champion in the fourth century of the doctrine of the equal divinity of Father and Son – most commonly called them simply three 'things'.
87. Boethius, *Against Eutyches and Nestorius* 3.
88. See above, p. 161.
89. See Andrew Linzey, *Animal Rights: A Christian Assessment of Man's Treatment of Animals*, London: SCM Press, 1976, and *Christianity and the Rights of Animals*, London: SPCK, 1987.
90. Thomas Aquinas accepts and defends Boethius' definition of 'person' in ST I 29.1. 'Thomas thus measures the process of human maturation largely by the capacity to reason ... Children are only temporarily incomplete, not essentially inferior, for childhood imperfection is something one outgrows': Traina, 'Person in the Making', p. 111.
91. Thus, among feminist theologians, 'connections to others and a fluid selfhood are prized over views of the self as separate and self-sufficient', according to Bonnie J. Miller-McLemore, '"Let the Children Come" Revisited: Contemporary Feminist Theologians on Children', in Bunge (ed.), *Child*, pp. 446–73, at p. 466.
92. That the child was so regarded – on both sides of the religious divide – in Reformation Europe is maintained by the historian Steven Ozment, *When Fathers Ruled: Family Life in Reformation Europe*, Cambridge, MA: Harvard University Press, 1983, pp. 138–9. I owe the reference to Strohl, 'Child in Luther's Theology', p. 149.
93. The phrase comes from Lewis Bayly – Bishop of Bangor under James I and author of *The Practice of Piety*, which was enormously popular in Puritan circles; the phrase is cited by Anthony Fletcher, 'Prescription and Practice: Protestantism

and the Upbringing of Children, 1560–1700', in Diana Wood (ed.), *The Church and Childhood*, Studies in Church History, 31, Oxford: Blackwell, 1994, pp. 325–46, at p. 326.

94. Karl Rahner, 'Ideas for a Theology of Childhood', *Theological Investigations*, vol. 8, tr. David Bourke, London: Darton, Longman & Todd, 1971, pp. 33–50, at p. 37. See the very useful discussion of this important essay by Hinsdale, '"Infinite Openness"'.

95. The author of Hebrews makes theological capital of this in order to connect the idea of a new covenant with the death of Christ (Heb. 9:16–17).

96. John Calvin, *Institutes of the Christian Religion* (1559 edn), 4.16.21 and 4.16.9. I quote from the translation of Ford Lewis Battles, 2 vols, Library of Christian Classics, 20 and 21, Philadelphia: Westminster Press, 1960. These passages are unchanged from the 1539 edition of the *Institutes*.

97. Calvin, *Institutes* (1559 edn), 2.10.2.

98. So Claus Westermann says of Genesis 9:10, 'It is this very verse, which extends the "covenant" to all species of animals, that makes clear that there can be no question of what is usually understood by covenant or of what is later called the promise. This assurance requires no acceptance or approval of any kind': Claus Westermann, *Genesis 1–11: A Commentary*, tr. John J. Scullion, London: SPCK, 1984, p. 471.

99. See Saul Berman, 'Noachide Laws', in Cecil Roth et al., *Encyclopaedia Judaica* (16 vols), Jerusalem Publishing House, 1971–2, vol. 12, cols 1189–91.

100. Irenaeus, *Against the Heresies* 3:11:8.

101. The Hebrew word *berith* is first used in Genesis 6:18 and then not again until 9:9.

102. Cronin, *Rights and Christian Ethics*, p. 230. See his very sympathetic development of a covenant model of rights, pp. 209–32.

103. Ibid., p. 231.

104. An instance would be a number of influential studies that draw on texts from ancient Egypt and Mesopotamia which describe the king as the image of (a) god and his representative of earth. See, for example, H. Wildberger, 'Das Abbild Gottes, Gen. 1: 26–30', *Theologische Literaturzeitung*, 21 (1965), pp. 245–59 and 481–501.

105. See Westermann, *Genesis 1–11*, pp. 145–7. Note that in Genesis 5:3 Adam is said to beget a son, Seth, 'in his likeness, according to his image': the same two nouns and the same two prepositions

are used, but the order of the nouns has been reversed and the preposition that goes with each has been swapped.

106. For surveys of different theories, see Karl Barth, *Church Dogmatics*, III, *The Doctrine of Creation*, Part One, tr. J. W. Edwards et al., Edinburgh: T&T Clark, 1958, pp. 192–7, and Westermann, *Genesis 1–11*, pp. 147–55. For the ancient Church in particular, there is a useful review in Walter J. Burghardt, *The Image of God in Man according to Cyril of Alexandria*, Studies in Christian Antiquity, 14, Woodstock, MA: Woodstock College Press, 1957, pp. 1–6, 12–21.

107. Philo, *De Opificio Mundi* 69.

108. Athanasius, *De Incarnatione* 3.

109. See Augustine, *83 Quaestiones* 51.

110. Thomas Aquinas, ST I 93.2 and 4.

111. The phrase comes from Porter, *Recovery of Virtue*, p. 140, citing the introduction to ST Ia IIae.

112. Martin Luther, 'Genesisvorlesung' on Genesis 1:26, *Werke, Kritische Gesamtausgabe*, vol. 42, Weimar: Hermann Böhlaus Nachfolger, 1911, pp. 45–7.

113. Calvin, *Institutes* (1559 edn) 1.15.3–4 (Battles translation).

114. Calvin, *Institutes* 3.7.6 (Battles translation).

115. Barth, *Church Dogmatics* III, 1, p. 184.

116. Dietrich Bonhoeffer, *Creation and Fall: A Theological Interpretation of Genesis 1–3*, tr. John C. Fletcher, London: SCM Press, 1959, p. 36. These passages are used by Barth in the development of his own position: *Church Dogmatics*, III, 1, p. 195.

117. Barth, *Church Dogmatics*, III, 1, p. 185.

118. Ibid., III, 1, p. 196.

119. Ibid., III, 1, p. 198.

120. At least he records the fact that in his youth he had heard the aged bishop of Smyrna, Polycarp (*Adversus Haereses* III.3.4).

121. The persecution is vividly described in the contemporary *Letter of the Churches of Lyons and Vienne*, preserved in Eusebius' *Ecclesiastical History* V.1–3.

122. *Against the Heresies* V.6.1. The word we have translated here as 'humankind' is *homo* in the Latin version in which Irenaeus' text has come down to us. It means both a particular human being (Adam) and human beings generically. It is difficult to capture both meanings at once in English if we reject 'man' on the grounds of non-inclusivity.

123. Ibid.

124. St Irenaeus, *Proof of the Apostolic Preaching*, tr. Joseph P. Smith, Ancient Christian Writers, 16, Westminster, MA: Newman Press, 1952, 12.

125. Ibid. 14.

126. Ibid. 12.

127. *Against the Heresies* V.10.1.

128. Denis Minns, *Irenaeus*, Outstanding Christian Thinkers Series, London: Geoffrey Chapman, 1994, p. 61 – an excellent and very readable introduction to Irenaeus and his world.

129. See *Against the Heresies* III.20.2; IV.14.2; IV.21.3, 'accustoming his heritage to obey God and to make their pilgrim way in the world and to follow his Word'.

130. *Against the Heresies* V.16.2.

131. *Against the Heresies* III.16.6.

132. *Against the Heresies* III.22.3.

133. Irenaeus thinks that Jesus was nearly fifty when he died, arguing (in part) from John 8:57: 'you are not yet fifty years old' (*Against the Heresies* II.22.5–6).

134. *Against the Heresies* II.33.4.

135. *Against the Heresies* III.18.1.

136. *Against the Heresies* IV.38.1.

137. *Against the Heresies* IV.37.7.

138. In rejecting the idea of children as apprentice adults, we do not mean to reject Karl Bath's romantic but rather attractive evocation of a childhood in which the young 'are not by nature their [the parents'] property, subjects, servants, or even pupils, but their apprentices, who are entrusted and subordinated to them in order that they might lead them into the way of life': Barth, *Church Dogmatics* III, *The Doctrine of Creation*, Part Four, tr. A. T. Mackay et al., Edinburgh: T&T Clark, 1961, p. 243.

139. For Marcellus and his theology, the theological author would like to refer to his wife's forthcoming book: Sara Parvis, *Marcellus of Ancyra and the Lost Years of the Arian Controversy*.

140. On Athanasius' theology in general, see Khaled Anatolios, *Athanasius, the Coherence of His Thought*, London: Routledge, 1998, and, for his theology of the body in particular, see Alvyn Pettersen, *Athanasius and the Human Body*, Bristol: Bristol Press, 1990.

141. See above, p. 324.

142. John Calvin, 'Commentarius in Genesin', in *Opera Quae Supersunt Omnia*, ed. Guilielmus Baum, Eduardus Cunitz and Eduardus Reuss, vol. XXIII = Corpus Reformatorum,

vol. LI, Braunschweig: C. A. Schwetschke and Son, 1882, cols 26–7 (on Gen. 1:26). Calvin makes a very similar remark in *Institutes* I.15.3.

143. Ibid., col. 26.

144. John Calvin, *Opera Exegetica*, vol. XV, *Commentarii in Secundam Pauli Epistolam ad Corinthios*, ed. Helmut Feld, Geneva: Libraire Droz, 1994, p. 66 (on 2 Cor. 3:18).

145. Calvin, 'Commentarius in Genesin', cols 25–7. See also *Institutes* I.15.4.

146. Calvin, *Institutes* I.15.3.

147. Calvin, *In Secundam Pauli Epistolam ad Corinthios*, p. 66.

148. Calvin, 'Commentarius in Genesin', col. 26; *Opera Exegetica*, vol. XVI, *Commentarii in Pauli Epistolas ad Galatas, ad Ephesios, ad Philippenses, ad Colossenses*, pp. 448–9 (on Col. 3:10); *Institutes* I.15.4.

149. Calvin, *In Secundam Pauli Epistolam ad Corinthios*, p. 66.

150. See above, p. 317.

8

Children's Rights and Human Destiny

8.1 Childhood and the Kingdom

In the last chapter we looked at children's rights, asking what they are and how they work, and how they can be backed up theologically. In this chapter we want to ask what it is all for – what kind of a life it is that our efforts to nurture and protect are meant to foster, what kind of a goal it is that they presuppose and are directed towards. Those are questions that can be answered on different levels and within different frames of reference. Individual human lives have a goal, and it is at that level that decisions affecting the future of individual children have to be made. That will be the focus of the later sections of this chapter. What sort of human teleology is implicit in our efforts on behalf of the child? What is it that we are trying to facilitate or to enable?

But human life as a whole also has a goal, and that goal turns out to be related in important ways to the theology of childhood. We will try to articulate that connection by looking, in this first section of the chapter, at what the Gospels, and in particular the sayings of Jesus recorded in the Gospels, have to say about children. That will bring into play some of the considerations that have to be borne in mind as we try to frame a teleology of childhood today.

8.1.1 *The Vocabulary of Childhood*

The most common word for 'child (male or female)' in the Greek in which the Gospels were written is *paidion*.[1] It appears forty-six times in all – eighteen in Matthew, twelve in Mark, thirteen in Luke and three in John. Related words (*pais* and *paidarion*) appear a further seventeen times in Matthew and Luke and twice in John.

Those raw statistics already have a story to tell. John's Gospel stands out in many ways from the three so-called Synoptic Gospels – Matthew, Mark and Luke. For one thing, it is more heavily 'theologised', in the sense that there is in John a more self-conscious level of theological reflection and a greater degree of abstraction, less narrative and fewer stories and parables of everyday life.

The paucity of references to children would seem to fit in with that. But a closer look shows that it is not quite so simple: the abundance of references to children in the Synoptics are not just a reflection of the ubiquity of children in ordinary, everyday life in Roman Palestine.

In the Synoptics the use of the words falls into three main groups. Jesus himself is described as a child. He heals children. And there are two sets of sayings about children. We shall start with the sayings and then return to them again at the end of this section.

8.1.2 *Becoming and Receiving*

In Mark 9:33–7 we read:

> (33) And they came to Capernaum. And once they were in the house, he began to ask them, 'What were you talking about on the road?' (34) But they were silent since on the road they had been talking to one another about who was the greatest. (35) And he sat down and called the twelve and said to them, 'Anyone who wants to be first will be last of all and servant of all'.
>
> (36) And he took a child and placed the child in the midst of them. And he put his arms around the child and said to

them, (37) 'Whoever receives one child like this in my name receives me. And whoever receives me, doesn't receive *me*, but the one who sent me.'

There are parallels in Matthew 18:1–5 and Luke 9:46–8.

The other set of sayings is found in Mark 10:13–16/ Matthew 19:13–15/Luke 18:15–17. In Mark's version this reads:

(13) And they were bringing children to him so that he could touch them, but the disciples told them off. (14) Jesus was annoyed when he saw that and said to them, 'Let the children come to me. Don't block them. For to such belongs the kingdom of heaven. (15) Truly I say to you, whoever does not receive the kingdom of God like a child will not come into it. (16) And he took them in his arms and blessed them by putting his hands on them.'

What do these two sets of sayings have to say about childhood and the kingdom?[2] The first set, in its context in the Gospels, is clearly about humility, whatever else it may be saying. In all three versions – Matthew, Mark and Luke – Jesus' words are triggered by a debate among the disciples about greatness. And in Matthew's version Jesus adds the words, 'So whoever humbles himself like this child – he is the one who is greatest in the kingdom of the heavens' (18:4). It is normally thought by New Testament scholars that Mark's Gospel is the earliest of the three and was used as a source by the other two. In this instance, Matthew's addition seems to make explicit what Mark actually means.

But there is a curious feature of this group of sayings. There is a shift of focus halfway through. Or, in the words of W. D. Davies and Dale Allison, 'The narrative logic is a bit awkward.'[3] The first part of the saying (Mark 9:33–6) looks as if it is going to be about *becoming like* a child. And that is, again, made explicit in Matthew: 'Truly I say to you, unless you turn and become like children, you will not come into the kingdom of the heavens' (18:3). But the second part is about *receiving* children rather than becoming like them.

What is the 'narrative logic' here? It is sometimes said that 'the reception of a child' is 'really an illustration of the humility'.[4] But that would make the receiving of the child a sort of moral visual aid. It would reduce it to the status of a paternalistic or even patronising act – I am so humble that I will welcome and accept *even* a child like this. And that cannot be meant as an instance of real humility.

We would like to suggest that the answer may lie in giving due weight to the phrase 'in my name'. Receiving a child 'in my name' means welcoming him, accepting him 'as if he were me'. Christ is, then, identified with the child just as the Father is, in turn, identified with Christ ('whoever receives me, doesn't receive *me*, but the one who sent me'). And this identification means that the child is to be accorded the status, the dignity, the honour of Christ himself. To enjoy that sort of company is to be 'great' in the kingdom.

An interpretation along those lines would fit in very well with our second set of texts and might in fact help to shed some light on them. In Mark's version of that second cluster of texts Jesus says, 'Truly I say to you, whoever does not receive the kingdom of God like a child will not come into it' (10:15). The wording in Luke (18:19) is identical, while in Matthew there is – as we will see in a moment – no direct parallel.

This verse is usually taken to mean 'unless you receive the kingdom *as a child receives it*, you will not enter'. But in Greek (as in English) the phrase 'like a child' is radically ambiguous. It could just as well mean 'unless you receive the kingdom *as you receive a child*, you will not enter'. Grammar cannot decide the matter for us since the two ways of construing the sentence are equally plausible. So should we take 'like a child' with 'whoever' or with 'kingdom'?

It looks as if Matthew understood the sentence in the way in which it is normally taken. As we have seen, his version of the *second* set of sayings (Matt. 19:13–15) has nothing corresponding to Mark 10:15 or Luke 18:19. But Matthew's version of the *first* set of sayings has in it the saying on humility we cited above: 'Truly I say to you, unless you turn and become like children, you will not come into the kingdom of the heavens' (18:3). And that saying has no direct parallel in either Mark's version or Luke's version of the *first* set of sayings. In other words, it looks as if that is the bit of Matthew that corresponds to Mark 10:15 and Luke 18:19. 'Truly I say to you, unless you turn and become like children, you will not come into the kingdom of the heavens' (Matt. 18:3) is Matthew's version of 'Truly I say to you, whoever does not receive the kingdom of God like a child will not come into it' (Mark 10:15 and Luke 18:19). Matthew – or the tradition of the community on which he drew – has simply moved it from the second set of sayings on children into the first set.

If that is right, it means that Matthew took the saying to mean 'unless you receive the kingdom *as a child receives it*'. Putting the sayings side by side makes that clear.

Mark 10:15/Luke 18:19   Whoever does not receive the kingdom of God *like a child* will not come into it.

Matthew 18:3   Unless you turn and become *like children* you will not come into the king-dom of the heavens.

But is that the way Mark and Luke understood it? Here we can see the significance of the fact that the *first* set of sayings suddenly shifts from a discussion of relative pecking order in the kingdom to an affirmation of the significance of receiving a child. It is the latter that determines the former – or, rather, receiving the child just is what it means to be great in the kingdom – precisely because receiving the kingdom is like receiving the child.

So we would like to suggest that Mark and Luke understood the saying the other way – not the way that Matthew or his tradition took it, not the way it has been most commonly understood.[5] We would like to suggest that Mark and Luke meant that you will not enter the kingdom unless you receive it as you receive a child. That might, at the very least, be the right reading *for us* in view of the questions and concerns we bring to the text.

What, then, is the point of the comparison? How is receiving a child like receiving the kingdom? In order to try to answer that question, we shall look at how children are depicted in other Gospel texts.

8.1.3 Being Weak and Being Strong

8.1.3.1 The Need to Be Healed

In Mark's Gospel the most common use of the word *paidion* is in healing stories. It is used four times in Mark 5:39–41, in the story of the ruler of the synagogue who is given the name Jairus in Luke's version. His twelve-year-old daughter dies and is restored to life.

The word is also used (Mark 7:30) in the story of the Syro-Phoenician woman whose daughter was possessed by a 'demon' or 'unclean spirit'. The woman is a Gentile, an outsider, and seems to have to cajole Jesus into working the cure. But he does so, speaking from afar, and her daughter is healed.

Finally, as Jesus comes down from the mountain of the Transfiguration he is approached by a man whose son – *paidion* (9:23) – is possessed by a 'voiceless spirit' which convulses him and makes him foam at the mouth and gnash his teeth. Jesus addresses the 'voiceless and mute spirit' and casts it out and raises the boy up and restores him.

In all of these stories children are, in another sense, possessed by a 'voiceless' spirit. They are weak and powerless and another has to speak for them. But in each case the child is healed. And the two stories in which Jesus is actually there end with his raising the child up – in the one case from the deathbed on which she lay (9:41–2) and in the other from the death-like collapse in which the child had been left by the last convulsion (9:27).

So powerlessness and weakness is met by healing and raising up. Other uses of words for 'child' in the Gospels also have associations of powerlessness.

John 4:46–54 is the story of the healing of the 'son' of a 'royal official'. But that story corresponds quite closely to the story in Matthew 8:5–13 and Luke 7:1–10 of the healing of the 'slave' of a 'centurion'. In John, the 'son' is referred to by the related words *paidion* (4:51) and *pais* (4:49). In Matthew and Luke, the 'slave' is called only *pais* (Matt. 8:6, 8, 13; Luke 7:7).

The two versions of that story point to a linguistic overlap. The basic meaning of *pais* is 'child', but it was often used in everyday Greek to refer to a slave. Luke uses it that way at 12:45 and 15:26. The former is the parable of the overseer, himself a slave, who abuses his power and begins to beat 'the male slaves and the female slaves' – literally, 'the children [with a masculine definite article in front of it] and the little girls'. The latter is from the parable of the Prodigal Son. When the curmudgeonly elder son returned from the fields, he 'summoned one of the boys' and asked him what all this meant.

This usage is quite like the contemptuous way in which 'boy' was used in apartheid South Africa or in the American South of segregationist days. And that linguistic overlap – the way in which the same word could be used to refer either to children or to slaves – has a lot to say about the powerlessness of both groups and about the dismissive way in which both were treated in ordinary speech and everyday life in the ancient world.

Again, in both Matthew and Luke, Jesus uses the image of children playing an ineffectual game. 'This generation' is 'like children sitting in market-places who call out to others and say, "We played the flute and you did not dance; we sang a dirge and you did not lament"' (Matt. 11:16; Luke

7:32 differs slightly in wording). The picture is of children playing weddings and funerals and trying in vain to get others to join in their game.[6]

Another, and more tragic, image of the powerlessness of children is found in Matthew 2:16. There the word *pais* refers to 'all the children in Bethlehem and its whole district two years old and younger', who are slaughtered by Herod.

8.1.3.2 *Insight and Promise*

So in the Gospels *paidion* and related words are most commonly linked with weakness, powerlessness and vulnerability. But that is far from being the only association.

The word 'child' also evokes God's promises to his people. The songs of the first chapter of Luke's Gospel recall how God has 'helped his child [*pais*] Israel' (1:54) 'in the house of his child David' (1:69).

And the word is used of Jesus. Of course he became a child himself and is described in the narratives of Matthew 2 and Luke 2 as both *pais* and *paidion*.[7] With this child are associated both vulnerability and promise. He is sought by Herod (Matt. 2:8 and 13) and is taken in flight to Egypt (Matt. 2:14). But his birth is proclaimed by angelic hosts (Luke 2:17) and marked by the arrival of astrologers from the East (Matt. 2:9 and 11). And as he grew 'the grace of God was upon him' (Luke 2:40). In all those verses the word *paidion* is used.

But in addition to these literal descriptions of Jesus as a child, the word *pais* could also be used as a title. It was one of the categories which the men and women of the Early Church used to try to gain some insight into who Jesus was.

Matthew applies to Jesus a verse of Isaiah: 'Behold my *pais* whom I have chosen, my beloved in whom my soul is well-pleased' (Matt. 12:18, citing Isa. 42:1). There is in that use of the word and in that application of Isaiah 42:1

a double referent. We have seen that in ordinary Greek the word *pais* could mean either 'child' or 'servant/slave'. So here, there is a reference, on the one hand, to the Suffering Servant of the prophecy of Isaiah and, on the other, to Jesus as *pais* in a unique sense, the one of whom the voice at the baptism said, 'This is my *Son*, the beloved, in whom I am well-pleased'[8] – another verse that echoes in its wording Isaiah 42:1.

There is a similar, though less sharply pointed, ambiguity in the phrases from the songs of Luke 1 which we looked at a moment ago – phrases that recall God's mercies of old toward 'his child Israel' 'in the house of his child David'. Again there is an elasticity of use, for both Israel and David are at once servants and more than servants.

In these passages the word *pais* serves as a link between the Old Covenant and the New and provides a way of talking about those whom God has specially chosen, those through whom his purposes are being worked out in history. A natural, human relationship has become a powerful metaphor of intimacy and dependence, and that metaphor in turn has become a theological category. Identifying Jesus as the *pais* of God gave the men and women of the very earliest Church a way of working out who Jesus was, a way of reading the signs of the times.

There is one passage in the Gospels in which children – real children, not metaphorical ones – do manage to read the signs of the times far better than the powerful adults around them. In Matthew 21:15–16 children themselves have a privileged insight into the meaning of what is happening.

In the last week of Jesus' earthly life, at the cleansing of the Temple,

> when the scribes and pharisees saw the marvellous things he did and the children who were crying out in the Temple and saying, 'Hosanna to the son of David', they were annoyed and said to him, 'Do you hear what these kids[9] are saying?' And Jesus said to them, 'Yes. Have *you* never

read, "From the mouth of infants and children at the breast
I will fashion praise?"'

The words Jesus quotes are from Psalm 8:1–2, cited in
Matthew as it appears in the Septuagint – the version of the
Greek Old Testament which was treated as the canonical
standard of the Early Church. And the words the children
recite are a part of what the crowd shouted at Jesus' triumphal
entry into Jerusalem, echoing Psalm 118:25–6.

There is a further link to Old Testament tradition. At
the time of the Exodus, so it was believed, when Israel had
crossed the Red Sea, children sang a hymn of praise to God.
The apocryphal or deutero-canonical Wisdom of Solomon
– probably written a century or so before the time of Jesus
– says that then 'Wisdom opened the mouth of the dumb
and made the tongues of infants articulate' (10:21). And the
idea that on the shores of the Red Sea little children sang
God's praises is developed in later rabbinic tradition.[10]

These connections help us see what is going on when the
children in the Temple cry 'Hosanna to the son of David'.
They – unlike their elders and betters – recognise who Jesus
is, and so, for Matthew and the first readers of his Gospel,
their words inevitably point ahead – to the death and resurrection of Jesus that are so soon to follow and to the life of
the Christian community that confesses his name and, like
the children, recognises who he is. But their words also point
back – back to the book of Wisdom in the intertestamental
period, back to the book of Psalms, back to the Exodus itself
– the great foundational event of Israel's history.

So the children in the Temple link the present to the past
and the future – as children always do.

There is one final passage in the Gospels to which we
would like to draw attention here, and that is John 21:5.
It is after the resurrection, and the disciples are fishing on
the Sea of Tiberias. Jesus appears, unrecognised, on the
shore and calls out to them. The word he uses to address
them is *paidion*.

Now, the words we have been considering, *pais* and *paidion*, are – as we have seen – often used interchangeably. But *paidion* was originally the diminutive of *pais* – that is, it meant 'little child' rather than just 'child'. By the New Testament period the distinction between the two words was largely lost, but it occasionally surfaces. In Luke 2, for example, the baby Jesus is a *paidion*, while the 12-year-old in the Temple is described by the more grown-up word *pais*.

Here in John, *paidion* is used of a group of adults. It has an informal, colloquial tone. It is the sort of matey word friends might use for each other – like 'lads' in modern usage. So when Jesus on the shore calls out and says, 'Lads, you wouldn't have something to eat, would you?' – no doubt in a broad Galilean accent – we are meant to pick up, from the words John quotes, the intimacy, the joy, the easy familiarity of our fellowship with the risen Lord.

From this survey we can see that the image of children in the Gospels is not a particularly sentimental one. It is not primarily a picture of innocence or simplicity or gentleness or even humility. What is stressed is, rather, powerlessness and vulnerability, but also insight, hope and promise.

8.1.3.3 *Like a Child*

We can now return to the saying of Jesus in Mark 10:15 and Luke 18:19: 'Whoever does not receive the kingdom of God like a child will not come into it.' Let us – in the light of our earlier discussion – take it as meaning 'Whoever does not receive the kingdom of God *as he receives a child* will not come into it'. Let us take it that way at least for now, and see what meaning it might have for us. How, then, is the kingdom like a child? What is the point of comparison?

In the Gospels, the nature of the kingdom is disclosed above all through parables. A parable is a story or an image that suddenly lets us see something we had not seen before. So perhaps the first thing to be said is that according to this saying the child – each child – is herself a sort of parable. Her story both conceals and conveys insight into the meaning of things.

The kingdom of the parables is small but is destined to grow in size and in complexity. It is like a 'mustard seed, which, when it is sown, is the smallest of all seeds on the earth but after it has been sown grows and becomes bigger than all other shrubs and puts forth great branches' (Mark 4:30–2 (Matt. 13:31–2; Luke 13:18–19)).

Its operation is now concealed, for it is like 'leaven which a woman took and hid in three measures of flour until the whole was leavened' (Matt. 13:33 (Luke 13:20–1)).

It will grow in ways we do not know and cannot control. It is like what happens when 'someone sows seed on the ground; he sleeps and rises, and the seed springs up and becomes tall, he knows not how, for the earth bears fruit by itself' (Mark 4:26–8). Or again, it is like a field sown with good seed and bad, wheat and tares. The two cannot be separated and simply have to be left to grow up together (Matt. 13:24–30).

But it is of inestimable value and worth any sacrifice, for it is like 'treasure hidden in a field which someone found and hid again and in his joy went and sold everything he had and bought that field' (Matt. 13:44). Or again, it is 'like a merchant looking for fine pearls; when he found one most precious pearl, he went and sold everything he had and bought it' (Matt. 13:45–6).

8.1.4 Towards the Kingdom

All of that suggests that to receive the kingdom like a child means to welcome each of them – the kingdom and the child – as something of infinite worth which is with us now but which will grow and change and develop in ways that we cannot know and cannot control. Each of them must be accepted with joy as it is and for what it is, here and now. And above all each must be given space to grow.

There are of course differences between the kingdom and a child. The child has a fragility and a vulnerability which the kingdom, even now, does not. And that means that the child cannot simply be left to grow like seed sown in the field that 'springs up and becomes tall, for the earth bears fruit by itself'. In that way giving a child space to grow is not like giving the kingdom space to grow. In the case of the child, the field must be protected and hedged round and tended with care and wisdom and love. Nonetheless, the child and the kingdom both have an autonomy of their own. They are what they are and are to be accepted as such. And they will become what they will become and are to be loved as such.

The growth of the kingdom is mysterious and we can only imagine what it will in its fullness be like. But we do have some clues.

For one thing, the image of kingdom itself has implications. It is the central model in the Gospels for what it might be like to stand in the presence of God. It is not the picture of an isolated individual thinking about God. It is not even the picture of an intimate community like the family. Rather, the model is of a large and complex human society.

If the model of kingdom gives us some purchase on the final goal of human life, it suggests the centrality of community and the need to learn to function within such a society.

Perhaps we can say more than that if we look beyond the Gospels. In the brilliant passage of 1 Corinthians in which Paul develops the idea of the triad of faith, hope and love, he starts from a consideration of the need to grow.

> For we know in part and prophesy in part. But when that which is full-grown comes, that which is partial will no longer be of use. When I was a little child, I spoke like a little child, I looked at things like a little child, I thought like a little child. But when I became a man, I ceased to use the things that characterized the little child.
>
> For now we see with the puzzling image in a mirror, but then we will see face to face. Now I know in part, but then

I will know even as I have been known. And now faith,
hope, love remain – these three. But the greatest of these is
love. (1 Cor. 13:9–13)

In that community which is the goal of human life we will
enjoy in their fullness knowledge and love – insight into the
true nature of things as they are and love for one another
and for the God who made us.

Knowledge and love, then, are skills that have to be
developed for the kingdom. In preparation, we might say,
they have to be fostered and facilitated now, as we grow
– as we as individuals grow from childhood to old age and
as our human family grows 'into the measure of the stature
of the fullness of Christ' (Eph. 4:13).

'Whoever does not receive the kingdom of God like
a child will not come into it.' In using the comparison
the way we have, we are of course, in one sense, using it
the wrong way around. In its immediate context in the
Gospels, the image of the child is meant to elucidate the
meaning of the kingdom. The movement – as in all parables
– is from the concrete and particular to that which lies
mysteriously ahead, from the known or imaginable to the
unknown and incomprehensible. But we have been using
such glimpses as the parables give us of the nature of the
kingdom to suggest some of the goals that childhood is
aimed at. The next sections of this chapter will try to
make that more concrete by focusing on the teleology of
children's rights today.

Before we move on to that, however, we should like to
draw attention to two implications that can be drawn for
us and our attitude to children from the Gospel material
we have looked at in this section. They are the need for
commitment and the need for repentance.

First, everywhere in the Gospels the need to be healed
is met by a commitment to heal. No-one who approaches
Jesus in the Gospels with a request for healing is sent away
empty. That is true even of the Syro-Phoenician woman, to

whose request Jesus accedes only after a little dialogue on the relationship between Jew and Gentile: 'Lord, even the dogs under the table eat from the crumbs that the children leave' (Mark 7:28). Where we perceive a need, we must respond.

Second, the wording of Matthew 18:3, which we looked at at the beginning of this section, is significant. 'Truly I say to you,' Jesus says, 'unless you *turn* and become like children, you will not come into the kingdom of the heavens.'

Underlying Matthew's Greek there are often Semitic turns of phrase as Hebrew or Aramaic expressions were passed down in the tradition or affected the speech patterns of Matthew's community. In Hebrew or Aramaic 'turn and become' is one way of saying 'become again'. But 'turn' is also the normal way of talking about repentance.

In the Greek of the New Testament and later Christian usage, the normal words for repentance were connected with thinking. 'To repent' was, literally, 'to rethink' or 'to think your way through and come to a new understanding'. But the Hebrew and Aramaic imagery was more concrete: repentance meant turning around, turning away, turning back to God.

The context in Matthew is a debate on who is the 'greatest' in the kingdom of Heaven (18:1). Perhaps Matthew means us to understand Jesus as saying that we must repent of our self-regarding concern with dominance and imitate the unselfconsciousness of little children.

We can, in any event, hear the text as a call to repentance. 'Repent and become like children.' Repent of what? Repent, perhaps, of the things that alienate us from our own childhood, that have turned us away from what we once were and might have been. Repent, perhaps, of the indifference and self-absorption that alienate us from children now. Repent too, perhaps, of the ways in which we and our society have contributed to the vulnerability of children and exploited their powerlessness and weakness.

8.2 Visions of Human Destiny

In 1951, Jacques Maritain referred to the notion of an international consensus on human rights as a kind of 'secular faith'.[11] 'Visions' of human destiny are not limited to the religious sphere. Indeed we noted in Chapter 4 that early Bolshevism, for example, had a distinctly eschatological character.[12] We asked how it was possible to frame a 'universal declaration of human rights' acceptable to the upholders of divergent visions, and noted the comment during the 1947 consultation that: 'Yes, we agree about the rights *but on condition that no one asks us why.*'[13]

Human rights aim to secure the necessary conditions for leading a minimally good life. Perceptions of what constitutes the 'good' may differ. Orientation towards the 'Kingdom of God' in the terms set out above represents a specifically Christian aspiration. However, the history of their development and articulation has shown that statements of human rights can provide an agreed set of minimum conditions and aid meaningful dialogue about problems and disagreements, even when such statements are viewed by some as the products of human agreement and by others as reflections of reason, a transcendent order or revealed truth.

Some visions will focus on personal fulfilment during the course of a human life; others on relationships within a human community; and yet others on personal 'salvation', with greater or lesser emphasis on the communal dimension of the kingdom of God.

The Convention on the Rights of the Child also presents a vision, of a child:

> fully prepared to live an individual life in society, and brought up in the spirit of the ideals proclaimed in the Charter of the United Nations, and in particular in the spirit of peace, dignity, tolerance, freedom, equality and solidarity.[14]

In pursuit of that vision:

The child, for the full and harmonious development of his or her personality, should grow up in a family environment, in an atmosphere of happiness, love and understanding.[15]

For religious communities, as noted in the conclusion to Chapter 2, acceptable secular statements such as the Convention will tend to be regarded as secondary frameworks consistent with their primary religious perspective, an approach that we consider wholly legitimate. Indeed one of the purposes of this book is to encourage believing individuals or communities who are hesitant about the Convention to accept it as a compatible vision and a useful mechanism both for promotion of the Christian agenda and for dialogue with those of other faiths and with the secular world.

In Chapter 7, we identified the Irenaean model of the bodiliness of a humanity growing from childhood to maturity as that providing the firmest foundation for a theology of children's rights. The 'vision' it pursues is that of increasing approximation to the paradigmatic image of God in Jesus Christ, a vision that reaches out to a fulfilment beyond our physical life, but also sanctifies the present moment and commands respect for the child's human dignity. We noted John Chrysostom's portrayal of parents as the 'sculptors' of this image in their children, and Wesley's view that education was to be directed towards recovery of the image of God through the 'breaking of wills'. This raises the question whether the efforts of parents are to be directed towards production of a uniform representation of the image; are children to be chiselled into one shape – that of the perfect Christian, or is there room for diversity – for respecting the grain of the stone?

As indicated at 6.6 above, Article 29 of the Convention heads its list of the aims of education with the following:

The development of the child's personality, talents and mental and physical abilities to their fullest potential.

This secular requirement to 'respect the grain of the stone' makes sense also in a religious context. Beauty is achieved, not by doing violence to the material but by releasing the potential within.

At the risk of being whimsical, one might imagine a world populated with statues of God running, singing, dancing, playing and working on a variety of tasks, rather than a warehouse full of stone clones.

8.3 Paths to Fulfilment

Are children merely the passive recipients of the chiselling of their parents with the help of the community, or do they shape, or even contribute to shaping, their own destiny?

The static picture of children as statues must be balanced by the dynamic portrayal in 8.1 above of a child as a 'parable', indeed as the mustard seed that 'will grow in ways we do not know and cannot control'. Or like a field sown with good seed and bad, wheat and tares which cannot be separated until the harvest.

What this suggests is that the paths to fulfilment of the destiny of the child operate both from the outside-in and the inside-out. Outside the child are the material and structural conditions for development, and the careful labour of wise parental artists. This is the realm of the human rights of the child, the field of operation of the 'necessary conditions for leading a minimally good life' already referred to.[16] Inside are the child's own gifts and potential for autonomous action. The inside of the child can be nurtured by education and shaped by virtue in the direction of fulfilment of her potential. Rights and virtues do not conflict but complement each other in facilitating the child's progress to human fulfilment.

At 6.6 above, we discussed the child's right to freedom of thought, conscience and religion, and the implications for education. We noted the differences between the 'freedom from' constraints on autonomy, characteristic of secular individualism, and the 'freedom for' fulfilment of a destiny, characteristic of religious belief. The Convention on the Rights of the Child does indeed list some 'freedoms from' in articles 13 to 15; but Article 29 was described as in some ways closer to the religious view in setting some goals of human development, which, it is argued, are compatible with the Christian perspective. Article 12 also requires that the child's view be given due weight when any decisions are being made about him. The question then arises: at what stage does a child become mature enough to make decisions about his or her own education and human formation? How does one balance the 'now and future' freedoms of the child?

The Convention has no hesitation in setting limits to some activities of the child, whether apparently consensual or not, that would damage his future freedoms by depriving him of general education, making him dependent upon drugs, or exposing him to other forms of exploitation, including sexual exploitation.[17] That apart, there still remains the difficulty of identifying the point at which a child's right to freedom of conscience and participation in all decisions should outweigh adult views about what is best in terms of, for example, education, religious observance or medical treatment.

The difficulty of this enterprise should not, however, cause us to set it aside. It may seem simpler to impose order through obedience, but we must ask whether this impedes the child's ability to choose virtue through autonomy.[18] One might indeed argue that the decision for heteronomy (submission to God, parents or any kind of authority) is the ultimate exercise of autonomy. It comes from within. 'Breaking the will' of a child may impose obedience, but it can hardly be described as virtue.[19] Karl Barth, for example, observed that true obedience 'is to be achieved in free, differentiated decision'.[20]

8.4 What does that Mean for Children and their Human Rights?

The debate about the balance of now and future freedoms should not, however, lead us to conclude that the defining characteristic of childhood is preparation for adulthood. Children are not mere 'adults in the making' but human persons in their own right.

The conclusion to Chapter 2 raised the question of the existence and identification of any 'God-given rights and responsibilities of parents to raise their children', and the compatibility of any such rights with the Convention. Chapter 6 observed that parental 'rights' existed only to support parents in the exercise of responsibilities towards their children, and were thus qualified by the rights of the child: to the provision of services to promote survival and development; to protection from abuse, neglect and exploitation; and to participation in matters affecting the child. From a theological perspective, Chapter 7 concluded that the concept of the rights of the child was compatible with Christian thought and was a useful mechanism for promoting central Christian concerns in the modern world. It was shown that the authority of parents to demand obedience from their children had been almost universally subject to the qualification that what was commanded was consistent with the law of God, and even with less Biblical standards of justice and perceived religious probity.[21] God gives for God's own purpose, and God's purpose is the establishment of the kingdom. The first section of this chapter presented the kingdom as 'the final goal of human life', suggesting, 'the centrality of community and the need to learn to function within such a society'. Such learning comes partly, but not solely, through the imposition of rules. At 7.2.1 above, it was concluded that, 'virtues and rules or virtues and rights are not competing for space. They inhabit different floors within the structure of morality.' One might indeed argue that rights empower the vulnerable to choose and develop the path of virtue, the path most consistent with the kingdom of God as 'within' (Luke 17:21).²²

It is our conclusion that any God-given rights of parents are qualified by the God-given rights of children, reflecting the expectation that they will be helped and supported towards fulfilment of their destiny within God's kingdom. The Convention on the Rights of the Child, properly understood, promotes respect for the minimum standards of human dignity necessary for the fulfilment of a spectrum of human visions, including that of Christianity, with which it is entirely compatible.

Notes

1. Another normal word for 'child' – both in the New Testament and in ordinary, secular Greek – is *teknon*. The two can often be used interchangeably, but *paidion* primarily means 'child' in terms of age while *teknon* primarily means 'child' in terms of biological relationship (it is connected with the verb that means 'to give birth to'). So, for example, *teknon* is used as a mode of address regardless of age (see Mark 2:5 (Jesus to the paralytic) or Luke 15:31 (the father to the elder brother of the prodigal son)) and is the natural word to use in a phrase like 'children of Abraham' (John 8:39; see also Luke 16:25).

2. We should say a word on what we mean here by 'kingdom'. The concept of the kingdom is central to the teaching of Jesus. In Mark, the preaching of Jesus began when he 'came into Galilee proclaiming the good news of God and saying, "The time is fulfilled and the Kingdom of God is at hand. Repent and believe in the good news"' (Mark 1:14-15, with a parallel in Matt. 4:17). Mark and Luke speak of the kingdom *of God*, while Matthew typically speaks of the kingdom *of the heavens*, but with no real difference in meaning. (In the Judaism of the time of Jesus it was quite common to avoid referring to God directly – out of reverence – and to use a round-about expression, like 'the heavens', instead.) The kingdom is the reign of God, announced and inaugurated by Jesus. It is both present reality and future promise: present among us now in hidden and enigmatic ways, it will be fully revealed in glory and power when all things reach their final end.

3. W. D. Davies and Dale C. Allison, Jr, *A Critical and Exegetical Commentary on the Gospel according to Saint Matthew*, The International Critical Commentary (3 vols) Edinburgh: T&T Clark, 1988–97, vol. 2, p. 759.

4. Ibid.

5. Though the 'receive the kingdom as a child receives it' interpretation has been far more common, scholars have on occasion taken the text as we would like to take it. See F. A. Schilling, 'What Means the Saying about Receiving the Kingdom of God as a Little Child', *Expository Times*, 77 (1965), pp. 56–8, and V. K. Robbins, 'Pronouncement Stories and Jesus' Blessing of the Children', *Semeia*, 29 (1983), pp. 43–74.

6. The image has often been interpreted as if those issuing the call to lamentation correspond to John the Baptist, while those issuing the invitation to dance correspond to Jesus, but, as Davies and Allison point out, it is 'this generation' – not John and Jesus – that is compared to the two groups of children: 'on this approach to the passage, the contemporaries of John and Jesus are like disagreeable children who complain that others will not act according to their desires' (*Matthew*, vol. 2, p. 262).

7. Jesus is called *paidion* at Matthew 2:8, 9, 11, 12 (twice), 14, 20 (twice), 21; Luke 2:17, 27, 40; and *pais* at Luke 2:43 (of Jesus at the age of 12). *Paidion* is also applied in Luke's Infancy Narrative to John the Baptist (1:59, 66, 76, 80).

8. Matthew 3.17; the parallels in Mark 1:11 and Luke 3:22 are identical apart from making the words addressed directly to Jesus himself: 'You are ... '

9. There is no word for 'kids' in the Greek of Matthew 21:16, but the use of 'these' is contemptuous or dismissive.

10. See the references in Davies and Allison, *Matthew*, vol. 3, p. 142, note 59.

11. Traer, *Faith in Human Rights*, p. 10, quoting Maritain, *Man and the State*, p. 111.

12. See 4.12 above.

13. See 4.6 above.

14. Preamble.

15. Preamble.

16. Indeed, at 6.3.2 above, reference was made to the view of Dickens that parental rights 'exist to preserve and prepare children for adulthood and emerging autonomy'.

17. Articles 32 to 36.

18. See M. de Blois, 'The Foundation of Human Rights: A Christian Perspective', in P. R. Beaumont, *Christian Perspectives on Human*

Rights and Legal Philosophy, Carlisle: Paternoster Press, 1998, pp. 7–29 (15): 'Mankind is therefore created with freedom to choose, to make decisions, to choose a path of life, in short he is a moral being we have to respect as such.'

19. See MacIntyre, *After Virtue*, pp. 175–6, comparing the 'external' reasons for a child playing chess – the promise of candy as a reward, and the internal reasons that might develop, connected with achievements of a particular kind of skill. This leads on to his first definition of 'virtue,' on p. 178, as 'an acquired human quality the possession and exercise of which tends to enable us to achieve those goods which are internal to practices and the lack of which effectively prevents us from achieving such goods'.

20. Barth, *Church Dogmatics*, III, 4, p. 252.

21. See 7.1.1 above.

22. Noting here that some translations say 'in the midst of you'. Luke's Greek can mean either 'within you' or 'in the midst of you', and there has been a great deal of scholarly discussion about which is the preferable option. It would also be possible to take the former interpretation in the sense 'within your reach'. That is the way it was understood by the North African theologian Tertullian about the year 200. Tertullian says, 'It is "within you" – that is, in your hand, in your power, if you hear, if you do the command of God' (*Against Marcion* IV.35.12). Tertullian then goes on to cite the very relevant parallel in Deuteronomy 30:11–14.

9

Concluding Perspectives

9.1 Introduction

In Chapter 1, we set out the 'starting positions' of our professional backgrounds and interests, and we promised to return to these at the end of the book in order to assess the extent to which our perspectives had been changed by this joint work. The following paragraphs represent our concluding reflections.

9.2 Concluding Perspective of Legal Author

One of the first surprises on working with theologians was the discovery of some resistance to the concept of 'the individual' as a focus of concern. I approached this work with an assumption that the rights of the individual were central, and that an important aim of the law was to protect the individual from oppression by those with power; whether at the level of a nation state, a local administration, a commercial or criminal enterprise, or a dysfunctional family. Resistance to the rights of the individual seemed to me to be a reactionary stance in the context of human rights, and one with sinister potential; although I was too polite to articulate my concerns in that way. My study of the philosophic consultations associated with the Universal Declaration of Human Rights helped me to understand that my perspective was an unidentified and unacknowledged

365

legacy of the Enlightenment, and that most cultures before, and many after, have had a much more community-focused view of life.

My surprise, not to mention concern, was heightened by the discovery that some viewed the 'Enlightenment' as a 'bad thing', as the point at which the broader and deeper religious vision had been rejected in favour of the materialist superstition of physical science. So, not only was my perspective more time-conditioned than I had thought, but it was conditioned by an influential period during which truth was seen as having been shrunk to the point of distortion.

I have learned to be more appreciative of the community-focused view, particularly where it reflects a theological emphasis on the community as the 'Body of Christ' and salvation history as a story of the 'People of God', rather than individuals. Nevertheless, I retain my concern that those structures which have the potential to be salvific and life giving have also the power to be oppressive and destructive; and that the life of the whole is well served by challenges to such abuse of power from within its very body. In our 'fallen' world, all power is liable to abuse, and much of that abuse will come to pass. Communities that acknowledge the rights of their members to challenge oppression, and provide mechanisms for it, are doing themselves a favour.

During the 1947 philosophic consultation, a comment was made that all bills of rights 'take their cue from recent abuses'.[1] The Universal Declaration was drafted in the years following the extreme abuses of totalitarian regimes during the Second World War. We are perhaps just far enough away from that now to be in danger of forgetting why the protection of the individual was felt to be so necessary in the first place. The debates at the time also show why there was less emphasis placed upon human duty than many argued for then and still insist upon today. While some may wish to redress the balance a little, we should keep in mind the dangers of moving towards a duty-based understanding of the world.

The protective rights of children set out in the 1924 Declaration of the Rights of the Child were also a response largely to the experience of war and its impact on children, a matter that has never ceased to be important but, as indicated in Chapter 1, is at the time of writing very visible in terms of the war in Iraq. The more recent Convention on the Rights of the Child might be viewed, partly at least, as a response to our increasing knowledge and understanding of the extent of abuse of children by those who care for them and therefore have power over them. Children need rights to counter the potentially abusive power of adults. We must not forget that either.

That brings me to my last point. My research into the dialogues between religious states and the UN Committee, and my reading of Church documents (reported in Chapter 2), left a deep impression of their 'idealistic' portrayals of family life. I found the theological author's description in 7.2.1 of the 'different floors in the structure of morality' helpful in understanding the different characters of the discourse of lawyers and theologians, who often use the same words, but in different contexts and for different ends. This reinforces my 'mission', set out in Chapter 1, to ensure that the high discourse of philosophy, theology and religious exhortation is not unthinkingly transported to the 'floor' of law and rights, where mere mortals try to hold at bay the worst effects of human fallibility.

9.3 Concluding Perspective of Theological Author

What have we learned and what changes have there been to our thinking? For the theological author, there are three things that stand out.

The first is that words are meant to do things. The legal author has throughout been insistent that ideas about children and children's rights are meant to achieve something and that it is essential to see how care and concern can be implemented.

That emphasis is important because philosophical ethics and moral theology *can* degenerate into the abstraction and unreality of intellectual shadow-boxing. Of course it should not be so and need not be so, but the danger is there. And that is all the more important in dealing with acute human problems such as the vulnerability and the deprivation to which children's rights are a response.

A second thing that has been brought home to me with renewed force during this work is the interconnectedness of theological discourse. Reflection on the rights of children – a very modern idea – has taken us back to the theology of the second century, and beyond that again to Scripture. It has taken us into Christology, Christian anthropology and eschatology. And that is a reminder that those –ologies are not separate academic disciplines, but are different facets of the way in which the one God has acted, is acting and will act within the world that God has made. No area of theological discourse can be isolated from any other.

If that is true of theological discourse in general, it is true not least of the theology of childhood. I have – as a third consequence – emerged from this work with a deepened appreciation of the centrality of the child in Christian theology.

We saw in Chapter 7 that the understanding of the image in which humankind is made has down the centuries reflected contemporary ideas of what it is that makes a human being human and what it is that imperils human fulfilment. The same is true of the understanding of childhood. We might think of John Chrysostom's analogy between a parent and a painter or sculptor – which we also looked at in Chapter 7. That analogy symbolises well the attitude to childhood in an age dominated by a Platonic world-view. The sculptor elicits the ideal form hidden within his block of stone just as the mind struggles to elicit intelligible reality amid the change and flux of the material world. Or, to take an example closer to home, we might look to the highly sentimentalised view of the innocence of childhood propounded by the Victorians and conclude that that view was the reflection of an age obsessed by a hollow front of public propriety and torn by the tension between reserve and emotion. So the theology of childhood always tells us a lot about ourselves.

Or, to take another instance of the centrality of the theology of childhood, I was quite struck by the way in which our survey of the uses of the word 'child' in the Gospels led us to so many major themes of New Testament theology.

The theology of childhood is not an appendix to 'normal' theology, but an integral part of it. It is a sensitive index to our view of the nature and goal of human life and is an unavoidable part of our reflections on what it means to say that the people of God grow through time 'into the measure of the fullness of the stature of Christ'.

This sense of the centrality of childhood is something new in our Christian culture, but it also the recovery of something that has been lost, something old, something new, as we said above. We can see that from interest in Jesus as a child.

For us, the childhood of Jesus has been largely senti-mentalised. It is perhaps a Victorian phenomenon that we should be left with the 'meek and mild' infant of the hymn and cloying, Christmas-card images.

But it was not always so. There was in the Early Church a whole family of infancy gospels – popular (indeed, enormously popular) accounts which gave imaginary and legendary reconstructions of the birth and childhood of Jesus.

We can, for example, look at a text called 'The Stories of Thomas the Israelite Philosopher on the Childhood of the Lord'. It was probably first written about the time Irenaeus was writing – toward the end of the second century – and its tales were told and retold, reworked and reworked again, throughout antiquity and the Middle Ages.[2]

In the Gospel of 'Thomas the Israelite' the child Jesus is certainly not sentimentalised. He is playful, mischievous and dangerous. Thus, at the age of five he makes toy sparrows out of clay and then turns them into real, living birds (2.2 and 4). Those who cross him or annoy him are crippled or struck dead or struck blind (though eventually 'all who had fallen under his curse were healed' (8.2)). He talks back to his teachers and gets in trouble with his 'father' Joseph, who at one point pulls his ear (5.2) and on another occasion has to tell Mary not to let him outside the house (14.3). But we also see him 'playing with other children too' (17.2).

The work ends with a retelling of the Gospel story from Luke 2 of the finding of Jesus in the Temple. What is the point of it all? And why were these stories so popular? In the gospel of 'Thomas the Israelite' as a whole, there is a development in the portrait of Jesus. He moves from conflict with his parents to submission, from conflict with other children to playing with them, from the destructive use of his strange powers to their constructive use for healing. It is as if the writer and his readers were struggling to come to terms with what it might mean for the divine to come into our world, for God to live a human life. And to try to understand that mystery, they modelled it on the ordinary processes of the socialisation of a child.

These infancy gospels were popular throughout the Middle Ages. And the high Middle Ages saw an outpouring of interest in the birth and childhood of Jesus which found expression in the imaginative worlds of art and visionary experience. And it is above all women whose faith was articulated and made concrete in this way.

For example, the fourteenth-century mystic Bridget (or Birgitta) of Sweden had a vision of the birth of Jesus which stressed the physicality of it all and which heavily influenced the way the Nativity was depicted in medieval and later art. Whenever we see a picture of Mary kneeling with the naked, newborn child on the floor in front of her, we are seeing the influence of Bridget. [3]

Or, to take another example from the later Middle Ages, those women in the Low Countries known as beguines, who lived a life of quiet devotion alone or in small groups, established an emotional and physical contact with Christ through small statues of the naked infant Jesus, which they could hold and dress.[4]

Behind these florid visions, behind this exuberant piety, was a sense of the importance of affirming and celebrating the solidarity of Jesus with us in our physicality. A study of children's rights reminds us of the centrality of a theology of childhood. And that in turn reminds us that the gospel is the story of one who came into our world weak and vulnerable. Our response, then, must be to reach out in care and concern for the weakness and vulnerability of others.

Notes

1. See 4.6 above.
2. For discussion and translation, see Oscar Cullman, 'Infancy Gospels', in Wilhelm Schneemelcher, *New Testament Apocrypha* (revised edn), tr. R. McL. Wilson (2 vols), Cambridge: James Clarke & Co, 1991–2, vol. 1, pp. 439–43 (introduction) and 444–51 (translation and notes).
3. For Bridget's vision, see her *Revelations* 7.21: Birgitta of Sweden, *Life and Selected Revelations*, ed. Marguerite Tjader Harris, tr. Albert Ryle Kezel, Classics of Western Spirituality, New York: Paulist Press, 1990, pp. 202–4.
4. See Joanna E. Ziegler, 'Reality as Imitation: The Role of Religious Imagery among the Beguines of the Low Countries', in Ulrike Wiethaus, *Maps of Flesh and Light: The Religious Experience of Medieval Women Mystics*, Syracuse, NY: Syracuse University Press, 1993, pp. 112–26, especially pp. 113 and 125–6.

The United Nations Convention on the Rights of the Child

Preamble

The States Parties to the present Convention,

Considering that, in accordance with the principles proclaimed in the Charter of the United Nations, recognition of the inherent dignity and of the equal and inalienable rights of all members of the human family is the foundation of freedom, justice and peace in the world,

Bearing in mind that the peoples of the United Nations have, in the Charter, reaffirmed their faith in fundamental human rights and in the dignity and worth of the human person, and have determined to promote social progress and better standards of life in larger freedom,

Recognizing that the United Nations has, in the Universal Declaration of Human Rights and in the International Covenants on Human Rights, proclaimed and agreed that everyone is entitled to all the rights and freedoms set forth therein, without distinction of any kind, such as race, colour, sex, language, religion, political or other opinion, national or social origin, property, birth or other status,

Recalling that, in the Universal Declaration of Human Rights, the United Nations has proclaimed that childhood is entitled to special care and assistance,

Convinced that the family, as the fundamental group of society and the natural environment for the growth and well-being of all its members and particularly children, should be afforded the necessary protection and assistance so that it can fully assume its responsibilities within the community,

Recognizing that the child, for the full and harmonious development of his or her personality, should grow up in a family environment, in an atmosphere of happiness, love and understanding,

Considering that the child should be fully prepared to live an individual life in society, and brought up in the spirit of the ideals proclaimed in the Charter of the United Nations, and in particular in the spirit of peace, dignity, tolerance, freedom, equality and solidarity,

Bearing in mind that the need to extend particular care to the child has been stated in the Geneva Declaration of the Rights of the Child of 1924 and in the Declaration of the Rights of the Child adopted by the United Nations on 20 November 1959 and recognized in the Universal Declaration of Human Rights, in the International Covenant on Civil and Political Rights (in particular in articles 23 and 24), in the International Covenant on Economic, Social and Cultural Rights (in particular in article ten) and in the statutes and relevant instruments of specialized agencies and international organizations concerned with the welfare of children,

Bearing in mind that, as indicated in the Declaration of the Rights of the Child, 'the child, by reason of his physical and mental immaturity, needs special safeguards and care, including appropriate legal protection, before as well as after birth',

Recalling the provisions of the Declaration on Social and Legal Principles relating to the Protection and Welfare of Children, with Special Reference to Foster Placement and Adoption Nationally and Internationally; the United

Nations Standard Minimum Rules for the Administration of Juvenile Justice ('The Beijing Rules'); and the Declaration on the Protection of Women and Children in Emergency and Armed Conflict,

Recognizing that, in all countries in the world, there are children living in exceptionally difficult conditions, and that such children need special consideration,

Taking due account of the importance of the traditions and cultural values of each people for the protection and harmonious development of the child,

Recognizing the importance of international cooperation for improving the living conditions of children in every country, in particular in the developing countries,

Have agreed as follows:

Article 1 (Definition of a Child)

For the purposes of the present Convention, a child means every human being below the age of 18 years unless, under the law applicable to the child, majority is attained earlier.

Article 2 (Non-discrimination)

1. States Parties shall respect and ensure the rights set forth in the present Convention to each child within their jurisdiction without discrimination of any kind, irrespective of the child's or his or her parent's or legal guardian's race, colour, sex, language, religion, political or other opinion, national, ethnic or social origin, property, disability, birth or other status.

2. States Parties shall take all appropriate measures to ensure that the child is protected against all forms of discrimination or punishment on the basis of the status, activities, expressed opinions, or beliefs of the child's parents, legal guardians, or family members.

Article 3 (Best Interests of the Child)

1. In all actions concerning children, whether undertaken by public or private social welfare institutions, courts of law, administrative authorities or legislative bodies, the best interests of the child shall be a primary consideration.

2. States Parties undertake to ensure the child such protection and care as is necessary for his or her well-being, taking into account the rights and duties of his or her parents, legal guardians, or other individuals legally responsible for him or her, and, to this end, shall take all appropriate legislative and administrative measures.

3. States Parties shall ensure that the institutions, services and facilities responsible for the care or protection of children shall conform with the standards established by competent authorities, particularly in the areas of safety, health, in the number and suitability of their staff, as well as competent supervision.

Article 4 (Implementation of Rights)

States Parties shall undertake all appropriate legislative, administrative, and other measures for the implementation of the rights recognized in the present Convention. With regard to economic, social and cultural rights, States Parties shall undertake such measures to the maximum extent of their available resources and, where needed, within the framework of international cooperation.

Article 5 (Parental Guidance and the Child's Evolving Capacities)

States Parties shall respect the responsibilities, rights and duties of parents or, where applicable, the members of the extended family or community as provided for by local custom, legal guardians or other persons legally responsible for the child, to provide, in a manner consistent with the evolving capacities of the child, appropriate direction and guidance in the exercise by the child of the rights recognized in the present Convention.

Article 6 (Survival and Development)

1. States Parties recognize that every child has the inherent right to life.
2. States Parties shall ensure to the maximum extent possible the survival and development of the child.

Article 7 (Name and Nationality)

1. The child shall be registered immediately after birth and shall have the right from birth to a name, the right to acquire a nationality and, as far as possible, the right to know and be cared for by his or her parents.
2. States Parties shall ensure the implementation of these rights in accordance with their national law and their obligations under the relevant international instruments in this field, in particular where the child would otherwise be stateless.

Article 8 (Preservation of Identity)

1. States Parties undertake to respect the right of the child to preserve his or her identity, including nationality, name and family relations as recognized by law without unlawful interference.
2. Where a child is illegally deprived of some or all of the elements of his or her identity, States Parties shall provide appropriate assistance and protection, with a view to speedily re-establishing his or her identity.

Article 9 (Separation from Parents)

1. States Parties shall ensure that a child shall not be separated from his or her parents against their will, except when competent authorities subject to judicial review determine, in accordance with applicable law and procedures, that such separation is necessary for the best interests of the child. Such determination may be necessary in a particular case such as one involving abuse or neglect of the child by the parents, or one where the parents are living separately and a decision must be made as to the child's place of residence.

2. In any proceedings pursuant to paragraph 1 of the present article, all interested parties shall be given an opportunity to participate in the proceedings and make their views known.

3. States Parties shall respect the right of the child who is separated from one or both parents to maintain personal relations and direct contact with both parents on a regular basis, except if it is contrary to the child's best interests.

4. Where such separation results from any action initiated by a State Party, such as the detention, imprisonment, exile, deportation or death (including death arising from any cause while the person is in the custody of the State) of one or both parents or of the child, that State Party shall, upon request, provide the parents, the child or, if appropriate, another member of the family with the essential information concerning the whereabouts of the absent member(s) of the family unless the provision of the information would be detrimental to the well-being of the child. States Parties shall further ensure that the submission of such a request shall of itself entail no adverse consequences for the person(s) concerned.

Article 10 (Family Reunification)

1. In accordance with the obligation of States Parties under article 9, paragraph 1, applications by a child or his or her parents to enter or leave a State Party for the purpose of family reunification shall be dealt with by States Parties in a positive, humane and expeditious manner. States Parties shall further ensure that the submission of such a request shall entail no adverse consequences for the applicants and for the members of their family.

2. A child whose parents reside in different States shall have the right to maintain on a regular basis, save in exceptional circumstances personal relations and direct contacts with both parents. Towards that end and in accordance with the obligation of States Parties under article 9, paragraph 1, States Parties shall respect the right of the child and his or her parents to leave any country, including their own, and to enter their own country. The right to leave any country shall be subject only to such restrictions as are prescribed by law and which are necessary to protect the national security, public order (*ordre public*), public health or morals or the rights and freedoms of others and are consistent with the other rights recognized in the present Convention.

Article 11 (Illicit Transfer and Non-return)

1. States Parties shall take measures to combat the illicit transfer and non-return of children abroad.

2. To this end, States Parties shall promote the conclusion of bilateral or multilateral agreements or accession to existing agreements.

Article 12 (The Child's Views)

1. States Parties shall assure to the child who is capable of forming his or her own views the right to express those views freely in all matters affecting the child, the views of the child being given due weight in accordance with the age and maturity of the child.

2. For this purpose, the child shall in particular be provided the opportunity to be heard in any judicial and administrative proceedings affecting the child, either directly, or through a representative or an appropriate body, in a manner consistent with the procedural rules of national law.

Article 13 (Freedom of Expression)

1. The child shall have the right to freedom of expression; this right shall include freedom to seek, receive and impart information and ideas of all kinds, regardless of frontiers, either orally, in writing or in print, in the form of art, or through any other media of the child's choice.

2. The exercise of this right may be subject to certain restrictions, but these shall only be such as are provided by law and are necessary:

   (a) For respect of the rights or reputations of others; or

   (b) For the protection of national security or of public order (*ordre public*), or of public health or morals.

Article 14 (Freedom of Thought, Conscience and Religion)

1. States Parties shall respect the right of the child to freedom of thought, conscience and religion.

2. States Parties shall respect the rights and duties of the parents and, when applicable, legal guardians, to provide direction to the child in the exercise of his or her right in a manner consistent with the evolving capacities of the child.

3. Freedom to manifest one's religion or beliefs may be subject only to such limitations as are prescribed by law and are necessary to protect public safety, order, health or morals, or the fundamental rights and freedoms of others.

Article 15 (Freedom of Association)

1. States Parties recognize the rights of the child to freedom of association and to freedom of peaceful assembly.

2. No restrictions may be placed on the exercise of these rights other than those imposed in conformity with the law and which are necessary in a democratic society in the interests of national security or public safety, public order (*ordre public*), the protection of public health or morals or the protection of the rights and freedoms of others.

Article 16 (Protection of Privacy)

1. No child shall be subjected to arbitrary or unlawful interference with his or her privacy, family, home or correspondence, nor to unlawful attacks on his or her honour and reputation.

2. The child has the right to the protection of the law against such interference or attacks.

Article 17 (Access to Appropriate Information)

States Parties recognize the important function performed by the mass media and shall ensure that the child has access to information and material from a diversity of national and international sources, especially those aimed at the promotion of his or her social, spiritual and moral well-being and physical and mental health. To this end, States Parties shall:

(a) Encourage the mass media to disseminate information and material of social and cultural benefit to the child and in accordance with the spirit of article 29;

(b) Encourage international cooperation in the production, exchange and dissemination of such information and material from a diversity of cultural, national and international sources;

(c) Encourage the production and dissemination of children's books;

(d) Encourage the mass media to have particular regard to the linguistic needs of the child who belongs to a minority group or who is indigenous;

(e) Encourage the development of appropriate guidelines for the protArtection of the child from information and material injurious to his or her well-being, bearing in mind the provisions of articles 13 and 18.

Article 18 (Parental Responsibilities)

1. States Parties shall use their best efforts to ensure recognition of the principle that both parents have common responsibilities for the upbringing and development of the child. Parents or, as the case may be, legal guardians, have the primary responsibility for the upbringing and development of the child. The best interests of the child will be their basic concern.

2. For the purpose of guaranteeing and promoting the rights set forth in the present Convention, States Parties shall render appropriate assistance to parents and legal guardians in the performance of their child-rearing responsibilities and shall ensure the development of institutions, facilities and services for the care of children.

3. States Parties shall take all appropriate measures to ensure that children of working parents have the right to benefit from child-care services and facilities for which they are eligible.

Article 19 (Protection from Abuse and Neglect)

1. States Parties shall take all appropriate legislative, administrative, social and educational measures to protect the child from all forms of physical or mental violence, injury or abuse, neglect or negligent treatment, maltreatment or exploitation, including sexual abuse, while in the care of parent(s), legal guardian(s) or any other person who has the care of the child.

2. Such protective measures should, as appropriate, include effective procedures for the establishment of social programmes to provide necessary support for the child and for those who have the care of the child, as well as for other forms of prevention and for identification, reporting, referral, investigation, treatment and follow-up of instances of child maltreatment described heretofore, and, as appropriate, for judicial involvement.

Article 20 (Protection of Children without Families)

1. A child temporarily or permanently deprived of his or her family environment, or in whose own best interests cannot be allowed to remain in that environment,

shall be entitled to special protection and assistance provided by the State.

2. States Parties shall in accordance with their national laws ensure alternative care for such a child.

3. Such care could include, inter alia, foster placement, Kafala of Islamic law, adoption, or if necessary placement in suitable institutions for the care of children. When considering solutions, due regard shall be paid to the desirability of continuity in a child's upbringing and to the child's ethnic, religious, cultural and linguistic background.

Article 21 (Adoption)

States Parties that recognize and/or permit the system of adoption shall ensure that the best interests of the child shall be the paramount consideration and they shall:

(a) Ensure that the adoption of a child is authorized only by competent authorities who determine, in accordance with applicable law and procedures and on the basis of all pertinent and reliable information, that the adoption is permissible in view of the child's status concerning parents, relatives and legal guardians and that, if required, the persons concerned have given their informed consent to the adoption on the basis of such counselling as may be necessary;

(b) Recognize that inter-country adoption may be considered as an alternative means of child's care, if the child cannot be placed in a foster or an adoptive family or cannot in any suitable manner be cared for in the child's country of origin;

(c) Ensure that the child concerned by intercountry adoption enjoys safeguards and standards equivalent to those existing in the case of national adoption;

(d) Take all appropriate measures to ensure that, in intercountry adoption, the placement does not result in improper financial gain for those involved in it;

(e) Promote, where appropriate, the objectives of the present article by concluding bilateral or multilateral arrangements or agreements, and endeavour, within this framework, to ensure that the placement of the child in another country is carried out by competent authorities or organs.

Article 22 (Refugee Children)

1. States Parties shall take appropriate measures to ensure that a child who is seeking refugee status or who is considered a refugee in accordance with applicable international or domestic law and procedures shall, whether unaccompanied or accompanied by his or her parents or by any other person, receive appropriate protection and humanitarian assistance in the enjoyment of applicable rights set forth in the present Convention and in other international human rights or humanitarian instruments to which the said States are Parties.

2. For this purpose, States Parties shall provide, as they consider appropriate, cooperation in any efforts by the United Nations and other competent intergovernmental organizations or non-governmental organizations cooperating with the United Nations to protect and assist such a child and to trace the parents or other members of the family of any refugee child in order to obtain information necessary for reunification with his or her family. In cases where no parents or other members of the family can be found, the child shall be accorded the same protection as any other child permanently or temporarily deprived of his or her family environment for any reason, as set forth in the present Convention.

Article 23 (Handicapped Children)

1. States Parties recognize that a mentally or physically disabled child should enjoy a full and decent life, in conditions which ensure dignity, promote self-reliance, and facilitate the child's active participation in the community.

2. States Parties recognize the right of the disabled child to special care and shall encourage and ensure the extension, subject to available resources, to the eligible child and those responsible for his or her care, of assistance for which application is made and which is appropriate to the child's condition and to the circumstances of the parents or others caring for the child.

3. Recognizing the special needs of a disabled child, assistance extended in accordance with paragraph 2 of the present article shall be provided free of charge, whenever possible, taking into account the financial resources of the parents or others caring for the child, and shall be designed to ensure that the disabled child has effective access to and receives education, training, health care services, rehabilitation services, preparation for employment and recreation opportunities in a manner conducive to the child's achieving the fullest possible social integration and individual development, including his or her cultural and spiritual development.

4. States Parties shall promote, in the spirit of international cooperation, the exchange of appropriate information in the field of preventive health care and of medical, psychological and functional treatment of disabled children, including dissemination of and access to information concerning methods of rehabilitation, education and vocational services, with the aim of enabling States Parties to improve their capabilities

and skills and to widen their experience in these areas. In this regard, particular account shall be taken of the needs of developing countries.

Article 24 (Health and Health Services)

1. States Parties recognize the right of the child to the enjoyment of the highest attainable standard of health and to facilities for the treatment of illness and rehabilitation of health. States Parties shall strive to ensure that no child is deprived of his or her right of access to such health care services.

2. States Parties shall pursue full implementation of this right and, in particular, shall take appropriate measures:

   (a) To diminish infant and child mortality;

   (b) To ensure the provision of necessary medical assistance and health care to all children with emphasis on the development of primary health care;

   (c) To combat disease and malnutrition including within the framework of primary health care, through inter alia the application of readily available technology and through the provision of adequate nutritious foods and clean drinking water, taking into consideration the dangers and risks of environmental pollution;

   (d) To ensure appropriate pre-natal and post-natal health care for mothers;

   (e) To ensure that all segments of society, in particular parents and children, are informed, have access to education and are supported in the use of basic knowledge of child health and nutrition, the advantages of breast-feeding, hygiene and environmental sanitation and the prevention of accidents;

(f) To develop preventive health care, guidance for parents and family planning education and services.

3. States Parties shall take all effective and appropriate measures with a view to abolishing traditional practices prejudicial to the health of children.

4. States Parties undertake to promote and encourage international cooperation with a view to achieving progressively the full realization of the right recognized in the present article. In this regard, particular account shall be taken of the needs of developing countries.

Article 25 (Periodic Review of Placement)

States Parties recognize the right of a child who has been placed by the competent authorities for the purposes of care, protection or treatment of his or her physical or mental health, to a periodic review of the treatment provided to the child and all other circumstances relevant to his or her placement.

Article 26 (Social Security)

1. States Parties shall recognize for every child the right to benefit from social security, including social insurance, and shall take the necessary measures to achieve the full realization of this right in accordance with their national law.

2. The benefits should, where appropriate, be granted, taking into account the resources and the circumstances of the child and persons having responsibility for the maintenance of the child, as well as any other consideration relevant to an application for benefits made by or on behalf of the child.

APPENDIX I   389

Article 27 (Standard of Living)

1. States Parties recognize the right of every child to a standard of living adequate for the child's physical, mental, spiritual, moral and social development.

2. The parent(s) or others responsible for the child have the primary responsibility to secure, within their abilities and financial capacities, the conditions of living necessary for the child's development.

3. States Parties, in accordance with national conditions and within their means, shall take appropriate measures to assist parents and others responsible for the child to implement this right and shall in case of need provide material assistance and support programmes, particularly with regard to nutrition, clothing and housing.

4. States Parties shall take all appropriate measures to secure the recovery of maintenance for the child from the parents or other persons having financial responsibility for the child, both within the State Party and from abroad. In particular, where the person having financial responsibility for the child lives in a State different from that of the child, States Parties shall promote the accession to international agreements or the conclusion of such agreements, as well as the making of other appropriate arrangements.

Article 28 (Education)

1. States Parties recognize the right of the child to education, and with a view to achieving this right progressively and on the basis of equal opportunity, they shall, in particular:

   (a) Make primary education compulsory and available free to all;

(b) Encourage the development of different forms of secondary education, including general and vocational education, make them available and accessible to every child, and take appropriate measures such as the introduction of free education and offering financial assistance in case of need;

(c) Make higher education accessible to all on the basis of capacity by every appropriate means;

(d) Make educational and vocational information and guidance available and accessible to all children;

(e) Take measures to encourage regular attendance at schools and the reduction of drop-out rates.

2. States Parties shall take all appropriate measures to ensure that school discipline is administered in a manner consistent with the child's human dignity and in conformity with the present Convention.

3. States Parties shall promote and encourage international cooperation in matters relating to education, in particular with a view to contributing to the elimination of ignorance and illiteracy throughout the world and facilitating access to scientific and technical knowledge and modern teaching methods. In this regard, particular account shall be taken of the needs of developing countries.

Article 29 (Aims of Education)

1. States Parties agree that the education of the child shall be directed to:

(a) The development of the child's personality, talents and mental and physical abilities to their fullest potential;

(b) The development of respect for human rights and fundamental freedoms, and for the principles enshrined in the Charter of the United Nations;

(c) The development of respect for the child's parents, his or her own cultural identity, language and values, for the national values of the country in which the child is living, the country from which he or she may originate, and for civilizations different from his or her own;

(d) The preparation of the child for responsible life in a free society, in the spirit of understanding, peace, tolerance, equality of sexes, and friendship among all peoples, ethnic, national and religious groups and persons of indigenous origin;

(e) The development of respect for the natural environment.

2. No part of the present article or Article 28 shall be construed so as to interfere with the liberty of individuals and bodies to establish and direct educational institutions, subject always to the observance of the principles set forth in paragraph 1 of the present article and to the requirements that the education given in such institutions shall conform to such minimum standards as may be laid down by the State.

Article 30 (Children of Minorities or Indigenous Peoples)

In those States in which ethnic, religious or linguistic minorities or persons of indigenous origin exist, a child belonging to such a minority or who is indigenous shall not be denied the right, in community with other members of his or her group, to enjoy his or her own culture, to profess and practise his or her own religion, or to use his or her own language.

Article 31 (Leisure, Recreation and Cultural Activities)

1. States Parties recognize the right of the child to rest and leisure, to engage in play and recreational activities appropriate to the age of the child and to participate freely in cultural life and the arts.

2. States Parties shall respect and promote the right of the child to participate fully in cultural and artistic life and shall encourage the provision of appropriate and equal opportunities for cultural, artistic, recreational and leisure activity.

Article 32 (Child Labour)

1. States Parties recognize the right of the child to be protected from economic exploitation and from performing any work that is likely to be hazardous or to interfere with the child's education, or to be harmful to the child's health or physical, mental, spiritual, moral or social development.

2. States Parties shall take legislative, administrative, social and educational measures to ensure the implementation of the present article. To this end, and having regard to the relevant provisions of other international instruments, States Parties shall in particular:

   (a) Provide for a minimum age or minimum ages for admissions to employment;

   (b) Provide for appropriate regulation of the hours and conditions of employment;

   (c) Provide for appropriate penalties or other sanctions to ensure the effective enforcement of the present article.

Article 33 (Drug Abuse)

States Parties shall take all appropriate measures, including legislative, administrative, social and educational measures, to protect children from the illicit use of narcotic drugs and psychotropic substances as defined in the relevant international treaties, and to prevent the use of children in the illicit production and trafficking of such substances.

Article 34 (Sexual Exploitation)

States Parties undertake to protect the child from all forms of sexual exploitation and sexual abuse. For these purposes, States Parties shall in particular take all appropriate national, bilateral and multilateral measures to prevent:

(a) The inducement or coercion of a child to engage in any unlawful sexual activity;

(b) The exploitative use of children in prostitution or other unlawful sexual practises;

(c) The exploitative use of children in pornographic performances and materials.

Article 35 (Sale, Trafficking and Abduction)

States Parties shall take all appropriate national, bilateral and multilateral measures to prevent the abduction of, the sale of or traffic in children for any purpose or in any form.

Article 36 (Other Forms of Exploitation)

States Parties shall protect the child against all other forms of exploitation prejudicial to any aspects of the child's welfare.

Article 37 (Torture and Deprivation of Liberty)

States Parties shall ensure that:

(a) No child shall be subjected to torture or other cruel, inhuman or degrading treatment or punishment.

Neither capital punishment nor life imprisonment without possibility of release shall be imposed for offences committed by persons below 18 years of age;

(b) No child shall be deprived of his or her liberty unlawfully or arbitrarily. The arrest, detention or imprisonment of a child shall be in conformity with the law and shall be used only as a measure of last resort and for the shortest appropriate period of time;

(c) Every child deprived of liberty shall be treated with humanity and respect for the inherent dignity of the human person, and in a manner which takes into account the needs of persons of his or her age. In particular every child deprived of liberty shall be separated from adults unless it is considered in the child's best interest not to do so and shall have the right to maintain contact with his or her family through correspondence and visits, save in exceptional circumstances;

(d) Every child deprived of his or her liberty shall have the right to prompt access to legal and other appropriate assistance, as well as the right to challenge the legality of the deprivation of his or her liberty before a court or other competent, independent and impartial authority, and to a prompt decision on any such action.

Article 38 (Armed Conflicts)

1. States Parties undertake to respect and to ensure respect for rules of international humanitarian law applicable to them in armed conflicts which are relevant to the child.

2. States Parties shall take all feasible measures to ensure that persons who have not attained the age of 15 years do not take a direct part in hostilities.

3. States Parties shall refrain from recruiting any person who has not attained the age of 15 years into their armed forces. In recruiting among those persons who have attained the age of 15 years but who have not attained the age of 18 years, States Parties shall endeavour to give priority to those who are oldest.

4. In accordance with their obligations under international humanitarian law to protect the civilian population in armed conflicts, States Parties shall take all feasible measures to ensure protection and care of children who are affected by an armed conflict.

Article 39 (Rehabilitative Care)

States Parties shall take all appropriate measures to promote physical and psychological recovery and social reintegration of a child victim of: any form of neglect, exploitation, or abuse; torture or any other form of cruel, inhuman or degrading treatment or punishment; or armed conflicts. Such recovery and reintegration shall take place in an environment which fosters the health, self-respect and dignity of the child.

Article 40 (Administration of Juvenile Justice)

1. States Parties recognize the right of every child alleged as, accused of, or recognized as having infringed the penal law to be treated in a manner consistent with the promotion of the child's sense of dignity and worth, which reinforces the child's respect for the human rights and fundamental freedoms of others and which takes into account the child's age and the desirability of promoting the child's reintegration and the child's assuming a constructive role in society.

2. To this end, and having regard to the relevant provisions of international instruments, States Parties shall, in particular, ensure that:

(a) No child shall be alleged as, be accused of, or recognized as having infringed the penal law by reason of acts or omissions that were not prohibited by national or international law at the time they were committed;

(b) Every child alleged as or accused of having infringed the penal law has at least the following guarantees:

(i) To be presumed innocent until proven guilty according to law;

(ii) To be informed promptly and directly of the charges against him or her, and, if appropriate, through his or her parents or legal guardians, and to have legal or other appropriate assistance in the preparation and presentation of his or her defence;

(iii) To have the matter determined without delay by a competent, independent and impartial authority or judicial body in a fair hearing according to law, in the presence of legal or other appropriate assistance and, unless it is considered not to be in the best interest of the child, in particular, taking into account his or her age or situation, his or her parents or legal guardians;

(iv) Not to be compelled to give testimony or to confess guilt; to examine or have examined adverse witnesses and to obtain the participation and examination of witnesses on his or her behalf under conditions of equality;

(v) If considered to have infringed the penal law, to have this decision and any measures imposed in consequence thereof reviewed by a higher competent, independent and impartial authority or judicial body according to law;

(vi) To have the free assistance of an interpreter if the child cannot understand or speak the language used;

(vii) To have his or her privacy fully respected at all stages of the proceedings.

3. States Parties shall seek to promote the establishment of laws, procedures, authorities and institutions specifically applicable to children alleged as, accused of, or recognized as having infringed the penal law, and, in particular:

(a) the establishment of a minimum age below which children shall be presumed not to have the capacity to infringe the penal law;

(b) whenever appropriate and desirable, measures for dealing with such children without resorting to judicial proceedings, providing that human rights and legal safeguards are fully respected.

4. A variety of dispositions, such as care, guidance and supervision orders; counselling; probation; foster care; education and vocational training programmes and other alternatives to institutional care shall be available to ensure that children are dealt with in a manner appropriate to their well-being and proportionate both to their circumstances and the offence.

Article 41 (Respect for Existing Standards)

Nothing in the present Convention shall affect any provisions which are more conducive to the realization of the rights of the child and which may be contained in:

(a) The law of a State Party; or

(b) International law in force for that State.

Article 42 (Making the Convention Known)

States Parties undertake to make the principles and provisions of the Convention widely known, by appropriate and active means, to adults and children alike.

[Articles 43 to 54 set out the procedure for ratification and amendment of the Convention, and for monitoring of implementation by the UN Committee on the Rights of the Child.]

Appendix 2

Sources of Statements about Freedom of Religion, etc.

Section 6.6, above, set out a list of statements relating to a child's right to freedom of thought, conscience and religion, and the implications for education. These had been extrapolated from a number of international instruments, whose sources are set out below.

Key

1924	League of Nations: Declaration of the Rights of the Child
1948C	UN: Declaration on the Rights of the Child
1948U	UN: Universal Declaration of Human Rights
1950	Council of Europe: European Convention on Human Rights
1959	UN: Declaration of the Rights of the Child
1966CP	UN: International Covenant on Civil and Political Rights
1966ESC	UN: International Covenant on Economic, Social and Cultural Rights
1981	UN: Declaration on the Elimination of All Forms of Intolerance and of Discrimination Based on Religious Belief
1989	UN: Convention on the Rights of the Child

Children have a right to spiritual development (1924; 1948C; 1959; 1989).

Every child has a right to freedom of thought, conscience and religion (1948U; 1950; 1966CP; 1981; 1989). No child should be coerced in matters of religion or belief (1966CP; 1981).

Parents have both a right and duty to direct the child in the exercise of their right to freedom of thought, conscience and religion, in a manner consistent with the evolving capacities of the child (1989). They should take account of the views of their children (1989).

Practices of religion or belief in which a child is brought up must not be injurious to the physical or mental health or full development of the child (1981).

The religious, moral or philosophical character of a child's education should be determined primarily by the parents (1948U; 1950; 1959; 1966CP and ESC; 1981; 1989?), but guided by the child's best interests (1959; 1981; 1989). Parents and educators should take account of the views of children (1989).

Parents have the right to organise their family life in accordance with their religion and belief (1981). They should take account of the views of their children (1989).

The religious character of any alternative care (including adoption) should take due account of any expressed wishes of the parents (1981), and the need for continuity in the life of a child (1989). The best interests of the child should be 'the guiding principle' (1981), and 'a primary consideration' (1989). In adoption it should be the 'paramount consideration' (1989). Account should also be taken of the views of the child (1989).

Bibliography

Amnesty International, *Reviewing the Vienna Declaration and Programme of Action and the 50th Anniversary of the Universal Declaration of Human Rights*, www.amnesty.org/ailib/intcam/unchr50/review.htm

Anatolios, Khaled, *Athanasius, the Coherence of His Thought*, London: Routledge, 1998.

Atkinson, C. W., ' "Wonderful Affection": Seventeenth-Century Missionaries to New France on Children and Childhood', in Bunge (ed.), *Child*, pp. 227–46.

Baehr, P. B., *Human Rights: Universality in Practice*, London: MacMillan, 1999.

Bainham, A., *Children, Parents and the State*, London: Sweet & Maxwell, 1988.

Barth, Karl, *Church Dogmatics*, III, *The Doctrine of Creation*, Part One, tr. J. W. Edwards et al., Edinburgh: T&T Clark, 1958.

Barth, Karl, *Church Dogmatics*, III, *The Doctrine of Creation*, Part Four, tr. A. T. Mackay et al., Edinburgh: T&T Clark, 1961.

Beaumont, P. R., (ed.), *Christian Perspectives on Human Rights and Legal Philosophy*, Carlisle: Paternoster Press, 1998.

Bendroth, Margaret, 'Horace Bushnell's *Christian Nurture*', in Bunge (ed.), *Child*, pp. 350–64.

Bentham, Jeremy, 'Anarchical Fallacies: Being an Examination of the Declaration of Rights Issued during the French Revolution', in Waldron (ed.), *'Nonsense upon Stilts,'* pp. 46–76.

Bentham, Jeremy, *A Critical Examination of the Declaration of Rights*.

Berman, Saul, 'Noachide Laws', in Cecil Roth et al., *Encyclopaedia Judaica* (16 vols), Jerusalem Publishing House, 1971–2, vol. 12, cols 1189–91.

Best, E., *A Critical and Exegetical Commentary on Ephesians*, International Critical Commentary, Edinburgh: T&T Clark, 1998.

Birgitta of Sweden, *Life and Selected Revelations*, ed. Marguerite Tjader Harris, tr. Albert Ryle Kezel, Classics of Western Spirituality, New York: Paulist Press, 1990.

Blackstone, W., *Commentaries on the Laws of England*, accessed at www.yale.edu/lawweb/avalon/blackstone/

Bonhoeffer, Dietrich, *Creation and Fall: A Theological Interpretation of Genesis 1–3*, tr. John C. Fletcher, London: SCM Press, 1959.

Brekus, Catherine A., 'Children of Wrath, Children of Grace: Jonathan Edwards and the Puritan Culture of Child Rearing', in Bunge, *Child*, pp. 308–28.

Brett, Annabel S., *Liberty, Right and Nature: Individual Rights in Later Scholastic Thought*, Cambridge: Cambridge University Press, 1997.

Brown, R. E., J. A. Fitzmyer, and R. E. Murphy (eds), *The New Jerome Biblical Commentary*, Student Edition, London: Geoffrey Chapman, 1993.

Bunge, Marcia J. (ed.), *The Child in Christian Thought*, Grand Rapids, MI: Wm. B. Eerdmans Publishing Co., 2001.

Bunge, Marcia J., 'Education and the Child in Eighteenth-Century German Pietism: Perspectives from the Work of A. H. Franke', in Bunge (ed.), *Child*, pp. 247–78.

Burghardt, Walter J., *The Image of God in Man according to Cyril of Alexandria*, Studies in Christian Antiquity, 14, Woodstock, MA: Woodstock College Press, 1957.

Calvin, John, 'Commentarius in Genesin', in *Opera Quae Supersunt Omnia*, ed. Guilielmus Baum, Eduardus Cunitz and Eduardus Reuss, vol. XXIII = Corpus Reformatorum, vol. LI, Braunschweig: C. A. Schwetschke and Son, 1882.

Calvin, John, *Institutes of the Christian Religion*, tr. Ford Lewis Battles, 2 vols, Library of Christian Classics, 20 and 21, Philadelphia: Westminster Press, 1960.

Calvin, John, *Opera Exegetica*, vol. XV, *Commentarii in Secundam Pauli Epistolam ad Corinthios*, ed. Helmut Feld, Geneva: Libraire Droz, 1994.

Calvin, John, *Opera Exegetica*, vol. XVI, *Commentarii in Pauli Epistolas ad Galatas, ad Ephesios, ad Philippenses, ad Colossenses*, ed. Helmut Feld, Geneva: Librarie Droz, 1992.

Campbell, T., K. D. Ewing and A. Tomkins (eds), *Sceptical Essays on Human Rights*, Oxford: Oxford University Press, 2001.

Canon Law Society of Great Britain and Ireland, *The Code of Canon Law in English Translation*, London: Collins Liturgical Publications, 1983.

Carr, E. H.. 'The Rights of Man', in UNESCO, *Human Rights*, p. 19–23.

Catechism of the Catholic Church. London: Geoffrey Chapman, 1994.

Catholic Bishops Conference of England and Wales, *A Programme for Action: Final Report of the Independent Review on Child Protection in the Catholic Church in England and Wales*, London: Catholic Media Office, 2001.

Charlesworth, James H. (ed.), *The Old Testament Pseudepigrapha* (2 vols), London: Darton, Longman & Todd, 1983–5.

Chung-Shu Lo, 'Human Rights in the Chinese Tradition', in UNESCO, *Human Rights*, pp. 186–90.

Cohen, A. (ed.), *The Soncino Chumash: The Five Books of Moses with Haphtaroth*, Soncino Books of the Bible, London: Soncino Press, 1947.

Congregation for Catholic Education, *The Religious Dimension of Education in a Catholic School*, 1988, accessed via Vatican website.

Coppock, V., 'Medicalising Children's Behaviour', in Franklin (ed.), *New Handbook of Children's Rights*, pp. 139–54.

Croce, B., 'The Rights of Man and the Present Historical Situation', in UNESCO, *Human Rights*, pp. 93–5.

Cronin, K., *Rights and Christian Ethics*, New Studies in Christian Ethics, Cambridge: University Press, 1992.

Cullman, Oscar, 'Infancy Gospels', in Wilhelm Schneemelcher, *New Testament Apocrypha* (revised edn), tr. R. McL. Wilson (2 vols), Cambridge: James Clarke & Co, 1991–2, vol. 1, pp. 439–51.

Davies, W. D., and Dale C. Allison, Jr., *A Critical and Exegetical Commentary on the Gospel according to Saint Matthew*, The International Critical Commentary (3vols), Edinburgh: T&T Clark, 1988–97.

Dawkins, R., *The Selfish Gene*, Oxford: Oxford University Press, 1989.

De Blois, M., 'The Foundation of Human Rights: A Christian Perspective', in P. R. Beaumont, *Christian Perspectives on Human Rights and Legal Philosophy*, Carlisle: Paternoster Press, 1998, pp. 7–29.

De Chardin, P. T., 'Some Reflections on the Rights of Man', in UNESCO, *Human Rights*, pp. 105–7.

De Madariaga, Don S., 'The Rights of Man or Human Relations?', in UNESCO, *Human Rights*, pp. 47–53.

Denzinger, H., and A. Schönmetzer (eds), *Enchiridion Symbolorum, Definitionum et Declarationum de Rebus Fidei et Morum* (24th edn), Barcelona: Herder, 1967.

Detrick, S. (ed.), *The United Nations Convention on the Rights of the Child: A Guide to the Traveaux Preparatoires*, Dordrecht: Martinus Nijhoff, 1991.

DeVries, Dawn, '"Be Converted and Become as Little Children": Friedrich Schleiermacher on the Religious Significance of Childhood', in Bunge (ed.), *Child*, pp. 329–49.

Dibelius, Martin, *Die Briefe des Apostels Paulus*, II, *Die neun kleinen Briefe*, Handbuch zum neuen Testament III, Tübingen: J.C.B. Mohr (Paul Siebeck), 1913.

Dickens, B. M., 'The Modern Function and Limits of Parental Rights', *The Law Quarterly Review*, 97 (July 1981), pp. 462–85.

Diemer, A., 'The 1948 Declaration: An Analysis of Meanings', in UNESCO, *Philosophical Foundations of Human Rights*.

Dixon, M., *Textbook on International Law* (2nd edn), London: Blackstone Press, 1990.

Dworkin, Ronald, 'Rights as Trumps', in Waldron, *Theories of Rights*, pp. 153–67.

Dworkin, Ronald, *Taking Rights Seriously* (revised edn), London: Duckworth, 1978.

Eekelaar, J. M., 'What Are Parental Rights?', *The Law Quarterly Review*, 89 (April 1973), pp. 210–34.

Etzioni, A. (ed.), *The Essential Communitarian Reader*, New York: Rowman & Littlefield Publishers, Inc., 1998.

Etzioni, A., *The New Golden Rule: Community and Morality in a Democratic Society*, New York: Basic Books, 1996.

Etzioni, A., *The Spirit of Community: Rights, Responsibilities and the Communitarian Agenda*, London: Fontana Press, 1995.

Farson, R., *Birthrights*, Harmondsworth: Penguin, 1978.

Fay, Thomas A., 'Maritain on Rights and Natural Law', *The Thomist*, 55 (1991), pp. 439–48.

Feinberg, J., 'The Nature and Value of Rights', *Rights, Justice and the Bounds of Liberty: Essays in Social Philosophy*, Princeton: Princeton University Press, 1980, pp. 143–57.

Finnis, John, *Natural Law and Natural Rights*, Oxford: Clarendon Press, 1980.

Flannery, A. (ed.), *Vatican Council II: The Conciliar and Post-conciliar Documents*, Leominster, Hereford: Fowler Wright Books, 1981.

Flannery, A. (ed.), *Vatican Council II: More Post-conciliar Documents*, Leominster, Hereford: Fowler Wright Books, 1982.

Fletcher, Anthony, 'Prescription and Practice: Protestantism and the Upbringing of Children, 1560–1700', in Wood (ed.), *The Church and Childhood*, pp. 325–46.

Fortin, Jane, *Children's Rights and the Developing Law*, London: Butterworths, 1998.

Franklin, B. (ed.), *The New Handbook of Children's Rights: Comparative Policy and Practice*, London and New York: Routledge, 2002.

Fraser, P., *A Treatise on the Law of Parent and Child* (3rd edn, by J. Clark), Edinburgh: W. Green & Sons, 1906.

Fredman, Sandra, 'Scepticism under Scrutiny: Labour Law and Human Rights', in Campbell, Ewing and Tomkins (eds), *Sceptical Essays on Human Rights*, pp. 197–213.

Freeman, M. D. A., *The Rights and Wrongs of Children*, London and Dover, NH: Frances Pinter (Publishers), 1983.

Fry, M., 'Human Rights and the Law-Breaker', in UNESCO, *Human Rights*, p. 246–9.

Gallagher, R., *Children and Young People's Voices: The Law, Legal Services, Systems and Processes in Scotland*, Edinburgh: The Stationery Office, 1999.

Gandhi, M., 'Letter to the Director-General of UNESCO', in UNESCO, *Human Rights*, p. 18.

Gerard, R. W., 'The Rights of Man: A Biological Approach', in UNESCO, *Human Rights*, pp. 205–9.

Gewirth, A., *The Community of Rights*, Chicago and London: University of Chicago Press, 1996.

Glendon, M. A., *Holy See's Final Statement at Women's Conference in Beijing*, 15 September 1995, accessed via www.its.caltech.edu/~newman/women-cp/beijing3.html, on 11 October 2001.

Goldstein, J., A. Solnit, S. Goldstein and A. Freud, *The Best Interests of the Child: The Least Detrimental Alternative*, New York: The Free Press, 1998.

Greven, P., *The Protestant Temperament: Patterns of Child-Rearing, Religious Experience, and the Self in Early America*, New York: Alfred A. Knopf, 1977.

Greven, Philip, *Spare the Child: The Religious Roots of Punishment and the Psychological Impact of Physical Abuse*, New York: Alfred A. Knopf, 1991; New York: Vintage Books, 1992.

Guroian, Vigen, 'The Ecclesial Family: John Chrysostom on Parenthood and Children', in Bunge (ed.), *Child*, pp. 61–77.

Haesaerts, J., 'Reflections on Some Declarations in the Rights of Man', in UNESCO, *Human Rights*, pp. 96–104.

Hardwig, John, 'Should Women Think in Terms of Rights?', *Ethics*, 94 (1984), pp. 441–55.

Harris, J. W. (ed.), *Legal Philosophies* (2nd edn), London, Edinburgh, Dublin: Butterworths, 1997.

Hauerwas, Stanley, *A Community of Character: Toward a Constructive Christian Social Ethic*, Notre Dame: University of Notre Dame Press, 1981.

Hauerwas, Stanley, *Suffering Presence: Theological Reflections on Medicine, the Mentally Handicapped, and the Church*, Notre Dame: University of Notre Dame Press, 1986.

Heitzenrater, Richard P., 'John Wesley and Children', in Bunge (ed.), *Child*, pp. 279–99.

Hersch, J., 'Human Rights in Western Thought: Conflicting Dimensions', in UNESCO, *Philosophical Foundations of Human Rights*.

Hessen, S., 'The Rights of Man in Liberalism, Socialism and Communism', in UNESCO, *Human Rights*, pp. 108–41.

Hinsdale, Mary Ann, '"Infinite Openness to the Divine": Karl Rahner's Contribution to Modern Catholic Thought on the Child', in Bunge (ed.), *Child*, pp. 406–45.

Hodgkin, R., and P. Newell, *Implementation Handbook for the Convention on the Rights of the Child* (rev. edn), New York/Geneva: UNICEF, 2002.

Hohfeld, W., *Fundamental Legal Conceptions*, ed. W. W. Cook, New Haven: Yale University Press, 1919.

Holy See, *Charter of the Rights of the Family*, 22 October 1983, accessed via Vatican website: www.vatican.va/roman_curia/

Horsley, Richard A., 'The Law of Nature in Philo and Cicero', *Harvard Theological Review*, 71 (1978), pp. 35–59.

Hountondji, P. J., 'The Master's Voice: Remarks on the Problem of Human Rights in Africa', in UNESCO, *Philosophical Foundations of Human Rights*.

Huber, Wolfgang, 'Human Rights – a Concept and Its History', in Alois Müller and Norbert Greinacher (ed.), *The Church and the Rights of Man*, Concilium, New York: Seabury Press, 1979, pp. 1–10.

Humphrey, J., and R. Tuck, 'The International Bill of Rights', in UNESCO, *Philosophical Foundations of Human Rights*.

Hurlbert, H., *UN Convention on the Rights of the Child: A Treaty to Undermine the Family*, on the website of Concerned Women for America, September 2001.

Inagaki, R., 'Some Aspects of Human Rights in Japan', in UNESCO, *Philosophical Foundations of Human Rights*.

Irenaeus, *Proof of the Apostolic Preaching*, tr. Joseph P. Smith, Ancient Christian Writers, 16, Westminster, MA: Newman Press, 1952.

Kabir, H., 'Human Rights: The Islamic Tradition and the Problems of the World Today', in UNESCO, *Human Rights*, pp. 191–4.

Karolis, R., *The Convention on the Rights of the Child: The Making of a Deception*, www.biblebelievers.org.au/right1.htm, accessed 24 October 2001.

Kilkelly, U., *The Child and the European Convention on Human Rights*, Aldershot (England): Ashgate and Brookfield (USA): Dartmouth, 1999.

Koester, Helmut, 'NOMOS PHYSEOS: The Concept of Natural Law in Greek Thought', in Jacob Neusner (ed.), *Religions in Antiquity*, Leiden: Brill, 1968, pp. 521–41.

Küng, H., and H. Schmidt (eds), *A Global Ethic and Global Responsibilities: Two Declarations*, London: SCM Press, 1998.

Lane, Anthony N. S., *John Calvin, Student of the Church Fathers*, Edinburgh: T&T Clark, 2000.

Laski, H. J., 'Towards a Universal Declaration of Human Rights', in UNESCO, *Human Rights*, pp. 78–92.

Lauren, P. G., *The Evolution of International Human Rights: Visions Seen*, Philadelphia: University of Pennsylvania Press, 1998.

Lewis, J., 'On Human Rights', in UNESCO, *Human Rights*, pp. 54–71.

Lien, A. J., 'A Fragment of Thought concerning the Nature and Fulfilment of Human Rights', in UNESCO, *Human Rights*, pp. 24–30.

Lightfoot, J. B., *Saint Paul's Epistles to the Colossians and to Philemon* (3rd edn), London: Macmillan and Co., 1879.

Linzey, Andrew, *Animal Rights: A Christian Assessment of Man's Treatment of Animals*, London: SCM Press, 1976.

Linzey, Andrew, *Christianity and the Rights of Animals*, London: SPCK, 1987.

Lomasky, Loren E., 'Person, Concept of', in Lawrence C. Becker (ed.), *Encyclopedia of Ethics* (2 vols), Chicago: St James Press, 1992, vol. 2, pp. 950–6.

Lorenzen, T., *The Rights of the Child*, Baptist World Alliance, Human Rights Booklet No. 2/1998, Virginia: Baptist World Alliance, 1998.

Loughlin, Martin, 'Rights, Democracy and Law', in Campbell, Ewen and Tomkins (eds), *Sceptical Essays on Human Rights*, pp. 41–60.

Luther, Martin, 'Genesisvorlesung', *Werke, Kritische Gesamtausgabe*, vol. 42, Weimar: Hermann Böhlaus Nachfolger, 1911.

MacCormick, D. N, *Legal Right and Social Democracy: Essays in Legal and Political Philosophy*, Oxford: Clarendon Press, 1982.

MacCormick, D. N., 'Rights in Legislation', in P. M. S. Hacker and J. Raz (eds), *Law, Morality and Society: Essays in Honour of H. L. A. Hart*, Oxford: Clarendon Press, 1977, pp. 189–209.

MacIntyre, A., *After Virtue: A Study in Moral Theory* (2nd edn), London: Duckworth, 1985.

McKenna, K. E., *A Concise Guide to Canon Law*, Notre Dame, Indiana: Ave Maria Press, 2000.

McKeon, R., 'The Philosophic Bases and Material Circumstances of the Rights of Man', in UNESCO, *Human Rights*, pp. 35–46.

Maguire, R., and K. Marshall, *Education and the Rights of the Child*, Glasgow: University of Glasgow Centre for the Child & Society, 2001.

Maritain, J., 'Introduction', in UNESCO, *Human Rights*, pp. 9–17.

Maritain, J., *Man and the State*, Chicago: University of Chicago Press, 1951.

Maritain, J., 'On the Philosophy of Human Rights', in UNESCO, *Human Rights*, pp. 72–7.

Markovic, M., 'Differing Conceptions of Human Rights in Europe – towards a Resolution', in UNESCO, *Philosophical Foundations of Human Rights*.

Marshall, K., *Children's Rights and Family Values: Complement or Conflict*, Glasgow: Blackfriars, 2002.

Marshall, K., *Children's Rights in the Balance: The Participation–Protection Debate*, Edinburgh: The Stationery Office, 1997.

Marshall, K., C. Jamieson and A. Finlayson, *Edinburgh's Children: The Report of the Edinburgh Inquiry into Abuse and Protection of Children in Care*, Edinburgh: City of Edinburgh Council, 1999.

Marshall, K., E. K. M. Tisdall and A. Cleland, *Voice of the Child under the Children (Scotland) Act 1995: Giving Due Regard to Children's Views in Matters that Affect Them*, Edinburgh: Scottish Executive Research Unit, 2002.

Marx, Karl, 'On the Jewish Question', in Waldron (ed.), *'Nonsense upon Stilts,'* pp. 137–50.

Mason, J. K., and R. A. McCall Smith, *Law and Medical Ethics* (4th edn), Edinburgh: Butterworths, 1994.

Mathieu, V., 'Prologomena to a Study of Human Rights from the Standpoint of the International Community', in UNESCO, *Philosophical Foundations of Human Rights*.

May, W. E., *The Difference between a 'Right' and a 'Liberty' and the Significance of This Difference in Debates over Public Policy on Abortion and Euthanasia*, accessed on 6 March 2003, at www.christendom-awake.org/pages/may/rights.html.

Meyer, L. R., 'Unruly Rights', *Cardozo Law Review*, 22:1 (2000), pp. 9–12.

Miller, Alice, *For Your Own Good: Hidden Cruelty in Child-Rearing and the Roots of Violence*, tr. Hildegarde and Hunter Hannum, New York: Farrar, Straus & Giroux, 1983.

Miller, Keith Graber, 'Complex Innocence, Obligatory Nurturance, and Parental Vigilance: "The Child" in the Work of Menno Simons', in Bunge (ed.), *Child*, pp. 194–226.

Miller-McLemore, Bonnie J., '"Let the Children Come" Revisited: Contemporary Feminist Theologians on Children', in Bunge (ed.), *Child*, pp. 446–73.

Minns, Denis, *Irenaeus*, Outstanding Christian Thinkers Series, London: Geoffrey Chapman, 1994.

Morrison, C., and C. McCulloch, *All Children All Ages: The NGO Alternative Report (Scotland) to the UN Committee on the Rights of the Child*, Edinburgh: Scottish Alliance for Children's Rights, 2000 (Based at Save the Children, Scotland Office, in Edinburgh).

Muddiman, John, *A Commentary on the Epistle to the Ephesians*, Black's New Testament Commentaries, London: Continuum, 2001.

Muirhead, J., *Historical Introduction to the Private Law of Rome* (2nd edn, revised and edited by H. Goudy), London: Adam and Charles Black, 1899.

Newell, P., *Children are People Too: The Case against Physical Punishment*, London: APPROACH, 1992.

Oaks, D. H., 'Rights and Responsibilities', in Etzioni (ed.), *Essential Communitarian Reader*, pp. 98–9.

Office of the High Commissioner for Human Rights, *The Situation Analysis of Children and Families in Poland: 6 November 1993*, United Nations Human Rights website, Treaty Bodies Database: accessed 12 October 2001.

Omari, C. K., and D. A. S. Mbilinyi, *African Values and Child Rights: Some Cases from Tanzania*, Dar es Salaam: DUP (1996) Ltd, 1997.

Ozment, S., *When Fathers Ruled: Family Life in Reformation Europe*, Cambridge, MA: Harvard University Press, 1983.

Pandeya, R. C., 'Human Rights: An Indian Perspective', in UNESCO, *Philosophical Foundations of Human Rights*.

Parvis, Sara, *Marcellus of Ancyra and the Lost Years of the Arian Controversy*, forthcoming.

Perry, Michael J., *The Idea of Human Rights: Four Inquiries*, New York: Oxford University Press, 1988.

Pettersen, Alvyn, *Athanasius and the Human Body*, Bristol: Bristol Press, 1990.

Pitkin, Barbara, '"The Heritage of the Lord": Children in the Theology of John Calvin', in Bunge (ed.), *Child*, pp. 160–93.

Pontifical Council for the Family, *The Family and Human Rights*, 9 December 1999, accessed via Vatican website: www.vatican.va/roman_curia/

Pope John Paul II, *Catechesis Tradendae: On Catechesis in Our Time*, 16 October 1979, in Flannery (ed.), *Vatican Council II: More Post Conciliar Documents*, pp. 762–814.

Pope John Paul II, *Familiaris consortio: The Christian Family in the Modern World*, 22 November 1981, in Flannery (ed.), *Vatican Council II: More Post Conciliar Documents*.

Pope John Paul II, *Let Us Give Children a Future of Peace: Message of His Holiness Pope John Paul II for the XXIX World Day of Peace*, 1 January 1996, accessed via Vatican website: www.vatican.va/holy_father/

Pope John Paul II, *Letter to Families*, 1994, accessed via Vatican website.

Pope Paul VI, *Evangelii Nuntiandi: Evangelisation in the Modern World*, 1975, in Flannery (ed.), *Vatican Council II: More Post-conciliar Documents*, pp. 711–61.

Porter, Jean, *Natural and Divine Law: Reclaiming the Tradition for Christian Ethics*, Saint Paul University Series in Ethics, Grand Rapids: William B. Eerdmans, 1999.

Porter, Jean, *The Recovery of Virtue: The Relevance of Aquinas for Christian Ethics*, London: SPCK, 1994.

Puntambekar, S. V., 'The Hindu Concept of Human Rights', in UNESCO, *Human Rights*, pp. 195–8.

Rahner, Karl, 'Ideas for a Theology of Childhood', *Theological Investigations*, vol. 8, tr. David Bourke, London: Darton, Longman & Todd, 1971, pp. 33–50.

Rawls, John, *Political Liberalism*, New York: Columbia University Press, 1996.

Raz, J., *Law Morality and Society: Essays in Honour of H. L. A. Hart*. Oxford: Clarendon Press, 1977.

Richman, H., *UN Child Rights Treaty*, reprint of an article published in the Opinion Page of the *Pittsburgh Tribune-Review*, 13 June 1995, obtained from www.pahomeschoolers.com/untreaty.html

Riezler, K., 'Reflections on Human Rights', in UNESCO, *Human Rights*, pp. 156–7.

Robbins, V. K., 'Pronouncement Stories and Jesus' Blessing of the Children', *Semeia*, 29 (1983), pp. 43–74.

Robinson, Mary, High Commissioner for Human Rights, *Human Rights: 'On the Eve of the Twenty-First Century',* The Paris Meeting, 7 December 1998.

Russell, B., *A History of Western Philosophy*, London: Unwin Paperbacks, 1984.

Schilling, F. A., 'What Means the Saying about Receiving the Kingdom of God as a Little Child', *Expository Times*, 77 (1965), pp. 56–8.

Schürer, Emil, *The History of the Jewish People in the Age of Jesus Christ (175 B.C. – A.D. 135)*, revised edn by Geza Vermes et al. (3 vols in 4), Edinburgh: T&T Clark, 1973–87.

Scott, G. R., *The History of Corporal Punishment*, London: Senate, 1996 (first published as *Flagellation*, by Tallis Press Ltd, in 1968).

Scottish Law Commission, *Report on Family Law* (Scot Law Com No 135), Edinburgh: HMSO, 1992.

Scottish Law Commission, *Report on the Legal Capacity and Responsibility of Minors and Pupils*, Scot Law Com No 110, Edinburgh: HMSO, 1987.

Scottish Office, *Evaluation of the Hamilton Child Safety Initiative* (known as the Hamilton Curfew), Edinburgh: Scottish Office Central Research Unit, 1999.

Sloss, D., 'The Domestication of International Human Rights: Non-Self-Executing Declarations and Human Rights Treaties', 24 *Yale Journal of International Law*, 129 (1999).

Storrar, William, and Andrew Morton (eds), *Public Theology for the 21ˢᵗ Century*, Edinburgh: Saint Andrew Press, forthcoming.

Strack, Hermann L., and Paul Billerbeck, *Kommentar zum neuen Testament aus Talmud und Midrasch*, III, *Die Briefe des neuen Testaments und die Offenbarung Johannis*, München: C. H. Beck, 1926.

Strohl, Jane E., 'The Child in Luther's Theology: "For What Purpose Do We Older Folks Exist, Other Than to Care for ... the Young?"', in Bunge (ed.), *Child*, pp. 134–59.

Sutherland, E. E., *Child and Family Law*, Edinburgh: T&T Clark, 1999.

Tanner, Norman P. (ed.), *Decrees of the Ecumenical Councils* (2 vols), London: Sheed & Ward, 1990.

Taylor, C., 'Human Rights: The Legal Culture', in UNESCO, *Philosophical Foundations of Human Rights*.

Tay, A. E., and E. Kamenka, 'Human Rights: Perspectives from Australia', in UNESCO, *Philosophical Foundations of Human Rights*.

Tergel, Alf, *Human Rights in Cultural and Religious Traditions*, Uppsala Studies in Faiths and Ideologies, 8, Uppsala: Uppsala University, 1998.

Thomas Aquinas, *Summa Theologica*, accessed via www.newadvent.org/summa/

Tierney, Brian, *The Idea of Natural Rights: Studies on Natural Rights, Natural Law and Church Law, 1150–1625*, Atlanta: Scholars Press, 1997.

Tomkins, A., 'Introduction: On Being Sceptical about Human Rights', in Campbell, Ewing and Tomkins (eds), *Sceptical Essays on Human Rights*, pp. 1–11.

Traer, R., *Faith in Human Rights: Support in Religious Traditions for a Global Struggle*, Washington, DC: Georgetown University Press, 1991.

Traer, R., *Fight over the Rights of the Child*, www.geocities.com/Athens/Parthenon/7185/Ratification/ushr.fight.child.htm

Traina, Cristina L. H., 'A Person in the Making: Thomas Aquinas on Children and Childhood', in Bunge (ed.), *Child*, pp. 103–33.

Tuck, Richard, *Natural Rights Theories: Their Origin and Development*, Cambridge: Cambridge University Press, 1979.

UNESCO, *Human Rights: Comments and Interpretations*, London & New York: Allan Wingate, 1949.

UNESCO, *Philosophical Foundations of Human Rights*, Paris: UNESCO, 1986.

Verhellen, E., *Convention on the Rights of the Child* (2nd edn), Leuven-Aledoorn: Garant, 1997.

Waldron, Jeremy, 'Inalienable Rights', *The Boston Review* (April/May 1999).

Waldron, Jeremy (ed.), *'Nonsense upon Stilts': Bentham, Burke and Marx on the Rights of Man*, London: Methuen, 1987.

Waldron, Jeremy (ed.), *Theories of Rights*, Oxford Readings in Philosophy, Oxford: Oxford University Press, 1984.

Werpehowski, William, 'Reading Karl Barth on Children', in Bunge, *Child*, pp. 386–405.

Wesley, J., *Explanatory Notes upon the New Testament*, London: Epworth Press, 1950.

Westermann, Claus, *Genesis 1–11: A Commentary*, tr. John J. Scullion, London: SPCK, 1984.

Whybray, R. N., *The Book of Proverbs: A Survey of Modern Study*, History of Biblical Interpretation Series 1, Leiden: E. J. Brill, 1995.

Wildberger, H., 'Das Abbild Gottes, Gen. 1:26–30', *Theologische Literaturzeitung*, 21 (1965), pp. 245–59 and 481–501.

Wilkinson, A. B., and K. McK. Norrie, *The Law relating to Parent and Child in Scotland*, Edinburgh: W. Green/Sweet & Maxwell, 1993.

Williams, Rowan, *Lost Icons: Reflections on Cultural Bereavement*, Edinburgh: T&T Clark, 2000.

Wood, Diana (ed.), *The Church and Childhood*, Studies in Church History, 31, Oxford: Blackwell, 1994.

Woodward, J.,'The UN Quietly Wages War on Religion', *Calgary Herald* (11 August 2001).

World Council of Churches, *The Message and Reports of the First Assembly of the World Council of Churches*, London: World Council of Churches/SCM Press, 1948.

Wright, Q.,'Relationship between Different Categories of Human Rights', in UNESCO, *Human Rights*, pp. 143–51.

Zane, J. M., *The Story of Law* (2nd edn), Indianapolis: Liberty Fund, 1998.

Ziegler, Joanna E., 'Reality as Imitation: The Role of Religious Imagery among the Beguines of the Low Countries', in Ulrike Wiethaus, *Maps of Flesh and Light: The Religious Experience of Medieval Women Mystics*, Syracuse, NY: Syracuse University Press, 1993, pp. 112–26.

Miscellaneous Websites

Amnesty International: www.amnesty.org/

Amnesty International USA: www.amnesty-usa.org/children/crn_faq.html

Baptist Peace Fellowship of North America: www.bpfna.org/openltro1.htm

CBS News: www.cbsnews.com

Children Are Unbeatable: www.childrenareunbeatable.org.uk/

Crown Office: www.crownoffice.gov.uk/publications/CO_Pcode.pdf

Episcopal Church USA, Children's Charter Information and Bibliography: www.dfms.org/myp/ccres.html

European Court of Human Rights: www.echr.coe.int/Eng/Judgments.htm

Leadership U: www.leaderu.com/issues/fabric/chap16.html

Physical punishment issues: www.stophitting.com/religion/

UNICEF UK, Convention on the Rights of the Child: Frequently Asked Questions: www.unicef.org/crc/faq.htm

United Methodist Church General Board of Church and Society: www.umc-gbcs.org/

United Methodist News Service: http://umns.umc.org/News97/mar/jscience.htm

United Nations: documents accessed via the website of the Office of the High Commissioner for Human Rights: www.unhchr.ch/

The Vatican: www.vatican.va/

WCC News: www.wcc-coe.org.wcc/what/interreligious/cd35-21.html

World Alliance of Reformed Churches: www.warc.ch.23gc/report/pub.html and www.warc.ch.23gc/proced.html

Index